UNDERSTANDING
BODY DYSMORPHIC
DISORDER

UNDERSTANDING BODY DYSMORPHIC DISORDER

AN ESSENTIAL GUIDE

KATHARINE A. PHILLIPS, M.D.

Professor of Psychiatry and Human Behavior
Alpert Medical School of Brown University
Director of the Body Dysmorphic Disorder Program
Butler Hospital, Providence, RI

OXFORD
UNIVERSITY PRESS
2009

OXFORD
UNIVERSITY PRESS

Oxford University Press, Inc., publishes works that further
Oxford University's objective of excellence
in research, scholarship, and education.

Oxford New York
Auckland Cape Town Dar es Salaam Hong Kong Karachi
Kuala Lumpur Madrid Melbourne Mexico City Nairobi
New Delhi Shanghai Taipei Toronto

With offices in
Argentina Austria Brazil Chile Czech Republic France Greece
Guatemala Hungary Italy Japan Poland Portugal Singapore
South Korea Switzerland Thailand Turkey Ukraine Vietnam

Published by Oxford University Press, Inc.
198 Madison Avenue, New York, New York 10016
www.oup.com

Oxford is a registered trademark of Oxford University Press

Library of Congress Cataloging-in-Publication Data

Phillips, Katharine A.
Understanding body dysmorphic disorder : an essential guide / Katharine A. Phillips.
    p. cm.
Includes index.
ISBN-13: 978-0-19-537940-2 (pbk. : alk. paper)
1. Body dysmorphic disorder—Popular works.   I. Title.
RC569.5.B64P483 2009
616.85'2—dc22
2008031527

9 8 7 6 5 4 3 2 1
Printed in the United States of America
on acid-free paper

For my patients and for everyone who has participated in BDD research; your courage, trust, and generosity have immeasurably increased understanding of BDD and have made this book possible

Dr. Phillips is a member of the DSM-V Task Force and Chair of the DSM-V Work Group on Anxiety, Obsessive-Compulsive Spectrum, Post-Traumatic, and Dissociative Disorders. Information or views expressed in this book do not necessarily represent the views of the DSM-V Task Force or Work Group.

CONTENTS

Preface		xi
Acknowledgments		xiii
1.	Patients Speak	3
2.	What Is Body Dysmorphic Disorder?	13
3.	How Do I Know If I Have Body Dysmorphic Disorder?	25
4.	Body Dysmorphic Disorder Comes in Many Forms	43
5.	Painful Obsessions	57
6.	Compulsive Behaviors: Mirror Checking, Grooming, Camouflaging, Dieting, and Others	67
7.	How Body Dysmorphic Disorder Affects Lives: Social Avoidance, Problems with School and Work, Violence, Suicide, and Other Consequences	89
8.	Gender and Body Dysmorphic Disorder across the Life Span	115
9.	What Causes Body Dysmorphic Disorder? Clues to an Unsolved Puzzle	127
10.	Getting Better: A Brief Treatment Guide	141
11.	How to Successfully Treat Body Dysmorphic Disorder with Medication	155
12.	Cognitive-Behavioral Therapy for Body Dysmorphic Disorder	189
13.	Cosmetic Treatments: Surgery, Dermatologic, Dental, and Other Treatments	233
14.	Anorexia Nervosa, Obsessive Compulsive Disorder, and Other Psychiatric Disorders—What's Their Relationship to Body Dysmorphic Disorder?	243

15. Advice for Family Members and Friends 251

16. Getting Help for Body Dysmorphic Disorder 265

Glossary 277

Index 287

PREFACE

I've written this book for people who have body dysmorphic disorder (BDD) and for their family and friends. It's also for anyone who wants to understand this relatively common, yet underrecognized, disorder. If you've been diagnosed with BDD—or if you worry about how you look to the point where it upsets you a lot or causes problems for you—then this book is for you.

People with BDD (sometimes called "dysmorphophobia") worry about how they look. They think, for example, that their skin is blemished or scarred, their hair is thinning, their nose is too big, their breasts are too small—*any* body part can be disliked. Most people with BDD compare themselves with other people, try to hide or cover up the body parts they hate, and check mirrors a lot. But BDD is more than a bad hair day.

When it's severe, BDD is devastating. It can completely destroy a person's life. Some people can't leave their house or hold down a job because they're so distressed by their worries about how they look. Many are socially isolated. Some even commit suicide. Others aren't as severely affected. The severity of BDD ranges from fairly mild to extremely severe. On average, people with BDD suffer a lot and have substantial problems with their daily functioning. BDD isn't vanity. It's a serious—and treatable—illness.

BDD has been neglected for far too long. It's been described around the world for more than a century, and it affects men as well as women, children as well as adults, and people from all races and walks of life. Yet, BDD has only recently come to the attention of the people who have it and the professionals who treat it. Since the early 1990s, I've been privileged to hear countless stories of people's struggles with BDD—their suffering, their emotional pain, and their triumphs. Their stories spurred me on to learn more about this often-secret disorder and to write this book.

Since I founded my BDD clinical and research program, I've evaluated or treated more than 1000 people with BDD. In this book, I describe what BDD is like, in the words of those who suffer from it. To protect confidentiality, all names are fictional, some minor details of stories have been changed, and longer stories are combinations of several peoples' experience. Otherwise, the stories are accurate, as are the quotations. They are from BDD sufferers themselves.

Hearing these stories, and the suffering that BDD causes, motivated me to spend nearly the last 20 years doing scientific research on this disorder. I've been on a quest to solve key BDD mysteries: what are the symptoms, who gets it, how common is it, what causes it, how does it affect peoples' lives, and—most important—how can people get better? Studies I've spearheaded or collaborated on, and which have led to published scientific reports on BDD, have involved nearly 2000 people. Additional BDD research has been done by researchers around the world. This work has taught us a lot about this often-devastating disorder and how people can overcome it.

I've written this book to bring you up-to-date on what's been learned about BDD in recent years, including effective treatments. This book is an updated and shorter version of my first book on BDD, *The Broken Mirror: Understanding and Treating Body Dysmorphic Disorder*, which I wrote in 1996. At that time, virtually no one had heard of BDD, and little was known about it. Since then, we've made tremendous strides in understanding this disorder. In 2005, I revised and expanded *The Broken Mirror* to include new knowledge acquired over the decade since I wrote the first edition. The present book is a more recent update that's geared more toward BDD sufferers, family, and friends—however, I hope that professionals and anyone else interested in learning about BDD finds it helpful. Readers who want more detailed information about BDD will still find *The Broken Mirror* informative.

I hope you find this book a helpful guide, whether you struggle with BDD yourself or care about someone who does. I hope it helps you understand this difficult illness, guides you or your loved one on the journey to wellness, and inspires you to maintain hope. With the right treatment, most people can overcome BDD!

Acknowledgments

I'd like to thank many people and organizations who helped make this book possible. Many colleagues have collaborated with me on research studies that generated information discussed in this book. While it isn't possible to mention all of them here, I'd like to give special thanks to some of my early collaborators and mentors—Drs. Susan McElroy, Harrison Pope, and James Hudson—who helped me get my BDD research off the ground while I was still a trainee nearly 20 years ago. They believed in me and the importance of BDD at a time when researching this little-known disorder was considered unconventional (fortunately, this has changed!). Thanks also to Drs. Steven Rasmussen, Jane Eisen, Eric Hollander, and Andrew Nierenberg, and to Dr. Barbara van Noppen and Leslie Shapiro, whose input contributed to the chapter for family members and friends.

Special thanks goes to Dr. Sabine Wilhelm of Massachusetts General Hospital/Harvard Medical School, who has been a wonderful collaborator on BDD treatment research. Dr. Wilhelm has taken a leading role in developing the cognitive-behavioral therapy treatment described in this book. Thanks also to Dr. Gail Steketee, who collaborated with us in developing this treatment. Other researchers and clinicians, too, deserve credit for their contributions to what is known about cognitive-behavioral therapy for BDD. They include Drs. David Veale, Fugen Neziroglu, James Rosen, and Rocco Crino.

I'd like to acknowledge and thank the research staff and volunteers I've worked over the years, especially William Menard, who I've been very fortunate to have on my team for nearly a decade. And special thanks to the other truly outstanding faculty members and research staff who work with me now, especially Dr. Elizabeth Didie, Dr. Megan Kelly, Christina Fay, Chris Walters, Lindsay Kurahara, and Dee Moniz. They deserve additional thanks for commenting on an earlier draft of this book. Thanks also to the talented editors in my family—my sister Carol Phillips Ewin, and my father, Harry Scott Phillips—for their comments and suggestions.

Most of all, I'd like to thank Dr. Larry Brown, my fiancé. I am so grateful for his insightful comments on a draft of this book, his unending support, and his selfless understanding of my commitment to my work and the long hours it requires.

Financial support from the following organizations has made it possible for me to do research on BDD, have enough time to listen to patients, and write this book. Most of all, I'd like to thank the National Institute of Mental Health, which has provided invaluable support over the years for my BDD research, including treatment studies. Thanks also to The National Alliance for Research on Schizophrenia and Depression (NARSAD), the American Foundation for Suicide Prevention, The Food and Drug Administration, Butler Hospital, and the Alpert Medical School of Brown University. Forest Laboratories, Solvay Pharmaceuticals, UCB Pharma, and Eli Lilly and Company provided unrestricted educational grants for much-needed treatment studies that I designed and conducted. Gate Pharmaceuticals provided medication for an additional treatment study.

I'd also like to thank members of the media for their role in bringing BDD out of the shadows. Being on Oprah, the Today Show, Dateline NBC, 20/20, Good Morning America, National Public Radio, CNN, and many other shows over the past 15 years has enabled me to reach millions of people and get the word out about this often-devastating illness. Many journalists, producers, television show hosts, reporters, and others have produced compelling, accurate, and helpful stories about BDD. Through these critically important efforts, millions of people have learned about BDD, and many have gotten effective treatment.

Most of all, I'd like to thank my patients and everyone who has participated in my research and other BDD researchers' studies over the years. It's only through your generous participation that we've learned so much about this devastating illness and how to treat it. By participating in research studies, you've immeasurably increased understanding of BDD, and you've diminished the suffering of countless people.

UNDERSTANDING
BODY DYSMORPHIC
DISORDER

1. PATIENTS SPEAK

■ Jennifer's Story

"This is incredibly embarrassing," Jennifer began. "It's really hard for me to talk about this. I don't want to be here." She had in fact canceled her first two appointments with me and had finally agreed to come to see me only at her mother's insistence.

I asked Jennifer if she could explain what was so embarrassing. "I don't like talking about my problem," she said. "You'll probably think I'm silly or vain. But I'm not," she said with tears in her eyes. "This is a very serious problem. I can't even tell you how bad it is." She sat silently for a minute. "Well, I guess I should tell you what it is. I think I'm really ugly. In fact, I think I'm one of the ugliest people in the whole world."

Jennifer was, by anyone's standards, attractive. She was a 22-year-old woman with long strawberry-blond hair, large green eyes, and a beautiful complexion. What could she possibly believe was wrong with how she looked? I couldn't see any flaws anywhere.

At first, Jennifer was reluctant to discuss the details. "Well, I just think I'm not pretty," she said. I know what you're going to say. You're probably going to tell me I look fine—everyone does—but I know it's not true. I look terrible!"

"What upsets you so much about how you look?" I asked. "My skin," she replied, after some hesitation. "See all these pimples and scars and marks?" she asked, jabbing her finger at her cheek and nose. I really couldn't see what she was describing. When I looked very closely, I could discern some small blemishes, but I had to be within a foot of her to see them.

Jennifer went on to describe how, since her early teenage years, she'd been preoccupied with the "acne" and "marks" she'd just pointed out. She also thought her skin was too pale. "I look like a ghost. Everyone else looks really good; I stick out like a sore thumb."

"When did the problem start?" I asked her. "When I was around 11," she replied. "It started with my nose. One of my nostrils stuck out more than the other. I remember catching a view of myself in the mirror one day and panicking. I thought, 'Is that what you look like? You look terrible, like a freak!'"

"My nostrils don't really bother me anymore. My skin took over for them. Now all I think about is how bad my skin looks. I think about it for most of the day. People can see it from 50 feet away!"

In high school, Jennifer thought so much about her supposed ugliness that she couldn't concentrate in class. Her preoccupations crowded her mind and sapped her energy. "I dressed up a lot, I got really tanned, wore blue eye shadow, and did a lot of things with my hair to distract people from my skin. But it didn't work. It was too hard for me to stay in school," she said. "I started calling my mother in the middle of the day to pick me up. She didn't want to; but I was so upset and cried so much she'd come and take me home."

While doing her homework, Jennifer spent so much time examining her face in a mirror she kept on her desk that she couldn't complete her assignments. "I had to see how my skin looked," Sometimes I'd get stuck there for hours, examining it for imperfections.

"I'd pick at it, too," she added, "which just made it worse. Sometimes I'd pick and pick with pins dipped in alcohol trying to get rid of the pimples and get the pus out. Sometimes I'd be up doing this at 1 or 2 in the morning, and then I'd fall asleep in class the next day, if I even went."

Because of her skin concerns, Jennifer's grades slipped from As and Bs to Ds, and she was put in a class for students with academic difficulties, even though she was bright. After missing many days of school, she dropped out of the 9th grade, even though she'd wanted to go to college.

Jennifer also missed parties because, as she explained it, "No one would want to hang out with me because I'm so ugly." When her friends encouraged her to go, telling her how pretty she was, Jennifer didn't believe them. "They were just feeling sorry for me and trying to be nice. How could I go when I looked so horrendous?"

She did date one boy after she'd dropped out of school but saw him mostly in her own house. "I hardly ever went out with him because I didn't want anyone to see my skin. When he came over, I pulled all the shades down and turned down the lights so he couldn't see how bad my skin looked. But I stopped seeing him, because I figured he'd just leave me anyway when he found out how bad I looked."

After dropping out of high school Jennifer tried waitressing three different times, but each time she quit or was fired because she missed so much work. "I wouldn't go if I had even one pimple. Sometimes I left in the middle of the day, because I thought the customers were making fun of my skin behind my back." A job as a filing clerk was more tolerable, since she didn't have to be around other people as much, but she had trouble with that job, too. She thought about her skin for most of the day and secretly checked it in a pocket mirror over and over. "I tried not to." Sometimes I was so totally panicked seeing all those pimples and marks I had to leave work and go to bed for the rest of the day."

When Jennifer had to work in a room with several other people and sit under fluorescent lights, she quit her job. "I remember the day I quit—all I could think of was that those awful lights showed up all the marks and pimples and holes in my face. I tried to calm myself down, but I was panicked. I ran out of that room and never went back."

Jennifer went on medical disability because she couldn't work, and she continued to live with her parents, even though she wanted to live on her own. They bought her most of what she needed, and she rarely went out. "Sometimes I go to a 24-hour grocery store at midnight, when I know no one else will be there. For a long time I've bought most of my clothes through catalogs. I'm too scared to go out—everyone will see how ugly I am," she explained. When she did venture out, she first spent at least 2 hours putting on makeup. "I look as though I'm wearing a mask, but at least I sort of cover up the pimples and scars," she said.

"It's getting worse," she said. "Last week, I got up my courage and decided to go out in the daylight, which I hardly ever do. I started driving to the store, and got stuck in a major traffic jam, and these people in the other cars were looking at me. All I could think was that they were looking at my face, thinking 'That poor girl; look how ugly she is. How can she go out in public when her skin looks so bad?' I was sweating and shaking, and I couldn't stop thinking they were laughing at me. I got so panicked I left my car in the middle of the traffic jam. I ran until I found a phone booth. I called my mother and I stayed there hiding until she got me. That's how bad it got."

Jennifer thought her problem was physical, not psychiatric, so she'd seen at least 15 different dermatologists. Some gave her antibiotics and other medications, but most said she didn't need treatment. "I'm every dermatologist's nightmare," Jennifer said, "I keep going back to see them, asking them over and over if my skin looks okay. I didn't believe them when they said my skin was fine. A lot of them refused to see me anymore. They're probably all seeing therapists because of me!"

One of the dermatologists had in fact called to refer Jennifer to me for treatment. He told me that Jennifer had beautiful skin but was so obsessed with it that she might benefit from seeing a psychiatrist. But, at that time, Jennifer preferred to see dermatologists and finally convinced one to do dermabrasion, a painful face peel usually reserved for treating severe acne. "She really didn't want to do it," Jennifer said, "but I was so desperate that she gave in." After the dermabrasion, Jennifer felt better about her skin for several months, even though her friends asked her what had happened to it. "They all thought it looked worse because it was red for a while," she said. "But I was thrilled—at least the pimples and marks went away." But within several months Jennifer's preoccupation returned and was even worse. She then had another dermabrasion, although the dermatologist was reluctant to repeat it. But Jennifer felt desperate. That procedure didn't help her feel any better, and she became so depressed that she considered suicide.

When she first saw me, Jennifer still believed her problem was physical, and she didn't want to see a psychiatrist. But her mother had insisted. "All my daughter does is ask me if she looks okay, over and over again, all day long," she told me. She had even told Jennifer that she'd have to move out of the house if she didn't stop her questioning. "It might be hard for you to believe this, Doctor, but this problem is ruining our family—the constant questioning, the constant tears. She won''t go out. We've tried to be patient, but nothing we do seems to help. We love our daughter and want to help her, but we can't take it anymore!"

■ BDD: When Appearance Worries Become a Problem

Jennifer's story isn't unusual. She has body dysmorphic disorder, also known as BDD. Although her BDD was severe, her long struggle is typical of what many people experience. So many people have told me, after reading **"The Broken Mirror,"** my first book about BDD, "I'm just like Jennifer!" BDD is an emotionally painful, yet, underrecognized psychiatric disorder—one in which normal-looking or even attractive people are preoccupied with one or more defects or flaws in their appearance. However, the defects aren't visible—or are barely visible—to others. People with this disorder may, for example, think that their hair is too curly, too straight, or too thin. Or that they have "veins" on their cheeks, scars on their nose, or skin that's too red or too pale. Some think that their nose is too big, their lips are too thin, their hips are too big, or their breasts are too small. Any body part can be disliked.

People with BDD not only focus on one or more physical flaws that other people don't notice—they think about them excessively. They worry. They obsess. Their appearance worries cause them emotional suffering and interfere with their life. BDD isn't just a bad hair day.

BDD often makes little sense to other people. How can someone with no perceptible flaw, or only a minimal flaw, in his or her appearance focus so excessively on something others don't notice? How can an attractive young woman like Jennifer think she's "one of the ugliest people in the whole world"?

The good news is that we're learning much more about BDD, and BDD is becoming better known—by professionals and the public alike. Also, most people get better with the right treatment. The bad news is that so many people are still unaware that it's a serious and common disorder. Many people with BDD have gone from doctor to doctor—without ever finding out that BDD was their problem. Many professionals still haven't heard of BDD. Even though this has been changing, BDD is still underrecognized.

■ Chris's Story

One of my first patients with BDD was a shy, articulate young man named Chris, who made an appointment with me to be evaluated for depression. When I first met with him, he told me that depression was his problem— that he'd been feeling down, unmotivated, uninterested in things he usually enjoyed. He was having trouble sleeping, and found it difficult to concentrate on his job. His girlfriend had recently left him.

Chris seemed to have a fairly straightforward case of depression. But when I asked if he was bothered by anything else, he was silent for several minutes. "There **is** something else bothering me. I wasn't sure I'd be able to tell you about it, but I should because it's why I'm here. It's my main problem. I'm depressed because of my hair.

"This is really embarrassing for me to talk about, but I'm devastated over my hair. I think it's falling out and that I look terrible. I realize I'm probably distorting—but I can't stop worrying about it." Chris had recently joined a hair club and had tried many hair tonics, which cost him $300 a month—a significant financial burden. But none of these remedies had diminished his preoccupation. Now he was considering a hair weave and was saving his money to pay for it.

Chris also worried that his nose was too wide and too long. "I'm so worried about my nose, and especially my hair, that I can't concentrate at work. I had a big assignment last month, and I was so distracted by these thoughts and by the fear that I was going to be bald that I was a week late with the assignment. What was really hard was that my boss called me in to talk about my lateness and ask me what the problem was. Of course I couldn't tell him what it was. I'd be totally mortified. I made up an excuse about a close friend being sick, even though I hate to lie."

Chris was also very nervous going to parties and bars with his girlfriend. "Before my hair problem began, I didn't have much trouble talking to people when I went out. But it's really hard for me now because of how I look. I can't concentrate on the conversation. All I can think about is whether my hair looks okay and whether people are noticing how thin it is. I constantly check out their hair and compare it to mine. Then I usually feel worse because I think their hair looks better. That's why my girlfriend left me. She said she can't stay with me if I stay home or leave parties early because of my hair. She thinks I look fine, and she can't understand why I can't just forget about it.

"The final straw for her came last month," he continued. "I was supposed to be in her brother's wedding. I went to the dress rehearsal, but on the morning of the wedding I panicked. I looked in the mirror and I thought 'Where's your hair?' I thought I looked balder than ever. I spent about an hour frantically putting gel in it, combing it, and blow drying it, trying to make it look fuller, but it didn't look right. I kept trying to convince myself that people would be looking at the bride and groom, not at my hair. But I just couldn't go. I felt so demoralized and desperate."

I wondered how Chris's hair and nose could have caused him such difficulties. His hair was a little thin, but not so thin that I'd noticed it when I met him. And his nose looked fine. How had it gotten so bad that he missed the wedding and his girlfriend had left him?

■ Keith's Story

Soon after I saw Chris, another patient, Keith, called me. "Dr. Phillips," he began, "I'm calling about something that's making me feel really panicked. It's been a problem for a while, but I haven't been able to tell you about it." I asked him what it was. "Well, I couldn't tell you about it in person because it's too embarrassing. But maybe I can over the phone. I'm...I'm upset about my hair." I was puzzled. His hair had always seemed fine. And two men with hair problems in the same month?

Keith went on to explain that he was very worried that his hair was too thin. "I try to stop thinking about it, but I can't." I wondered whether Keith might actually be losing his hair for some medical reason. But I was wrong. "It's actually not my overall hair—it's my bangs," Keith explained. "They're too thin, and the shape is wrong. I don't think my hair is falling out. I just think my bangs look **really bad.**"

Keith was extremely embarrassed about this. "I'm afraid you're thinking I'm silly to be worried so much about my hair, but I can't help it. I think I look like a dork!" I wondered whether Keith, like Chris, might have BDD. As it turned out, he did.

When I next met with Keith I was surprised to learn that he had **many** worries about his appearance. He thought that his ears were "too pointy—like Mr. Spock's," (the character from the TV show Star Trek). He also worried that he had "lines" on his face, and that his eyes were "small and beady." His most embarrassing concern was that his chest and buttocks were "shaped like a woman's." I'd known Keith for more than 2 years and had worked closely with him. But this problem had been too embarrassing for him to discuss. I commented that he'd seemed comfortable talking about other personal matters—what made this one so hard to discuss? He replied that it was somehow much easier to talk about his depression or his mania—even his sexual problems. For reasons he found difficult to explain, he was particularly ashamed of his appearance concerns. He was afraid I'd think he was superficial and vain. He also feared that by talking about his "ugly" body parts, he'd call attention to them. He finally summed it up: "I just didn't have the guts to tell you. I can't believe I brought it up."

■ The Ugliest Girl in Sparta

When I saw Keith, Chris, and Jennifer, BDD was largely unknown among professionals and the public alike. In all of my years of medical training, I hadn't heard of it. But when I tried to figure out what their problem was and how to help them feel better, I learned that BDD had actually been described for more than a century. For the previous 100 years, BDD was more commonly known as **dysmorphophobia,** a term coined in the 1880s by Enrico Morselli, a brilliant Italian psychiatrist. This term is still sometimes used. Dysmorphophobia comes from **dysmorfia,** a Greek word meaning ugliness, specifically of the face, which first appeared in the Histories of Herodotus. It refers to the myth of the "ugliest girl in Sparta," who, upon being stroked by the hand of a goddess, became the "fairest of all Spartan ladies" and later married the Spartan king. Herodotus writes, "Thither the Nurse would bear the child every day to the Shrine and set her by the Statue and pray the Goddess to deliver her from her ill looks."

"Beauty hypochondria" and "one who is worried about being ugly" are other colorful labels used in the 1930s to describe a BDD-like preoccupation with perceived ugliness. "Dermatologic hypochondriasis" depicted a BDD-like syndrome that focused on perceived defects of the skin and hair. BDD first formally entered the mental health field's classification of mental disorders only as recently as 1987. At that time, its name was changed to body dysmorphic disorder.

Vivid descriptions of BDD written during the past century from around the world bear testimony to this disorder's long history and the fact that people from a variety of countries and cultures suffer from it. Indeed, BDD is well known in some countries—Japan, for example—but has escaped adequate recognition in many others, including, until very recently, the United States.

■ A Secret Obsession

A likely reason that BDD's been largely unknown is that it's often kept secret. People with this illness are often too ashamed of their obsession to tell anyone about it. If they finally muster up the courage to reveal their concern to someone they trust, but are told they look fine, they feel misunderstood. So they may never mention it again. Or they may not mention it because they worry they'll be considered "crazy." But people with BDD aren't crazy—they have a treatable medical problem.

Others don't realize that their problem is psychiatric. They think they have a very noticeable physical problem. They go to surgeon after surgeon, dermatologist after dermatologist, hair club after hair club seeking a cosmetic cure for what is actually a mental health problem. This, too, has contributed to BDD's underrecognition. In addition, until recently, scientific research on BDD has been limited. Thus, we knew very little about it, including how to identify it in people who have it. But thanks to lots of recent research, this has changed.

BDD isn't rare. Research done so far suggests that BDD affects nearly 1% to 2.4% of adults in the general population. It's been found to affect more than 2% to 13% of students, 13% to 16% of people hospitalized in a psychiatric hospital, 9% to 14% of people seeking treatment from a dermatologist, and 3% to about half of people who receive cosmetic surgery.

These numbers translate into many millions of people in the United States alone. I and other researchers have been surprised by how many people seem to have BDD. When stories about BDD have run in newspapers and magazines, I've been deluged with calls and letters. I hear from people who wonder if they have BDD and want treatment, from family members who think a loved one may be suffering from the disorder, and from professionals asking for information and, sometimes, for help for their own family members.

■ Hope for People with BDD

Much more scientific research is urgently needed so we can learn more about BDD. At this time, there are still many questions. What causes BDD? Is it rooted in a person's genes, their life experience, or societal pressures? Why do some people get it but others don't? Is it related to eating disorders, like bulimia and anorexia nervosa (see Glossary for definitions), which also involve distorted body image? Or is it related to obsessive compulsive disorder (OCD), a disorder in which people have obsessive thoughts (for example, about contamination or harm) and compulsive behaviors that, like those of BDD, often involve checking and reassurance seeking? (See Glossary.)

And where exactly should we draw the line between BDD and the normal concern with appearance that so many people have? Is BDD simply a more intense and problematic version of these normal, common concerns? Or is it something quite different?

Yet we aren't totally in the dark. There's a lot that we **do** know—what symptoms people with BDD have, what other problems and disorders they commonly experience in addition to BDD, how BDD affects peoples' lives. We know that this disorder often improves with certain mental health treatments. The suffering of many people with BDD has been significantly alleviated by these treatments. Some are now completely free of their tormenting symptoms.

Jennifer got better with an antidepressant medication known as an SRI (serotonin-reuptake inhibitor). SRIs (also known as SSRIs) are a type of antidepressant medication that also diminish obsessional, repetitive thoughts (such as appearance preoccupations) and compulsive repetitive behaviors (such as mirror checking) as well as other symptoms such as depression and anxiety. These medications are not habit forming, and they are usually well tolerated. Currently, the SRIs are recommended as the first-choice medication treatment for BDD. Seven of them are currently marketed in the United States. I say much more about these medications in Chapter 11.

After several months of taking an SRI medication, Jennifer began to notice that she thought about her skin much less often, and it became much easier to resist peeks in the mirror. Her preoccupation no longer tormented her. As she explained, "I've put this problem in perspective. I don't love my skin, but I can accept it. It no longer ruins me." She's been able to leave her house, go into stores to shop, and look for a job.

Keith also improved with a SRI plus a type of therapy known as cognitive-behavioral therapy (CBT). CBT is a practical, "here-and-now" treatment that is currently the first choice psychotherapy for BDD. CBT helps people learn skills to stop compulsive behaviors, such as mirror checking. It also makes it easier to face situations that cause anxiety, such as social situations. I say much more about CBT in Chapter 12. With CBT and a SRI, Keith stopped worrying about his appearance almost entirely. Like Jennifer, it's now much easier to go out in public because he no longer thinks that everyone is staring at him.

The fields of mental health and neuroscience are rapidly advancing; some things we now know about the workings of the brain were barely imaginable even a decade ago. Many advances—such as those in brain imaging and genetics—will be used to study BDD and are likely to exponentially increase our understanding of this serious disorder and lead to even better treatments. In the meantime, we already know a lot about BDD, and most people can substantially improve with the treatments described in this book. There's lots of hope for those who suffer from BDD!

2. What Is Body Dysmorphic Disorder?

■ "My Problem Isn't Very Severe": Do I Even
Have Body Dysmorphic Disorder?

Sarah, a 24-year-old medical student, called me after she'd seen a story on body dysmorphic disorder (BDD) on TV. "My problem isn't very severe; I'm not sure I have body dysmorphic disorder. My concern with my appearance isn't that extreme, but it probably **is** excessive. It's a problem for me."

At this point I'd seen many people with more severe BDD—people like Jennifer—but fewer people with mild BDD, and I was interested in what Sarah would have to say. It sounded as though she had milder BDD. Or were her appearance concerns so minimal that she didn't even have BDD?

When I first saw Sarah I had no idea of what her concern could be. She was very appealing—quiet yet also animated—with a lovely smile. She did have a few small pimples on her chin, but they were barely noticeable. Nonetheless, this is a concern that many people with BDD have—perhaps it was hers.

But it wasn't. We started off talking about medical school and the hospital rotation she was on. She was trying to decide what her specialty would be—perhaps pediatrics. "My work is going well," but I'm having problems with my social life. It's hard for me to get into relationships because of my appearance worries."

Sarah went on to describe what bothered her. "I don't like my thighs. They're flabby and they have this rippling look. I also worry a lot about varicose veins on my legs and ankles. They're dark purple, and some of them bulge out of my legs. They bother me a lot. I get very upset when I think about these things—very nervous and anxious."

I asked her if there was anything else that bothered her. "Well, my hair too," she replied. "It's just not right. I can spend a lot of time combing it. And I've never been very happy with my weight. I'm always on a diet. But my weight doesn't stop me from doing things the way my other concerns do."

"Do your other concerns cause you problems?" I asked. "Yes, they do," she answered. "I avoid the beach even though I love it. If I go, I worry about my thighs and my veins the entire time. And I wear pants even on really hot summer days. It probably looks pretty strange. It also makes my feel phony—why can't I just be myself? Why do I care so much about how I look? I try to talk myself out of my concerns, but I can't.

"But the bigger problem is that I've avoided dating because of these things. I finally got up the courage to go out with someone; I like him a lot, and I want the relationship to continue, but my appearance is interfering. It sounds stupid, but I'm afraid he'll reject me when he sees my veins and my thighs! This worry is a burden and a hindrance. I'm afraid I'll never be able to get married because of it." Sarah stopped at that point, and she looked upset. "I'd really like to get married sometime," she said. "I don't want this to get in the way. The big problem right now is that I haven't told my boyfriend about these things. I try to hide my legs, but that's pretty hard to do when you're romantically involved with someone."

I asked Sarah if there were other factors that might be contributing to her relationship problems. "Maybe there **are** other reasons for my intimacy problems. My parents didn't have a good marriage, so maybe I'm unconsciously afraid of getting seriously involved with someone. I've always been somewhat sensitive to rejection, so I do think I hold back to some degree before getting involved with men. But my appearance concerns are a **big part** of my relationship problems.

"People tell me I'm attractive and that men find me attractive, but I find it hard to believe them. Actually, **overall** I think I look fine. But the things I told you about are very upsetting."

It did sound as though Sarah had BDD. She was very distressed over her concerns, and her relationships had suffered because of them. I wondered how bad the flaws that she described really were. Were they slight or non-existent, or as grotesquely unsightly as she thought? I couldn't see her legs because she was wearing pants, but Sarah told me that her sister thought they looked fine.

I also wondered about her hair. I couldn't see anything wrong with it. It was a beautiful deep auburn and was cut fashionably short. I asked her to tell me about it. "Yes, my hair's a problem, too. It really bugs me because it never looks right. First it's too flat. Then one side sticks out more than the other. But it's more than a bad hair day. It's upsetting." Sarah went on to describe how she sometimes got stuck in the mirror, literally for hours, trying to get her hair right—combing and restyling it.

I wondered how she managed to function as a medical student. "Has this gotten in the way of your work at all?" I asked her. "Well I try really hard not to let it," Sarah replied. "I try not to ever look in the mirror when I'm at work, but if my hair looks bad, I can't resist fiddling with it, and then the whole routine can start. I've actually been late for rounds and lectures because I got stuck. My friends have even come looking for me in the bathroom. That was really embarrassing!"

Many people with BDD don't like to admit the problems their symptoms cause them. Many try to ignore them and go on with their job, with raising children, with their lives. Some make a valiant effort to keep a stiff upper lip. But it's usually a struggle, even when BDD is relatively mild.

Despite her useful strategy of not checking mirrors, Sarah still encountered a problem when she got up each morning. "I need to look in the mirror to get myself ready for the day," she explained. "And that's a problem because I can get stuck there, and I've been late for work. But I try to just comb my hair and walk out after a few minutes. I'm petrified that my hair looks terrible, but I tell myself it probably looks fine and that the anxiety is nothing compared to what I feel when I get caught up in the grooming."

Sarah also avoided shopping malls with lots of mirrors and kept her distance from mirrors when buying clothes. "Getting my hair cut is especially hard—I **hate** getting it done. I keep my eyes glued to a newspaper or magazine the whole time so I don't get too upset."

Like Sarah, most people with BDD have a special and torturous relationship with mirrors. Most check excessively, and some get stuck in them for hours each day. Because excessively looking in mirrors can generate such intolerable anxiety, people who've found ways to stop this say they're better off.

Sarah returned to talking about how her symptoms affected her work. "My legs cause less of a problem at work because I can cover them. But they still bother me. When I see patients' legs I think of my own and how ugly they are. But I'm very serious about my work, and I just try to get my mind back on what I'm doing. I usually manage."

Sarah was in fact doing very well in medical school, and her patients liked her a lot. She was especially commended for her sensitivity to her patients' suffering. "Maybe it's because I myself suffer with this problem," she said. "You may think that sounds really bad.... How can I compare my appearance problems to the suffering of my patients who have cancer or are amputees? But, you know, even though I think I have a pretty mild case of BDD, it still causes me a lot of emotional pain. I try to tell myself that it's silly—but it still bothers me a lot. I worry that I'll always be alone in life because of this problem."

■ A Spectrum of Severity: From Mild to Life-Threatening

Milder BDD symptoms, like Sarah's, can be distressing and can interfere to some extent with living. By definition, to be considered BDD, the symptoms must cause clinically significant distress or impairment in functioning. (I'll discuss this further later.) But milder BDD is more manageable.

People with milder BDD may be productive; some are high achievers. Some manage well, despite their suffering.

A colleague of mine wondered if one of her patients had BDD but thought he probably didn't because he seemed to be functioning well in his daily life. It turned out that the patient, a professor at a college, did have BDD. He managed to perform well at work because he tried so hard to stay focused and keep his symptoms from interfering with his job. Yet the professor considered his functioning to be less than optimal. He hadn't applied for a job he'd wanted because he feared he'd be turned down because of his "awful" appearance. "Even though I'm very high functioning and successful," he explained, "I'm not working up to my capacity, although no one would ever know it."

BDD can also be more moderate in severity, and in some cases it's extremely severe. When BDD is severe, it can destroy virtually every aspect of one's life. Some people, like Jennifer, stop working and are stuck in their homes, sometimes for years. Some adolescents drop out of high school or college. Parents may stop caring for their children because they're so preoccupied with their appearance that they can't focus on their children's needs. Some people with BDD think they look so ugly that they never date or marry.

Some even get into life-threatening accidents. One man stared so intently at his reflection while washing windows that he fell off a three-story ladder. A young woman was so distressed by the shape of her breasts that she repeatedly slashed them with a knife. Some suffer so intolerably that they attempt suicide. Some people kill themselves.

So the severity of BDD spans a spectrum, ranging from milder symptoms to very severe and even life-threatening symptoms. In this way, BDD is like any other medical or mental health problem. Depression can be severe and life-threatening but can also be milder. Some depressed people, despite their suffering, manage to function adequately. BDD is similar. When it's severe, it's as crippling as any serious psychiatric or medical illness.

Some people have told me that they thought they didn't have BDD because their symptoms "weren't that bad." Others thought they might not have the disorder because their symptoms were **so severe** that there couldn't possibly be other people with the same problem, who suffered as much as they did. But they all had BDD.

BDD varies from person to person in other ways. Some people are preoccupied with their hair, others with their buttocks, legs, genitals, breasts, or eyebrows. Any body part can be the focus of concern. Even among people concerned with the same body part, exactly what they dislike can differ. One person may think his skin is too red, whereas another thinks he has terrible acne. Some people pick their skin or compulsively groom themselves, whereas other people don't.

Although no one with BDD has exactly the same experience as anyone else with BDD, all people with BDD have important things in common:

Everyone with BDD is preoccupied with some aspect of their appearance that they consider ugly, unattractive, or "not right," and everyone is distressed or doesn't function as well as they might because of their appearance preoccupations. The symptom severity and the details may differ from person to person, but these basic themes are shared by all.

■ How Is BDD Defined?

BDD's basic features are described by its diagnostic criteria. These criteria, shown in Table 2–1, are from DSM-IV (the *Diagnostic and Statistical Manual, Fourth Edition*). DSM-IV is the manual used by health professionals in the United States and many other countries to make psychiatric diagnoses. DSM provides "diagnostic criteria," which define a disorder's basic, most fundamental characteristics.

As shown in Table 2–1, BDD's diagnostic criteria indicate that people with BDD look normal, but are preoccupied with the idea that their appearance is defective or abnormal. This preoccupation causes them significant distress or interferes with their daily functioning.

I'll now go through each of BDD's diagnostic criteria.

Criterion 1: Preoccupation

Criterion 1 describes the preoccupation with appearance that occurs in BDD. People with BDD worry that some aspect of their appearance looks defective. They may describe the body area or areas as ugly, unattractive, flawed, "not right," deformed, disfigured—even as grotesque, hideous, repulsive, or monstrous. People with BDD have more than an occasional thought that they don't look right—they're preoccupied. They think excessively about their supposed appearance problem. Generally they spend at least an hour a day thinking about the supposed appearance flaws; on average, they spend between 3 and 8 hours a day.

TABLE 2–1   *Definition of Body Dysmorphic Disorder*

1. Preoccupation with an imagined defect in appearance. If a slight physical anomaly is present, the person's concern is markedly excessive.
2. The preoccupation causes clinically significant distress or impairment in social, occupational, or other important areas of functioning.
3. The preoccupation is not better accounted for by another mental disorder (e.g., dissatisfaction with body shape and size in anorexia nervosa).

Reprinted with permission from the *Diagnostic and Statistical Manual of Mental Disorders, Fourth Edition, Text Revision* (Copyright 2000), American Psychiatric Association

The definition notes that the appearance flaw is imagined or slight. In reality, the flaws that the BDD sufferer perceives are nonexistent—the disliked body areas usually look completely normal. Or, in some cases an imperfection is present, but it's slight, and not anything that would typically be noticed at conversational distance. Yet the BDD sufferer considers it to be very prominent and clearly visible to others.

In other words, people with BDD have **a problem with body image—with how they view their physical appearance—not with how they actually look.** Body image is the picture of our body that we have in our mind. Research on body image more generally (not just BDD) shows that the view from the "inside" (our body image) usually doesn't match that from the "outside" (other people's view of how we look). Many homely people think they look fine, and many attractive people think they're unattractive. In BDD, this mismatch is greatly magnified.

In this way, people with BDD are like those with anorexia nervosa: they see themselves very differently than other people see them. Even though people with anorexia are painfully thin, they see themselves as fat. Even though people with BDD see themselves as having ugly appearance flaws, they look normal to other people.

Sometimes, the disliked body areas are actually very attractive. One beautiful young woman had been asked to work as a model, and as a child she'd been told that she would someday be Miss America. However, she believed people told her this out of pity for her ugliness.

The "imagined" part of the BDD definition is complicated. Some people with BDD think they **really do** look bad, and they balk at the word "imagined." They worry that if they're imagining their defect, they may be considered "crazy." Some insist that because they're not imagining the flaw, they must not have BDD. One person who had BDD asked me, "My problem is really there; it's true. Do you deal with true things or only imaginary things?" He thought that if I dealt only with "imaginary things," then I wasn't the doctor he should be seeing.

It isn't known why people with BDD see themselves differently than other people do. This may be due to problems with visual processing (how a person's brain "sees" their environment). People with BDD appear to overfocus on details and minor aspects of appearance, which "take over" and dominate their view of themselves. In addition, people with BDD may interpret their appearance differently than others do, considering the body part ugly or unattractive when other people don't. The question isn't so much whether the defect is "real" versus "imagined," but rather **why** people with BDD view their appearance differently than other people do and see their appearance as so flawed (I'll say more about this in Chapter 9).

Yet another knotty issue is how to determine whether a "defect" is "slight," which the definition requires. If the defect is very obvious to others, then by definition, the person doesn't have BDD. But what if the defect is more subtle? Reality and distortion can't always be clearly differentiated. If someone with BDD thinks her legs are huge, but I think they're only "slightly" big, who is right? In some cases, I notice the flaw only if the BDD sufferer points it out. Is such a defect "slight" or "nonslight?"

It's helpful to consider what **most people** observe. I often have corroboration from others—health care professionals, family members, or friends—who agree that the defect is nonexistent or slight. The most common reason people with BDD are turned down for surgery or other cosmetic treatment for BDD concerns is that the physician considers the treatment unnecessary and won't provide it. Many patients have been brought to me by family members who recognize that their loved one has an inaccurate view of how they look. I and several dermatologists did a study in which we independently rated the severity of skin defects and found that we had good agreement about which defects were slight and which were clearly noticeable. This suggests that such judgments can be made with reasonable agreement and objectivity.

Occasionally BDD sufferers themselves agree that the defect is really only slight and that they have a distorted view of how bad it is. They're more likely to recognize this after they've improved with mental health treatment.

To go back to Criterion 1, if the defect is slight, then BDD's definition requires that the person's concern is "markedly excessive"—that is, they must be preoccupied. And typically, they overreact to the minor defect in terms of how it affects their life. Charles, a college student, left his dorm room only once during a 2-week period when his mild acne worsened. He missed his classes and avoided social activities. Charles qualified for BDD because his mild acne wasn't particularly noticeable, and his concern was excessive.

What if the severity of the perceived flaw can't be assessed because of its location? Many people with an "unassessable" defect have another perceived defect that can be assessed, which allows BDD to be diagnosed. For example, although I didn't evaluate one patient's buttocks, I could see that his concern with his "crooked" eyes was unfounded and a symptom of BDD. In other cases, an "unassessable" defect has been assessed by someone else who thinks it looks normal. Men with penis concerns often say that spouses and doctors alike have told them the size is normal. This information also allows a presumptive diagnosis of BDD to be made.

Making the diagnosis can also be complicated if skin picking, a common symptom of BDD, has caused noticeable scarring. If it can be determined that the acne or scarring was fairly mild before the picking began, and that the person is picking to try to make their skin look better, they are a candidate for the BDD diagnosis.

Yet, in my experience, the need to make difficult judgment calls, like those I just discussed, is the exception rather than the rule. For example, of the patients I've seen, only 3% have had an unassessable "defect" without also having others that could be assessed. In most cases, the perceived defect is clearly nonexistent or minimal.

Criterion 2: Distress or Impairment in Functioning

As shown in Table 2–1, to warrant the diagnosis of BDD the appearance pre-occupations must cause significant distress or cause problems with func-tioning. This criterion helps to guard against overdiagnosis of BDD by drawing a line between normal appearance concerns (which shouldn't be considered a mental illness) and excessive, problematic appearance concerns (BDD).

Criterion 2 mentions distress, which is emotional suffering. It can include feelings of depression, sadness, anxiety, worry, fear, panic, and other nega-tive thoughts and feelings. If a person experiences at least moderate distress because of how they look, this is compatible with a diagnosis of BDD. More severe distress—such as severe anxiety, depression, or suicidal thinking due to appearance concerns—clearly signals the presence of BDD.

Impairment in functioning can include problems with any aspect of social functioning that's caused by BDD, such as problems with relationships, socializing, intimacy, or being around other people. It also includes prob-lems with ability to function in a job, academically, or in one's role in life (such as being a parent). If you avoid anything because you dislike how you look—for example, dating, school, or any social situations—this is consistent with having BDD. You may also qualify for BDD if your appearance concerns interfere with your functioning in other ways. For example, work or school performance can be impaired because BDD thoughts or behaviors interrupt concentration, make you late, or make you miss school or work.

People with BDD commonly experience interference in their daily func-tioning in areas such as the following. They may avoid these situations par-tially or completely, or they may have other types of problems in these areas because of BDD symptoms:

- Friendships (ability to have friends)
- Spending time with friends
- Dating
- Intimacy and sexual relationships
- Relationship with spouse or partner
- Attending social functions and events
- Doing things with family
- Having a job or being able to be in school
- Going to school or work each day
- Being on time for school or work
- Focusing on school or work
- Being productive and meeting expectations at school or work
- Doing homework or maintaining grades

- Carrying out other important role activities, such as caring for children or elderly parents
- Maintaining a household, doing errands, going shopping
- Other daily activities, recreational activities, or hobbies

Criterion 3: Differentiating BDD from Other Disorders

Finally, to have BDD, the preoccupation with appearance can't be better accounted for by another mental disorder, such as anorexia nervosa or bulimia nervosa (see Glossary for definitions). In other words, symptoms of anorexia or bulimia shouldn't be misdiagnosed as BDD. Anorexia and bulimia are both eating disorders in which people are excessively concerned with weighing too much or being too fat, and they try to lose weight by restricting their eating or other methods. However, it's important to realize two things: (1) some people with BDD worry about their weight or being too fat but **don't** have an eating disorder—instead, they have BDD; and (2) some people have **both** an eating disorder **and** BDD (also disliking nonweight-related aspects of their appearance). (See Chapter 14 for further discussion.)

"A Sign on the Road"

The DSM-IV criteria for BDD that are shown in Table 2–1 provide a useful common language for BDD sufferers, clinicians, and researchers. They allow the diagnosis to be made, which, in turn, guides treatment. As a man with BDD said to me, "I read DSM to find out what was wrong with me. It was a relief to know what I had. Finally, I'd found the road and a sign on the road telling me where I was."

While the criteria are useful guidelines, they don't fully convey the experience of people with BDD. They don't tell us about their lives—the private torment, the fears, the isolation, or what is unique about each person's experience.

Sarah, for example, had certain things in common with Jane, whose story follows. They both fulfilled the diagnostic criteria for BDD, but, in some ways, their experiences were different. Sarah's symptoms were relatively mild, and she functioned well despite them. Jane's symptoms, in contrast, were very severe. Because of them, she couldn't work and had been hospitalized. She had even considered suicide.

■ "My Biggest Wish Is to Be Invisible"

I clearly remember meeting Jane. She was in her mid-thirties, fashionably dressed, tall, thin, and stately. She looked kind and earnest—but very timid and anxious. She explained that a friend had driven her to my office because she was too afraid to drive alone—which had everything to do with why she had come to see me.

"My biggest wish is to be invisible," she began. Despite her severe anxiety, she got straight to the heart of the matter. "Why do you want to be invisible?" I asked. "So no one will laugh at me and think I'm ugly. That's my biggest fear." On the one hand, Jane's statements were hard to understand, but by now I had seen scores of people with BDD and knew this was how many of them feel.

"I think I have this disorder you're studying, and I'm **totally** paralyzed by it. I've left my house only once in six years. That's why I couldn't come alone—I was much too scared."

"My hatred of my appearance began when I was 12," she began. "I became obsessed with my nose; I thought it was too big and shiny. It started when I heard a boy in my class make a comment about the actor Jimmy Durante's nose. The boy was snickering, and I thought he might be making fun of **me**—of **my** nose. I kept worrying that maybe there **was** something wrong with my nose. After that I started lifting up my lips to raise my nose so it wouldn't look so big. I didn't do my final eighth-grade project because I couldn't stand up in front of the class and have people see my nose. All my grades dropped— I went from straight As to Ds and Fs. I got very withdrawn, and I stopped seeing my friends."

"What were you like before then?" I asked. "I really wasn't very concerned with how I looked," she replied. "But I was always very sensitive. And I wasn't very interested in boys and wondered if something was wrong with me. Then the nose problem started, and my life went downhill. I've thought about it every day since.

"When I was 16 things got even worse. I had a slight scar on the top of my lip, but it never really bothered me until then, when I got it surgically revised. After the operation, I noticed a funny irregularity in a certain light, and it's been a disaster ever since. I think about it 24 hours a day. I even have dreams about it. In my dreams people ask me things like, 'What's that thing on your lip?' and they make nasty comments about it."

Jane's concern with her faint scar started at the time she was having problems with her boyfriend. "Maybe it was the stress," she said. "But I don't want you to misunderstand. Some of my therapists have tried to convince me that my appearance concerns are just a symptom of other problems—that they aren't my real problem. I've finally decided that they're wrong. **My obsessions have a life of their own.** They're not just a symptom of other problems.

"I've been incredibly frustrated when I've been told that this isn't my real problem. **This** is the biggest problem in my life, the one that's kept me in my house for six years. Sometimes it feels **chemical**, totally out of my control." Jane had fortunately found a therapist and a psychiatrist who took her concerns seriously and who treated her BDD as a legitimate disorder.

Jane then pulled her suede jacket up over her chin and mouth so I couldn't see her face from the nose down. She smiled slightly, through her tears. "I have to hide my face before I tell you about this one," she said. Then she became completely serious. "In my early twenties I started worrying about my jaw when a surgeon I'd seen for a nose job said my nose was fine but my jaw was too big. I was totally devastated by that comment, and I've been haunted ever since."

Jane had also worried about other things—that her breasts were too small and her buttocks too "big and round." "I tried to go to school to become a fashion designer, but I had to drop out. I couldn't let people see how bad I looked. So many of my body parts were totally unpresentable. Then I tried working, but I stayed only a few weeks at each place. I felt I was really ugly and really unlikable. It got worse and worse. I stopped dating, and then I stopped going out at all.

I started spending my entire day in my parents' house. When relatives come over, I hide upstairs. I don't even see them on holidays. I feel over-whelmed and hopeless and out of control. Sometimes I panic, and I think 'I'm going to die. I have to kill myself. I wish I could be put to sleep.'

"The hardest part of this is the isolation. I didn't see my own mother for two years, even though she lived in the same house with me. I was so ashamed of my appearance that I completely avoided her. My family has no idea that I have this problem. I've kept the BDD a secret."

Jane then described the one time she'd left her house in six years. "I got sick. I tried putting off going to the doctor, but the pain got pretty intense. When I finally went, I covered my face with bandages, so no one could see how I looked.

"So coming here today was a big event. I haven't been out in **so** long. Sometimes when I drive I get especially freaked out because I think everyone is looking at me as they drive by and that they're thinking how ugly I am. Sometimes I think my face will frighten them so much that they'll crash their cars."

Jane had received a lot of treatment. A nose job didn't help her feel any better about her nose, so she had it redone—which didn't help either. The revision of the scar on her lip actually triggered a new obsession. She continued to seek surgery but finally stopped after four surgeons refused to do any further procedures.

"Later, when I realized my problem was psychiatric, it was still really hard for me," Jane said. "The first time I was hospitalized, the doctors and nurses on the psychiatry ward hadn't heard of BDD, so it was hard for them to understand me or take me seriously. No one knew my inner torment. They tried to reassure me and talk me out of my concern, telling me I looked fine, but this just made me feel pathetic. It felt patronizing. If I'd had any other problem, they would never have taken that approach."

Jane had been treated with cognitive-behavioral therapy as well as many psychiatric medications. A type of antidepressant known as a monoamine oxidase inhibitor was very helpful for several years but then stopped working. Because she then became so severely depressed over her appearance, Jane received electroconvulsive therapy (ECT), also known as shock therapy. This treatment did temporarily help her depression somewhat but not her BDD. "It's still on my mind all the time," she said, "and I still consider suicide because of it."

Jane had been in several support groups for people with a variety of mental health problems such as anxiety and depression. "Everyone else was pretty open about their problems, and I was to a certain extent. But I couldn't discuss my appearance, even though I was in the group for four years. It was too humiliating, and I was afraid they wouldn't understand. I was afraid they'd focus on my defects more and notice how horrendous they looked. And I was afraid of their reaction, which I'd hear negatively, no matter what. My **biggest** fear was that they'd **validate** my concern. I couldn't take the risk. So my isolation continued."

At the time she saw me, Jane was considering a cingulotomy, a type of brain surgery that patients with severe psychiatric disorders sometimes undergo when other treatments haven't worked. "I really don't want to have brain surgery," she said, "but I can't go on suffering like this."

I didn't treat Jane, but I spoke with her several times after I'd seen her. I'd recommended to her and her doctor that she postpone the neurosurgery consultation and first try a new combination of medications. With the new medication, she gradually felt better, and 4 months after I'd seen her she gave me a call. "You won't believe this," she said. "The medications have helped immensely. I can get out of the house, and I'm doing volunteer work as a receptionist. I still have BDD feelings," she said, "but I can view it more rationally. I can tell myself that people aren't looking at me. It's a real triumph to allow people to get so close to my face."

But about a year and a half later, she called to tell me that she'd been feeling tired and more depressed. She had decided to stop her medications, and her BDD symptoms gradually came back. But when I next talked with her, she had good news: she had tried a serotonin-reuptake inhibitor medication and had restarted cognitive-behavioral therapy—and she was feeling great again.

3. How Do I Know if I Have Body Dysmorphic Disorder?

■ BDD Is Fairly Common

Body dysmorphic disorder (BDD) isn't rare. In fact, Table 3–1 on the next page indicates that it's fairly common. Studies from several countries, including the United States, have found that nearly 1% to 2.4% of adults in the general population have BDD. This makes BDD about as common as, or even more common than, many other serious mental disorders, such as bipolar disorder, panic disorder, and schizophrenia. Studies of students have found even higher rates. Overall, these studies indicate that millions of people in the United States alone suffer from BDD.

BDD is even more common in clinical settings. Two studies of hospitalized psychiatric patients found that a surprisingly high percentage—13% and 16%—had BDD. In one of these studies, BDD was more common than schizophrenia, obsessive compulsive disorder, social phobia, eating disorders, and many other disorders. Reported rates of BDD among outpatients receiving mental health treatment are often high, depending on the group being assessed. A small study of patients with anorexia nervosa, for example, found that 39% also had BDD. In studies of depression, BDD was more common than a host of other mental disorders among patients with depression.

In a study I and my colleagues did of people who went to a dermatologist, 12% had probable BDD. Other studies have found that 9% to 14% of acne patients have BDD. And studies of people seeking cosmetic surgery have found that from 3% to about half have BDD.

Some of my patients are convinced that these rates of BDD are falsely low. "Those are the ones who confess," one man told me. "If someone did a survey and asked me if I had BDD, I'd deny it. I'd be too embarrassed and ashamed. Also, if I was stuck in my house, how would I be in a survey? I wouldn't answer the door."

BDD affects both men and women as well as people of all ages, from children to the elderly. It also affects a broad range of racial and ethnic groups, and it has been reported in countless countries around the world. If you have BDD, you aren't alone!

TABLE 3–1   *How Common Is BDD?*

Studies Have Found That BDD Occurs in Approximately....

- A little under 1%–2.4% of adults in the general population
- 2.2%–13% of students
- 13%–16% of patients who are psychiatrically hospitalized
- 14%–42% of outpatients with atypical major depression*
- 11%–12% of outpatients with social phobia.*
- 3%–37% (average of 17%) of people with obsessive compulsive disorder (OCD)*
- 39% of hospitalized patients with anorexia nervosa*
- 9%–14% of patients seeking treatment from a dermatologist
- 3%–about half of patients seeking cosmetic surgery

*See Glossary for a definition of these disorders; outpatients are people who seek treatment without being hospitalized.

■ BDD Is Underrecognized

Health care professionals, however, often overlook BDD. As a result, BDD sufferers may not find out that they have the disorder, and treatment may not succeed because it doesn't target BDD. In the two studies of psychiatric inpatients just mentioned, none of the patients who had BDD had raised their BDD symptoms with their doctor or received the diagnosis while in the hospital. In a study I did of 200 people with BDD, more than half of those who'd been treated with psychiatric medication had never revealed their BDD symptoms to their doctor, even though their symptoms were a major problem. Other studies have similarly found that BDD usually goes undiagnosed, even among people who are receiving mental health treatment.

These findings are very consistent with what I've heard for nearly two decades from my patients and people participating in my research studies. A staggeringly high proportion of those who have suffered with BDD for years, even decades, were never diagnosed, even though they'd seen plenty of doctors and therapists.

So why is BDD so underrecognized and underdiagnosed? Here are some likely reasons.

■ Why BDD Is Underrecognized and Underdiagnosed

Secrecy and Shame

BDD is often a secret disorder. Sufferers don't reveal their appearance concerns, and health professionals often don't ask. Many patients I've seen have never mentioned their appearance concerns to anyone at all, not even their spouse or closest friend. And many who've been in treatment with a mental health professional haven't revealed their symptoms, even though they're a serious problem. It takes courage to mention BDD concerns and discuss them with someone else.

Many people with BDD are too ashamed to raise their appearance concerns. If a friend, family member, or health care professional doesn't ask if the person has such concerns, the sufferer may not reveal them.

Reasons for secrecy and shame include the following:

- Fear of being negatively judged. BDD can be confused with vanity, and some sufferers worry they'll be considered superficial, silly, or vain, so they keep their worries to themselves;

- Worry that once the perceived defect is mentioned, others will notice it and scrutinize it even more, causing more embarrassment and shame;

- Fear that disclosure of the worry will be met with reassurance that the BDD sufferer looks fine. Many people with BDD interpret this response to mean that they were foolish to have mentioned it, or that their emotional pain isn't being taken seriously or understood—and they may not mention it again.

One research study found that people with BDD **want** their health care professional to ask if they have such concerns and that they **want** to discuss them. They're just too embarrassed to raise the topic themselves.

BDD Can Be Mistaken for Vanity or Trivialized

BDD isn't vanity. It's a legitimate and often-severe illness that can seriously disrupt a person's life (see Chapter 7). Most people with BDD aren't narcissistic or vain.

BDD can also easily be trivialized in other ways. Why should he care so much about a few pimples? How could she be so worried about her face when she's so pretty? The fact that BDD sufferers generally look fine, combined with the fact that normal appearance concerns are so common in the general population, contribute to its trivialization. But research indicates that people with BDD feel much more unattractive and are much more dissatisfied with their appearance than other people are. And anyone who knows someone like Jennifer or Jane is only too aware of how serious—even life-threatening—the disorder can be.

Lack of Familiarity with BDD

Many people, including health care professionals, still aren't aware that BDD is an actual disorder that often improves with psychiatric treatment. So they may not ask patients about it. Despite its long history, BDD entered psychiatry's diagnostic manual (DSM) only a few decades ago, and BDD is still among the lesser-known psychiatric disorders. Sufferers and family members, too, often don't realize that it's a treatable disorder that other people have too, so they don't discuss the symptoms with a health care professional.

BDD Can Be Misdiagnosed as Another Disorder

People with BDD may also have depression, social anxiety, or other symptoms that may be less embarrassing to discuss. Thus, they may receive the diagnosis of depression or social phobia, but not BDD. Moreover, patients who reveal their BDD symptoms are sometimes told that their real problem is low self-esteem, a relationship problem, or another issue. Although people with BDD may have some of these problems, BDD itself should also be diagnosed and treated. Sometimes, these problems are actually **due** to BDD. In these cases, it's even more critical to diagnose BDD.

Pursuit of Surgical, Dermatologic, and Other Cosmetic Treatment

Many people with BDD see dermatologists, plastic surgeons, and other physicians rather than mental health professionals such as psychiatrists and psychologists. They search, usually unsuccessfully, for a cosmetic solution to a body image problem, unaware that BDD is a known psychiatric disorder for which mental health treatment is often effective.

■ Screening Questions for BDD

How do you know whether you or someone you know has BDD? At present, psychiatric diagnoses—including BDD—are made primarily by asking questions that ascertain that the DSM criteria for the disorder are fulfilled. As of yet, there are no blood tests, brain-scanning techniques, or other tools sufficient to diagnose BDD.

I've developed several questionnaires, or scales, for BDD, which consist of questions useful in making the diagnosis. One, the Body Dysmorphic Disorder Questionnaire (BDDQ), is filled out by the patient (Box 3–1). A second set of questions (the BDD Diagnostic Module) is asked by a clinician (Box 3–2). Both of these scales mirror the DSM-IV diagnostic criteria for BDD discussed in the last chapter, and they determine whether these criteria are fulfilled. Versions of these scales for children and adolescents are provided in Chapter 8.

You're likely to have BDD if you give the following answers on the BDDQ

- Question 1: Yes to both parts
- Question 3: Yes to any of the questions
- Question 4: Answer b or c

BOX 3–1 *Body Dysmorphic Disorder Questionnaire (BDDQ) for Adults*

Name _____

This questionnaire assesses concerns about physical appearance. Please read each question carefully and circle the answer that best describes your experience. Also write in answers where indicated.

1. Are you very concerned about the appearance of some part(s) of your body that you consider particularly unattractive?   Yes   No

   • If *yes*: Do these concerns preoccupy you? That is, you think about them a lot and wish you could think about them less?   Yes   No

   • If *yes*: What are they? _____

   Examples of areas of concern include: your skin (e.g., acne, scars, wrinkles, paleness, redness); hair (e.g., hair loss or thinning); the shape or size of your nose, mouth, jaw, lips, stomach, hips, etc.; or defects of your hands, genitals, breasts, or any other body part.

   • If *yes*: What specifically bothers you about the appearance of these body part(s)? (Explain in detail):

   _____

   _____

   (NOTE: If you answered "No" to either of the above questions, you are finished with this questionnaire. Otherwise please continue.)

2. Is your main concern with your appearance that you aren't thin enough or that you might become too fat?   Yes   No

3. What effect has your preoccupation with your appearance had on your life?

   • Has your defect(s) caused you a lot of distress or emotional pain?   Yes   No

   • Has it significantly interfered with your social life?   Yes   No

     • If *yes*: How? _____

     _____

     _____

   • Has your defect(s) significantly interfered with your school work, your job, or your ability to function in your role (e.g., as a homemaker)?   Yes   No

     • If *yes*: How? _____

     _____

     _____

   • Are there things you avoid because of your defect(s)?   Yes   No

     • If *yes*: How? _____

     _____

     _____

4. How much time do you spend thinking about your defect(s) per day on average? (add up all the time you spend) (circle one)

(a) Less than 1 hour a day   (b) 1–3 hours a day   (c) More than 3 hours a day

On the BDDQ, question 1 establishes whether preoccupation is present, and question 3 determines whether it causes significant distress or impairment in functioning. Question 4 is useful, even though the BDD diagnostic criteria don't require that the perceived defect be thought about for a specified amount of time a day. If you spend **at least** 1 hour a day thinking about perceived appearance flaws, the diagnosis is more likely. But if it's less than an hour a day, in total, this probably isn't enough time or preoccupation to fulfill criterion 1 for the diagnosis.

A note of caution about the BDDQ: It's intended to screen for BDD, not diagnose it. What this means is that the BDDQ can suggest that BDD is present but can't necessarily give a firm diagnosis. The diagnosis is ideally determined by a trained clinician in a face-to-face interview. There are several reasons for this. First, clinical judgment should be used to confirm that (1) answers on the BDDQ (a self-report questionnaire) indicate the presence of a disorder (for example, that any distress or impairment reported on the questionnaire is problematic enough to warrant a psychiatric diagnosis); (2) the physical defect is nonexistent or slight; and (3) the appearance concerns aren't better accounted for by an eating disorder. A "yes" answer to question 2 raises the possibility that an eating disorder might be a more accurate diagnosis. (See Chapter 14.)

■ Scales for Diagnosing BDD

Your doctor or therapist can use the BDD Diagnostic Module which has questions they can ask you to determine whether you have BDD. The questions mirror the DSM-IV criteria for BDD (as well as the BDDQ questions). The clinician asks the questions on the left-hand side to determine whether each diagnostic criterion, shown on the right-hand side, is fulfilled. If the person answers "yes" to the top question on the left, which means that they meet the diagnostic criterion across from it (preoccupation), the clinician asks the next question on the left and then the next. If the person's answers indicate that all of the diagnostic criteria are met, they are diagnosed with BDD.

The questions on the left should be asked as written, but further questions can be asked to clarify whether the criterion is met. It's helpful, for example, to ask about various body areas to be sure problematic concerns aren't missed. It's also important to ask about how the person is functioning in different areas of their life to determine whether they're experiencing enough impairment to qualify for the diagnosis. Criterion C doesn't have any questions next to it because the clinician is expected to know about eating disorders and how to differentiate BDD from an eating disorder (although some people have both disorders). BDD can also be diagnosed

---

BOX 3–2   *Body Dysmorphic Disorder Diagnostic Module for Adults*

Questions	DSM-IV Criteria for BDD
Have you ever been very worried about your appearance in any way? *If yes*: What was your concern? Did you think (body part) was especially unattractive?	A. Preoccupation with an imagined defect in appearance. If a slight physical anomaly is present, the person's concern is markedly excessive
What about the appearance of your face, skin, hair, nose, or the shape/size/ other aspect of any other part of your body? Did this concern preoccupy you? That is, you thought about it a lot and wished you could worry about it less? (Did others say that you were more concerned about _____ than you should have been?)	**Note:** *Give some examples even if person answers no to these questions* Examples include skin concerns (e.g., acne, scars, wrinkles, paleness), hair concerns (e.g., thinning), or the shape or size of the nose jaw, lips, and so on Also consider perceived defects of hands, genitals, or any other body part
What effect has this preoccupation had on your life? Has it caused you a lot of distress? Has your concern had any effect on your family or friends?	B. Preoccupation causes clinically significant distress or impairment in social, occupational, or other important areas of functioning **Note:** *If slight physical defect is present, concern is clearly excessive*
(If concern is completely attributable to an eating disorder, do not diagnose BDD)	C. The preoccupation is not better accounted by another mental disorder (e.g., dissatisfaction with body shape and size in Anorexia Nervosa)

---

using the Structured Clinical Interview for DSM-IV (SCID). This widely used diagnostic measure contains many mental disorders, including BDD.

■ Determining the Severity of BDD

One way to get a sense of how severe your BDD is to use the first three items of a scale I and my colleagues developed, called the **Yale-Brown Obsessive-Compulsive Scale Modified for BDD** (BDD-YBOCS). The first 3 items of this 12-item scale mirror the DSM-IV diagnostic criteria for BDD (they also mirror the questions on the BDDQ and the BDD Diagnostic Module). A difference, however, is that with the BDD-YBOCS you can get a total score that reflects the severity of your BDD. It's best to have a qualified clinician ask you the questions on these scales, especially to help score interference in your functioning.

Here are the first three items on this scale:

1. *Time* **occupied by thoughts**
   about body defect
   How much of your time is
   occupied by THOUGHTS
   about a defect or flaw in your
   appearance (*list body parts*
   of concern)

   0 = None
   1 = Mild (less than 1 hr/day)
   2 = Moderate (1–3 hrs/day)
   3 = Severe (greater than 3 and
       up to 8 hrs/day)
   4 = Extreme (greater than 8 hrs/day)

2. *Interference* **due to thoughts**
   about body defect
   How much do your
   THOUGHTS about your body
   defect(s) interfere with your
   social or work (role) functioning?
   Is there anything you aren't
   doing or can't do because
   of them?

   0 = None
   1 = Mild, slight interference with social
       or occupational activities, but over-
       all performance not impaired
   2 = Moderate, definite interference
       with social or occupational per-
       formance, but still manageable
   3 = Severe, causes substantial
       impairment in social or
       occupational performance
   4 = Extreme, incapacitating

3. *Distress* **associated with**
   thoughts about body defect
   How much distress do your
   THOUGHTS about your
   body defect(s) cause you?

   0 = None
   1 = Mild and not too disturbing
   2 = Moderate and disturbing
   3 = Severe and very disturbing
   4 = Extreme and disabling distress

The following scores are compatible with a diagnosis of BDD: (1) a score of 2 or higher on item 1 (thinking about your appearance flaws for a total of at least 1 hour a day), plus (2) a score of 2 or higher on either item 2 or 3 (at least moderate distress or moderate impairment in day-to-day functioning). Assuming you qualify for BDD (using these guidelines as well as one of the diagnostic scales mentioned above), Table 3–2 is a rough guide to interpreting your BDD-YBOCS score.

■ How to Differentiate BDD from Normal
   Appearance Concerns

I'm often asked how to differentiate BDD concerns from normal appearance concerns. In fact, concern with physical appearance is very common; most of us care about how we look. In a nationwide body image survey, only 7% of women and 18% of men had little concern about their appearance and didn't

TABLE 3–2   *Interpreting Your BDD-YBOCS Score*

Total Score on the First 3 BDD-YBOCS Items	BDD Severity
4 or 5	Mild BDD
6	Mild to moderate BDD
7	Moderate BDD
8	Moderate to severe BDD
9	Severe BDD
10	Severe to extremely severe BDD
11 or 12	Extremely severe BDD

Roughly equivalent scores on the scale's full 12-item version are as follows: score of 5 on the first three items is roughly equivalent to a 20 on the full version, a 6 is roughly equivalent to a 24, a 7 to a 28, an 8 to a 32, a 9 to a 36, a 10 to a 40, an 11 to a 44, and a 12 to a 48 (the highest possible score). The full scale is available in *"The Broken Mirror: Understanding and Treating Body Dysmorphic Disorder"* or by contacting my program.

do much to improve it. The vast majority thought about, attended to, valued, and actively worked on their looks.

Most of us even **dislike** how we look. A landmark 1997 survey found that more than half of all women—56%—and nearly half of all men—43%—said they were dissatisfied with their overall appearance. Even more people than this were dissatisfied with particular body areas. Moreover, many people have a **distorted** view of how they look, involving the body as a whole, specific parts (typically the waist and hips), and body weight. BDD echoes normal appearance dissatisfaction and distortion. So how do we differentiate BDD from these common body image problems and concerns? At present, the best answer is to use the DSM-IV criteria for BDD, which the BDDQ and BDD Diagnostic Module assess: **preoccupation, distress,** and **impairment in functioning.**

To have BDD, the person must be preoccupied. Everyone I've given the diagnosis to has at some point worried about their appearance for at least an hour a day. I'm reluctant to diagnose BDD in anyone who worries less than this, because their preoccupation may not be excessive enough to warrant a psychiatric diagnosis. On average, people with BDD worry about their appearance for 3 to 8 hours a day, and some worry all day long.

To qualify for BDD, appearance concerns must also cause clinically significant distress or impairment in functioning. Most people with BDD experience both. The term "clinically significant" implies that a health professional determines that the distress (emotional suffering) or impairment in life functioning are problematic to a significant degree. Most people with BDD experience a degree of preoccupation, distress, and impairment in functioning that is clearly greater than what most people experience.

On the first 3 items of the BDD-YBOCS, which I discussed earlier, most people with BDD have a total score of at least 5 or higher. (On the full 12-item scale, the usual cutpoint to differentiate full-fledged BDD [meeting all DSM-IV criteria] from non-BDD appearance concerns is a total score of at least 20 or higher.)

It's interesting that people with BDD themselves often differentiate their BDD symptoms from normal appearance concerns using the same benchmarks: preoccupation, distress, and impairment. Kathleen disliked her "wide" nose, "fat" stomach, and "grotesque" veins on her legs. She considered her nose concerns to constitute BDD, but her stomach and vein concerns to be "normal." "My nose takes up much more of my time. I think about it a lot, and it's getting in the way of my life," she said. "My stomach and legs bother me, but they don't cause me such intense anxiety and pain. They don't keep me from socializing."

Kathleen's nose concerns were more intense and severe than normal appearance concerns. She worried too much and suffered. Many people with BDD have some additional normal concerns about their appearance, which they can usually easily differentiate from their BDD.

But sometimes, in people with mild BDD, it can be hard to determine where normal concern leaves off and BDD begins. In other words, the difference between BDD and normal appearance concerns may be somewhat blurry and a matter of degree. Does a man whose slightly thinning hair makes him feel anxious around women and nervous about asking them out have BDD? The same issue applies to certain other mental disorders and medical disorders. The boundary between normal blood pressure and high blood pressure is also a matter of degree, with "mild" high blood pressure being just one point higher than normal blood pressure. It isn't hard, however, to differentiate moderately severe or severe BDD from normal appearance concerns. The man who quits job after job because he thinks his buttocks are asymmetrical, clearly has BDD.

There are good reasons to think that BDD also differs in other ways from the more common and normal appearance concerns that so many people have. For example, people with BDD may "see" their environment and process visual information differently than people without BDD. More specifically, they overly focus on and try to extract greater detail from faces and abstract drawings. They also appear more likely to misinterpret facial expressions as contemptuous and angry, and they may have subtle differences in brain structure (see Chapter 9). Those with BDD commonly dislike their skin, hair, or face, whereas, people in the general population most often dislike their weight or weight–related aspects of appearance, such as the size of their abdomen, hips, or thighs. Also, BDD symptoms often diminish with the right medication. We wouldn't expect normal appearance concerns to improve with medication, because the medication normalizes a "chemical imbalance" in the brain. If a chemical imbalance doesn't exist in the first place, medication wouldn't be expected to work.

■ Clues That Someone May Have BDD: Mirror Checking, Excessive Grooming, Skin Picking, and Other Behaviors

The BDDQ and the BDD Diagnostic Module ask about the core definitional features of BDD—what's required for the diagnosis. But BDD has some additional features that aren't required for the diagnosis but which many people with BDD have. These behaviors can provide clues that a person may have BDD: frequent mirror checking, excessive grooming, skin picking, reassurance seeking, and other behaviors. Some (although not all) of these behaviors are "normal" things that most people do, but in BDD they're done excessively and are hard to control (I discuss these behaviors further in Chapter 6).

I've sometimes observed strangers doing things that have made me wonder if they have BDD. I once saw a young man in a parking lot repeatedly checking his hair in a side-view mirror, frantically combing and recombing it. He appeared extremely agitated and distressed over the state of his hair. And I once drove behind a woman on a busy highway for about 20 miles who spent most of the time looking in her rearview mirror fixing her hair rather than looking at the road. Did either of these people have BDD? Without talking with them, I couldn't be sure. But their behaviors were clues that they might.

Table 3–3 lists some of the more common clues to BDD. Most people with BDD don't do **all** of these things, but most people with BDD do **at least some** of them. A "yes" answer to any of the questions in Table 3–3 doesn't necessarily mean that you have BDD. But "yes" answers—especially many "yes" answers—suggest that BDD may very well be present. In this case, it's a good idea to get an evaluation from a professional who's knowledgeable about BDD.

■ Additional Clues to BDD: Depression, Social Anxiety, and Other Symptoms

There are other clues that a person may have BDD. Many people with BDD are depressed. Others have problems with alcohol or drugs. Many are anxious, and some have panic attacks. Indeed, people with BDD often have other psychiatric symptoms and disorders, which can provide additional clues that a person may have BDD.

The most common mental disorder than coexists with BDD is major depressive disorder—three-quarters of those with BDD suffer from it at some point in their life. In some cases, the depression and the BDD seem to be somewhat "separate." But often, the depression seems largely due to BDD. As

TABLE 3–3   *Clues to the Presence of BDD*

1. Do you often check your appearance in mirrors or other reflecting surfaces, such as windows?

2. Do you frequently check your appearance without using a mirror, by looking directly at the disliked body part?

3. Do you frequently compare yourself to others and often think that you look worse than they do?

4. Do you often ask—or want to ask—other people whether you look okay, or whether you look as good as other people?

5. Do you try to convince other people that there's something wrong with how you look, but they consider the problem nonexistent or minimal?

6. Do you spend a lot of time grooming—for example, combing or arranging your hair, tweezing or cutting your hair, applying makeup, or shaving? Do you spend too much time getting ready in the morning, or do you groom yourself frequently during the day? Do others complain that you spend too much time in the bathroom?

7. Do you pick your skin, popping pimples or trying to get rid of blackheads or blemishes, because you're trying to make it look better?

8. Do you spend a lot of time or money on finding beauty products (e.g., makeup, hair growth tonics, acne treatment) or clothes to try to solve your appearance problem?

9. Do you often change your clothes, trying to find an outfit that covers or improves disliked aspects of your appearance? Do you take a long time selecting your outfit for the day, trying to find one that makes you look better?

10. Do you try to cover or hide parts of your body with a hat, clothing, makeup, sunglasses, your hair, your hand, or other things? Is it hard to be around people when you haven't done these things?

11. Do you try to hide certain aspects of your appearance by maintaining a certain body position—for example turning your face away from others? Do you feel uncomfortable if you can't be in your preferred positions?

12. Do you tan to try and fix a problem with your skin color, acne or blemishes, or another appearance problem?

13. Do you frequently measure parts of your body, hoping you'll find they're as small as, as large as, or as symmetrical as you'd like?

14. Do you spend a lot of time looking for information or reading about your appearance problems in the hope that you'll reassure yourself about how you look or find a solution to your problem?

15. Have you wanted to get cosmetic surgery, dermatologic treatment, dental treatment, or other cosmetic treatment to fix your appearance when other people (for example, friends or doctors) have told you such treatment isn't necessary? Have doctors been reluctant to give you the treatment because they say the defect is too minor or they're afraid you won't be pleased with the results?

(continued)

TABLE 3–3   *Clues to the Presence of BDD (continued)*

16. Have you had cosmetic surgery or dermatologic treatment and been disappointed with the results? Or have you had multiple surgeries, hoping that with the next procedure your appearance problems will finally be fixed?

17. Do you work out excessively to improve your appearance?

18. Do you spend a lot of time lifting weights or give up important activities to make time for lifting?

19. Do you diet, even though others tell you it isn't necessary?

20. Do you often touch disliked body areas to check if they look okay?

21. Do you avoid mirrors because you dislike how you look?

22. Do you avoid having your picture taken because you think you look so bad?

23. Do you get depressed or anxious because of how you look?

24. Do you feel more comfortable going out at night or sitting in a dark part of the room, because your appearance flaws will be less visible?

25. Do you have panic attacks or get very anxious when you look in the mirror because of how you look?

26. Have you felt that life wasn't worth living because of your appearance?

27. Do you get very frustrated or angry because of how you look?

28. Have you ever hurt yourself because you feel so angry or hopeless over how you look?

29. Do you get down on yourself because of how you look?

30. Have you been aggressive toward property or people because you're so angry over a problem with how you look?

31. Does it take you longer to do things because you're distracted by appearance worries or related behaviors such as mirror checking?

32. Do you have trouble concentrating because you're distracted by appearance worries?

33. Do you have trouble doing school work or your job because of appearance worries? Or are you unable to go to school or hold a job for this reason?

33. Do appearance worries cause problems with other people—such as your partner, family, or friends?

34. Do you avoid dating because of how you look?

35. Do your appearance worries interfere with managing your life, leisure activities, caring for others, or self-care?

many patients have said to me, "Wouldn't you be depressed if you were really ugly?!" Conversely, BDD appears fairly common in people with depression, especially those with a certain type of depression known as "atypical" depression (see Glossary). Onset of depression at an early age and a long duration of depressive symptoms are clues that someone who is depressed may have BDD in addition to depression.

Most people with BDD have social anxiety that results from their BDD. They fear being rejected and ridiculed because of how they look. Furthermore, more than one-third of people with BDD have the disorder social phobia (also known as social anxiety disorder) in addition to BDD. Social phobia is an excessive fear of social or performance situations due to a fear of doing something embarrassing or humiliating (see Glossary). So social anxiety and avoidance can be a clue that a person may have BDD.

Certain other disorders commonly co-occur with BDD and may be a clue to BDD's presence. About one-third of people with BDD also have obsessive compulsive disorder (OCD), characterized by obsessions (intrusive, recurrent, unwanted thoughts that are difficult to dismiss despite their disturbing nature) and compulsions (repetitive behaviors that are intended to reduce the anxiety caused by obsessions).

Nearly half of people with BDD have had problems with alcohol or drugs. One study that investigated the converse—the percentage of people with an alcohol or drug problem who also had BDD—found that 26% of them also had BDD. This percentage is surprisingly high. So it's important to determine if people with these symptoms or disorders also have BDD.

■ How to Avoid Misdiagnosing BDD as Another Disorder

In addition to being **under**diagnosed, BDD can easily be **mis**diagnosed as another mental disorder. This occurs because BDD can produce symptoms that mimic another disorder, such as social phobia, as noted earlier. Table 3–4 lists some of the disorders that are most commonly confused with BDD.

It's important to note that all of the disorders in this table can **coexist** with BDD. In other words, as I noted earlier, a person with BDD can have other disorders **in addition to** BDD. In fact, people with BDD often also have depression, social phobia (social anxiety disorder), or OCD as well as BDD. If a person with BDD also has other mental disorders, **both** these disorders **and** BDD should be diagnosed and focused on in treatment.

■ So Do You—Or Someone You Care About—Have BDD?

BDD is usually easy to recognize by doing the following: (1) Asking questions in the BDD Diagnostic Module or filling out the BDDQ; (2) Being alert to the BDD clues described in this chapter and shown in Table 3–3; and (3) Keeping in mind reasons for misdiagnosis and underdiagnosis that are discussed earlier. In addition, if your experience is similar to that of the people I describe in this book, you may very well have BDD.

TABLE 3–4 *Misdiagnosis and How to Avoid This*

Disorder That's Been Diagnosed Instead of BDD	Brief Definition*	Why BDD May Be Misdiagnosed As Another Disorder	How to Avoid Misdiagnosing BDD
Major depression	Depressed mood, decreased interest, and other symptoms such as sleep and appetite disturbance for at least several weeks at a time	Depressive symptoms that coexist with BDD are diagnosed, but BDD is missed; **or** BDD symptoms are considered a symptom of depression, and BDD isn't diagnosed. In my clinical experience, this is the most common diagnostic error.	• Look for BDD in people with depression. • Don't assume that appearance concerns are simply a symptom of depression. • Diagnose BDD if it's present.
Social phobia (Social anxiety disorder)	An excessive fear of social or performance situations due to fear of doing something embarrassing or humiliating	BDD often causes social anxiety, withdrawal, and avoidance; the social anxiety may be quite noticeable, but the BDD may be kept secret. This can lead to misdiagnosis of BDD as social phobia or avoidant personality disorder.	• Don't assume that social anxiety or avoidance is just due to social phobia. • If social anxiety or avoidance are largely due to BDD, BDD rather than social phobia should be diagnosed. • Some people have **both** BDD and social phobia, in which case both diagnoses should be given.
Agoraphobia	Anxiety about being in places or situations from which escape might be difficult or embarrassing, or in which help might not be available, in the event of having a panic attack or panic-like symptoms	Because some people with BDD think they're too ugly to leave their house, or because they fear that others are taking special notice of their perceived defect, they may feel anxious in and avoid a variety of situations.	• People with features of agoraphobia should be asked whether they're anxious in and avoid situations because of how they look. If the avoidance is largely because of BDD, BDD should be diagnosed instead of agoraphobia.

(continued)

39

TABLE 3–4 *Misdiagnosis and How to Avoid This (continued)*

Disorder That's Been Diagnosed Instead of BDD	Brief Definition*	Why BDD May Be Misdiagnosed As Another Disorder	How to Avoid Misdiagnosing BDD
Obsessive compulsive disorder (OCD)	Obsessions and/or compulsions that are time-consuming, distressing, or impairing	Because BDD and OCD are both characterized by obsessions and repetitive behaviors, BDD can be misdiagnosed as OCD.	• If the obsessions (preoccupations) and behaviors focus on physical appearance, BDD is the more accurate diagnosis.
Panic disorder	Recurring panic attacks that come out of the blue followed by concern about having more attacks, worry about the consequences of the attacks, or a significant change in behavior related to the attacks	People with BDD can have panic attacks as a result of BDD. They may feel intensely uncomfortable and fearful—and experience physical symptoms, such as a pounding heart, sweating, or trouble breathing—because they're so upset by how they look. These attacks of extreme anxiety can be triggered by the mirror or thinking someone is staring at the person or mocking their looks.	• To receive a diagnosis of panic disorder, the panic attacks must come "out of the blue"—not triggered by BDD or another disorder. • If BDD is the cause of panic attacks, BDD should be diagnosed. Panic attacks maybe be the initial clue that leads to the diagnosis of BDD.
Trichotillomania	Recurring hair pulling, resulting in noticeable hair loss	Some people with BDD remove their hair (body, head, or facial hair) to try to improve their appearance.	• If the purpose of the hair pulling is to improve a perceived "defect" in appearance, BDD should be diagnosed rather than trichotillomania.

(*continued*)

TABLE 3–4   *Misdiagnosis and How to Avoid This (continued)*

Disorder That's Been Diagnosed Instead of BDD	Brief Definition*	Why BDD May Be Misdiagnosed As Another Disorder	How to Avoid Misdiagnosing BDD
Schizophrenia	Symptoms such as delusions, hallucinations, disorganized speech; behavior that is grossly disorganized or abnormal	BDD beliefs are often delusional, and many people with BDD believe other people take special notice of them (referential thinking) (see Chapter 5 for more information).	• If the delusional beliefs and referential thinking are limited to appearance, and there are no other symptoms of schizophrenia, BDD is the more accurate diagnosis.

*See the Glossary for a more detailed definition of these disorders.

If you're trying to figure out if someone else has BDD, it's important to **ask about and listen to** their appearance concerns. Do this in a noncritical and nonjudgmental way. Take their worries seriously. Don't simply say they look fine and change the topic. BDD is too emotionally painful and problematic to dismiss. In Chapter 15, I'll say more about helpful approaches that family members and friends can try.

As I discussed in the last chapter, a major stumbling block is that many people with BDD think they have a physical problem rather than BDD, and they may resist the diagnosis of BDD. If you're someone who thinks this way, I encourage you to give the BDD diagnosis a chance. In other words, if you think you might **possibly** have BDD, or if other people think you do, read the rest of this book to become more informed about BDD, and see a qualified professional to find out if you have this disorder. There's no down side to doing this. (I say more about this in Chapter 10.) It could be lifesaving.

The main thing is that, regardless of how you think you actually look, if you're **preoccupied** with flaws in your appearance, and this preoccupation causes you **emotional distress or interferes with your day-to-day functioning**, you may have BDD. If other people think you may have BDD, you owe it to yourself to consider the diagnosis and, with a qualified and knowledgeable health professional, give the right treatment a try. There's no need to continue to suffer. Trying the right treatment could make you a lot more satisfied with your life, a lot more productive, and a lot happier.

4. BODY DYSMORPHIC DISORDER COMES IN MANY FORMS

■ Overview of Disliked Body Areas and Behaviors

People with body dysmorphic disorder (BDD) describe their appearance problem in various ways. They may say that the disliked areas are ugly, unattractive, or abnormal looking. Or that they look defective, flawed, wrong, odd, not right, or "off." Some people use words like "deformed," "monstrous," or "hideous." One man said he looked like a cartoon character; another described himself as looking like a terrible burn victim. A woman said that she resembled a distorted figure from a Salvador Dali painting.

Some people with BDD want to be unusually attractive or look "perfect." But in my experience, most don't—they simply want to look normal. What they're obsessed with is getting rid of the perceived defects. They say things like, "I just want to look average—I don't need to look like Brad Pitt," or "I don't want to look tanned like the actor George Hamilton; I just want to look **not pale**. My goal is to be acceptable."

Every time I meet someone with BDD and listen to their story, I hear familiar themes. In some ways, their story is similar to that of other people with BDD. But each person's experience is also in some ways unique. This is shown by Table 4–1, where I've listed 15 examples of people with BDD, the body areas they were preoccupied with, the BDD behaviors they performed, and consequences of their BDD symptoms.

As you can see, people with BDD can dislike virtually any part of their body. The average person reports that they're excessively concerned with five different body parts over time. As Table 4–1 illustrates, most people also perform a variety of behaviors to cope with their appearance concerns, such as mirror checking, excessive grooming, skin picking, and reassurance seeking. I'll say more about these behaviors in Chapter 6.

■ Which Body Parts Are Disliked?

People with BDD are usually preoccupied with specific parts of the body. Table 4–2 which reflects data from more than 500 people who participated in my research

TABLE 4–1   *Examples of Preoccupations, Behaviors, and Consequences of BDD**

Appearance Concerns	Associated Behaviors and Consequences
Carol:	
Thighs too flabby	Believes others take special notice of appearance
Nose misshapen	Avoids mirrors
	Avoids swimming, social activities, and dating
	Had nose surgery
	Diets
Enrique:	
Thinning hair	Excessive hair combing
	Checks mirrors excessively
	Problems with girlfriend
	Social avoidance
	Consulted a dermatologist
Lauren:	
Hair "never right"	Checks mirrors and windows excessively
Body shape abnormal	Buys excessive amounts of hair products
(hips too wide, shoulders	Gets lots of haircuts and perms
too narrow, waist too	Questions others about her appearance
high and wide)	Wears baggy clothing
	Avoids gym class, swimming, and social activities
Zach:	
Beard growth asymmetric	Believes others take special notice of his appearance
Eyes too small	Checks mirrors excessively
"Blotchy" skin	Compares self with others
	Shaves excessively
	Picks skin
	Wears tinted glasses to hide eyes
	Grew long hair to cover face
	Avoids magazines, social activities, dating
	Housebound
Tiffany:	
Lines around mouth	Believes others take special notice of her appearance
Hair loss	Excessively checks mirrors
Chin too prominent and	Compares self with others
asymmetric	Seeks reassurance
Teeth crooked, curved, and	Avoids social activities and dating
too large	Difficulty working
Cheeks sunken	Had braces several times
Nose too large	
Alan:	
Facial skin and muscle tone	Checks mirrors and other reflecting surfaces excessively
flabby	Frequent makeup application
Hair too curly	Compares self with others
Dark circles under eyes	Avoids shopping, school, social situations,
Acne	dating, and sex

(continued)

44

Appearance Concerns	Associated Behaviors and Consequences
Maria:	
Nose bumpy and too small at tip after surgery	Believes others take special notice of her appearance
	Excessively checks mirrors
Facial and body hair excessive and dark	Avoids dating
	Had teeth filed
One tooth longer than another	Saw an endocrinologist to evaluate body hair
	Had electrolysis
Body too fat	Diets
	Excessively exercises
Jim:	
Thinning hair	Avoids mirrors
Shrunken and sagging facial muscles	Excessively lifts weights
	Wears a hat
Facial skin too loose	Stuffs shorts and wears shirts down to knees to cover crotch
Lips too thin	
Cheekbones asymmetric	Grew a beard to cover face
Penis too small	Missed school
Body build too small	Avoids shopping and social activities
	Leaves the house only at night
	Uses numerous hair tonics
Luana:	
Ugly face	Checks mirrors, car bumpers, and windows excessively
Facial scar	Camouflages scar with makeup
	Late for school
	Difficulty interviewing for jobs
Tyrone:	
Penis too small	Believes others take special notice of appearance
Wrists and body build too small	Checks mirrors excessively
	Compares self with others
Pot belly	Avoids showers in gym class
	Covers crotch with long clothes and wears bulky clothes
	Lifts weights excessively
	Avoids dating and sex
	Consulted urologist for penis surgery
Alisha:	
Nose too large	Believes others take special notice of her appearance
Hair too curly	Checks nose, brushes hair, and applies makeup excessively
Forehead too high	
Face too long	Asks others for reassurance
Breasts too small	Wears padded bras
	Holds head in certain positions so nose looks smaller
	Covers forehead with bangs
	Spends large sums of money on hair products
	Unable to go to school, work, swim, or socialize

(continued)

TABLE 4-1 *Examples of Preoccupations, Behaviors, and Consequences of BDD** (continued)

Appearance Concerns	Associated Behaviors and Consequences
Jeff:	
Waist too fat	Believes others take special notice of appearance
Nose too wide	Checks mirrors and store and car windows
Chest hair asymmetric	Changes clothes frequently
Pubic, underarm, and leg hair ugly	Sits and stands only in certain positions so waist isn't visible under clothing
Skin too white	Shaves body hair
	Wears bronzer
	Avoids commercials and ads with "gorgeous people"
	Avoids dating, sex, swimming, shopping, and public transportation
	Had several nose jobs and liposuction
Lilly:	
Circles and puffiness under eyes	Believes other take special notice of appearance
	Checks mirrors and other reflecting surfaces excessively
Lines on face	Seeks reassurance
Stomach too fat	Compares self with others
Buttocks misshapen	Avoids salty foods
	Takes diuretics (water pills)
	Camouflages with makeup
	Avoids swimming
	Had liposuction
Dave:	
Thinning hair	Believes others take special notice
Hips too slim	Compares self to others
Acne scarring	Avoids haircuts
Large pores on face	Got a hair weave
Shoulders too broad	Picks skin
Zoe:	
Nose unattractive	Believes others take special notice of her appearance
Chin and neck too large and wide	Avoids mirrors
	Worries nose will break or otherwise be damaged
Facial rash and acne	Compares with others
Body too fat	Covers face with hands
	Seeks reassurance
	Picks skin
	Sleeps and uses alcohol to avoid thinking about appearance
	Avoids restaurants, other public places, and dating
	Housebound

*The descriptions are examples of what people with BDD experience; they don't provide a comprehensive list of all BDD concerns.

TABLE 4–2   *Location of Perceived Defects in BDD*

Body Part	Percent (%) of Patients with Concern*
Skin	73
Hair	56
Nose	37
Weight	22
Stomach	22
Breasts/chest/nipples	21
Eyes	20
Thighs	20
Teeth	20
Legs (overall)	18
Body build/bone structure	16
Ugly face (general)	14
Face size/shape	12
Lips	12
Buttocks	12
Chin	11
Eyebrows	11
Hips	11
Ears	9
Arms/wrists	9
Waist	9
Genitals	8
Cheeks/cheekbones	8
Calves	8
Height	7
Head size/shape	6
Forehead	6
Feet	6
Hands	6
Jaw	6
Mouth	6
Back	6
Fingers	5
Neck	5
Shoulders	3
Knees	3
Toes	3
Ankles	2
Facial muscles	1

* The percentages add up to more than 100% because people are usually concerned with more than one aspect of their appearance.

studies, illustrates that BDD can strike virtually anywhere. The skin, hair, and nose are most often disliked. It's likely that people underreport worries about certain body areas—for example, breasts and genitals—because they're embarrassed, and that the true percentages for such areas are higher than those listed here.

I've found that skin concerns are most frequent. Two-thirds of people with skin concerns obsess about perceived acne or scarring. This is followed by concerns with marks (in one-third) and skin color (in one-quarter), with people typically thinking their skin is too red or too white. But virtually any aspect of the skin can be disliked—facial pores that are considered unusually large, veins, capillaries, or other skin flaws. Others obsess about wrinkles, lines, sagging, shriveling, or stretch marks, which they may consider a sign of aging.

Some people have multiple skin concerns. Ellen was obsessed with supposed facial acne and scars, as well as veins, which were barely discernible to other people. She excessively checked mirrors and repeatedly asked her mother for reassurance, asking "Do you think this pimple will go away? Will I have a scar?" To improve her skin, Ellen spent lots of time applying makeup and picking at her face, sometimes using pins. She also compulsively washed her hands to avoid causing pimples while she picked. Treatment from a dermatologist temporarily diminished her preoccupation, but, as she described it, she became "more sensitive to smaller imperfections," resulting in no overall improvement.

Hair concerns are also very common. The most common worries focus on hair loss, thinning, or balding (a concern of one-third of people who dislike their hair) and excessive facial or body hair (also one-third). But hair obsessions may focus on virtually any aspect of the hair: it's too curly, too straight, too full, not full enough, uneven, messy, or dirty. James, a teacher, feared that his hair was thinning and that other people laughed at him because he was going bald. Each day he applied hair potions that cost him hundreds of dollars a month. When a thousand-dollar hairpiece he bought didn't help, he destroyed it in a fit of rage.

While men are more likely to worry about thinning hair, women have this concern as well. One woman feared she would eventually look even worse than her mother, who had very thin hair, and would become completely bald.

Getting a haircut is usually very distressing for people with hair concerns. "I'm terrified of getting my hair cut," Jon told me. "Getting the right haircut is **crucial**. How I feel and function depends on how I happen to look and the quality of my haircut."

Hair concerns may also involve other body hair. Men may be preoccupied with supposedly uneven, light, or heavy beard growth. Men or women may think they have too much or too little body hair. Marie, an attractive 24-year-old nursing student, worried that she had "excessive" and "dark" hair on her arms and nose. She thought about her hair nearly "all day every day," tweezed it at work, and, using special lights, checked her facial hair in mirrors for an hour a day. She tried to hide her hair with makeup, had electrolysis, wore long sleeves in the summer, and covered her face with her hands. Marie said that she felt "masculine" and "like a freak" whom no one would ever love.

Nose concerns are also very common. About 60% of people with nose concerns worry that their nose is too large. More than a quarter worry that it's bumpy or misshapen. People with nose concerns are especially likely to have surgery—often repeated surgeries. One woman first thought her nose was too large, and then, after surgery, believed it was too small.

BDD can also involve larger body areas. Some people dislike virtually their entire body. About one-quarter of men with BDD are preoccupied with their overall body build, thinking they look too small or inadequately muscular. This form of BDD is called "**muscle dysmorphia**" (see description below). Others—often women—are concerned that they're too large or overweight. Of the people in my studies, 22% were excessively concerned with their weight.

■ Disliked Body Areas over Time

Sometimes concerns with different body areas are present simultaneously, and sometimes sequentially. I've identified three common patterns:

(1) About 30% of people are concerned with one body part—or one set of body parts—over time. One man was concerned with his receding chin and never developed another concern. Another became concerned simultaneously with his "sunken" eyes and "swollen" nipples; he remained concerned only with these two things.

(2) Approximately 40% are concerned with one body part and then add new parts over time. At age 13, Ted worried that his ears stuck out, at 18 he started to worry about his crooked lip, and at 25 he started worrying about a scar on his neck. At 25, he had all three concerns.

(3) The third pattern is more complex, and occurs in about 30%. Over time, concerns with one or more body parts disappear, and new concerns emerge. Jane (see Chapter 2), fit this pattern. Her concern about her buttocks disappeared but she started worrying about a scar on her lip and then her jaw and breasts.

Most people with BDD think they look bad all the time. But some think that they sometimes look okay. As one woman said, "When my hair looks okay, I think I look attractive. But when it's bad, which it often is, I think I'm really ugly." People who are worried about minor acne may think they look fine when their skin is better—but when it's "broken out," it's a disaster.

■ "I'm Just One Big Pimple!"

While people with BDD judge their "defective" body areas very negatively, they evaluate other aspects of their physical appearance less negatively and more accurately. However, most are very dissatisfied with their overall appearance. When asked to rate how they look **overall,** 4% say they're attractive, 23% say they look average, and 73%, unattractive. When considering their overall appearance, they seem to focus more on the disliked body areas and give them more "weight." In other words, their negative view of their "defects" unduly impacts their view of how they look overall.

They're so focused on the perceived defect, they believe it's the most obvious and important part of how they look. They view themselves not as an attractive person with a small bump on their nose, but as one whose most prominent feature is a grotesque nose. This was the case with Matthew, who was so focused on his mild acne that it was all he could "see." He told me, "I'm just one big pimple, without any feet or even any toes!"

Self-portraits of people with BDD illustrate this. They tend to emphasize the perceived defect while giving only cursory attention to other body parts. One woman drew a massive, messy, and detailed head of hair while portraying the rest of her body as a stick figure. A man's self-portrait consisted only of three different views of his nose, covered with huge and gaping holes.

In fact, some people with BDD don't seem to notice or be bothered by aspects of their appearance that would probably concern most people. A young woman I treated had large, deep, red ulcers on her legs caused by a medical illness. But they didn't particularly bother her, and she often wore shorts. Instead, she was preoccupied with her supposedly wide nose and her "sunken and dull" eyes, which other people considered attractive.

■ Different Forms of BDD

Muscle Dysmorphia: An Especially Worrisome Form of BDD

One of the most important and common forms of BDD is called **muscle dysmorphia.** Most people with muscle dysmorphia are men, although I've seen a few women who have it. In my studies, nearly one-quarter of men with BDD have this form of BDD (most of them additionally had nonmuscle dysmorphia appearance preoccupations).

Men with muscle dysmorphia fear that their body build is too small and not lean or muscular enough. Even though they look normal, or in some cases very muscular, these men want to become even more muscular. They also worry about not gaining fat.

Mark, a muscular man in his 20s, believed his upper body was too thin and that he looked "dwarfed and wimpy." To build himself up, he drank protein drinks every day and lifted weights for hours daily. At least 20 times a day he asked his father, "Do I look okay? Am I getting bigger?" Mark always wore long-sleeved shirts to hide his "skinny" arms and avoided going to the beach. When I met him, he was wearing five layers of T-shirts and sweatshirts to look bigger.

Men with muscle dysmorphia obsess about their muscularity and body size, and they perform typical BDD behaviors, such as excessively checking mirrors to see how they look, asking other people if they look muscular enough, and measuring their body to see how big they are. Many of these men camouflage with clothing to hide body areas they don't like. Some try to look bigger by wearing big, bulky clothes or many layers of clothes.

In one small study, my colleagues and I found that 71% of men with muscle dysmorphia lifted weights excessively, 64% exercised excessively, and 71% dieted. Some men lift weights and exercise so much that they don't have time for other activities or their families, and some seriously injure their bodies (see Chapter 6). Men with muscle dysmorphia are much more likely to engage in these behaviors than men who have BDD but not the muscle dysmorphia form of BDD. Thus, these behaviors may be clues that a man has muscle dysmorphia.

Fernando also had muscle dysmorphia. He was in his early 30s and was quite muscular. However, he was convinced that he looked "unattractive, emaciated, and dwarfed." Fernando thought about his appearance for an estimated 17 hours a day. He painstakingly planned his diet and frequently checked mirrors to see how big he was. He also wore bulky clothes, and he compared his body size and muscularity with other men's bodies and with men in muscle magazines.

Fernando was so petrified that he looked tiny that whenever he had a spare second he compulsively lifted weights. When he was at his job in a restaurant and had a few minutes of privacy, he frantically lifted big stacks of dishes back in the kitchen. "I just keep hoping that someone won't walk in and see me doing this," he said. "I also sneak into the bathroom at work to do push-ups. People come banging on the door to see where I am and what I'm doing. I know I should be working, but I just can't stop."

Fernando was so distressed over his appearance that he injected himself with anabolic steroids to try to bulk up. He knew that this was potentially dangerous but felt compelled to do it anyway. As he said, "I have to get bigger—I can't stand looking so bad!" His obsessive thoughts about his body and his compulsive behaviors were so distressing and time consuming that he had to drop out of college. He didn't date because he thought no woman would want to be with him because he looked so small.

Many people with muscle dysmorphia use food supplements, such as protein powders and creatine, to gain muscle and lose fat. Some use potentially dangerous methods such as human growth hormone, diuretics (water pills), and ephedrine. Of great concern, about 20% of men with muscle dysmorphia use anabolic steroids, which are illegal when used for this purpose and are potentially dangerous to one's physical and emotional health. If dirty or shared needles are used to inject these drugs, there's a risk of getting an infection or abscess—even AIDS, hepatitis, or other life-threatening diseases.

In one small study my colleagues I found that an alarming 86% of men with muscle dysmorphia had a problem with other street drugs or alcohol (i.e., a substance use disorder), and that 50% had attempted suicide.

BDD by Proxy: Obsessing about Someone Else's Appearance

This is another important form of BDD. People with BDD by proxy worry about someone **else's** appearance. They obsess, for example, that their son's ears are sticking out or that their boyfriend's hair looks wrong, when in fact these body areas look okay. They may insist that their loved one get unnecessary surgery. In some cases, the object of this concern starts to worry about their appearance too.

A woman who was frantic over her daughter's nose had BDD by proxy. "I worry that it doesn't look right, that it's crooked," she told me, "even though everyone else says it looks fine. **She** doesn't worry about it, but **I** do! I keep pushing on it to make it straight, and I'm afraid I'm ruining her self-esteem."

I'm aware of a very sad case in which a man in his 50s was convinced his daughter was going bald and that he was the cause. His daughter actually looked normal. He was in such despair over this that he killed himself. This brings home how serious this form of BDD can be.

"I Hate Everything about My Looks!"

A common misconception is that BDD has to involve one, or just a few, specific body areas. But some people actually hate most of their body. They say things like, "My entire body is ugly," or "I hate everything about how I look." One man intensely disliked and was preoccupied with 33 body areas!

Some people who say they hate everything about their body actually have more specific concerns, but they're too embarrassed to talk about them. Instead, they discuss their appearance concerns in more general terms. After all, it's much easier to say, "There's something wrong with how I look" than "I think my penis is too small." As one woman said, "I told my doctor about my aging fears, but not about the wrinkles or hair. It's easier to talk in generalities."

The first two times I saw Larry, he told me, "I just don't like my face; I don't like how it looks. It feels different from everyone else's." It wasn't until the third time I saw him that he felt comfortable enough to reveal the specifics: his nose was too wide, his forehead too small, and his eyes too beady. "I was much too embarrassed to tell you these things before," he said.

"My Face Is Asymmetrical"

One-third of the people in my studies worried that at least one area of their body was asymmetrical. Most often, symmetry concerns focus on the hair, breasts, or nose. One woman was preoccupied with having more freckles on one side of her face than the other. A teenager was concerned that one eyelid hung over one of his eyes more than the other one.

Some people worry that their hair is uneven and may spend hours a day cutting it to make it perfectly even. A college student told me, "I'm obsessed with having my hair an even length. I cut it every morning, and then I carry scissors with me and cut it throughout the day. I've even hit my hands with a hammer and slammed them in a car door so I'd stop cutting. But that didn't work either. I **have** to make my hair even so it will look better!"

"My Face Is Falling"

Most people describe the perceived appearance flaw in quite specific terms—for example, "My ears are pointed," "My hairline is receding," or "My waist is too wide." But others express it in a vague, hard to understand way. One man was preoccupied with his "inadequately firm eyes." A woman I interviewed was extremely distressed because her "face was falling." After much discussion, it seemed that she thought that her facial muscles were wasting away and her facial skin was sagging.

"I Look Like a Gorilla"

Some people find it easier and more accurate to describe their appearance concerns in terms of animals, other people, or even food. One man obsessed about his "egg shaped" head. Another said he looked like a chicken. This was, in his view, the best description of his appearance and was as important as his specific concerns—wrinkles on his face, a large nose, a thin face, and sunken cheekbones. Another person complained of "chipmunk cheeks." A woman concerned about excessive facial hair described herself as a gorilla.

Some people compare themselves to other people or fictional characters, stating that they look like a burn victim or the Hunchback of Notre Dame. One man who disliked his hair said he looked like Kramer on the TV show *Seinfeld*. Other people associate their perceived defect with a family member or relative. "My looks remind me of my father, who I dislike," a 40-year-old woman told me. "He was ugly emotionally and physically." Some men who are concerned with thinning hair fear that they'll end up looking like their bald father.

"I'm Not Feminine Enough"

Some people link their perceived appearance flaws with other characteristics they consider negative, such as aging or a lack of masculinity or femininity. In the same breath, they may mention their worry about wrinkles and aging. While they're concerned with the perceived ugliness of the wrinkles, they're also upset because they consider them a sign that they're getting old. One young woman I saw had been hospitalized because she was so desperate over the belief that her appearance had changed, and that new lines on her face made her look 10 years older than she actually was.

Some women are concerned about not being feminine enough. Often, they're worried that excessive facial hair makes them look masculine. A young woman who worried that her breasts were too small said that she felt she "really wasn't a woman, because breasts symbolize femininity." Even though men frequently asked her out on dates and told her she was quite feminine, she didn't believe them.

Similarly, men who worry that their penis is too small may say they feel unmasculine and that women don't find them desirable. "It makes me feel like I'm not masculine enough," one young man told me. "It's embarrassing and something I feel I need to hide. What I obsess about is I'm half of a man."

Fear of the Future: "Soon I'll Be Totally Bald!"

Fear of the future is a prominent theme for some people with BDD. They worry that their perceived defect will become worse and uglier with time. "No one will want to hire me when I'm older and even uglier," Olivia told me. Eric feared that his hair would get thinner and thinner and that he would soon be completely bald. "Bald guys are total rejects. My life will be over when I lose all my hair."

Fear of the future sometimes focuses on a belief that the person used to look fine but now their looks have been ruined and will continue to deteriorate. "Sometimes when I look in the mirror I get an image of how I used to look," Ed said. "Then I see how I look now, and I worry about next week and next year. Will I get even uglier?"

"I Look Depressed"

Jacob had a less common form of BDD. "I look depressed," Jacob told me. "I feel my mouth is unattractive and that I'm not likable because I look depressed, which is something people don't want to see." Jacob thought he looked depressed because his mouth was turned down, and he'd considered surgery to straighten it.

"My Fingers Are Getting Shorter"

"Sometimes my hand gets fat, and all of my fingers get shorter," Jim told me. "I actually **see** them change. It happens two or three times a day. It can happen when I'm around other people, especially good-looking people, or when I'm feeling nervous. Some of my doctors thought maybe I had a seizure disorder or another neurological problem, but I don't. I know it's impossible for this to happen, but it's what I see."

Occasionally people have an experience like Jim's—their body parts seem to change shape or size and become unattractive in the process. Experiences like these, while unusual, raise the question of a neurological disorder. But if one isn't present, BDD may be the explanation.

"I'm Afraid My Nose Will Break!"

About 15% of people with BDD think that the unattractive body part is fragile and in danger of breaking or that it doesn't work correctly. "I have a nose problem," Julie said when I first met her. "I hope you're an expert on noses." In the past, Julie had worried that her nose was too big and bumpy. But now her concern was different. "This is very humiliating because it sounds so silly. I'm totally obsessed that my nose is fragile and is going to break," she told me.

"Whenever I bump it or brush against something, I panic. I think I've ruined it. Sometimes I even think that I've hurt it by crinkling it up or letting cigarette smoke get near it." Julie also developed what she called a "sniffing obsession." "When I was wondering if I'd hurt my nose, my nose felt funny when I sniffed, so I had to keep sniffing to see if I'd damaged it."

The problem had started when Julie had had nose surgery 20 years earlier to remove a small bump. After surgery, the surgeon commented, "I worked really hard on your nose, so take care of it and don't damage it." Julie took this to mean that her nose was fragile, and for the next 8 years, she secretly visited her surgeon as often as twice a week seeking reassurance that it wasn't broken. "When he reassured me, I felt a little better, but only for a few minutes."

When she first saw me, Julie was more worried than usual, because she'd just seen a TV show on "botched" nose jobs. "I've been so preoccupied that I haven't been able to keep up the house or keep a job," she said. "And it's hard for me to enjoy social activities. I'm afraid my nose problem will flare up and I won't be able to go out. It's a huge problem in my marriage, too. My first husband left me because of it."

During childbirth, Julie was so petrified that her nose would be damaged that she hadn't even felt labor pains. While having dental work, she refused Novocain. This way, if the dentist damaged her nose by bumping it, at least she'd know that the damage had occurred.

"The Walking Concept Was Erased"

Occasional people with BDD worry that their supposedly ugly body part doesn't work correctly. They believe, for example, that their lip is misshapen **and** their speech is slurred. Or that their nose is crooked **and** they make whistling noises when they breathe. Ben was concerned not only that his legs "looked funny" but also that he couldn't walk normally. The problem began with pain in his right foot. A diagnosis of a fallen arch frightened Ben, and he incorrectly assumed that he'd never be able to walk again. He worried about this all day long.

Eventually, Ben began to think that he really couldn't walk normally. "The walking concept was erased," he said. He also started worrying that the muscles in his legs "were becoming thin like toothpicks and disappearing." Several doctors tried to reassure him that his walking, as well as the appearance of his legs, was normal, but Ben couldn't be reassured. "I felt crippled," he said. "The damage was already done."

Concerns such as these—as well as those involving bodily fragility—resemble typical BDD beliefs in that they are distressing preoccupations about one's body. But they differ from typical BDD concerns in that they don't focus only on appearance per se. Most of the patients I've seen with such concerns also had a more typical BDD concern that involved the same body part; that is, they worried that the fragile or malfunctioning body part was also unattractive or deformed looking.

"I'm Shrinking Because I Have Cancer"

A few patients I've seen attributed the perceived appearance defect to an underlying medical illness. Kelsey, who believed that her shoulders and upper body were shrinking, attributed this to cancer. She'd seen countless physicians and had had numerous tests, all of which were normal. Ben, the young man who worried that his legs were becoming thin and atrophied, thought these changes were due to multiple sclerosis. Both Kelsey and Ben received a diagnosis of hypochondriasis in addition to BDD.

Tactile Sensations

About a quarter of people with BDD experience tactile sensations such as itching in the area of perceived blood vessel markings, tightness where they see acne, "gritting where fat rubs together," or "too much air" where they think their hair is thinning. Usually, these sensations are fairly mild and not problematic. But sometimes they're troubling because they're a reminder of the defect or because they're painful. The woman who thought cancer was causing her shoulders and upper body to shrink also had prominent and constant shoulder pain, which was itself a troubling problem.

5. Painful Obsessions

■ "I Can't Get It Out of My Mind"

I'm obsessed about my appearance," a 50-year-old secretary told me. "I think about it all the time. It's like a clock ticking. It's always there, taunting and haunting me."

About one-third of people with body dysmorphic disorder (BDD) think about their appearance flaws for 1 to 3 hours a day, nearly 40% for 3 to 8 hours a day, and about a quarter for more than 8 hours a day. The remaining 5% think about the defect for less than an hour a day, but for a substantial period in the past they thought about it for at least an hour a day.

Some people think about their perceived flaws "all day, every day." One woman said, "My BDD is a shadow—it's always with me. I can't get rid of it." Others say that they "actively" think about it for only part of the day, but their concern is always in the back of their mind. Some say they always have "two reels going." With one reel, they focus on the matter at hand; with the other, they're thinking about how they look.

One man described his preoccupation with his "small" head as follows: "I can't get it out of my mind. It's like a monkey on my back. I even obsess in my sleep." And another said, "It's always there, like a radio that's always on. You may not hear it for a while, but you know it's there." Ray told me, "I was very preoccupied. My mind would go back and forth from the hair to the chest and from the chest to the hair, back and forth like a yo-yo."

Most people with BDD realize that they spend too much time thinking about their appearance. But for others the thoughts are so much a part of their lives that they don't realize that they worry too much. They think that **everyone** worries about their appearance for hours a day.

What do the thoughts consist of? They vary, but they're usually quite negative—for example: "There's a pimple on your face; everyone's going to see it and think you're ugly," or "I'm disfigured. It's ugly. I deviate." One person thought, "You stick out in a crowd; you look ridiculous. People are looking at you funny because of your ears."

Some people ruminate about surgery they think was botched. "I **constantly** think about the operation I had on my nose," Greg said, "Now it's too short and too thin, like a woman's nose, not a man's. And I obsess about how angry I am at the doctor. I also think a lot about what all the different surgeons have told me. Things like 'Don't do anything to it; it could get worse.'"

One reason preoccupations with the perceived appearance flaws take up so much time is that they're difficult to resist and control. Many people do try to resist them by trying to focus on something else. But others find their preoccupations so powerful that they don't even try to divert their attention away from them. Yet degree of resistance can fluctuate, with more of an effort made to resist the thoughts at some times than at others.

Most people have only limited control over the thoughts, and virtually no one with BDD says they have complete control over them (unless they've been successfully treated). This is a particularly difficult aspect of BDD. "I try to ignore them, but I can't," one man told me. "It's like trying to will away a headache; you can't just make them stop." A woman told me, "One of the hardest things about this disorder is that I can't control my own thoughts. They have a life of their own. I feel powerless over them."

Sometimes people with BDD are told to just stop worrying about how they look. If only it were this simple! People with BDD can't just stop worrying by trying not to worry—it's hard to control their negative thoughts. They'd love to have their problem disappear—they, more than anyone else, would like to end their suffering. But they can't—**this is what BDD is all about.**

One small study found that a majority of people with BDD also experience negative recurrent appearance-related images, which are often visual in nature. They are often vivid and detailed. Many of these images are linked to stressful memories, such as being teased about appearance.

Brian described these images as "like a videotape—I have an incredibly vivid picture in my mind of people who made comments about my hair. It's like it's happening now, even though it really happened 20 years ago. I feel embarrassed, humiliated, and angry." Brian "replayed" the tapes in his head, over and over again, trying to figure out what the person really meant or trying to reassure himself that the comment wasn't so bad. "But it never works," he told me. "I just feel even worse."

Similarly, some people have nightmares about their appearance—dreams in which their worst fears come true. One woman described nightmares of getting her hair cut. "All of my hair is getting cut off the front. I wake up in a panic." Another woman who disliked her hair described this dream: "...A friend of mine with beautiful long hair was getting married. The bride told me I couldn't be in the wedding unless I wore a wig. I couldn't even be in the church because of my hair, and I had to leave."

■ "It's Like an Arrow through My Heart"

When I met Bill, a 40-year-old landscaper, he was in a darkened room in the hospital and was so profoundly distressed over his appearance that he couldn't put his pain into words. He was wearing a baseball cap pulled down to partially cover his eyes. His head was down on his knees.

Hesitantly, he started to tell me about his problems. He had no friends, and he'd just been fired from his job. He felt that life wasn't worth living. "It's really hard to talk about this, Doctor. It's too embarrassing, and it hurts too much."

Eventually, he told me that he worried about his nose, which he thought was covered with huge pockmarks and pores. Except for the pores, he thought he looked fine. But he believed the pores made him grotesque, like the Elephant Man. He'd thought about them for hours a day for the past 15 years. He wore the hat to hide them.

"I can't begin to describe this to you," he said. "It's humiliating. Who am I to complain, when so many people are worse off than me? To lose control over your life because of marks on your face—it's embarrassing, and it seems ridiculous! But every morning when I get up, I want to die. I rush to the mirror and see the marks. I can't face it anymore. Maybe it's how cancer victims feel. It's like an arrow through my heart.

"It ruined my life. I got very depressed. I stopped seeing people. I was so obsessed I couldn't work, and I got fired. It crushed me. Before I came into the hospital, I went to a hotel room to kill myself. I kept looking at myself in the mirror, thinking I couldn't live with the marks. I was scared, because I wanted to die, and I hated myself. I paced around the room, arguing with myself, telling myself it was stupid to be so worried about the marks. But everyone could see them—I couldn't hide them! I decided I couldn't go on living like this, and I tried to suffocate myself."

Bill got much better with a serotonin-reuptake inhibitor medication and cognitive-behavioral therapy (CBT). So much better, in fact, that he told me his life had completely changed. "I'm really happy," he told me. "I have my life back!" He really didn't care how his skin looked. After feeling well for many years, he decided to stop the medication because he thought he had some side effects. A month later, he killed himself.

■ Painful Feelings

BDD thoughts and preoccupations cause very painful feelings. A young man told me, "The pain is unbearable, unremitting. My life is a devastation. It's so painful it's hard to put it into words. Every day is hell."

Many people with BDD experience a lot of emotional pain. Common BDD-related emotions include depression, sadness, hopelessness, anxiety, worry, fear, shame, embarrassment, disappointment, self-disgust, anger, frustration, and guilt (I discuss some of these emotions further in Chapter 7). Many are hesitant to describe their emotional suffering and even apologize for it, thinking they're selfish or silly for suffering as much as they do.

The distress and emotional pain may be less severe than Bill's. It spans a spectrum of severity. Occasionally, it's mild, but usually it ranges from moderate to severe to extreme and disabling distress.

I've tried to understand why people with BDD suffer so much. One reason is that the thoughts are so often present and hard to control. Spending so much time thinking unwanted thoughts interferes with concentration and robs time from enjoyable or important activities. And of course, the content of the thoughts—believing you don't look right, or even look disfigured—is very distressing. One man tried to explain: "Think about how you'd feel if someone cut your nose off. That's how I feel about how I look."

In fact, many people with BDD wish they were worried about some *other* body part instead, because they think it would be less emotionally painful. A young woman who thought she was losing her hair said, "I wish I worried about something else, like my skin. At least I could cover it with makeup. But I can't change my hair." But a young woman who hated her skin said, "I wish I worried about something else, like my hair, because I could wear a wig. But I can't change my skin. The scars are there forever." The source of this pain is a belief that the disliked body part is unchangeable, making the person permanently flawed, which creates feelings of helplessness and despair.

BDD thoughts are also very painful because they're about the person themselves—as being defective, inadequate, inferior, and even unlovable. Many BDD sufferers feel they're fundamentally flawed as a person. As a result, they have feelings of depression, sadness, and despair. People with BDD typically have low self-esteem and deep feelings of shame.

"I've always disliked myself so much I can't imagine people liking me or how I look," Sonya told me. "My appearance concerns are all tied up in feelings of inferiority, feeling like damaged goods." "My face is the source of all the pain in my life," a 35-year-old artist said. "I feel hopeless about it. It's a feeling I'll never belong anywhere or be happy. It's a feeling I'm unacceptable. I feel the outside world sees me as unlovable, rejected, unacceptable, ugly."

Shame is very common in BDD and appears to be a core aspect of the disorder. Feelings of shame make sense because BDD involves strongly negative feelings about oneself as unappealing, defective, and inferior. This view of a supposedly defective body part often extends to the person more generally. Shame is due to an internal sense of the self as being inferior to others. As one woman said, "Whenever I see myself, I see something very inadequate. The one word I associate with my body is shame." Men may be ashamed because they consider it unmasculine to worry so much about how they look.

Another source of shame can be thought of as "external"—a worry that other people will scrutinize, humiliate, or reject the BDD sufferer because they look so awful. As a high school teacher said, "Shame is central to my appearance concerns. BDD equals ridicule." Worries of being rejected or ridiculed by others can also cause feelings of anxiety, fear, or anger.

Some people with BDD feel guilty. They blame themselves for ruining their appearance. "I look in the mirror, and I say 'What did I do!?'" Tina said. "I get really down on myself because I destroyed my looks by picking at my skin." Others feel guilty because they think they should be able to fix the problem—for example, by dieting or working out enough. Still others feel guilty because their symptoms seem "selfish" to them, or because they feel it's wrong—even immoral—to be so focused on how they look. This is what I call the "double whammy" of BDD: not only do BDD sufferers have distressing thoughts they can't control, they also berate themselves for having those thoughts. Many feel guilty because they're so preoccupied with something they feel is so trivial.

As one woman told me, "I shouldn't be so worried about this. I get down on myself because I am. Appearance shouldn't matter. I don't want to be the kind of person who cares so much about something so superficial. I'm so ashamed of it, I refer to it as 'you know what.'" Another woman said, "It sounds very superficial. I feel ridiculous thinking about it. I feel spoiled and shallow. I feel guilty because I could be blind or crippled. I **try** not to think about it, but I can't."

But other people with BDD don't consider their appearance concerns trivial. They point out that attractiveness is important and highly valued in our society. Thus, their concerns seem justified to them. They may also feel angry that other people don't understand their appearance concerns and why they're so upset over them.

But more common are feelings like the following: "I feel like a horrible, terrible person because I'm so concerned with my breasts. How could I be so vain?" This woman berated herself even more when she learned that her best friend had breast cancer. "Here I was obsessing about how big my breasts were when she had to have a mastectomy. I'm the one who deserved the mastectomy!"

Rather than a problem of excessive vanity or selfishness, BDD should be viewed as a serious illness like depression or anorexia nervosa or heart disease. It doesn't reflect moral weakness. If people could simply stop thinking about their appearance, they would. The self-blame only adds to their suffering.

Sadness and depression are very common. BDD sufferers typically feel defective and unlikable, and they often isolate themselves from others. A college student didn't go home for the holidays because she thought her family would be repulsed by her skin and wouldn't love her. As she said, "I fear being an outcast." A young man told me, "Maybe people, especially women, would like me more and accept me more if I were better looking. I'm overwhelmingly lonely."

Contributing to the isolation are feelings that other people don't seem to understand or take their appearance concerns seriously. After all, people with BDD actually look fine, so other people tend to be reassuring or even incredulous. "I feel foolish talking about my concern," one man said. "The usual reaction is 'What?!'" When someone has a medical problem, they usually have observable symptoms that confirm the illness is real. The same is true for many psychiatric disorders. A panic attack, for example, is observable and obviously not under the person's control. Symptoms such as rapid breathing or sweating are obvious and "real" to anyone who might witness them. Even though others may not fully understand the symptoms, they know something is wrong and that the person is suffering and needs help.

But BDD is different. Because the BDD sufferer looks fine, it's hard for others to understand the preoccupation and emotional pain it causes. How can someone be so obsessed with something that, in the eyes of others, doesn't exist? Or if a slight defect is present, why can't the person just forget about it? So people with BDD often feel misunderstood and alone.

"I've been very isolated with my concern because people thought I was crazy," one man told me. "They didn't understand, so I've kept it largely to myself. It's an extremely private inner turmoil. I feel alone." "The pain is as bad as when my dog who I'd had for 15 years was put to sleep," a college student told me, "but that was easier because people can understand your grieving. People can't understand BDD."

■ "Everyone is Staring at Me!"

A very distressing aspect of BDD for many sufferers is their belief that other people take special notice of—and even mock—their appearance. If someone glances in their direction, they think they're being looked at in horror or with disgust. One man who was concerned about a minimal scar on his neck said, "I know people are smirking at me when they see me. When I cross at a crosswalk I think people in cars are thinking, 'I wonder what happened to him. Look how ugly he is.'" Another man, who worried about mild acne, said, "When I go out, I think everyone's noticing it. I think they're thinking 'What's that ugly thing on his face?' Everywhere I go I feel like a neon sign is pointing at my face!"

People with BDD usually think that others can see the defect, but what I'm describing here—known in psychiatric terms as **referential thinking**—is that others take **special notice** of the defect. Benign events in the environment that are unrelated to the person's appearance are misinterpreted as referring to the flaw in a negative way. About 60% of the people in my studies have had such experiences—for example, thinking others are staring at them, talking about them, or making fun of how they look. About half of the 60% think that other people **probably** are taking special notice of them, and about half are **completely convinced** of this. Some use the term "paranoia" to describe their experience. This was a serious problem for Jennifer, who left her car in the middle of a traffic jam because she thought other people were horrified by her skin (see Chapter 1).

Conversations may be erroneously interpreted to refer to the disliked body areas. "Whenever people talk about shaving or beards, I think they might be referring to **my** beard," Bart told me. "They're really mean." And some BDD sufferers think others can see the defect from impossibly long distances. A man who sang in a choir thought the entire audience could see a small scar on his neck.

These experiences are similar in some ways to what we all experience. We've all noticed that someone is looking at us, and we may wonder why. Do we remind them of someone they know? Are they interested in the book we're reading? Are they noticing our glasses because they're thinking of buying a similar pair? It's possible that they're observing our appearance—perhaps something negative. But it's also possible that they're noticing something positive about how we look. Or are they even noticing us at all? Perhaps they're looking in our direction but thinking about something else, like what they need to buy at the supermarket. The possible explanations are endless. But most people with BDD don't consider other possible explanations. They assume the person is scrutinizing the defect and thinking about it in a negative way. They **see themselves** in terms of their imperfect appearance and assume that others must be doing the same. Often, it's only after they improve with mental health treatment that they can consider other explanations and actually believe them.

Steven's experience was a poignant example of referential thinking. He was often pursued by women who found him very attractive, but he was convinced that he was ugly—in particular, that his facial structure "wasn't sophisticated or full enough." When he was around others, especially young women, he thought that they took special notice of him—but in a negative, not a positive, way. He was sure they were laughing at the shape of his face, and he felt mortified, deeply shamed, and sometimes angry. I would guess that, most of the time, any laughing Steven observed had nothing to do with him and that other people sometimes **did** notice Steven—in a positive way.

Some BDD sufferers describe a no-win variation on this theme. "If people look at me I think it's because I'm ugly," one woman told me. "If they **don't** look at me, it's because I must be ugly. And if they look at me and then look away, they must be thinking that I'm not worth looking at. I feel shut out and rejected."

These types of experiences reflect important aspects of BDD. One is that many, if not most, people with BDD erroneously believe that other people view the perceived defect—and them—negatively. Second, people with BDD generally experience interactions with other people in terms of their appearance. They look at the world through "appearance-tinted glasses" and assume the rest of the world does too.

One component of CBT treatment for BDD, which I describe in Chapter 12, is to help patients understand that most people value many different aspects of the people they know and love, such as their warmth, kindness, and personality. And when others do notice how the BDD sufferer looks, they're unlikely to focus on the perceived flaw.

■ Different Degrees of Certainty

Stephanie realized her view of her appearance wasn't accurate. "I have X-ray vision," she said. "No one else would see the marks on my face. My mind is playing tricks on me. It magnifies every crazy little thing! I look in the mirror, and a mark **jumps out** at me. I see it a mile away, but I know that's stupid." In fact, recent research indicates that people with BDD inappropriately try to extract details from faces and other visual stimuli (see Chapter 9).

Hal also realized that he had an inaccurate view of his skin. Sometimes the acne was actually there, but it was slight. But, in his mind, it would grow to hideous proportions. "My imagination goes haywire. In my mind, this little pimple becomes a massive ugly thing that everyone is staring at. That's how it seems to me, but I know I'm distorting how bad it is."

Stephanie and Hal have **good insight**—they recognize that their view of their appearance is inaccurate. Even though they worry about it a lot, they realize that they really aren't ugly. But most people with BDD don't have good insight. They think their view of how they look is **probably** accurate. They say things like, "It's **probably** as bad as I think it is." These people have **poor insight.**

Still others think their view of the defects is **definitely** accurate; they're **completely convinced** that they're right. In psychiatric terms, such thinking is considered **delusional (absent insight).** They say things like, "I'm 100% convinced that I'm right. I'm not exaggerating how bad it is. Everyone else is wrong. No one can talk me out of this." Or "If you said you didn't see it, I wouldn't believe you, because **I** see it." Or "I see it in pictures. I know what I see." One man said, "I'm as certain of what I see in the mirror as you are that the box on this table is rectangular, not round."

People with delusional thinking may try very hard to convince others of how terrible the defect looks. Some present photographs to document supposed changes in their appearance, or produce "evidence" that they're right— for example, hair on a towel or in the drain may be considered irrefutable evidence that hair loss is excessive. Frustrated friends and family members often bear testament to the tenacity of the beliefs, which they've vainly tried to argue the person out of.

One possible explanation for this view is that people with BDD actually **see** something different from other people. Another is that they see what we see but consider it very unattractive. Yet another possibility involves excessive focusing on a minimal defect, which might lead to a distorted view of the

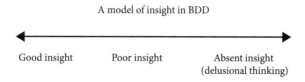

FIGURE 5-1 Insight in BDD.

importance, or even the appearance, of the supposed defect. I'll discuss these possible explanations further in Chapter 9.

Thus, insight in BDD ranges from excellent to good, to fair, to poor, to delusional thinking (absent insight), as shown in Figure 5–1. On average, insight is poor. More than a third of BDD sufferers have appearance beliefs that are currently delusional. People with delusional beliefs tend to have more severe BDD symptoms.

Most people with BDD think that most other people share their view of how they look. It's usually hard to talk people with BDD out of their view, and they only occasionally try to talk themselves out of it. Whereas some realize that their appearance beliefs have a psychological or psychiatric cause, many don't, thinking they're simply true. For this reason, some people with BDD are unwilling to accept the mental health treatment that could help them feel so much better.

For some people, insight can fluctuate between the different catego-ries shown in the diagram, rather than always remaining the same. A sales clerk told me, "Some days I think my skin's not so bad, but other days I'm convinced." Some people who realize they don't look so bad become con-vinced that they look terrible when they examine themselves in the mirror. Cassandra recognized that she had a distorted view of her freckles. "I know that no one else thinks they're hideous. But sometimes, they seem really bad. I look in the mirror, and I panic. I think, 'They really **are** that bad!'"

Sometimes insight gets poorer when the BDD sufferer is around other people. One man told me, "When I don't go out, I think I imagine the acne. But when I go out, I can become 100% certain that it's awful and hideous and that other people definitely see it." Sometimes, other kinds of stressors, and anxiety, also seem to temporarily decrease insight. And insight may improve with the right treatment (see Chapters 10–12). Hannah, who had been obsessed with acne and red and white facial discoloration, realized after she took a serotonin-reuptake inhibitor medication that her skin looked fine. She was so certain of this that she even went swimming, without makeup—something she'd never done before.

6. Compulsive Behaviors: Mirror Checking, Grooming, Camouflaging, Dieting, and Others

■ "I Have This Ritual Every Morning…"

Amanda grew up in a family where appearance didn't really matter. "So I don't know why I worry so much about it," she said. "But I do." Amanda thought that overall she looked acceptable, but disliked her hair, which she thought stuck out and "looked bizarre." She was also overly concerned about a faint scar on her face and thought her neck was too large.

To look better, Amanda spent hours a day arranging and combing her hair. "I have this ritual every morning, where I take a shower, and then I take at least an hour in front of the mirror getting ready to go to work. I stay in the bathroom looking in the mirror, combing and recombing my hair. I blow dry it and put gel on it, and then I comb it again. I try rearranging it in different ways so it doesn't stick out in the wrong places. I go through the whole process every morning at least five to ten times so I can look decent enough to leave the house. But it never really works."

Amanda also applied and reapplied makeup to cover her slight scar. Sometimes, she picked at it. She also checked mirrors at work. "I'm supposed to be waiting on people, but I'm in the mirror instead."

Amanda worked as a sales clerk in a clothing store and sometimes kept her customers waiting too long. "My boss isn't exactly pleased with my job performance. I'm surprised he hasn't fired me yet. I'm actually thinking of leaving, because it's not the right job for me. I meet new people all day long, and I'm sure they're thinking I look bad. I can't look people straight in the eye because I feel so self-conscious about how I look."

■ Common Compulsive and Safety-Seeking Behaviors

Amanda often did several typical compulsive BDD behaviors: mirror checking, excessive grooming, and skin picking. These behaviors are done to examine, hide, or improve the supposed defect, or to feel reassured that it doesn't look so bad. The behaviors are "compulsive" in that the person feels driven to do them, finds them hard to resist, and typically does them over and over again. They're sometimes called rituals. Sometimes, they're referred to as safety-seeking behaviors because their goal is to avoid or escape unpleasant feelings or prevent a feared event, such as being ridiculed by others.

Table 6-1 summarizes common compulsive BDD behaviors. Nearly everyone with BDD does at least one of them. The average number is 6, and some people do as many as 13. Most BDD sufferers, frequently and secretly,

TABLE 6-1 *Common Compulsive Behaviors (Rituals) in BDD*

Behavior	Percent (%) of People with Behavior
Camouflaging	91
With body position/posture	65
With clothing	63
With makeup	55
With hand	49
With hair	49
With hat	29
Comparing disliked body part with others/scrutinizing the appearance of others	88
Checking appearance in mirrors and other reflecting surfaces	87
Seeking surgery, dermatologic, dental, or other cosmetic treatment	72
Excessive grooming (combing hair, applying makeup, shaving, removing hair, etc.)	59
Questioning or reassurance seeking: seeking reassurance about the perceived flaw or attempting to convince others that it's unattractive	54
Touching the perceived flaw	52
Excessive clothes changing	46
Dieting	39
Skin picking to improve appearance	38
Tanning to improve a perceived flaw	22
Excessive exercise	21
Excessive weight lifting	18

compare themselves with others. Nearly 90% check their perceived defects in mirrors or other reflecting surfaces over and over again. More than half excessively groom themselves or question other people about how they look. Some go to doctor after doctor seeking cosmetic treatments. More than one-third compulsively pick at their skin. Although the behaviors in Table 6–1 are particularly common, there are others, such as repeatedly measuring the "defective" body part, reading about the problem area, and scouring the internet for cosmetic solutions such as hair growth potions.

Camouflaging the perceived defect with clothes, makeup, a hat, or in other ways is also common. In some cases this is done only once a day (for example, putting on a baseball cap to cover perceived hair loss) rather than over and over during the day.

Other behaviors are more avoidant than compulsive; they involve **not doing** rather than excessive doing. Some people avoid eye contact or keep their head down or turned away from other people. Others avoid having their picture taken. Or they cut their face out of photos or destroy all photos ever taken of them. One man avoided doing chores around the house because he feared any activity would enlarge his calves. Some people avoid showering or washing or brushing their hair because they fear more hair will fall out. Other types of avoidance behaviors (e.g., being housebound) are described in the next chapter.

■ "I Can't Resist"

Most compulsive BDD behaviors have certain things in common. They're usually time consuming and hard to resist or control. Typically, they're done over and over again. This is because there's doubt or dissatisfaction about what was seen or done. "My hair **still** isn't right! I can't go out till it is!" Or they may be done repeatedly because they bring some relief—although the relief is only temporary.

People with BDD can spend hours a day doing things, such as grooming, that most people do in minutes. Or they frequently do things, like seeking reassurance, that most people do rarely if at all. Table 6–2 shows the amount of time people with BDD spend each day on compulsive BDD behaviors.

Compulsive BDD behaviors are triggered by an upsetting thought, such as "How does my hair look today?" or "I know I look terrible, and I have to fix it!" Feelings of worry, anxiety, and tension drive the behaviors, which are carried out in an attempt to relieve these distressing thoughts and feelings.

There's usually a strong drive to perform the behaviors, which are difficult to resist or control. Some people try to resist, but others just "give in" or do them "automatically." As one woman said, "My rituals are like an itch that I have to scratch." As shown in Table 6–2, people most commonly report

TABLE 6-2 *Compulsive BDD Behaviors (Rituals): Time Spent, Resistance, Control, and Resulting Interference in Functioning*

	Percentage (%)
Time Spent on Behaviors	
None	0
Less than 1 hour a day	10
1 to 3 hours a day	42
More than 3 hours a day and up to 8 hours a day	39
More than 8 hours a day	10
Attempt to Resist Behaviors	
Always try to resist	2
Try to resist most of the time	14
Try to resist some of the time	27
Rarely try to resist	29
Never try to resist	29
Control Over Behaviors	
Complete control	1
Much control	5
Moderate control	23
Little control	44
No control	27
Interference in Functioning due to Behaviors	
None	4
Mild	19
Moderate	49
Severe	24
Extreme and disabling	5

Adapted with permission from the Yale-Brown Obsessive-Compulsive scale for BDD (BDD-YBOCS).

rarely or never trying to resist the urge to do their compulsive behaviors and having little control over them.

The degree of resistance or control may vary depending on the activity. Many people with BDD resist asking for reassurance. They may feel a strong urge to ask but worry that people will think they're vain or consider their question strange, so they don't. In contrast, BDD sufferers typically don't resist camouflaging. They simply do it. This may be because camouflaging doesn't necessarily take much time, and they may not feel worse after doing it.

Do the behaviors actually diminish tension and anxiety? Sometimes—in the short run. Many people **sometimes** feel less anxious right after mirror checking, if they think they look a little better than they expected. If anxiety and distress diminish after doing the compulsive behavior, the relief is only temporary. After some time has passed, the unpleasant feelings return.

People who pick their skin might feel better immediately after picking but later feel worse after surveying the skin damage they've caused. Reassurance seekers might feel better temporarily after being told they look fine, but their anxiety returns as they begin to doubt what they were told.

The temporary decrease in anxiety and distress may actually reinforce the behavior, compelling the BDD sufferer to perform the behavior once again in their quest for temporary relief. Over the longer run, these behaviors are counterproductive and just feed BDD. They have a rebound effect in which preoccupation and emotional distress may actually increase later after the behaviors are performed. They also feed BDD by keeping the sufferer focused on their appearance rather than on other things in their life.

But many people usually feel worse right after doing the compulsive behaviors. For example, mirror checking may, in their eyes, immediately confirm their belief that they look bad. The distress can be so unbearable that it fuels hopelessness and thoughts of suicide.

Why would someone who usually feels **more** anxious after mirror checking, or performing other compulsive BDD behaviors, keep doing it? The usual explanation is that they **sometimes** feel less anxious after doing the behavior, and they hope this will be one of those times. One man told me, "I check in the **hope** that I'll look better this time—that **this** will be one of the times that my fear and anxiety decrease. There's a small chance, a hope."

For fewer than 5% of people with BDD, compulsive BDD behaviors don't interfere with daily functioning or quality of life (see Table 6–2). But for most, the behaviors are a problem in and of themselves. They require enormous time and effort. A homemaker who spends 2 hours a day checking mirrors doesn't have as much time for her children and running the household. A salesperson may miss work because she was up picking at tiny pimples until the early hours of the morning, and can't bear for others to see the resulting disfigurement the next day.

BDD behaviors can create problems for family members and other loved ones, and strain even close relationships. Reassurance seeking is particularly likely to do this—the questioning can be so incessant that friends and family can't tolerate it. Requesting other people to join in rituals, and avoiding daily activities or special occasions so rituals can be done, can be very hard on loved ones. Sometimes, the strain ends friendships and causes divorce. Fortunately, the treatments I describe in Chapters 10 to 12 can greatly diminish or even stop these problematic behaviors.

■ The Mirror Trap

Most people with BDD have a torturous relationship with mirrors. Mirrors reflect their greatest hope—that they look okay—and their deepest fear—that there's something terribly wrong with how they look.

As shown in Table 6–1, nearly 90% of people with BDD excessively check mirrors or other reflecting surfaces. They examine the perceived defects in excruciating detail, often for long periods of time. As one man told me, "Sometimes I get stuck there inspecting myself and worrying. I can't leave. It's like I'm superglued." Those who don't check excessively usually avoid mirrors, generally to escape the disappointment, anxiety, and frustration their reflection triggers.

While checking is often done in a bathroom or bedroom mirror, virtually any reflecting surface will do: store windows, car bumpers, toasters, watch faces, clock faces, TV and computer screens, one's shadow, and the backs of spoons can become vehicles of hope and disappointment.

People with BDD typically get extremely close to mirrors, often within an inch or two. They zero in on the disliked body areas to get an even more microscopic look. Try holding your hand an inch or two from your face. What do you see? Lines jump out at you, the color looks uneven and splotchy, all kinds of tiny imperfections become magnified. This is what happens when BDD sufferers stare in the mirror: they get a very distorted view of how they look. Looking in nonmirror reflecting surfaces, such as car bumpers, also seriously distorts their image. The longer they look, the more self-focused they become, and the worse they typically feel.

Many people check mirrors in the hope that they'll look different or not as bad as they fear. Others check to make sure they know what they look like or to ensure that their view of the defect is correct. As one man said, "I check to see that I'm right, and that the scar is still there. It always is—I'm not stupid."

What do people actually do when they check? Typically they inspect the supposed defect, often in excruciating detail. A college student told me, "I examine the front of my hairline to see if the density is decreasing. Even on a daily basis I could see the changes." The inspection may be done from different angles or with different lights to get as good a look as possible. "I look at myself a lot at special angles," Eliza told me. "I have three mirrors in my bathroom so I can get a better look." Some people try to fix the perceived defect while inspecting themselves. They comb their hair, reapply their makeup, rearrange their hat, pick their skin, or pull on their nose. Others practice the best position to show in public, or use "mental cosmetic surgery" to feel better. One woman tilted her head, squinted her eyes, and covered the lower part of her face. "It made me look more like my old self," she said, "the way I want to look."

After mirror checking, many people sometimes feel better but often feel worse. If they feel better, the relief is temporary. If they feel worse it's because the mirror confirms their worst fear—that they look ugly. How they feel after checking may depend on factors such as lighting, whether the mirror is a "good" one, how well they've applied their makeup, or how their clothes look at that time.

One of the first patients I saw told me, "At least 10 times a day I have the urge to look in the mirror. There are many times when I just can't resist, and I go running. About 50% of the time, I don't feel so bad. I even feel somewhat relieved. I don't look that bad, and the problem doesn't seem to be getting worse. But about half the time, I look worse, and I have a panic attack. I have trouble breathing, I get sweaty, and sometimes I feel dizzy. Sometimes I feel so bad I go to bed for the day. Sometimes I don't go to work."

Mirror checking causes problems. As Jennifer (see Chapter 1) said, "It's the first thing I think of when I wake up in the morning. I immediately rush to the mirror, wondering 'How does it look?' How my skin looks in the morning completely determines how my day goes." A business executive stayed up most of the night, staring at a small scar on his cheek, and was always exhausted at work the next day. Mirror checking wastes precious time, and it can interfere with relationships and social activities. Many people get stuck in the mirror and don't go out because they feel too ugly to be seen.

Eating in restaurants or going to the mall, where there are lots of mirrors, can be especially hard. One person asked if I'd ever noticed how many restaurants have mirrors in them. "A lot do," he told me. "Or they have pictures with reflecting glass on them. It's easy to get distracted by checking out how I look." Going to museums can also be hard. "When I go to museums," he said, "I count my freckles in the reflections of the paintings instead of looking at the pictures."

Other people completely avoid mirrors. One man didn't look in even one mirror for 11 years because seeing his skin was so frightening. He combed his hair and shaved in his mirrorless basement for all those years. "Looking at myself in the mirror is like looking at a scary picture," he told me. The mirror is the enemy. I curse the person who invented it."

Yet others don't need mirrors to check. They simply look at the body part—such as their fingers—directly. Others frequently analyze their appearance in photographs or videos.

Occasionally, mirror checking triggers a suicide attempt. Seeing the hated defects reflected back can be too much to bear. The mirror itself can be used to inflict self harm, using broken shards of glass.

■ Comparing: "She Looks Better Than I Do!"

"I always look at other peoples' noses—mostly their pores—comparing myself to them to reassure myself," Bill said. "I see other people have pores and they're doing okay, so I should do okay. But I can't reassure myself. I just get more down on myself."

Comparing is the most common BDD behavior of all. As shown in Table 6–1, more than 90% of people with BDD do this. They frequently and silently compare their "ugly" body part with the same body part on others. They seem to have built-in radar for the body part of concern, quickly focusing in on it. As Mike described it, "I zero in on other peoples' ears and compare them to mine." One woman frequently compared herself to other women and also contrasted young people with old people to see if they had lines on their face. "I know every line and wrinkle on every person's face," she said.

BDD sufferers often feel worse when they compare. Aaron, who worried about his slightly receding hairline, told me, "I check out everyone's hair. And everyone looks better than me, even bald guys. I'm the one guy who can't lose his hair and keep any of his looks." He then added, "It's okay if other people are bald. They can look handsome, but I don't because I have a long face."

Aaron experienced the typical no-win situation. People with BDD generally think that other people look better than they do, which reinforces their feelings of defectiveness. To make matters worse, they overestimate the attractiveness of other people. Even if they see someone who they think looks as bad as they do, they still don't feel much better about themselves. Somehow they interpret the situation negatively, thinking such things as "He doesn't have much hair, but he's laughing and seems to be enjoying himself. Why can't I?" Or "She looks as bad as I do, but she has a boyfriend. What's wrong with me?" Comparing usually ends up reinforcing the BDD sufferer's own perceived shortcomings.

Comparing with people on TV or in magazines is common. "The models have thicker hair than I do," Jordan told me. "I think 'Why can't I look like that?' Then I feel even worse." Some people with BDD compulsively collect magazine pictures or videos of celebrities or attractive people and compare themselves with these images. It makes sense that comparing oneself with unusually good-looking people—which is what people with BDD often do—would make a person feel worse about their own looks.

Comparing can take lots of time and make it difficult to focus and concentrate. It's hard to focus on a conversation, or instructions your boss is giving you, if your attention is on the other person's physical attributes.

Some people with BDD assume that other important people in their life are also comparing them to others and finding them less attractive. This can wreak havoc in relationships. Linda compared her breasts with those of every woman she saw, and she assumed her husband was doing the same. "It was a terrible problem in our relationship, because I'd think he was constantly looking at other women, and I'd get insanely jealous and make all kinds of accusations. We even had to go into couples' therapy because it was such a problem. Now I realize that I was projecting my own behavior onto him. He wasn't comparing me with other women; I was!"

■ Grooming: Cutting, Combing, Teasing, Tweezing, and Washing

Each day, Daniel met his girlfriend, Angela, during her lunch break and drove to a nearby park. While sitting in her car, he instructed Angela to comb and style his hair so it would look fuller. She also applied expensive tonics that were supposed to stimulate hair growth.

"I had her do it because I couldn't see my hair well enough in the back. She followed the directions better than I did. And looking in the mirror is really traumatic for me. I'd also ask her if she saw any changes."

Daniel felt bad about asking Angela to do this, but he felt he had to. He had severe BDD and suffered tremendously. "Having her do it kept me going," he explained. "She wanted to leave me because I was so obsessed with my hair. I talked about my hair all the time, and we constantly fought over it. The relationship eventually deteriorated. But I tried to hold on to her because I needed her to do my hair and monitor me for hair loss."

Nearly 60% of people with BDD groom excessively. Often they do it in front of the mirror. They may do it at home, in the car, at work, at school, or in other people's homes. They can spend hours a day in the bathroom doing this. One woman spent at least 4 hours on her hair every morning—washing, setting, combing, and teasing it—so her family couldn't use the bathroom. She told me, "My hair looks horrendous if I don't do my hair ritual. It's too flat and not full enough." Todd performed a similar grooming ritual. "I fix my hair many times a day while I'm looking in the mirror. I comb it, brush it, and spray it, thinking 'Please just look normal!' I do it with my real hair and then with my hairpiece." A man who thought his hair was too curly first straightened it, then permed it, then straightened it, and finally shaved it all off in a fit of rage.

Some people cut and recut their hair, trying to get it exactly even or just the right shape. They may carry scissors with them and cut at work or school. Others have haircutting "binges," cutting in a frenzied burst of compulsive activity. Some people end up with extremely short hair.

Diane compulsively cut her hair for up to 8 hours a day. "I couldn't stop," she told me, "even though I had to take care of my children. I had to get it looking exactly even and right. I cut minuscule amounts so it wouldn't get too short, but it did get really short because of the time I was spending. I bought wigs because I was so embarrassed—I was practically bald—but I cut the wigs too, and I spent all of my money on them." "If she couldn't cut her hair," she told me, "I'd get so extremely upset that I'd have to be hospitalized."

Some people with BDD are concerned about excessive body hair and may spend hours a day tweezing it, removing it from their face, arms, or other body areas. Others have frequent electrolysis. Eyebrows may be repeatedly plucked or shaved to create the desired shape. Some men spend lots of time shaving to get their beard to look the way they want. One man shaved many times a day to get rid of his supposedly uneven shadow, to the point where he bled.

Other people apply and reapply makeup. "I use a lot of makeup, and I take a long time to put on my eyeliner and lipstick," Emma said. "I'm in agony if I can't do this. I need my fix! I'd guess that I reapply my makeup as often as 30 times a day."

Many people have complex and time-consuming skin routines. They may wash their face 10 times a day, or spend a half hour each time they wash it. Many use special soaps, cleansers, and acne products. Sheila tried to prevent acne by washing her face for hours a day, which damaged her skin.

Grooming rituals are especially problematic for people with BDD when they stay at other people's homes. Some in fact avoid traveling or staying with friends or family because it's so difficult to enact their grooming routine. "I won't stay overnight places because I need my special makeup lights," Anne Marie said. "I never visited my in-laws or my family because of my combing," one man told me. "I couldn't take up the bathroom for that long, and I needed to keep my problem a secret from them. I think it's one of the reasons my wife left me—we could never visit her family."

■ The Batman Mask and Other Forms of Camouflage

John was a 34-year-old electrician who thought he was good looking except for his skin. "I like to blend in with the crowd," he said. "But I can't with white skin." He'd had this concern since he was 12, when he dreaded going to gym class and the beach because people would see his skin. Over the years, his preoccupation became increasingly upsetting.

John's solution was to use a skin bronzer. "I spend at least an hour a day trying to paint a perfect picture, so no one knows it's makeup. I look jaundiced, but that's better than pale. It helps me get to work, and it makes my life bearable."

But it also created some problems. "First, it's much too much effort to do this every day," he said. "And it's very expensive. But the hardest part is how this affects my girlfriend. I couldn't be spontaneous with her. We couldn't just go out and do something. It's why I never moved in with her. It would be too degrading to put it on in front of her.

"It's especially hard wearing the stuff in the summer, because it runs. What put me into the deepest, darkest depression of my life was when I was watering the lawn with my girlfriend, and the hose split. I got covered with water, and the bronzing stuff ran. I've never been so humiliated in my entire life. I got very depressed, and I had to go into the hospital for my depression.

"After the hose accident, I realized I needed a better solution for my problem. So I decided to take some tanning pills. I was told they can damage your liver and gallbladder, but I was so desperate, I took them anyway. I had terrible stomach pain, but I kept taking them. A month later, I had to have my gallbladder taken out. I'm convinced it was because of the tanning pills. Before the operation, I made sure I put my bronzer on—all I could think about was how I'd look on the operating table, not that I could die!"

As Table 6–1 shows, 91% of the people in my research studies have, like John, used camouflaging. I use "camouflaging" to refer to attempts to minimize or conceal a perceived appearance flaw so it's less visible and noticeable to other people. It's a safety-seeking, protective behavior that aims to escape the threat of having certain body areas seen or scrutinized by others. Camouflaging methods are numerous and varied.

You may recall Bill, the landscaper I described in the last chapter, who wore a baseball cap pulled down over his forehead to try to cover pockmarks he perceived on his nose. He also turned his head to the right when he was with other people, so what he considered the bad side of his nose was turned away from them. He always kept the lights turned down so the pores weren't as visible. "But the only time I feel really good," he told me, "is on Halloween. When I give out candy to the neighborhood kids, I wear a Batman mask, which completely covers the pores. It's the only time I feel okay being around other people."

Hats, especially baseball caps, are used to cover thinning hair or other hair problems, the forehead, eyes, eyebrows, skin, nose, or some other facial feature. Joe had worn a hat to cover his hair for the past 15 years. "Just about the only time I take it off is when I sleep," he said.

Like hats, wigs may be used to cover hair that's considered thin or unattractive in some way. Some men with BDD join hair clubs and buy expensive hairpieces, which they usually don't like. Some buy hairpiece after hairpiece, trying to find the right look.

Camouflaging with makeup and with clothing is also common. Luisa hated her legs—especially her thighs, which she thought were flabby, misshapen, and "dimpling." To hide them, she wore "big, shapeless clothes." Jessica hated her supposed flat-chestedness. She was once teased about her breasts in junior high school and was mortified ever since. She always used padded bras to look bigger. She kept searching for the perfect bra, one that enhanced her breast size but also looked natural.

Men do similar things, trying to appear larger or taller. Some wear long shirts to cover their genital area; others wear shoes with lifts. Some wear only long-sleeved shirts or pants, even in the heat of summer, to cover "thin" wrists or arms or "misshapen" knees. And men with muscle dysmorphia, who think their body build is too small, often wear bulky clothing or extra layers of clothes to look larger. One man I met with was wearing six shirts. But clothing solutions, too, are often unsatisfactory, because they can lead to frequent clothes changing and endless shopping and spending in search of the perfect cover.

Body parts may be used to camouflage other body parts. Hair is combed over to cover an area that seems particularly thin. Bangs are pulled down to conceal a supposedly short or misshapen forehead. Men may grow a mustache or beard to hide a supposedly uneven lip or scar. One person's camouflage can be another's BDD: what one person considers excessively thick bangs, another might consider the perfect cover for forehead scarring.

Many people use their hands or body posture to conceal the disliked area. One man sat and stood only in certain positions so his shirt wouldn't rest against and reveal his "love handles." A very attractive woman stood in a certain way at her wedding so the congregation wouldn't see her face.

Camouflaging methods are virtually limitless. Rob sewed an extra pocket in his underwear so he could stuff it and make his penis look bigger. A teenage boy kept candy or wads of paper in the side of his mouth to widen his supposedly thin face.

People with BDD camouflage to try to decrease their anxiety and emotional distress. But camouflaging has its limits. It can be very time consuming. Men who wear makeup fear that people will detect it. And by always covering up, BDD sufferers don't give themselves the opportunity to learn that nothing terrible will happen if they don't.

Yet another problem is that camouflaging sometimes appears strange. A young man who thought his nostrils were too wide, even after having three nose surgeries to narrow them, camouflaged them with his hair, completely covering his face with a curtain of long bangs. Another man wouldn't leave his house without covering his entire head with a black hood, which terrified other people. And John's experience with his bronzer and tanning pills is a poignant example of the limitations of camouflaging.

■ Skin Picking: "I Can't Stop Destroying My Looks!"

Pamela, a 25-year-old music student, described herself as a "picker." She'd picked at her skin for the past 8 years, usually for several hours a day and sometimes all night, trying to remove tiny blemishes and imperfections that to her were "hideously ugly."

"I usually check a mirror first," she said. "I check in school with a pocket mirror, in store mirrors, or in my bathroom mirror. If I see a tiny blemish, I start obsessing that my skin looks ugly and that other people will notice it. I have to get rid of it, so I start. I **have** to start picking when I see anything wrong. I can't resist! Then, afterward, I check to see how I look. Usually, I look so terrible that I isolate myself."

Pamela's picking caused noticeable skin lesions that required dermatologic treatment. "The treatment helped my skin heal, but it didn't help me stop the picking," she said. "One dermatologist told me to just stop doing it. I've tried to stop a hundred times, but I can't. I've tried cutting my fingernails, and then I wore artificial fingernails and bandaids to avoid doing more damage to my face. It really didn't work. I can't stop destroying my looks!"

Pamela's boyfriend had recently broken up with her because of her picking. I was much too embarrassed to tell him what I was doing. The picking took a lot of time—I ran out of excuses about where I was and why I couldn't do things with him."

More than one-third of people with BDD pick their skin. This relatively high frequency isn't surprising, given that skin concerns are so common in BDD. People with BDD who pick are usually worried about minimal acne, scars, or scabs, or such things as "large" pores, "bumps," "small black dots," "white spots," "ugly things," or other supposed imperfections. While many use their hands to pick, pinch, or squeeze, others use tweezers, needles, pins, razor blades, staple removers, or knives.

Picking with implements like these can cause major skin damage. One woman picked an actual hole through her nose. Some people have to go to the emergency room, because they pick through their facial skin into major blood vessels and need stitches. Occasional people require medical hospitalization and surgery to repair wounds because they are picked at time and time again. A colleague told me about a patient who picked so deeply at a pimple on her neck with tweezers that she exposed her carotid artery, the major blood vessel to the head. She required immediate emergency surgery; the surgeon said that the picking nearly killed her.

Yet, it's important to realize that people with BDD don't intend to mutilate themselves. Instead, they're trying to improve how their skin looks. They're trying to make it smoother, clearer, more attractive. The problem is that the behavior is so compulsive that they can't stop, which is what causes the damage.

For most BDD sufferers who pick their skin, the picking is in and of itself a serious problem; some consider it their major problem. One woman attributed her suicide attempt and psychiatric hospitalization to her belief that she had "ruined (her) face because of picking." Two woman with BDD who I know of needed psychiatric hospitalization largely because of their picking and eventually committed suicide.

People with BDD who pick their skin differ in some ways from those with BDD who don't pick. Those who pick are more likely to be female, to be concerned with their skin, and to excessively groom and camouflage with makeup—perhaps because they sometimes do create actual skin defects. One study, but not another, found that people who pick are also more likely to have actual skin defects. A vicious cycle can occur in which a minimal skin defect leads to picking behavior, which then creates actual, noticeable defects and then more picking to try to get rid of them.

People who pick their skin are also more likely to be treated by a dermatologist. Although dermatologic treatment is sometimes needed to treat resulting skin damage or infections, it usually doesn't decrease the picking itself or other BDD symptoms. As I'll discuss further in Chapters 11 and 12, picking behavior often diminishes with medication or with a type of behavior therapy called **habit reversal.** Because the picking can be so time consuming, distressing, and damaging, it's important to treat it specifically.

Not all people who pick their skin have BDD. Skin picking can occur as a symptom of other mental disorders. In some cases, it's simply a habit rather than a symptom of a disorder. To determine whether picking is a symptom of BDD, ask the person why they pick. Do they pick to remove or minimize supposed defects or imperfections in their appearance, such as pimples, bumps, acne, or scars? If so, and the other diagnostic criteria for BDD are fulfilled (see Chapter 3), the picking behavior is a symptom of BDD. It's often a clue that a person has BDD.

But often the picking is kept secret. Many people are very ashamed of this behavior and don't reveal it to anyone. They can hide it with heavy makeup. But sometimes there are visible clues that a person picks their skin. They may have actual skin lesions, such as red spots, inflammation, or bloody scratches on their face. Or, if someone has been picking for many years, they may have noticeable facial scarring. Thus, skin pickers—if they have noticeable lesions or scarring due to the picking—are an exception to the rule that people with BDD look normal. They're nonetheless considered to have BDD because the skin flaws that triggered the picking in the first place are minimal, and when the person stops picking, their skin often returns to normal.

■ Questioning and Reassurance Seeking: "Do I Look Okay?"

Many people with BDD never breathe a word to others about their appearance concerns—largely because they'd be much too embarrassed to mention them. But about half of those with BDD frequently question other people about how they look.

Often, the questioning is a request for reassurance: "Do I look okay?" "Is the problem noticeable?" They want to be reassured that the supposed defect isn't as bad or as noticeable as feared. Kevin, who was preoccupied with his "large" lips, "small" legs, and "sparse" body hair, asked his mother 5 to 10 times a day whether he looked okay. "I call my friends and ask them too," he said, "and I have huge phone bills because of it. They always say I look fine. Sometimes I feel better, and sometimes I don't. When I'm feeling really bad, I think they're just trying to be nice."

A young man who was concerned that his penis was too small frequently asked his father whether the chart of penis sizes he'd gotten from a book was accurate. A woman who'd been in therapy for several years spent most of her therapy sessions asking her therapist if her nose looked all right. "It's just about all she talked about," her therapist told me. "I'd try to steer her away from the subject, but it was useless. No matter what I said, she couldn't be reassured that she looked fine. She thought I was just being nice."

Sometimes people with BDD don't directly question others because they're afraid people will think they're vain or that their question is strange. A man concerned with his body build explained, "I wanted to ask other people how I looked, but I didn't want them to know I cared so much about it. Instead, I hinted around the subject, talking about appearance or body size in a more general way, hoping to get them to say 'You look big.'"

Some BDD sufferers repeatedly try to convince others of the reality or ugliness of the defect: "Can't you see this on my face?" "Can't you see I'm ugly?!" Some people use photos to try to convince others of how drastically they've changed and how bad they now look. One woman handed me a several-year-old photo. "Can't you see how much I've changed?" she implored. She described at length how the photograph clearly demonstrated these changes, although I couldn't see them.

A third type of questioning consists of repeated requests for advice or help to improve the defect. The BDD sufferer may frequently ask other people how to straighten "excessively curly" hair or how to pay for liposuction.

Reassurance seeking typically causes problems. It can take up a lot of time and be very difficult for family members and friends. Whereas mirror checking, grooming, and picking can be done in private, questioning always involves someone else.

Peter, a 40-year-old unemployed carpenter who hated his ears, jaw, and eyes, questioned his wife so often that she divorced him. "All I did was complain about how I looked and talk about how I wanted plastic surgery," he said. "I didn't accept her reassurances. She ended up hating me because of my obsession and because I talked about my looks all the time. Once I drove her so crazy talking to her about it that she pulled a knife on me. She threatened me, 'If you think you need surgery, now you'll **really** need it!'"

One parent told me something that's been echoed by many other family members: "The most frustrating part of it is that no matter what I say, it doesn't really help." Indeed, responding to requests for reassurance is a no-win situation. Saying the person looks fine doesn't help. They usually don't believe you or think you're just trying to be nice. Or you didn't get a good enough look at the problem, or you need new glasses. A handsome young man told me that he could "just tell" that his parents think he's ugly, even though they tell him he's handsome, because it's "their moral obligation." Another told me that "reassurance doesn't really help, because why did everyone laugh at me at camp and in the locker room?"

But agreeing with the questioner and saying that the defect is there and looks bad is even worse. Family members or friends may say this in desperation because reassurance hasn't worked. On the one hand, BDD sufferers may welcome the agreement because someone is finally telling them they're right; at the same time, their worst fear has been confirmed.

Another response that doesn't work is something like the following: "Well, now that you point it out I can see it, but it's really not that bad. Before you showed it to me I didn't even notice it." The person with BDD usually hears it differently. The "really not that bad" and "didn't even notice it" parts go unheard or are considered untrue. Responses such as these can plunge the BDD sufferer into a serious depression. To summarize, the bind is this: no matter how you answer the question, it usually doesn't help. As I'll discuss further in Chapter 15, the best approach is not to comment on the perceived defect and to help the BDD sufferer focus their attention on something more enjoyable or productive.

■ Doctor Shopping: The Never-Ending Quest

I got a call one morning from a psychiatrist who needed some advice about a patient. "He's seeing all the ophthalmologists in town," he told me. "He thinks his eyes look cross-eyed, and he can't be reassured that they're not. They all tell him he looks fine, but he won't stop doctor shopping. He wants to get his eyes fixed."

This story isn't unusual. Many people with BDD seek non–mental health treatment, often dermatologic or surgical. They see dermatologists for slight or nonexistent hair loss or skin problems, requesting various types of treatment. They see surgeons to have their lips thickened, jaws widened, ears pinned, or breasts enlarged. They see endocrinologists for supposedly excessive or insufficient body hair, dentists for braces, orthopedic surgeons for a supposedly crooked spine, podiatrists for "bent" toes, and urologists for penis enlargement. They may see doctor after doctor, trying to find one who will provide the desired treatment. Others visit nonphysicians, seeking electrolysis, a hairpiece, or hair-growth tonics. There's no limit to the types of treatment requested.

"Seeing doctors is an obsession for me," Victoria told me. "I'm trying to find someone who can tell me why my feet are so misshapen, but they all tell me that nothing's wrong with my feet. One doctor said my problem was that I had an obsession with body image. I agree that I have a body-image problem because I'm so obsessed, but I also need to find out what's wrong with my feet."

A 20-year-old woman I saw had seen surgeons up and down the east coast. She was desperately seeking a surgeon who would agree to make her head bigger. She was a very attractive woman with a normal-sized head. Even though all of the surgeons had turned her down, she refused to give up her quest.

Dwayne had seen 5 dentists, 4 dermatologists, and 16 plastic surgeons. He disliked "everything" about his appearance, which he described in the following way: "I must be an alien from another planet because I look so strange. I was totally obsessed with getting surgery. None of the doctors wanted to treat me. The dentists said braces wouldn't help me. One of the dermatologists said I should just wash my hair more. Fifteen surgeons refused to treat me because they said I looked fine. One of the surgeons said it was a good thing I didn't have much money, because I'd be mutilated if I did."

Mac had been turned down for surgery many times because the surgeons said he looked fine. "But I kept going back to them, and going to new surgeons, trying to find one who would do it. I know when they saw me, they said, 'Oh no, it's **him** again!'" Finally, in desperation, Mac tried to break his nose with a hammer so a surgeon would agree to operate. "That way," he said, "something would have to be done."

■ Tanning

Excessive tanning is a common and risky BDD behavior. One quarter of people with BDD tan specifically to improve a BDD concern. They may do this to try to minimize the appearance of minimal acne or scarring, darken "pale" skin, or make "uneven" or "blotchy" skin a more homogeneous color. A young woman repeatedly sunburned and peeled her nose to try to make it smaller. Ironically, some people tan to diminish the appearance of wrinkles, even though tanning actually makes wrinkles worse.

Arnie was obsessed with getting a tan—not to darken his skin, but to distract women from what he considered his "jutting" jaw. "I look a little better when I'm tan," he explained. "I get positive feedback from people, so I spend a lot of time in tanning salons." Another man, who was housebound because of BDD, wanted to tan in his back yard but was worried that the neighbors would see his "pale" skin. The only way he could get up the courage to go out to tan was by first getting drunk. As a result, he developed an alcohol problem.

Some people with BDD carry tanning to such an extreme that they severely burn their skin, permanently discoloring and damaging it. Tanning also prematurely ages the skin, and—most worrisome of all—it is a well-established cause of skin cancer.

■ Buying Beauty Products and Clothes

The cosmetics industry fuels our economy and promises us sex appeal, youth, and eternal beauty. Many of us—men as well as women—feel we couldn't possibly survive without makeup, hair gel, and conditioners. Purchasing such products has become commonplace in our lives.

But for some people with BDD, this behavior is carried to an extreme. They spend lots of time and money buying products for grooming and camouflaging. One woman spent more than $100 a week on shampoos and conditioners. "I can't walk out of a drug store without one. I keep looking for the perfect product."

Ken went to the drug store every day, searching for an acne cure. He spent hours each time examining the different products, and sometimes spent more than $100 a week on them, even though he couldn't afford it. He described his behavior as compulsive. Several times, when his funds were low, he was so desperate that he shoplifted skin products.

Clothes shopping, too, can be expensive and time consuming. While some people avoid shopping because they get so anxious looking in mirrors and trying on clothes, others shop excessively, trying to find something that will improve their looks, distract others from their flaws, or provide the perfect cover. "Shopping was like an addiction," Maureen said. "It was a way to cope with my ugliness. I needed clothes to make me look good."

In fact, some people with BDD are diagnosed with "compulsive shopping." In some cases, BDD is the cause of the shopping problem. A waitress I treated had bought so much makeup that she was $9,000 in debt. I've seen people who were $40,000 in debt from BDD-related purchases, such as clothes, makeup, and other beauty products.

■ Clothes Changing

Nearly half of people with BDD compulsively change their clothes, frantically trying to find an outfit that will minimize their perceived flaws. One woman told me: "I change them four or five times a day because they don't look right. They make my legs look too fat and my shoulders look too broad. I get very anxious, and I think people are analyzing my appearance, so I have to change them."

Tiffany spent 3 hours each morning picking out clothes, putting them on, appraising herself in the mirror, then ripping them off and flinging them on her bed in disgust. "I can't leave the house without doing this," she told me. "It's horrible. I **try** to stop but I **can't.** My husband keeps accusing me of having an affair, because I'm so obsessed with picking the right outfit! But I'm not! I tell him that I'm just trying to find a way to stand my awful body."

■ Dieting

While dieting is a common behavior in the general population, and a symptom of eating disorders, it can also be a symptom of BDD. One young man with BDD severely starved himself in the hope that losing large amounts of weight would erase wrinkles from his face. Another lost 30 pounds to make his face less wide.

Other people with BDD diet for more conventional reasons. They try to flatten their stomach or slim their thighs or calves. Others eat special diets—for example, they avoid chocolate or greasy foods, or take herbal supplements—to try to make their skin clear. One man I treated went from 160 to 120 pounds because he worried his skin would break out if he ate anything greasy or oily; in fact, he avoided most foods. Men with muscle dysmorphia may eat high-protein, low-fat diets to become larger. One man who did this, however, didn't allow himself to get **too** large and muscular because he feared that compared to the rest of his body, his penis would look too small.

■ Weight Lifting, Aerobics, and Other Forms of Exercise

Some people with BDD exercise excessively. They may run or do aerobics to decrease cellulite or the perceived flabbiness of their thighs, or to make their arms or legs slimmer or larger. Others do sit-ups to flatten their stomach. These behaviors are carried to an extreme. A man I treated who had muscle dysmorphia was so worried about not exercising during his hour-long drive to see me, thinking his muscles would "shrivel up," that he joined five gyms between his house and my office, which he worked out at along the way.

Exercise often doesn't have the desired effect, and some people think it makes them look even worse. One woman did what she called "extreme exercises" to decrease supposed facial bloating. "But the exercise made my legs look bigger and worse. I became obsessed with my legs while I was waiting for them to decrease in size."

Men with muscle dysmorphia are especially likely to exercise and lift weights to excess. Nick, a 32-year-old former car mechanic, carried weight lifting to an extreme, severely damaging his body. Nick had severe muscle dysmorphia (see Chapter 4). To increase his body size, he ate massive quantities of food, weight-gain powders, and special vitamins. He also wore extra shirts and padded his clothes. "But the main thing I did," he said, "was lift weights. I lifted for hours a day." Lifting became the focus of Nick's life. I stopped working because of it, I dropped out of life....I couldn't concentrate on my work because all I was thinking about was lifting. I didn't see my friends—I just stayed in my basement lifting. I lost a lot of them because of it. Once, I got so upset thinking I wasn't big enough that I stayed in my basement for a month, lifting and lifting. I was so depressed, thinking I'd never be big enough, that I thought I'd rather be dead. I couldn't let anyone see my body."

Nick eventually severely injured himself. He was often in pain and even had difficulty walking. When I saw him, he was in physical therapy and had to use crutches to walk. "I totally ruined my body by lifting," he said. "I tore my muscles apart. The irony is that now I can't work out at all—not even a normal amount."

■ Measuring

Measuring is another form of checking and reassurance seeking. Those who think they're too short may repeatedly check their height. Muscle girth, breast size, and penis size may be measured over and over again.

One man measured his penis with a tape measure up to 10 times a day, even though a urologist had told him it was normal. If the measurement confirmed his fear that his penis was tiny, he felt devastated. When I asked why he kept measuring it when he was so often disappointed with the results, he responded. "I measure it because I **hope** it will be bigger this time."

■ Reading and Information Seeking

Some people with BDD compulsively seek, buy, and read any information they can find about their perceived appearance problems. Men with genital concerns may peruse every book, magazine, and website they can find, searching for information about genital size and how to make theirs bigger. Some people with hair concerns read voraciously about hair growth. They search medical textbooks and the internet, seeking information about agents purported to increase or speed the growth of hair.

Men and women with body size concerns may spend hours a day reading fashion magazines, weight-lifting magazines, and books on dieting or exercise. They compare themselves with models or search for a magical solution that will dramatically transform their body.

■ Touching

Rosa frequently touched her hair to make sure it was puffed up. If it didn't feel right, she rushed to the mirror to fix it. Another woman constantly touched her face to "cool it off" so it didn't look so red. Zach frequently touched his lips, which he thought were too small, tense, and "never in the right position," trying to make them look fuller, more relaxed, and more natural.

Frequently touching the disliked body part, which about half of people with BDD do, is another form of body checking. Touching may also involve manipulating the body part to make it look better. A nose may be pushed up to look shorter or sideways to seem less crooked. Judy frequently pressed on her eye to make it more symmetrical with her other eye. She put so much pressure on it that she gave herself a black eye.

Touching, like mirror checking and many other BDD behaviors, can actually fuel BDD obsessions and is best avoided. Sometimes it's a trigger for skin picking or hair plucking. Touching often increases emotional distress and may lead to more time-consuming and futile attempts to remove or improve the flaw.

■ Distraction Techniques

Close to 20% of people with BDD accentuate or try to improve certain aspects of their appearance to distract other people from the "ugly" body areas. The thinking goes like this: if I can make an acceptable or attractive body part look even better, other people's attention will be directed to the attractive body part rather than the ugly one. The most common distraction techniques are with makeup (in 10%) followed by clothes (9%), hairstyle (5%), and jewelry (4%). Tanning and getting cosmetic procedures to enhance one's appearance are other strategies.

A man I saw excessively combed his hair, which he considered one of his primary assets, to make it even more attractive and thereby distract people from his "sunken" eyes. A beautiful young woman who thought her breasts looked fine was nonetheless considering breast augmentation to distract people from her "ugly" nose.

■ More BDD Behaviors: Compulsive Hand Washing, Showering, and Others

There's no end to BDD behaviors. A woman I treated tensed and untensed her facial muscles to make them less "limp." Another person pushed on her eyeballs to improve their shape. Yet another returned literally hundreds of pillows to the manufacturers she'd bought them from because she was convinced that they worsened her facial wrinkles.

Symptoms commonly seen in obsessive compulsive disorder can also occur as a symptom of BDD. People may compulsively wash their hands to avoid getting dirt on their face, which they fear will cause acne. They may excessively shower as part of their hair ritual, washing their hair over and over to set the stage for yet more grooming.

To make his face look fuller, Frank slept without a pillow, ate lots of food, and drank more than three gallons of water a day. James tightly tied ropes around his calves to try to make them look smaller. Claudia swallowed water a certain way so the skin around her mouth wouldn't drop, making her lines worse. Dennis, who worried about hair loss, searched his pillow each morning for hair, saved his hairs in a plastic bag, and developed complex math formulas to determine the rate of his hair loss. He paradoxically sometimes pulled out his hair, to see how easily it would come out. Somehow the evidence always confirmed that his fear was true. These are only some of the countless examples of behaviors people with BDD may do to try to alleviate their intense emotional suffering.

7. How Body Dysmorphic Disorder Affects Lives: Social Avoidance, Problems with School and Work, Violence, Suicide, and Other Consequences

■ Ian's Experience: "It's Ruined My Life"

"I look like a freak of nature," Ian told me. "I look like the Elephant Man. This is the cause of my problems. It's why I went to California. I was trying to look better."

Ian came to see me after his parents discovered that he'd disappeared to California to get a tan. To scrounge up money for his trip, he had broken into houses across the country, stealing cash and credit cards. "I'm not a criminal," Ian said. "But I was hoping a good tan would distract people from my ugly face, and I was desperate to get one.

"Maybe I was also sort of trying to get back at society, because people were making fun of how I looked," he added. "I was also hoping to find a surgeon in California who would redo my whole face. The ones I saw here wouldn't do it because they said I looked fine and didn't need it. But I don't believe them. It's their moral obligation to say I look okay." When I asked how he would have gotten the money to pay for surgery, he replied, "I was thinking of robbing a bank."

Ian had been a good student, athlete, and musician in high school and had never gotten into trouble of any sort. His appearance concerns began in college. One day he went into the men's room after class, looked in the mirror, and felt incredibly ugly. "I feel like my whole face has changed." he said. "The skin under my eyes has gotten darker. My face is too wide. My nose looks ridiculous. I have this tape in my head that says 'I hate how I look.' I feel repulsed by what I see," he said angrily, covering his face with his hands. "It's ruined my life."

Because he thought he looked so ugly and felt so anxious about his appearance, Ian stopped going to classes and spent most of his time alone in his room. "All I thought about was my face. I didn't go to the dining hall to eat, and I didn't even know if I had classes. I thought about suicide every night," he said. As a result, Ian started failing in school. His professors and a dean met with him and encouraged him to go to class, but he couldn't. "They asked me what was wrong, but I couldn't tell them. I wanted to go to class, but I couldn't."

Ian also stopped dating and seeing his friends. He'd gone out on a date once in the past year and thought the woman had dated him because she'd felt sorry for him. "I don't go out with girls because I know they'll reject me. So I reject them before they have a chance."

Ian's despair got so severe that he attempted suicide after looking in the mirror at school and thinking he couldn't go on living any longer. He was hospitalized and then moved back home with his parents.

■ Carl's Experience: "I Pull Myself Together"

While people with more severe body dysmorphic disorder (BDD) may, like Ian, be unable to function because of their symptoms, others, like Carl, function fairly well despite their emotional pain. Carl was an intelligent man in his late thirties with a good sense of humor. He worked as a partner in a law firm, where he'd been very successful over the years. "I've been a fairly happy person, and I had a good life," he told me. "But a year ago that all changed dramatically.

"I was looking in the mirror one morning, and out of the clear blue sky I noticed unusual thinning of my hair, and I panicked. I feared I was starting to go bald. I looked hideous."

Carl started reading about hair loss in dermatology textbooks and seeing dermatologists. "I even talked one of them into giving me Rogaine to make my hair grow, which didn't do me any good. The other dermatologists I saw didn't understand why I was using it. I think about my hair 24 hours a day. It's like a feeling of hunger that's always there. When I comb my hair or look in the mirror, my focus on it becomes intense, and sometimes I have panic attacks."

In reality, Carl had a full head of thick, curly blond hair. "I realize I look worse to myself than I do to other people," he acknowledged. "I'm distorting my perception, but I also believe what I see.

"I never really liked how I looked when I was younger. I always thought I was the ugly one in my family," Carl told me. "But I gradually got to like my looks, especially my hair. Now I feel I've lost the best part of my appearance." Because of his concern, he felt depressed, and it was hard for him to concentrate at work. "It's affected every aspect of my life," he said. "I'm depressed and it's totally due to my hair."

Nonetheless, Carl managed to function well. "I do my best to pull myself together for work," he said. He had to put in some extra hours at the law firm to make up for decreased efficiency, but he performed his job adequately. "But," he acknowledged, "I'm afraid that if I continue to lose my hair, I'll be too embarrassed to be around clients."

"Socially, it's caused me some problems," he added. "It affects my relationships because I'm so wrapped up in my hair. I feel very self-conscious around women, but I force myself to go out on dates. I worry, though, that this will be an issue if I get into a serious relationship."

■ A Range of Consequences

The consequences for most people with BDD are somewhere between what Ian and Carl experienced. Most people have problems with relationships, their social life, school or work, and other aspects of their life. They may avoid social gatherings, dating, sexual intimacy, or places with lots of mirrors (e.g., stores), places where their body will be more exposed (e.g., the beach), or places with lots of people (e.g., malls). Some people avoid only certain situations, whereas others avoid virtually any situation where other people might see them. Depression and anxiety are common. Accidents and violent behavior can occur. Occasionally, people with BDD do surgery on themselves, with disastrous results. Some people contemplate—and attempt—suicide. Some actually kill themselves.

This isn't surprising if you consider what's known about the effects of actual physical deformities that are caused, for example, by birth defects, accidents, or illnesses. People who are visibly damaged often feel profoundly stigmatized by their deformity. They feel ashamed and rejected by others. They may feel deeply defective and try to fade into the background rather than stand out in the crowd. They struggle to maintain self-esteem and acceptance by others. Some cut off their relationships with the world and go into a closet existence. People with BDD aren't actually disfigured but **believe** they are—and many experience strikingly similar feelings, fears, and isolation.

Table 7–1 provides a summary of some of the problems that the more than 500 people in my research studies experienced since their BDD began. Their average age was in the early 30s, and on average they'd had BDD for 14 years. My impression is that these individuals—and the problems they experienced because of BDD—are fairly representative of people with BDD more generally. However, additional research is needed to confirm this. I'll discuss these and other problems in more detail in the rest of this chapter.

TABLE 7-1   *Interference in Functioning*

Problem	Percentage of People with BDD Who Experienced the Problem During Their Lifetime, Or Average Number*
Interference with social functioning (e.g., with friends, family, or intimate relationships) due to BDD	99%
Periods of avoidance of nearly all social interactions because of BDD	95%
Interference with work or academic functioning because of BDD	99%
Periods of complete avoidance of work, school, or one's role (e.g., maintaining a household) because of BDD	80%
Days of work missed because of BDD*	52 days
Not working currently due to mental illness**	39%
Receiving disability payments (currently)	23%
Not primarily due to BDD	13%
Primarily due to BDD	10%
Days of school missed because of BDD	49 days
Dropped out of school because of BDD	25%
Temporarily	14%
Permanently	11%
Completely housebound for at least 1 week because of BDD	29%
Ever felt depressed because of BDD	94%
Ever violent because of BDD	28%
Ever psychiatrically hospitalized	38%
Psychiatrically hospitalized at least once because of BDD	26%
Abuse of or dependence on alcohol or street drugs	40%

*Since BDD began.
**For most, BDD was their primary problem; 20% of this group had an additional reason they weren't working.

■ Effects on Relationships and Social Activities

"There are traffic lights longer than my social life," Jake said wearily when he met with me. "This problem is ruining my life." Jake was preoccupied with his arms and legs, which he thought were too skinny, and his "pale" skin. "I have no sex life or love life. I hardly ever go out. If I do go to a night club, I feel suicidal....It amazes me that no one faints when I get on the subway!"

Jake had been married but later divorced. "I married someone I felt no desire for. She was probably the worst woman in the whole world, but I didn't think anyone else would accept me because of how I look."

As shown in Table 7–1, the most common problem that BDD causes is interference with relationships and social activities. Ninety-nine percent of the people in my research studies reported that at some point their BDD symptoms negatively affected these things. When they considered the period when their BDD was at its worst, 4% said that BDD interfered with their social functioning only mildly, whereas 29% said it interfered moderately, 39% severely, and 28% extremely. Theresa's BDD symptoms caused severe interference: "I feel so ugly and unpresentable that I avoid parties and dates. I feel too anxious when I'm around other people. I think they're evaluating how ugly I am. I feel like a leper. This problem has utterly and completely limited my social life."

In one of my studies, 126 people with BDD completed a questionnaire called the Social Adjustment Scale (SAS-SR). On average, their answers indicated that their social functioning is severely impaired in all areas that the scale assesses (see Figure 7–1). The scores of those with BDD were, on average, worse than scores that have been reported for more than 95% of people in the community.

Additional recent research using another scale (The Inventory of Interpersonal Problems-64) indicates that, on average, people with BDD tend to be very socially inhibited.

People with BDD are often reluctant to go to parties, dances, clubs, weddings, class reunions, family get-togethers, or other types of social activities. They feel self-conscious and embarrassed to be seen, and they're usually very focused on how they look and how others are appraising their appearance. As one man said, "Ninety percent of your mind is on your obsession—you have only 10% left over to focus on what someone is saying."

BDD behaviors can also contribute to other problems in social situations. "When I first meet someone, I don't want to be seen," Jake said. "I'm morbidly self-conscious. Then I check out their arms and legs. I think they're lucky. Or if someone looks worse than me, I feel better for a short while—but not too many people look worse than me. I'm not listening to the conversation. I'm totally focused on whether they're noticing my arms and legs and how theirs look compared to mine."

People with BDD feel especially uncomfortable and anxious in situations in which the perceived defects are likely to be exposed. They may avoid swimming, the beach, or events requiring shorts or short sleeves. People with facial concerns feel anxious in most social situations. Many people say that their

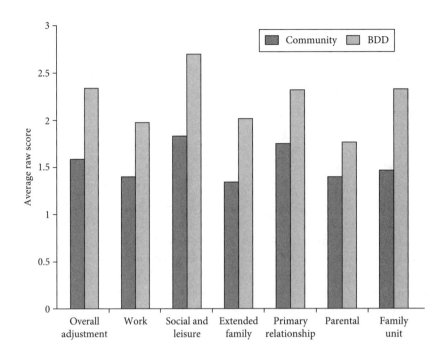

FIGURE 7–1 Social Adjustment Scale (SAS) scores in people with BDD and people from the community. Higher scores indicate poorer social functioning. On the SAS "Overall Adjustment" scale, the scores of 176 people with BDD were, on average, worse than the scores reported for more than 95% of people in the community.

symptoms typically worsen when they're around other people, which makes them avoid people even more.

Relationships and intimacy may be strained or avoided altogether. Spouses, boyfriends, or girlfriends usually have trouble understanding the self-consciousness and avoidance and may become irritated or even angry. "My husband is very frustrated that I don't want to go places with him where I'll have to dress up," Maria told me. She avoided situations in which she couldn't wear bulky sweatpants that covered her thighs. "He doesn't understand why I prefer to stay at home, and he's afraid that we're starting to lose our friends because of it."

BDD often stifles intimacy. "I've avoided dating because of it," Martha told me. "I finally got a boyfriend, after 20 years of not having one, and my worries about my feet and thighs are interfering with our relationship. It interferes with sex—I'm afraid he'll reject me because of my appearance." Martha never told her boyfriend about her appearance concerns, even after they got engaged. Because she was so self-conscious she tried to hide her body whenever she was around him. She undressed only in the dark, and she never allowed him to see her feet. "I wear socks at all times," she said.

On the other hand, some people with BDD indiscriminately seek out sexual relationships. They do this to obtain validation that their body is acceptable to others.

Randy attributed his impotence to his BDD. "I'm constantly judging the size of my penis negatively. I'm probably misperceiving, but I think it anyway. The intensity of the feeling is severe. No wonder I'm impotent."

Many people say that BDD caused the breakup of a relationship, even divorce. Jonathan's wife left him because of his BDD. "I don't blame her for leaving," he said. "I was totally obsessed. I'd spend weekends in bed, and I wouldn't go out with her because of my pimples. She called BDD 'the selfish disease.'"

Many people aren't in a relationship at all. About two-thirds of the people I've seen (who on average were in their early 30s) have never been married. Twenty two percent were currently married, and 12% were divorced. Many want to be in a relationship but aren't for various reasons—self-consciousness, fear of rejection, shyness, or low self-esteem.

Warren told me that he'd never been in a relationship with someone he liked because of his appearance. "I've felt undesirable," he said. "I've stayed single so I don't inflict myself on anyone else."

Avoiding dating and social activities can create a vicious cycle that makes people more and more isolated. A young man who refused to ask anyone out because of his hair was certain that no woman would ever want to date him, let alone marry him. When I pointed out that he might not ever date if he didn't ask women out, he was surprised. He had assumed that the reason he wasn't dating was because women found him so unappealing. He didn't realize the extent to which he himself was creating his dateless situation by avoiding women.

Many people with BDD have told me that they haven't had children—or never will—because of their BDD. As one patient told me, "I grew up praying that my brothers wouldn't look like me, and I was always reluctant to have children for the same reason." Like this man, many are afraid that their children will be ugly. Others worry that their children will have BDD and don't want them to suffer with such a painful illness.

BDD also often hurts friendships. Friends may find it hard to understand why social events are missed or attended only after much urging and encouragement. They may be puzzled and frustrated by lateness and last-minute cancellations. "I haven't seen my friends in the past 20 years," one woman said. "I'm afraid they'll see how I've aged and that my hair is thinner. It's gotten to the point where I totally avoid people."

Family get-togethers, weddings, and funerals may be anticipated with great trepidation and fear—or missed altogether. "I've missed a ton of social events because of my appearance," Guy told me. "To tell you how bad it is,

I missed my two best friends' weddings! I felt too ugly to go. I've humiliated my parents by not showing up at relatives.' It really bothers me. My family and friends never knew the extent to which I was worried about this."

Although not all social problems are necessarily due to BDD, people with BDD generally say that their BDD symptoms are the cause of their social problems or significantly contribute to them. My research shows that the more severe a person's BDD symptoms are, the poorer their social functioning and overall functioning are. In addition, more severe BDD symptoms predict poorer functioning in the future. The good news is that when BDD symptoms improve with mental health treatment, social functioning and relationships usually improve as well.

■ Effects on School and Work

"If I'm supposed to be in a meeting at work but I have blemishes, I don't want to go," Dan said. Alicia didn't work at all because of her appearance. "I'm too ugly," she said. "I don't want people to see me and comment negatively."

Table 7–1 shows that 99% of the people in my studies experienced interference with school or work at some point in their life because of BDD. When their BDD was at its worst, about 10% said that BDD interfered with work or school functioning only mildly, 30% moderately, about one quarter severely, and about one third extremely. Eighty percent had had at least one period when they avoided work or school.

Looking at current work functioning, my colleagues and I found that 89% of 141 adults with current BDD reported some impairment in work functioning (see Figure 7–2). Thirty nine percent of the 141 adults didn't work for at least one consecutive week in the past month due at least in part to mental illness (BDD was the primary diagnosis for most). Twenty three percent were currently receiving disability payments because they weren't able to work.

Of these 141 adults, one-third said that they wanted to attend school or take classes but weren't currently able to at least in part because of mental illness (BDD was the main problem for most). And virtually all of those who were in school reported experiencing impairment in their ability to do assigned school work (see Figure 7–2). People with BDD may have trouble concentrating on work or school because they're worrying about their appearance or caught up in rituals such as comparing or mirror checking. They may be late for school or work or not go at all because they don't want to be seen. Or they may be reluctant to interview for jobs because they assume they'll be rejected because of how they look. Those with more severe BDD may never even try to get a job or may quit school or work. They may become financially dependent on others.

Elizabeth, a fashion designer in her 30s, had been obsessed with her "rat's nest" hair for 10 years, ever since she'd gotten a bad haircut. It's the first thing

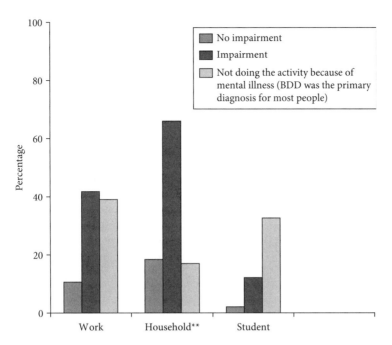

FIGURE 7–2 Current problems with functioning.*

* For 141 adults with current BDD; percentages in each category do not total 100% because some categories do not apply to certain people.
** Includes managing a household, shopping, paying bills, doing errands, caring for children, and other household duties.

I think of in the morning. It makes me feel desperate." Although Elizabeth had been widely acclaimed for her innovative work, she hadn't worked for the past 4 years. "I've passed up lots of opportunities, all because of my hair. I can't work because I'm so depressed and demoralized over my hair. I don't want people to see how I look."

People with BDD sometimes avoid taking a job they'd really like. Jobs that involve a lot of interaction with others, especially if the disliked body areas will be exposed, are especially avoided. I've seen many people who had a solitary job, such as a night watchman. As one person told me, "I can't do any kind of job where I have to be up close to people. I don't want people to see my facial abnormalities. I think they're noticing how ugly I am, and I worry that they'll think less of me because of it."

Tony always longed to be a high school teacher and football coach, but he hadn't pursued these jobs because of his chin. Instead, he'd worked at office jobs where he sat in a back room doing solitary work. "I haven't met my potential," he said. "When opportunities for advancement came along I turned them down. I didn't want a job where people would see me. I would have felt too ashamed."

Use of camouflage can also interfere with work. One young man, who wore a hat to cover his hair, told me, "I'm a pretty smart guy, and I should have a much better job than I do. But I can't look for a decent job and dress up in a jacket and tie with this ridiculous thing on my head!"

As Table 7–1 shows, people with BDD may drop out of high school or college—even elementary school—because of their BDD symptoms. Sean, at 24, was still enrolled in college but hadn't attended classes for the past 3 years. Instead, he'd gone back home to live with his parents. "First I started missing classes and school activities because my hair bothered me so much I couldn't go. I spend hours in front of the mirror combing it and trying to fix it. Once I had a perm, and it looked better for a while, but when it grew out I looked like a terrorist. First I started missing some classes, and my grades started dropping because I couldn't concentrate. Then I started missing so many classes that I took a year off. I didn't tell the school officials why because I was too embarrassed. I tried to go back, but I couldn't concentrate, so I dropped out again."

Gym class can be especially hard because of the need to change clothes or shower in front of peers, thereby exposing the perceived defects. Rita, who worried about her thighs, told me, "I always flunked gym because I wouldn't wear shorts." A young man I saw had avoided all sports and skipped gym class because of his shame over his genitals. He eventually dropped out of the ninth grade and never returned to school because he was so terrified of having a required physical exam, when the doctor would see him naked.

With the right treatment (see Chapters 11–13), many people find it easier to go to school or work. Grades and job performance often improve. And many of those who quit a job or school because of BDD—or never started in the first place—find they can now successfully do these things.

■ Other Problems: Caring for Children, Managing a Household, Leisure Activities, and Self-Care

BDD can also interfere with caring for children and managing a household. Ann Marie spent so much time worrying that her face was creased and her eyelids were shriveled that she couldn't care for her young son. "I've neglected him," she said. "My appearance problems are so time consuming and energy consuming. My ex-husband has to take care of him."

In my research study of 200 people with BDD, more than 80% currently had problems doing household duties, caring for their children or other family members, or doing errands because of BDD or another mental disorder (BDD was the primary problem for most of them) (see Figure 7–2).

Many people with BDD avoid many types of everyday situations and activities because they're so self-conscious, depressed, anxious, or fearful.

They may avoid public transportation, clothes and food shopping, leisure activities, restaurants, and going outside on windy days. Robert avoided all of these. "I'm afraid if people see me they might say 'Oh, gee, look at that guy. Isn't he gross looking?' I think people laugh at me. I avoid public transportation because of it. I can't get on the subway without hyperventilating. I usually go grocery shopping at night, because people won't see me."

Like Robert, some people get their mail, shop, and perform other necessary activities under cover of darkness or via the internet. They avoid clothing stores and shopping malls because there are so many mirrors. Others keep their distance from mirrors when trying on and buying clothes. One man stood about 20 feet from the mirror when trying on clothes. "Or, if I get up close, I have to look at the clothes with my head down so I can't see my face," he said. "Otherwise I'll freak out."

Many people, especially those concerned about facial defects, avoid bright lights. "At parties, I'm very uncomfortable hanging out in the kitchen with bright lights," a 26-year-old computer programmer told me. Some people quit their jobs, or never accept one in the first place, if they have to work under fluorescent lights.

"I restrict going places," Jerry said. He was a 45-year-old man who'd had BDD for 20 years. "When I go out, I feel worse and uglier. It's hard to go to the store. I have to boost myself to go. I'm afraid I won't fit in. I constantly worry that people are scrutinizing me and criticizing me. I try to convince myself it's not a big deal, but sometimes I leave the line in a panic, and I go and look at cookware because it calms me down."

Many people avoid swimming because the disliked body areas will be more exposed, or because the water will ruin camouflage and painstaking grooming. Greg avoided sports, even though he'd been an excellent athlete and had played on several varsity teams in high school. Although he was muscular and in excellent physical shape, he feared that people would see his "small and puny" body build, so he stopped playing altogether. Loni didn't play on her high school field hockey team because it would mess up her hair. Many of the people I've treated limit their recreational activities to things they can do alone in their house—such as watching TV or spending time on the internet—where people won't see them.

Reggie dropped out of his band because of his appearance worries. "I was too self-conscious to perform," he said, "and I couldn't groom my beard the way I wanted on the road. The other guys in the band thought I was crazy."

Some of my patients refuse to see their doctor for a regular check-up or even refuse to be checked out if they're not feeling well. They're too embarrassed to have the doctor see their body. This is worrisome, because physical problems may go undetected, and recommended preventive care may not be obtained.

■ Being Housebound

Being housebound is the most extreme kind of avoidance. Twenty-nine percent of the people in my studies have been completely housebound for at least a week because of their BDD symptoms. Many more stay in their house for briefer periods. Some are trapped in their house for years, petrified of going out and being seen.

"I've stayed home for weeks at a time because of my beard," Josh said. "It's the root of my paranoia." Kelly stayed in her house for 3 months. "This happened after I destroyed my looks by picking at my face at any tiny blemish," she said. "My skin is ugly. I didn't want anyone to see my face."

"I hide from people," Max told me, "especially after I get a bad haircut. I don't want to do anything. I just want to hide. There've been weeks when I didn't leave my house at all. I ate my roommates' food and ordered out. I was petrified of running into people. I'm afraid they'll think 'Here's this guy who looks awful. I don't want to have anything to do with him.'"

Kelly hadn't left her house for 15 years. Even though she was actually attractive, she thought she was so horrendously ugly that she'd dropped out of high school during her sophomore year. She hadn't gone to school, worked, or seen any friends since. Now age 30, she'll leave her room only about once a month, going downstairs to be with her parents—but only after covering her head with a veil so they can't see her face.

■ Poor Overall Functioning and Quality of Life

As the stories in this book convey, people with BDD, on average, function poorly and have very poor quality of life. Most feel distressed, don't get much enjoyment or satisfaction from life, and have difficulty functioning in important areas of their life.

In my prospective study of how people with BDD do over time, over nearly 3 years there was a very low chance of functioning reasonably well (having no more than slight impairment in functioning) for at least 2 months in a row. On one scale, only 6% of people had experienced good functioning, and on another scale, only 11%. The more severe a person's BDD was, the poorer their functioning tended to be. In a population-based survey in Germany (which included 2,552 individuals, 42 of whom had BDD), those with BDD tended to have higher rates of unemployment, lower financial income, and lower rates of living with a partner. Fortunately, there are effective treatments for BDD, which I discuss in Chapters 11 to 13.

In my research studies, people with BDD report unusually poor mental health status and mental health-related quality of life. On a scale called the SF-36, mental health-related quality of life for 176 people with BDD is much

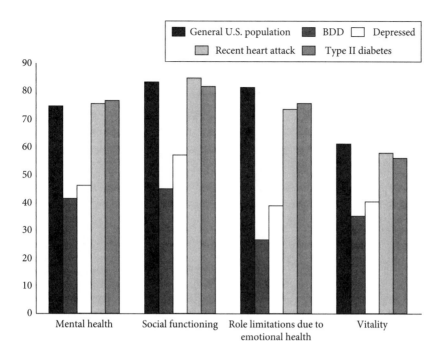

FIGURE 7–3 Quality of life scores on the SF-36 scale for people from the general U.S. population and for patients with BDD, depression, a recent heart attack, or diabetes. Lower scores indicate poorer quality of life. On average, on all of the scale items, scores for 176 people with BDD were worse than scores for 93% of people from the general U.S. population.

poorer than for the general U.S. population (see Figure 7–3). As Figure 7–3 shows, their mental health-related quality of life is also worse than for people with a recent heart attack (an acute medical condition), type II diabetes (a chronic medical condition), or clinical depression.

Those with BDD also have very poor quality of life as measured by the Q-LES-Q, another widely used measure of quality of life, compared to people in the community (see Figure 7–4). In fact, 95% of people from the community score better than the average BDD score. Only 5% of 176 with BDD had "normal" quality of life (within 10% of the community norm). As Figure 7–4 shows, quality of life is very poor in all areas assessed by the questionnaire. On both the Q-LES-Q and the SF-36, the more severe a person's BDD symptoms, the poorer their quality of life tends to be. Psychosocial functioning and mental health-related quality of life appear as poor as—or even poorer than—that of people with obsessive compulsive disorder (OCD).

The Q-LES-Q scores shown in Figure 7–4 reveal another important finding: people with BDD, on average, report poor physical health status and physical health-related quality of life. Scores on the SF-36 scale show the same finding. Compared to the general U.S. population, people with BDD have significantly poorer scores for general health, bodily pain, and ability to

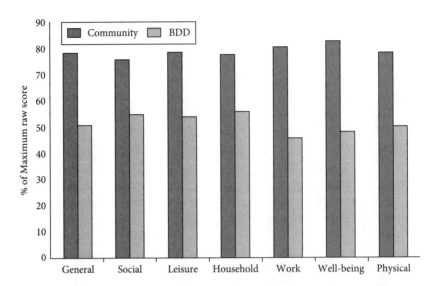

FIGURE 7–4 Quality of life scores on the Q-LES-Q scale for people with BDD versus people from the community. Lower scores indicate poorer quality of life. On average, on all of the scale items, scores for 126 people with BDD were worse than scores for 95% of people from the community.

function in one's role because of physical health problems. The more severe a person's BDD symptoms, the poorer they report their physical health to be. The reason for this isn't known, but one possibility is that the very high stress levels that people with BDD feel (see discussion below) may wear them out physically. Another possibility is that some people with BDD don't take good care of themselves by seeing their doctor regularly or when they're ill (see earlier discussion), which may compromise their physical health.

■ Low Self-Esteem, Depression, Anxiety, Panic Attacks, and Perceived Stress

In various groups of people—both ill and healthy people—body-image dissatisfaction and distortion are associated with depression, low self-esteem, and general psychological distress. The greater their body image distortion, the worse their self-esteem and depression tend to be. So it isn't surprising that most people with BDD have negative emotions such as low self-esteem, depression, and anxiety. For some, BDD causes panic attacks. The more severe BDD symptoms are, the worse self-esteem, depression, and anxiety tend to be. Many BDD sufferers say these negative feelings **result from** BDD. Others view them as part and parcel of their appearance worries and find it hard to say which causes which. Sometimes they seem to feed each other: negative emotions such as these seem to worsen BDD, and, conversely, BDD worsens these feelings.

Low Self-Esteem

People with BDD tend to have low self-esteem. This makes sense. Even in people who don't have BDD, physical appearance is important to the development of healthy self-esteem. The worse someone thinks they look, the lower their self-esteem tends to be. Similarly, research has found that people with BDD tend to judge themselves negatively as a person—for example, thinking they're uninteresting or undesirable—because of how they look. Furthermore, the perceived appearance defect has a major influence on how they judge themselves as a person, compared to other personal characteristics such as their personality or talents.

Self-esteem is poorer in those with more severe BDD symptoms, more severe depressive symptoms, and poorer insight regarding their appearance flaws. It's important to realize, though, that BDD isn't simply poor self-esteem. It's a legitimate mental disorder that needs to be diagnosed and treated.

Depression

Most people with BDD have symptoms of depression (see Table 7–1). On standard depressive symptom rating scales, scores tend to be fairly high. Those with more severe BDD tend to have more severe depressive symptoms. Three quarters of people with BDD have experienced major depressive disorder (see Glossary) at some point in their life, with BDD usually starting before the depression. BDD sufferers with current major depressive disorder tend to be more severely ill in a number of ways: they are more likely to have suicidal thoughts and behavior, and they have more severe social anxiety, poorer functioning, and poorer quality of life.

The relationship between BDD and depression is complex: some people say that their depression makes BDD worse, whereas many say that their BDD makes their depression worse—or even causes their depression. As one patient said: "If you thought you looked like a monster and that everyone was laughing at you, wouldn't you be depressed?" In my prospective research study, I found that the connection seems to be in both directions: improvement in major depression is often followed by improvement in BDD over the next weeks to months, **and, conversely,** improvement in BDD is often followed by improvement in major depression over the following weeks to months. However, not everyone whose depression gets better has improvement in BDD. Thus, BDD and major depressive disorder do **not** appear to be identical disorders. If they were, we'd expect BDD to always resolve when depression resolves. It's a mistake to consider them to be the same (also see chapter 14). BDD may be related to depression but is different in some important ways, and BDD requires somewhat different treatment approaches (see Chapters 10–12).

Anxiety, Fear, and Panic Attacks

People with BDD also typically experience anxiety. On standard anxiety scales, scores tend to be high. Anxiety may be psychological, consisting of worry and fear. It may also be physical, with symptoms such as headaches and stomach aches. People with BDD also tend to have high levels of social anxiety and distress, feeling anxious in social situations. In fact, levels of social anxiety are similar to those reported for people who have social phobia (social anxiety disorder). Among those with BDD, the more severe their BDD symptoms are, the more severe their social anxiety tends to be.

BDD can also cause panic attacks. Panic attacks consist of extreme fear as well as physical symptoms such as heart palpitations, difficulty breathing, and light-headedness. "The stress of BDD has caused me to have a lot of anxiety and even panic attacks," Henry told me. "It's also caused me many stress-related physical symptoms—burning in my stomach, high blood pressure, headaches for which I've had brain scans. I've seen a lot of doctors for these problems, but I couldn't ever tell them what the cause was."

"I get so anxious over my physical flaws that it wakes me up at night. I wake up thinking about them and feeling panicked," an interior decorator told me. Chuck, a contractor, told me: "It's like you were just told that you had inoperable, terminal cancer—that fear, that panic. That's what it's like **all** the time."

Panic attacks can be triggered by anything that makes the BDD sufferer suddenly feel worse about their appearance. They may be triggered by looking in the mirror and being horrified by the reflected image. Sometimes they're triggered by the belief that other people are staring at or mocking the BDD sufferer.

Perceived Stress

Research studies have shown that people with BDD have unusually high levels of perceived stress (i.e., feeling that their life is stressful). Levels of perceived stress are much higher than for people in the general population or for people with a variety of other psychiatric or medical conditions. The more severe BDD is, the higher the level of perceived stress tends to be.

These findings fit with Geoffrey's experience. "My worries about my mouth exhaust me," he told me. "Sometimes I'm afraid to get up in the morning because my mouth will consume all my energy and take my time. I've had

BDD for 16 years, and I honestly don't know how my body has withstood the enormous stress that this obsession causes me."

■ Problematic Alcohol and Drug Use

Many BDD sufferers have problematic alcohol or drug use. While the prevalence of this problem varies across studies, in the two largest studies that have been done on this topic I found that the rates were very high: 30% of 175 participants and 48% of 200 participants had a current or past substance use disorder (abuse or dependence on alcohol or drugs). Alcohol and marijuana are most commonly abused. Conversely, BDD may be common among those with a substance use disorder. One study found that among 34 adults with a current substance use disorder who were hospitalized on a psychiatric unit, 27% had BDD.

A very high percentage—70%—of people with BDD who have a substance use disorder say that BDD contributed to their problem, with 30% of them citing BDD as the main reason or a major reason for it. They may abuse alcohol or drugs as a way to try to decrease their appearance preoccupations, dull emotional pain, and lessen anxiety and self-consciousness in social situations.

BDD was a major cause of Rick's problem. "BDD is the absolute core of what led to my alcohol and drug use," he said. "I slept too much and did alcohol and drugs as an escape, to try to forget my scars." In fact, he'd been selling heroin to support his habit and had been in jail for this several times. He stopped using alcohol and heroin when a serotonin-reuptake inhibitor medication made his BDD better. Whenever he stopped the medication, he started using heroin again. Whenever he restarted the medication, he stopped his heroin use.

Emily told me, "The only thing that brought relief was drinking....My symptoms were totally debilitating, so intensely painful, and they were making me more and more depressed. No one knew I was suffering from BDD because I managed to look as though I was doing okay. I pulled it together, but the agony inside was totally overwhelming. I couldn't talk about it with other people....I finally went to my doctor. He told me when I stopped drinking I wouldn't be depressed. But that wasn't true for me. I drank and slept to deal with body dysmorphic disorder. What causes me the most pain now is the effects of my drinking on my son. I wasn't there for him."

Certainly, alcohol or drug abuse are serious problems in and of themselves. In addition, they may increase the risk for suicide attempts in people with BDD.

Men with muscle dysmorphia (see Chapter 4) appear to be at particularly high risk for a drug or alcohol problem. In one small study I found that 86% of men with muscle dysmorphia (most of whom also had additional nonmuscle-related BDD) had a problem with alcohol or drugs. This percentage is alarmingly high, and it's significantly higher than for men with non-muscle-focused BDD. Of the men with muscle dysmorphia, 79% had abused or were dependent on illegal street drugs, and 21% had used anabolic steroids to bulk up. Anabolic steroids are a family of drugs that includes the male hormone testosterone and numerous synthetic derivatives. These drugs are illegal in the United States and many other countries unless prescribed for specific medical conditions. They may increase risk for heart disease, stroke, and possibly other medical problems. They can also cause irritability, aggression, depression, and physical dependence.

To shed pounds or body fat, some people use ephedra-related products (such as ephedra, ephedrine, or ma huang). These dietary supplements are chemical relatives of speed. In high doses, ephedra may have very serious health risks. It can cause heart attacks, strokes, seizures, and even death.

■ Unnecessary Cosmetic Treatment

A majority of people with BDD seek and receive unnecessary cosmetic treatment—usually dermatologic or surgical. Doctors often refuse such treatment because the defect is nonexistent or so minimal they consider treatment unnecessary. Several men I've seen have even been turned down by hair clubs. As discussed in the last chapter, some people nonetheless persist in their search for a doctor who will give them the desired treatment. Some receive treatment after treatment—even surgery after surgery—hoping the next one will finally relieve their suffering. Sometimes, these treatments deplete life savings.

This behavior can take the place of living. Abby, who said she'd seen just about every dermatologist in Chicago, described her doctor shopping as "just about all I do. The doctors I saw said my skin wasn't so terrible and some thought I was crazy. So off I'd go to find another one. It's how I spend my days—going to skin doctors."

Research indicates that most people with BDD are disappointed with the outcome of cosmetic treatments, feeling that it didn't improve their appearance (see Chapter 13). Many blame themselves or the doctor for having made a serious mistake. For some, preoccupation and suffering diminish only temporarily—or shift to another body area. Some BDD sufferers are so dissatisfied they sue the treating physician, or are even violent toward them.

■ Self-Surgery

Some people with BDD are so desperate to fix their perceived defect that they do surgery on themselves. They can't afford to pay a doctor or find one willing to give them the treatment they want. One study found that more than one-third of 25 people who'd had cosmetic treatment for BDD had done such procedures on themselves to try to dramatically alter their appearance. In that report, people cut their thigh with a knife and tried to squeeze out the fat, attempted dermabrasion with course sandpaper, filed down teeth to change the appearance of the jaw line, and repeatedly removed blood with a syringe to lighten "overly red" skin.

I've seen people with BDD who filed down their teeth to make them even or cut their nipples off because they thought they were ugly. One man thought the fingers on his left hand were too long, so he cut them off. Another man was so desperate to improve the appearance of his nose that he cut his nose open with a knife and attempted to replace his own cartilage with chicken cartilage in the desired shape.

■ Bodily Damage and Self-Mutilation

Other types of bodily damage can occur. Sometimes this is intentional and sometimes not. Harsh chemicals used for acne or to stimulate hair growth can irritate and burn the skin. Excessive face washing can leave skin bleeding and raw. One young man superglued his "stuck-out" ears. To get rid of acne or white skin, severe, skin-damaging sunburns may be endured. Excessive weight lifting can cause back strain or more serious harm to muscles and joints. Skin picking can cause skin lesions, scarring, infection, or bleeding that requires stitches or even emergency surgery.

Some people with BDD are so desperate for surgery that they harm themselves intentionally, so surgery will have to be done. One man smashed his nose with a hammer so a surgeon would have to operate.

■ Accidents

BDD can cause accidents. Janet had several. "I'm a mirror-driven person," she said. "I check all the time. A few years ago I had a car accident because I was looking in the rearview mirror instead of the road." Some people, trying to stop this behavior, turn the rearview mirror away from them while driving, or remove it altogether—another setup for an accident. Others check a pocket mirror while driving instead of looking at the road.

■ Anger and Violence

Some people with BDD are very angry. They may be angry because they think they look ugly, feel it isn't fair that they're ugly, or can't fix their appearance problem. Others are angry because they think people are rejecting or mocking them. "I get angry because it isn't fair that I'm the one with the small penis," a college student told me. "And I get very angry at the people who laughed at me in the locker room in high school about my penis size."

Research shows that, on average, people with BDD have higher levels of anger/hostility than healthy people or people with another psychiatric disorder. The more severe BDD symptoms are, the higher the levels of anger/hostility are and the more likely a person is to have been violent. In my research studies, 28% of those with BDD say they've been violent—damaged property or physically harmed someone—specifically because of their BDD. A study in Italy found that 36% of 58 adults with BDD reported aggression/violence that was specifically attributed to their BDD symptoms.

While most people with BDD aren't aggressive or violent, some get so angry over their symptoms that they throw heavy objects like a brick or put their fist through a wall or door. A young man who thought that face cream had created dark spots on his face went on a rampage around his parents' house, attacking their furniture and splintering it with a hammer. Some people have such prominent referential thinking—believing that other people are mocking them—that they physically harm the person. In fact, one patient had to discontinue participation in one of my treatment studies because she had thoughts of killing someone who she thought was mocking her appearance. I heard from a man who was so angry at people he thought were making fun of his looks that he set off a bomb, for which he went to prison.

Occasionally, anger and even violence are directed toward a surgeon or dermatologist who provided unsatisfying cosmetic treatment. I know of one man who attacked his plastic surgeon with a knife because he was so upset over how his surgery turned out (he looked fine to everyone else). Another tried to murder his dermatologist because he thought the treatment didn't work. And there are published reports of people with apparent BDD who threatened, stalked, attempted to kill, or actually killed their dermatologist or plastic surgeon. In a survey of the American Society for Aesthetic Plastic Surgery, 12% of participants said they'd been threatened physically by a patient with BDD.

■ Illegal Activities

While most people with BDD are law abiding, BDD can spawn illegal behavior. As described earlier, Ian broke into houses across the country so he could get to California to get a tan. Todd shoplifted acne treatments from drug stores. Over several months, he'd stolen nearly $1,000 worth of items. "I'm afraid I'll get caught," Todd said. "But I can't resist. My acne is destroying my life. I have to make my skin look better!"

Another man I saw had done many illegal things, such as assaulting people and breaking and entering—in the **hope** he'd go to jail. He explained, "That way, no one would see me except the other inmates. And it's hard for me to keep a job because I look so bad, and I wouldn't have to worry about it in jail. Jail would be better than this hell I live in every day."

■ Hospitalization

BDD commonly causes psychiatric hospitalization and sometimes medical hospitalization. This may occur for various reasons, including severe BDD symptoms and resulting depression, accidents, or a suicide attempt. Nearly 40% of the people in my research studies have been psychiatrically hospitalized. Twenty-six percent attributed at least one psychiatric hospitalization primarily to their BDD symptoms.

I met Lawrence in the hospital after he'd tried to kill himself. He was agitated, anxious, and very depressed. "When I started graduate school in physics, I was troubled by not having many friends and also by a sense of my dramatically receding hairline. A few weeks ago I noticed excessive hair loss and decreased density in the front. I worried about how I would have to present myself with my new appearance to my old friends. I also worried about how I could meet new people with my hair the way it was. My self-esteem plummeted, and I felt like a social failure. I couldn't concentrate on my studies. I started to wonder if people were talking about me or laughing at me.

"In the past week I started to panic. I was worrying more and more about how I looked and what other people thought of me. I worried that it would get worse and that I'd become bald. I couldn't stop thinking about it, and I felt I was falling apart. I was crying, looking at myself in the mirror. I thought I was collapsing, eroding, and I tried to kill myself."

When his family came to visit him in the hospital, Lawrence couldn't tell them the real reason he was there. "I just told them I was depressed." This was easier for him to say. "I'm much too embarrassed to tell them about my hair," he said. "I'm afraid they won't take it seriously or they'll see me as vain. And if I bring it up, I'm afraid they'll notice how bad my hair is."

Even when BDD symptoms are this severe, many people never discuss them. They keep them a secret not only from family but also from hospital staff. BDD symptoms are usually never even mentioned in the medical record, even for patients whose main problem is BDD.

I'm aware of several young people who had such severe BDD that they were sent to permanently live in a nursing home. They hadn't improved with numerous treatments and hospitalizations, and they were so incapacitated by their BDD that neither they nor their family members could care for them.

■ The Economic Cost of BDD

The economic cost of BDD can be very high. It can include the cost of medical and psychiatric hospitalization, medical treatment for bodily harm and accidents, and ineffective medical and surgical evaluation and treatment. It also includes the cost of incomplete education, decreased work productivity, lateness and days lost from work, and disability payments. Table 7–1 and Figure 7–2 show the high rates of work impairment in people with BDD and the high proportion who are receiving disability payments.

Some people have significant financial problems for these reasons or because they spend so much money on wigs, clothes, makeup, or surgery. One woman was more than $10,000 in debt because she'd spent so much money on clothing and wigs.

Richard's experience illustrates how costly BDD can be. Richard had dropped out of school because he constantly went to the bathroom to check the mirror and couldn't concentrate on his studies. He tried several jobs, but quit each of them because of his symptoms. He then moved in with his family and started receiving disability payments from the government.

Richard had made three suicide attempts because he thought he looked so ugly and was hospitalized after each one. One led to a long stay in an intensive care unit. In the six months before I saw him, he'd been hospitalized four times. Richard had also undergone three costly operations on his lips. Two, in his view, had such devastating results that he had to be psychiatrically hospitalized. "I had to be hospitalized because after the surgery my lips were black and blue and swollen," he said. "They looked deformed. I went wild, screaming and smashing things. I thought they were worse than ever, and I thought I'd done irreparable damage to myself."

Although Richard had had BDD for only several years, the cost of his illness had been staggering—already well over $100,000. But the greater cost of BDD is the human cost—the severe suffering and pain. Years lost to the illness can't be replaced.

■ Suicide: The Most Devastating Consequence of All

The greatest cost of all is suicide—an irreversible act that reflects intolerable suffering and loss of hope. Most people with BDD have suicidal thoughts (also called suicidal ideation). About a quarter or more attempt suicide. And research done so far suggests that BDD is associated with a markedly high rate of completed (actual) suicide.

Suicidal Thoughts

Thoughts that life isn't worth living, a wish to be dead, or thoughts of killing oneself are alarmingly common in people with BDD. As shown in Table 7–2, about 80% of the people who participated in my studies have had these kinds of thoughts at some point in their life.

Comparisons with other disorders must be made cautiously; however, these suicidal ideation rates are higher than reported for any mental disorder

TABLE 7-2   *Suicidal Thoughts and Suicide Attempts in People with Body Dysmorphic Disorder**

Suicidality Variable	United States (n = 307)	United States (n = 200)	Italy (n = 58)	England (n = 50)	Germany (n = 42)**
Suicidal thoughts	81%	78%	—	—	—
Suicidal thoughts due to BDD†	68%	55%	45%	—	19%
Attempted suicide	24%	28%	—	24%	—
Attempted suicide due to BDD†	15%	13%	—	—	7%

* All percentages reflect lifetime (i.e., past or current) rates, except for the Italian study, which reported a current rate; the German study did not specify a period of time during which suicidal thoughts or suicide attempts occurred.

** 42 study participants had BDD; the total sample size was 2,552 (this was a large population-wide epidemiologic study).

† BDD was the primary reason, in the person's view.

— Indicates that the variable was not assessed.

The two U.S. studies were published by me, the Italian study by Perugi and colleagues, the British study by Veale and colleagues, and the German study by Rief and colleagues.

in an outpatient study, and higher than studies have found for schizophrenia or major depressive disorder.

A majority of those with BDD attribute their suicidal thoughts primarily to their BDD symptoms (Table 7–2). As one woman said, "My appearance is the source of all the pain in my life.…Sometimes I feel that life isn't worth living." Having more severe BDD symptoms, or major depressive disorder, increases the likelihood of having suicidal thoughts. (A possible explanation for the lower rate in the German study is that the time period was not specified; this was also the case for suicide attempts. Some people might have reported only current suicidal thinking rather than any they'd had at any point during their life.)

In my prospective study of 200 people with BDD, an average of 58% of participants reported having suicidal thoughts each year. This rate is about 10 to 25 times higher than in the general U.S. population. Thirty-six percent of all participants said they had suicidal thoughts over a year's time that they attributed primarily to BDD.

Juanita felt suicidal because of the hair she perceived on her face, arms, and legs. "It's **severely** upsetting," she told me. "I feel like a freak, a bad person because I have a defect in my appearance. I fear that no one will ever love me—that I'll be an outcast. So what's the point of going on? I've seriously considered buying a gun to kill myself."

Suicide Attempts

Luke attempted suicide after an acne medication (Accutane) failed to improve his skin. "It was my last hope," he said. "I got so upset that it didn't work that

I had a nervous breakdown. I was constantly grieving over how I looked. I had to be hospitalized because I tried to kill myself."

As shown in Table 7–2, research studies have found that about a quarter or more of people with BDD have attempted suicide. These suicide attempt rates are much higher than those for the general U.S. population (6 to 23 times higher, depending on the study). About half of all suicide attempters attributed at least one attempt largely or entirely to their BDD. Furthermore, among those who attempted suicide, the average number of attempts in one study was two and in another study was slightly more than three.

Although here, too, comparisons with other mental disorders should be made cautiously, the suicide attempt rates for BDD are within the range reported for depressed outpatients, and higher than those for a number of other mental disorders (generalized anxiety disorder, panic disorder, or agoraphobia).

In one small study, I found that an alarming 50% of men with muscle dysmorphia had attempted suicide; this rate was significantly higher than the rate for men with nonmuscle dysmorphia BDD (16%). In addition, people with BDD are more likely to have attempted suicide if they also have post-traumatic stress disorder (a six-fold increased risk of an attempt compared to those without post-traumatic stress disorder) or a substance use disorder (a three-fold increased risk). In addition, with each 1 point increase on a 9-point BDD severity scale, the likelihood of a suicide attempt increases by 50%.

In my prospective BDD study, 72% of suicide attempts were characterized by serious, very serious, or extreme intent to die. Each year an average of 2.6% of study participants attempted suicide. This rate is about 3 to 12 times higher than in the general U.S. population.

Viewed from another perspective, people with other mental disorders may be more likely to attempt suicide if they also have BDD. In a study of 122 psychiatrically hospitalized patients, those who had BDD were somewhat more likely than those without BDD to have attempted suicide (statistically, the difference was at a trend level). In a study of 41 inpatients with anorexia nervosa, those who also had BDD were three times more likely to have attempted suicide than anorexia patients who didn't also have BDD.

Completed (Actual) Suicide

It isn't known with certainty how many people with BDD kill themselves, but available research findings are alarming. In my prospective BDD study of 200 participants, in which people are interviewed once a year, 0.3% of participants killed themselves each year over a 5-year period. This is equivalent to about 1 in 300 people each year. This suicide rate (adjusted for age, gender, and geographic region) is about 37 times higher than in the U.S. population. This finding should be considered very preliminary, because it is based on a small sample size and only 5 years of follow-up interviews. Thus, comparisons with other disorders must be made with caution. Nonetheless, this suicide rate is higher than that reported for virtually any other mental disorder. While suicide rates vary in different studies, the rate in people with major depressive disorder is about 20 times higher than in the general population, and that for eating disorders is about 23 times higher.

One of the people who committed suicide was a 54-year-old man with very severe BDD (BDD was his primary diagnosis) as well as major depressive disorder. He was obsessed with his lack of "chin tone," asymmetrical ears, inadequately full beard, and off-centered lip. His appearance concerns began in late adolescence, and were triggered by hitting his lip on the edge of a table during a fall. He believed that subsequent cosmetic surgery ruined his looks. He was psychiatrically hospitalized four times for BDD and had attempted suicide because of his BDD symptoms. He committed suicide by stabbing himself. Another man, who hanged himself, had muscle dysmorphia as well as other appearance concerns and had abused anabolic steroids. Bill, whom I described in Chapter 5, had made more than 20 serious suicide attempts and finally killed himself after he stopped a serotonin-reuptake inhibitor medication, which had substantially improved his BDD symptoms. For all of these men, BDD was their main problem.

Published reports in psychiatry journals contain descriptions of people with BDD who committed suicide because they were so despairing over their perceived ugliness. And I know from colleagues of numerous people with BDD who committed suicide. Several were beautiful young women with BDD who were obsessed with their skin and compulsively picked it. Another was a young man obsessed with his "misshapen" forehead, and another a young man who hated his hair. One young man from a very loving family had severe BDD that focused on his skin. When he could no longer tolerate the emotional torment that his BDD caused, he hanged himself.

In a study of two dermatology practices in England, the most frequent causes of patient suicide were acne and BDD. I've talked with dermatologists who told me about BDD patients of theirs who committed suicide. One dermatologist said that six of his patients with probable BDD had committed suicide in the past year alone. And in a study of adolescents in an inpatient setting, my colleagues and I found that those with BDD scored significantly higher than those without BDD on the Suicide Probability Scale, which reflects suicide risk.

One man told me, "I think many people have committed suicide because of BDD. I know, because it's so painful. I made two suicide attempts at the time my symptoms were severe. I felt very isolated, and I lost hope."

Thus, BDD must be taken very seriously. It needs to be accurately diagnosed and appropriately treated. And people with BDD need to be asked if they are having any suicidal thoughts (see Chapter 15 for additional suggested approaches), so measures can be taken to try to prevent this terrible outcome from occurring.

Risk Factors for Suicide in People with BDD

These rates of suicidal thinking and behavior make sense. BDD involves very negative thoughts and beliefs about oneself. These beliefs are often firmly held (i.e., are delusional), such that sufferers can't obtain relief by recognizing that their beliefs are inaccurate. The time-consuming, obsessional, and intrusive nature of negative BDD-related thoughts further fuel emotional distress. In addition, BDD symptoms usually involve a deep sense of shame, low self-esteem, even self-loathing, and feelings of being unworthy, unacceptable, and unlovable. Many BDD sufferers believe that other people reject them—or even mock them—because of how they look, and they are often socially isolated.

In addition to limited social support, many people with BDD have poor functioning, co-occurring disorders such as major depression and substance use disorders, poor self-esteem, and high levels of anxiety, depression, anger/hostility, and impulsivity—all of which are risk factors for suicidal thinking or suicide attempts.

Hope for Suicidal People with BDD

Relatively little research has been done on suicidal thinking and behavior in BDD, and there is an urgent need for more research to increase knowledge of rates of suicidal thinking and behavior, risk factors, treatments to decrease suicidal thoughts and behavior, and prevention of suicide. In the meantime, I have no doubt that in many cases successful mental health treatment (serotonin-reuptake inhibitors and/or cognitive-behavioral therapy) can prevent suicide. In my treatment studies, suicidal thinking significantly diminished during treatment with a serotonin-reuptake inhibitor (see Chapter 11).

Juanita improved substantially with one of these medications. She called me years later to say that she'd gotten married and had a great job. She was no longer suicidal over how she looked. Luke also had an excellent response to the same medication plus cognitive-behavioral therapy. After treatment, his appearance no longer tormented him. He went on to a successful career in television, and gave up thoughts of suicide. "It's the furthest thing from my mind now," he told me. "I have a great life. Thank God I got treatment. I owe my life to it."

Many of the other negative consequences of BDD described in this chapter improve with the right treatment (see Chapters 10–12). A majority of people find it easier to function in their daily life and overcome the other problems I've described. So even though BDD typically causes many problems, and can even be devastating, there's lots of hope for those with BDD.

8. Gender and Body Dysmorphic Disorder across the Life Span

■ BDD and Gender

It's often assumed that body dysmorphic disorder (BDD) is much more common in women than in men. Aren't women more focused on their looks? And doesn't society place a particularly high premium on attractiveness in women? However, while several BDD studies contained more women than men, some studies had more men. In the two largest epidemiologic surveys of BDD, the disorder was present in 2.5% of women and 2.2% of men (a U.S. study) and in 1.9% of women and 1.4% of men (a German study).

I'm sometimes asked about the sexual orientation of people with BDD. In my study of 200 people, 5% were homosexual and 3% were bisexual. These percentages are somewhat higher than in the general population, but they indicate that the vast majority of people with BDD are heterosexual.

I and other researchers have found that men and women with BDD have many similarities, including most demographic and clinical characteristics, such as which body areas are disliked, what kinds of compulsive BDD behaviors are performed, BDD severity, suicidal thinking and suicide attempts, and coexisting mental disorders. Why men with BDD appear to have as high a rate of major depressive disorder as women with BDD is puzzling, as this disorder is usually more common in women. One possible explanation is that depression may often be "secondary" to BDD—that is, resulting from the distress and impairment that BDD causes. Another is that the same underlying biological and psychological mechanisms that cause BDD (see Chapter 9) also contribute to the depression that accompanies BDD.

Another interesting gender similarity is that men and women are equally likely to seek—and receive—cosmetic treatment, such as surgery or dermatologic treatment, for their BDD concerns. This finding differs from the general population, in which women are more likely to receive cosmetic treatments than men.

Yet there are some interesting differences between men and women with BDD. Three research studies have examined this question (two were done by myself in the United States and one was done in Italy). All three studies found that males are more likely to be preoccupied with their genitals, and females are more likely to have a coexisting eating disorder. The following differences were found in two of the three studies. Males were more likely to be single, have an alcohol or drug problem, and be preoccupied with thinning hair and small body build (thinking they're too small, skinny, or not muscular enough). Females were more likely to be preoccupied with their weight (nearly all thinking they weigh too much), hips, breasts, legs, and excessive body hair. They were more likely to use camouflaging of any type, use makeup or their hands for camouflage, check mirrors, and pick their skin. It's interesting that many of these differences reflect gender differences in the general population.

One of my gender studies examined daily functioning and quality of life in some detail. Men had a significantly worse score than women on one measure of overall functioning. Also, a significantly higher proportion of men weren't currently working because of mental illness and were receiving disability payments, including disability payments specifically for BDD.

■ BDD over Time

BDD usually begins during early adolescence, but it can start in childhood or adulthood. The more than 500 participants in my research studies developed full-fledged BDD at an average age of 16. Two-thirds were between 9 and 23 years old when BDD began. The most common age that full-fledged BDD began was 13. The earliest age of BDD onset was 4, and the oldest was 49 (see Figure 8–1).

The fact that BDD usually begins during early adolescence is, in a sense, not surprising. Puberty is a time of dramatic physical and physiological (e.g., hormonal) changes. Might such changes contribute to the development of BDD? Also, at puberty, across species, the brain seems to increasingly attend to indicators of social status, including appearance, as well as cues of social rejection. In addition, our society's messages that emphasize the importance of appearance are clearly important at this time.

An important question is how people with BDD do over time, as they get older. Does BDD tend to be life-long, or do people get over it by early or middle adulthood? Some research findings are discouraging. Looking back over time, more than 80% of people say that their BDD symptoms have been chronic. That is, they haven't been free, or nearly free, of them for at least a full month since their BDD began. When I ask, "What's the longest time you've gone without worrying about your defect since the problem began? the most common answer is "less than a day." Most of the people who say this, however, haven't received the right treatment for BDD.

Prospective studies, in which people are assessed forward over time (rather than by looking back over time), are the scientifically best way to see how people fare over time. In my prospective BDD study, participants

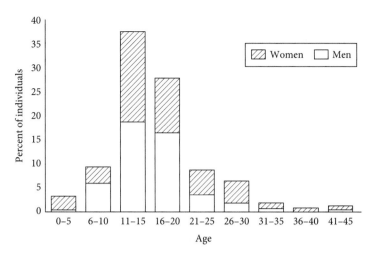

FIGURE 8–1 BDD age of onset*

*In the studies, age at onset was usually determined retrospectively (looking back over time, after BDD began) rather than prospectively (forward over time, before BDD developed). Because memory can be faulty, this approach is subject to error. Nonetheless, many people with BDD have very vivid memories of their early symptoms, suggesting that their recollections may be reasonably accurate.

were interviewed annually about their symptoms (187 people had at least one follow-up interview). Over 1 year, only 9% were free of BDD symptoms for at least 8 consecutive weeks during that year, and only 21% were partially free of BDD symptoms (i.e., they didn't meet full DSM-IV criteria). Over 2 years the corresponding rates were only 16% and 28%, and over 3 years they were 17% and 36%. These improvement rates are lower than similar studies have found for major depressive disorder, personality disorders, and most anxiety disorders.

While these numbers may sound dismaying, very few people in these studies had received adequate treatment for BDD. People who get the right treatment (see Chapters 10–12) tend to do much better. Among people I treated in my clinical practice, all of whom took medication and some of whom also received cognitive-behavioral therapy (CBT), 58% had improved with treatment after 6 or 12 months. After 4 years of treatment, 84% had improved.

More scientifically rigorous treatment studies also yield encouraging findings: in medication studies, more than half to three-quarters of people substantially improved with a serotonin-reuptake inhibitor (SRI) (see Chapter 11). Similarly, studies of CBT show significant improvement in BDD symptoms (see Chapter 12).

What factors influence whether BDD improves or worsens? In my prospective study, people who had more severe BDD at the beginning of the study or a personality disorder were less likely to recover from BDD. Many people say that their symptoms worsen with stress. Women not uncommonly say their BDD symptoms worsen premenstrually, suggesting that sex hormones (estrogen) may play a role for some women. Many people with some acne say that their appearance preoccupations get worse when their acne flares. For people with bipolar disorder (manic-depressive illness), BDD symptoms temporarily go away when they're manic. But many more research studies are needed to understand what factors influence BDD severity; understanding more about this may help prevent worsening of BDD and increase the chance of improvement.

■ BDD Occurs in Children and Adolescents

Johnnie was excessively worried about his hair, which he thought "wasn't right" or flat enough, his teeth, which he thought weren't white or straight enough, and his "pot" belly. He frequently checked mirrors and brushed his teeth. Throughout the day he touched and combed his hair, using special hair creams. "I wish the whole world was bald," he said, "including me, so I wouldn't have to worry about my hair!"

Over and over again, Johnnie asked his parents, "Is my hair okay?" "Am I fat?" His mother estimated that he spent at least 3 hours a day focused on his appearance and asking for reassurance. Johnnie was only 5 years old.

Holly, a shy and attractive 16-year-old high school student, was embarrassed to discuss her appearance concerns. "I think my problems first began with shyness. But then, a few years ago, I started worrying about my body shape. Then I got a terrible haircut, and I started worrying about my hair—that it's ugly and never looks right. It's a real rat's nest."

Holly thought about these perceived defects for several hours a day, and frequently checked them in mirrors and windows. She spent at least $40 a week on haircuts, permanents, and hair products, and wore loose-fitting clothes to cover her body. "Because I look so bad, I feel I don't fit in anywhere," she said. "I'm avoiding friends, and I hardly ever go to parties."

As Johnny's and Holly's stories illustrate, BDD occurs in adolescents and even young children. Many adults with BDD have surprisingly vivid memories of their early symptoms. A woman whose symptoms began at age 4 clearly remembered hating her "stubby" fingers and insisting on wearing mittens at her fourth birthday party. Another woman had refused to go to nursery school because she thought she looked so ugly. And another told me, "At the age of five I looked in the mirror and said, 'I'm ugly.' To hide my ugly face, I wore sunglasses to kindergarten."

We don't really know how common BDD is in children and adolescents, because so little research has been done. In a study of 208 adolescents hospitalized in a psychiatric hospital, 7% had definite or probable BDD. Most people with BDD—about 70%—develop it before age 18. So it's important to be aware that BDD can occur in this age group. It's also important to realize that not all appearance concerns in adolescents are normal or simply a passing "phase"—sometimes they're BDD.

■ Characteristics of BDD in Children and Adolescents

To increase knowledge of BDD in this age group, much more research is needed. Nonetheless, to the best of our knowledge, characteristics of BDD in adolescents and children are very similar to those in adults. Table 8.1 summarizes some BDD characteristics in 47 systematically assessed children and adolescents who were under age 18. Like adults, they have time-consuming, distressing preoccupations that can focus on any body area, and insight is often poor. A majority think that other people take special notice of them in a negative way because of how they look. Nearly all perform compulsive behaviors, such as mirror checking. For most, BDD symptoms cause substantial

TABLE 8–1   *Features of BDD in 49 Children and Adolescents**

Characteristic	Average, or Percent of Children/ Adolescents with this Characteristic
Age	15
Gender	90% female
	10% male
Body areas of concern (most common)	71% skin
	51% hair
	47% weight
Number of body areas of concern (past or present)	6
Behaviors (most common)	Camouflaging 92%
	Mirror checking 82%
	Comparing 80%
BDD severity (as assessed by BDD-YBOCS)	31 (moderately severe)
Ever socially impaired because of BDD	100%
Ever impaired at work or school because of BDD	100%
Currently impaired academically	86%
Dropped out of school due to BDD	18%
Ever psychiatrically hospitalized	39%
Ever housebound due to BDD	16%
Violent behavior due to BDD	38%
Past or current suicidal thoughts	73%
Attempted suicide	33%

*All were under age 18.

problems with functioning. In more severe cases, children and adolescents with BDD drop out of school, become housebound, require psychiatric hospitalization, and even attempt suicide.

When I and my colleagues compared 36 youth (under age 21) to 164 adults, we found that these two age groups didn't significantly differ in terms of most characteristics, such as body areas of concern, compulsive behaviors, and severity of BDD or depressive symptoms. However, a significantly higher proportion of youth than adults had attempted suicide (44% vs. 24%). Youth also had more delusional BDD beliefs. In addition, lifetime rates of coexisting mental disorders and impairment in functioning were similar in youth and adults—even though youth had had fewer years to have developed these problems because they were younger. These differences raise the possibility that youth may be somewhat more impaired than adults with BDD.

In a study that my colleagues and I did of 208 adolescents who were hospitalized in a psychiatric hospital, those who had BDD had significantly worse anxiety, depression, and suicidal intent than those without BDD—another indication that adolescents with BDD can be severely ill and impaired.

Kristin, a 17-year-old, had many of the classic BDD symptoms shown in Table 8–1. I met her in the hospital after she'd tried to commit suicide because she hated how she looked. Since age 13 she'd been excessively preoccupied with her nose, which she thought was too large; her breasts, which were too "small"; and her hair, which "wasn't right."

Kristin thought about her appearance "every second of every day." She constantly checked mirrors, store windows, and other reflecting surfaces. She avoided seeing friends and dating. To feel better about how she looked, she had a nose job, which diminished her nose concern, but then she worried more about her breasts. Eventually she dropped out of school. She described her concerns as "So horrible I get suicidal; it's why I overdosed. I couldn't stand the pain any more."

At age 14, Eric became preoccupied with the idea that he had severe acne, wrinkles around his eyes, and "stuck-out" ears. He often checked himself in mirrors, kept lights dimmed so his "defects" wouldn't be visible, covered his forehead with his bangs and a baseball hat, and wore makeup to hide his supposed acne. Eric used to have many friends and had been a very good student and a star soccer player. But eventually, he couldn't go to school and became housebound.

■ Suicidality and Other Risk Behaviors in Youth with BDD

Risky adolescent behaviors—while common among youth in general—may be particularly common among youth with BDD. As the bottom of Table 8–1 shows, nearly three quarters of children and adolescents with BDD have had suicidal thoughts. This is markedly higher than rates in the community of 15% to 27%. One-third of children and adolescents in my studies have attempted suicide, compared to community rates of 2% to 20%. In the study I mentioned earlier, hospitalized adolescents with BDD had greater suicidal intent than hospitalized adolescents without BDD. In addition, nearly 10% of the youth in one of my studies said that they mutilated themselves (for example, cut themselves) specifically because they hated how they look.

Lifetime aggression/violence due to BDD also appears to be common among children and adolescents (see Table 8–1). Furthermore, such behavior appears even more common in youth than in adults with BDD.

Also of great concern, many youth with BDD have a significant problem with alcohol or drugs. In one of my studies, only 6% had a past or current substance use disorder, but in my other study, an alarming 44% of those under age 21 had a substance use disorder. Sixty percent of them said that their BDD symptoms contributed to their substance use. The long-term effects of substance use on adolescent development, including their developing brain, are of particular concern.

Self-consciousness and social withdrawal can interfere with the development of healthy peer relationships—friendships as well as sexuality and intimate relationships. This can be accompanied by increased dependence on the family at a time when such dependence is usually decreasing. Having BDD during adolescence may also cause problems with identity formation, resulting in doubt, insecurity, and aimlessness. BDD may be particularly likely to interfere with the development of healthy self-esteem and identity. Of the domains of competence that appear to contribute most to global self-esteem in adolescence, physical appearance heads the list. Thus, youth with BDD, who **believe** their appearance is defective, may have particular difficulty developing healthy self-esteem.

My experience is that problems like these that occur during adolescence can have negative repercussions throughout adulthood. Compared to people who develop BDD in adulthood, those who develop it in adolescence are more likely to have been psychiatrically hospitalized, have a substance use disorder, experience suicidal thinking, and attempt suicide. I've also found that many adults who had severe BDD during adolescence, and who didn't get treated, missed out on important developmental milestones such as graduating from high school, moving on to college or a job, starting to date, or getting married. For some, it's been hard, if not impossible, to get back on track with work and relationships later in life.

It's important to find a licensed and qualified health care professional who is familiar with BDD and knowledgeable about its treatment (see Chapter 16). Early and successful treatment has the potential to minimize or even eliminate BDD symptoms and prevent the longer-term disability that the disorder

TABLE 8–2   *Why It's Important to Recognize BDD in Children and Adolescents*

- BDD can cause poor grades, dropping out of school, withdrawal from family and friends, suicidal thoughts, suicide attempts, violent behavior, and other serious problems.
- Normal development can be derailed by BDD symptoms.
- Long-term academic, occupational, and relationship problems can develop if BDD isn't treated early.

so often causes. It can enable a child or adolescent to get back on track, resume normal functioning, and live an enjoyable and healthy life (Table 8–2).

■ How to Diagnose BDD in Children and Adolescents

I'm sometimes asked whether BDD can even be diagnosed during adolescence, because this is a time when appearance concerns are so common. The answer is yes—it definitely can! In fact, BDD usually begins during adolescence. While it may sometimes be difficult to differentiate mild BDD from normal adolescent appearance concerns, more moderate and severe BDD can easily be diagnosed.

The BDDQ, the self-report screening questionnaire for BDD described in Chapter 3, has a version for adolescents, which is shown here (Box 8–1). The BDD Module, also described in Chapter 3, has an adolescent version which

---

BOX 8–1   *BDDQ for Adolescents*

This questionnaire asks about concerns with physical appearance. Please read each question carefully and circle the answer that is true for you. Also please write out your answers where asked.

(1) Are you very worried about how you look?	Yes	No
- If yes: Do you think about your appearance problems a lot and wish you could think about them less?	Yes	No
- If yes: Please list the body areas you don't like: _____		

_____

_____

_____

_____

(continued)

BOX 8–1 *BDDQ for Adolescents (continued)*

Examples of disliked body areas include: your skin (for example, acne, scars, wrinkles, paleness, redness); hair; the shape or size of your nose, mouth, jaw, lips, stomach, hips, etc.; or defects of your hands, genitals, breasts, or any other body part

(NOTE: If you answered "No" to either of the above questions, you are finished with this questionnaire.)

(2) Is your main concern with how you look that you aren't   Yes   No
      thin enough or that you might get too fat?

(3) How has this problem with how you look affected your life?

  - Has it often upset you a lot?   Yes   No
  - Has it often gotten in the way of doing things with

    friends or dating?   Yes   No
  - If yes: Describe how: _____

    _____

    _____

    _____

  - Has it caused you any problems with school or work?   Yes   No
  - If yes: What are they? _____

    _____

    _____

    _____

  - Are there things you avoid because of how you look?   Yes   No
  - If yes: What are they? _____

    _____

    _____

    _____

(4) How much time a day do you usually spend thinking about
    how you look? (Add up all the time you spend, then circle one)
    (a) Less than 1 hour a day (b) 1–3 hours a day (c) More than 3 hours a day

---

should be used to determine with greater certainty whether an adolescent has BDD (Box 8–2). See Chapter 3 for how these scales should be scored.

■ Treating BDD in Children and Adolescents

At present, it appears that the most effective treatments for children and adolescents are SRIs and CBT—the same treatments that appear effective for adults. Holly, Kristen, and Eric all improved with an SRI medication. After

---

BOX 8–2 *Body Dysmorphic Disorder Diagnostic Module for Adolescents*

Questions	DSM-IV Criteria for BDD
1. Are you very worried about how you look? **IF YES:** What don't you like? Do you think (body part) looks really bad? Is there anything else you don't like about how you look? What about your face, skin, hair, nose, or the shape, size, or other things about any other part of your body? Do you think about (body part) a lot? Do you wish you could worry about it less? (Do others say you worry about it too much?)	A. Preoccupation with an imagined defect in appearance. If a slight physical anomaly is present, the person's concern is markedly excessive **Note:** *Give some examples even if person answers no to these questions.* Examples include: skin concerns (e.g., acne, scars, wrinkles, paleness), hair concerns (e.g., thinning), or the shape or size of the nose jaw, lips, etc. Also consider perceived "defects" of hands, genitals, or any other body part **Note:** *List all body parts of concern*
2. How does this problem with how you look affect your life? Does it upset you a lot? Has your worry affected your family or friends?	B. Preoccupation causes clinically significant distress or impairment in social, occupational, academic or other important areas of functioning **Note:** *If slight physical defect is present, concern is clearly excessive*
3. (If concern is completely attributable to an eating disorder, do not diagnose BDD)	C. The preoccupation is not better accounted by another mental disorder (e.g., dissatisfaction with body shape and size in Anorexia Nervosa)

Adapted from R. Albertini, M.D., K. Phillips, M.D., Butler Hospital, Brown University, 7/30/97.

---

several months of treatment, Eric returned to school and started playing soccer again and seeing his friends. Kristin worried less about how she looked, went back to school, and no longer thought about suicide. And Holly stopped covering her body with oversized clothing and started swimming again.

Sally, a 17-year-old girl I treated, dropped out of high school in the ninth grade because she was completely convinced that her face was severely scarred and disfigured—in her words, she looked like a burn victim. She stayed in her bedroom, completely isolated, for the next 4 years because she thought she looked so hideous. She didn't go to school, receive tutoring, or see any friends. After taking an SRI medication for a month, Sally's BDD symptoms virtually disappeared. She left her bedroom, returned to school, and started doing things with family and friends. In my experience, children and adolescents respond to these medications similarly to adults (see Chapter 11), although much more research on this very important issue is needed.

CBT has also been used to treat adolescents with BDD (see Chapter 12). However, CBT needs to be modified somewhat to make it suitable for young people and so parents can participate. Other types of treatments may be helpful when combined with CBT and/or medication (see Chapter 12). For example, family therapy may help the adolescent and family members cope better with BDD. Or an adolescent who improves with treatment after being out of school for a while will probably benefit from therapy that helps him or her reenter school and reestablish friendships.

■ BDD in the Elderly

If BDD isn't treated earlier in life, it can persist into old age. Mildred was 80 years old and had had BDD for nearly 70 years. "I've always felt homely and ugly," she began. "Now when I see pictures of myself, I think I didn't look so bad back then. But I'm still too concerned with how I look."

Mildred grew up in a small town in the Midwest. "I remember sometimes crossing the street to avoid people because I was so ugly," she said. "I also remember being told that I looked like my mother. She wasn't a good person, and I thought she was unattractive. I hated to be identified with her.

"Seventy-five percent of my life has centered on how I look. I fought back. I think I might have done different things with my life if I hadn't been so preoccupied. I did raise wonderful daughters, but I would have had more energy for them and for other things, like my music. I was in therapy for many years, but I never brought it up or even told my husband about it because it would have been too difficult. I felt so ashamed, especially at my age."

Margaret, who was 70, had also struggled with BDD for many decades. Her concerns, too, had begun when she was a teenager. She'd had several surgeries for severe scoliosis (curvature of the spine), which improved and was hardly noticeable. Yet she was still preoccupied with it. "I think my back still looks very ugly, and I think about it for hours a day."

In fact, Margaret spent about 8 hours a day selecting and changing her clothes to hide her back, scrutinizing other people's backs, checking mirrors, and asking her husband whether she looked okay. "After all these years, I still think about it. It's one of the things that's made me depressed."

Because untreated BDD may be a fairly chronic disorder, it isn't surprising that the elderly can have it. It isn't known, however, how common BDD is in this age group. The average age of the people I've seen is the 30s; I've seen far fewer elderly people with BDD. Does BDD "burn out" as people age, becoming less severe or remitting altogether? Conversely, can it become more severe over time, and can the elderly be particularly distressed and impaired because of the cumulative effect of suffering over so many years? Further research is needed to answer these important questions.

9. What Causes Body Dysmorphic Disorder? Clues to an Unsolved Puzzle

■ Patients' Perspectives

"This problem is chemical," Bridget said. "I can't think of any reason for these gut-wrenching worries about how I look. It must be from a chemical imbalance in my brain." I started worrying too much about my skin when I was really stressed," Caroline told me. "But I think my worries have deeper roots, like how I was always put down when I was growing up."

"Maybe I learned looks were important," Brad said. "My family stressed the importance of looks. We always had to look our best and be well-manicured no matter what.... Everyone paid lots of attention to my brother—he was the champ of the family and my father's pet. I was always sensitive to criticism and rejection. I'm a perfectionist. I've always been hard on myself—since day one. I have high standards. My parents expected a lot from me. I was always the black sheep of the family."

People have various explanations for their body dysmorphic disorder (BDD) symptoms. Some believe the cause is biological. Others think the cause might be childhood experiences or personality traits such as perfectionism. Some blame society's emphasis on attractiveness. Some people attribute their symptoms to a comment about their looks or to stress. Others have no explanation for their symptoms, but they search for one, trying to make sense of their experience.

■ BDD Probably Has Many Causes

The question of what causes BDD is very important. Once we understand its causes, we'll be better able to treat it—and perhaps even prevent it from ever developing. At this time, BDD's cause remains largely unstudied, and there are no definitive answers. However, research is starting to shed some important light on this question.

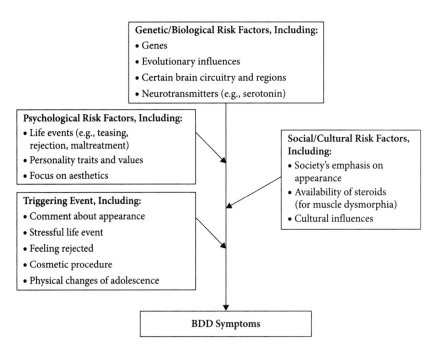

FIGURE 9–1 A possible pathway to the development of BDD

Most likely, BDD's cause will turn out to be very complicated. BDD probably has many causes, with many different factors contributing to its development. In this chapter, I've organized possible causes according to genetic and biological risk factors, psychological risk factors, and social/cultural risk factors (see Figure 9–1). In reality, these categories overlap to some extent. For BDD to develop, multiple risk factors from all three categories are probably needed. It's likely that each risk factor somewhat increases the chance of getting BDD. No one of them alone is likely sufficient to produce the disorder.

In this way, BDD is like other mental and medical disorders. To use blood pressure as an example, having certain genes makes a person more susceptible to developing high blood pressure. However, psychological factors, such as feeling stressed, and social/cultural factors, such as the widespread availability of salty, preprocessed foods, are additional risk factors. BDD, too, almost certainly doesn't have one single cause, such as one faulty gene or being teased during childhood.

Much more scientific research is needed to identify all of BDD's risk factors. In this chapter, I discuss each possible risk factor separately, but they probably interact with one another in complex ways over the course of a person's life to produce BDD. Research is needed to understand the complex mechanisms by which they produce BDD and keep it going once it's developed. At this point we have just a few pieces of the puzzle. Eventually, scientists will discover more puzzle pieces, put them together, and develop a whole and integrated picture of what causes BDD.

■ Possible Genetic and Neurobiological Risk Factors

A Likely Role for Genes

I'm starting with genetic factors, because it's likely that the genes a person is born with provide an essential foundation for BDD to develop. BDD probably isn't caused by one single gene. Instead, most likely, many different genes act together to increase the chance of getting BDD. Genes that increase risk for BDD may be common in the population and not necessarily defective.

Genes in turn probably increase the risk of developing many of the other risk factors I'll discuss subsequently. For example, having certain genes will increase the chance of having certain personality traits, whether certain brain circuits are hyper-reactive, and other characteristics that in turn may further increase the risk of getting BDD.

But before we consider specific genes, we need to look at whether BDD runs in families. I've found that about 20% of people with BDD have at least one first-degree relative (parent, sibling, or child) with BDD. About 6% of all first-degree relatives have BDD (although this is probably an underestimate because relatives weren't directly interviewed). This rate is an estimated three to six times higher than in the general population—thus, BDD seems to run in families. This is likely due to **both** genetic **and** environmental influences. In other words, BDD probably runs in families because family members share genes that increase the risk of getting BDD; in addition, if a family highly values appearance, for example, this might also increase family members' risk of getting BDD. Twin and adoption studies are needed to sort out genetic from environmental influences, but these studies haven't been done yet. It's likely, though, that a tendency to develop BDD—like other mental disorders—is at least partly genetic.

I and my colleagues did a preliminary genetics study in which we found that a certain form of a gene called the $GABA_A$-$\gamma2$ receptor gene was more common in people with BDD than in those without BDD. This finding, while needing replication, is interesting, because studies in mice suggest that this gene is associated with behavior indicative of anxious and depressive-like mood states. Gamma-aminobutyric acid (GABA) is a calming brain chemical (neurotransmitter) that inhibits the activity of nerves in the brain, like a brake. It's present throughout the brain and appears important in the development of some anxiety disorders.

Evolutionary Influences

Some researchers theorize that a universal preference for certain facial features may be innate—hard-wired into our collective brains over millions of years. Infants, for example, prefer attractive faces before they've had any significant exposure to cultural standards of beauty. A preference for bodily symmetry, a concern of one-third of BDD sufferers, may have biologically based, evolutionary underpinnings. Researchers have found that some animals prefer symmetry in their mate's appearance. For example, male Japanese scorpion flies with the most symmetrical wings obtain the most mates. Symmetry, or smooth unblemished skin, may have an evolutionary, neurobiological basis, signaling reproductive fitness or health or the absence of disease.

In the animal world, large body size confers some advantages, with larger animals tending to be more dominant. Indeed, animal and evolutionary models of social dominance and submissiveness may also be relevant to BDD, as people with BDD tend to be unassertive and feel inferior to others.

Certain animal behaviors also offer clues about possible neurobiological underpinnings of BDD. For example, dogs with a condition known as acral lick syndrome compulsively lick their fur, especially their paws, to the point of causing painful sores and infections. This is similar to compulsive grooming behaviors in BDD. Some birds compulsively pluck out their feathers, similar to compulsive grooming and skin picking in BDD. In animals, the brain chemicals serotonin and dopamine and some of the brain areas discussed later (the orbitofrontal cortex and striatum) are involved in excessive stereotypic behaviors like excessive grooming. It's interesting that in animals, these abnormal grooming behaviors may improve with serotonin-reuptake inhibitor medications, just as we find in BDD.

Selective Attention and Overfocusing on Details

People with BDD appear to selectively attend to, and overly focus on, specific aspects of their appearance or minor flaws. Little flaws become magnified. As one man said, "It's like when I put my thumb under a microscope—that's how I see my skin." Another said that by excessively focusing on tiny pimples, they would "grow to hideous proportions." This overfocusing is theorized to fuel negative thinking, dissatisfaction, and preoccupation with one's appearance. Other aspects of appearance fade into the background and may even be ignored. As a woman said, "I focus on the negative things; they become too prominent. I get tunnel vision."

These clinical observations led researchers to do neuropsychological studies, which found that people with BDD had more difficulty than those without BDD in drawing a complex abstract figure from memory. The reason is that those with BDD tended to overfocus on tiny details in the figure rather than its overall organization. They had trouble seeing the forest for the trees.

Another study similarly suggests that people with BDD tend to focus on details instead of the bigger picture. In this study, participants matched photos of other people's faces while they were in an MRI scanner. Some of the faces were altered to have more or less detail. The MRI scans showed that compared to people without BDD, those with BDD had greater activation of the brain's left hemisphere (lateral prefrontal cortex and lateral temporal lobe)—brain areas specialized for more "analytic," detail-focused visual processing—even when they looked at low-detail faces. Thus, people with BDD processed faces in a more piecemeal way that extracted details. The people without BDD, in contrast, tended to view the faces in a more global, "holistic," and "big picture" way, without zeroing in on details.

Overfocusing on details of specific facial features, while losing the larger overall context of the face, may play an important role in causing or maintaining BDD symptoms. It could lead to preoccupation and dissatisfaction with minor flaws. It might also feed a vicious cycle: selective attention and hypersensitivity to minor details or flaws may increase dissatisfaction with these body areas, which in turn feeds even more selective attention to appearance details and minor flaws. People with BDD may do this when looking at their own face or body. They may also assume that everyone else is as detail oriented as they are in their perceptions of appearance, which could contribute to self-consciousness and referential thinking. Cognitive-behavioral therapy (CBT) treatment helps people develop a more "holistic" view of their body, rather than zeroing in on tiny details (see Chapter 12).

A Bias for Threatening Interpretations?

In the MRI study I just described, those with BDD also had greater activation of their amygdala than healthy comparison participants while they were matching faces. The amygdala is a small almond-shaped structure deep in the brain that's the command center for the body's fear system. The amygdala communicates potential threats (e.g., perceived environmental threats) to other relevant brain areas so we can quickly respond to the threat. It's also involved in reacting to emotional facial expressions. The amygdala hyper-reactivity that occurred in BDD participants in this study suggests that people with BDD may automatically and rapidly process faces as being threatening. Feelings of being threatened, and feelings of anxiety and fear, may drive compulsive BDD behaviors (such as excessive grooming) and avoidance behaviors (such as avoiding social situations).

This MRI result is consistent with several cognitive processing studies. In one study, participants completed a questionnaire that presented various ambiguous situations (appearance-related, social, and general situations) and asked participants what thoughts occurred to them. Compared to healthy comparison subjects, those with BDD tended to interpret the situations as threatening. In other studies, people with BDD tended to be less accurate than comparison subjects in identifying facial expressions of emotion, misinterpreting facial expressions as angry. And when they thought the faces were looking at them, they tended to misidentify the facial expressions as being contemptuous and angry.

These results fit with what patients often say: that they feel negatively judged by other people and rejected. Misinterpreting other people as being angry or threatening might, in turn, reinforce beliefs about being ugly and undesirable. Additional research is needed to confirm these study results and to determine whether increased sensitivity to threat might contribute to the development of BDD, result from BDD, or both.

What Brain Regions Might Be Involved?

Body dysmorphic disorder (BDD) likely involves a complex interplay of dysfunction in several neural regions and systems of the brain. As discussed earlier, left-sided prefrontal and temporal regions involved in visual processing of faces, and amygdala hyper-reactivity, may play a role. Dysfunction in frontal-striatal brain circuits may also be involved. This is suggested by several neuropsychological studies as well as a small study in which my colleagues and I compared women with BDD to healthy women without BDD using MRI scans to visualize the brain's structure. We found that the BDD group's MRI scans differed in subtle ways from those of the comparison women. There were differences in the caudate, a C-shaped structure deep in the brain's core (the striatum), which regulates voluntary movements, habits, learning, and cognitions (thinking), and may be linked to repetitive behaviors such as BDD rituals. In OCD, the caudate is unable to properly filter out worrying ideas (obsessions) coming from other parts (the "frontal" part) of the brain, creating a "worry loop." This might also be the case in BDD. In support of this theory, there are several reports of successful neurosurgery in patients with BDD that targeted frontal-striatal brain circuits. In our MRI study, the BDD group also had greater total white matter (myelinated parts of nerve cells in the brain that carry messages between nerve cells), the meaning of which is unclear.

Studies indicate that in people with OCD, effective mental health treatment "calms down" the brain's worry loop and makes it normal again. Before treatment, brain scans showed that people with OCD had overactivation of their brain's worry loop; when they got better with a serotonin-reuptake inhibitor medication or CBT, their brain's worry loop functioned normally again.

Other brain regions might also be involved in BDD. A small neuroimaging study that used single photon emission computed tomography (SPECT) showed various areas of hyperactivation in diffuse areas of the brain—the frontal, temporal, occipital, and parietal lobes. While all of these areas may be involved, it makes sense that the fusiform face and extrastriate body areas in particular, which are located in the temporal/occipital area and are important in perception of body image and facial emotion perception, might play a role. Damage to these areas, as well as the parietal lobe, such as that caused by a stroke, can impair perception of bodies and faces.

The Serotonin Hypothesis and Other Neurotransmitters

People with BDD may have an imbalance in the brain chemical serotonin. In support of this theory, BDD often improves with serotonin-reuptake-inhibitor medications, which help boost serotonin in the brain to a healthy level. The brain consists of billions of nerve cells, and serotonin is a natural brain chemical (also known as a neurotransmitter, or chemical messenger) that carries information from nerve cell to nerve cell. Serotonin enables cells to communicate with one another and function.

Serotonin is especially abundant in certain parts of the brain that may be especially important in BDD. It's critical to many bodily functions, including mood, cognition (thinking), memory, sleep, appetite, eating behavior, sexual behavior, and pain. It inhibits aggressive and destructive behavior. Serotonin is involved in a variety of psychiatric disorders, including depression and OCD.

Serotonin is also involved in the visual system and visual processing, and it may help protect animals from overreacting to unimportant sensory input from the environment. This is interesting, given that people with BDD appear to overfocus on unimportant details of appearance and "over-react" to nonexistent threats (see preceding text). Serotonin-reuptake inhibitor medication helps people become less "over-reactive" and less focused on minor appearance flaws. Some people say that the flaws they used to perceive disappear when they take the medication. One man said that when he took a serotonin-reuptake inhibitor, he no longer saw the holes in his teeth. When we lowered his dose, he saw the holes again. In addition to possible effects on the visual system, serotonin-reuptake inhibitors might alleviate BDD symptoms by increasing serotonin release in the striatum and other key brain areas and by inhibiting an overactive amygdala.

It's likely that other neurotransmitters are also involved in BDD. One is dopamine, which may, in combination with serotonin, be particularly important in the delusional form of BDD. Another is GABA (see preceding text).

■ Possible Psychological Risk Factors

Early Life Experiences

Certain childhood experiences might increase the risk of getting BDD. If a child learns that physical appearance is very important, learns to associate physical attractiveness with being desirable or successful, or gets lots of positive attention or other rewards for being pretty or cute, this might increase the chance that they'll develop BDD. Some patients, but not all, say that they had these kinds of experiences. Occasionally, BDD symptoms seem to begin with a parent's excessive preoccupation with their child's appearance—what might be called "BDD by proxy" (see Chapter 4).

In one study, I found that on a standard questionnaire people with BDD reported lower-than-average levels of parental care. It isn't clear, however, whether they actually received less parental love and care than the average person, or whether they were unusually sensitive to feeling criticized, rejected, or uncared for.

Teasing

Teasing is a possible risk factor for BDD that can occur in childhood or at any point in life. Frequent teasing has been linked to greater body dissatisfaction more generally. My research indicates that about 60% of people with BDD report frequent or chronic teasing about their appearance during childhood or adolescence. It isn't known whether this percentage is higher than in the general population, but it's possible that people with BDD have been teased more than others. In fact, one small study found that people with BDD said they'd been teased more than mentally healthy participants, both in terms of their appearance and their competency. It's also possible that people with BDD are unusually sensitive to teasing, so when they're teased they pay more attention to it and are more easily hurt.

One small study found that people with BDD were more likely than healthy comparison participants to have negative, recurrent appearance-related images, which were linked to early stressful memories, such as being teased and bullied at school.

Childhood Maltreatment

Might childhood trauma, abuse, or neglect increase the risk of developing BDD? A recent study found that 79% of 75 people with BDD perceived that they had experienced maltreatment during childhood: emotional neglect (in 68%), emotional abuse (56%), physical abuse (35%), physical neglect (33%), or sexual abuse (28%). Another study found that patients with BDD reported higher rates of emotional and sexual abuse (but not physical abuse) than patients with OCD. These studies did not confirm that abuse actually occurred, and not everyone with BDD has experienced abuse. It's possible, however, that abuse, especially sexual abuse, might contribute to dislike of one's body and bodily shame.

Values and Personality Traits

While valuing appearance may to some extent be hard wired and evolutionarily based (see earlier discussion), some people value it more than others. Looking good, or not flawed, is especially important to their self-esteem. People who place more value on looking good, or perfect, may be more likely to get BDD.

Research suggests that people with BDD tend to be perfectionistic, both in terms of their appearance and more generally. In theory, perfectionism might increase selective attention to minor appearance flaws and fuel pre-occupation and dissatisfaction with one's looks. Perfectionism might also fuel BDD symptoms in another way. Research suggests that for people with BDD, there's a big discrepancy between how they think they **actually** look and (1) how they ideally would **like** to look and (2) how they think they **should** look. They tend to underestimate their own attractiveness and overestimate the attractiveness of other people, which may further increase this discrepancy. The more perfectionistic a person is, the bigger this "self-ideal" discrepancy may be, which might in turn fuel even more dissatisfaction with one's looks.

Many people with BDD are unassertive, emotionally overreactive to rejection and criticism, and have low self esteem. In addition, many are very introverted and socially inhibited. People with BDD tend to score very high on neuroticism, a personality trait that reflects anxiety, depression, self-consciousness, anger, and feelings of vulnerability.

It makes sense that personality traits and values such as these might increase the risk of getting BDD. It's also possible, though, that once someone gets BDD, the BDD symptoms themselves may cause or amplify some of these traits and values.

A Focus on Aesthetics?

Might a tendency to be "aesthetically focused" or "aesthetically sensitive" be a risk factor for BDD? One study found that people with BDD are more likely than those with certain other psychiatric disorders to have an occupation or education in art or design. Among 146 individuals with BDD, I found that the proportion of BDD subjects employed as an artist was approximately twice that in the general population.

These findings may reflect an appreciation of aesthetics, which may contribute to BDD's development in some patients. They may be less tolerant of aesthetically unappealing minor flaws. Another plausible explanation, however, is that rather than being a risk factor for BDD, people who get BDD may subsequently develop an interest in aesthetics.

■ Possible Social and Cultural Risk Factors

Society's Focus on Appearance

Our society's incessant messages about the importance of appearance may also contribute to the development of BDD. As one person with BDD put it, "You see models everywhere. How can you **not** think about how you look!" The marketing of beauty is a multibillion dollar industry that bombards us with unattainable images of physical perfection. Even children are exposed to unrealistic body ideals, such as Barbie's impossibly thin and curvy look or GI Joe's gigantic muscles. Studies in male and female adults show that being exposed to idealized bodies, such as those in the media, increases dissatisfaction with one's own appearance.

About a quarter of people in my research studies said that our society's focus on appearance is a major cause of their BDD symptoms. Muscle dysmorphia (see Chapter 4) is a form of BDD that seems especially likely to result in part from sociocultural pressures. Because muscle dysmorphia rarely occurred until recently, society's current messages that men should be big and muscular, combined with the availability of anabolic steroids, have probably channeled a vulnerability to BDD into this particular form.

However, sociocultural and media pressures are unlikely to be BDD's only cause. BDD has been described since the 1800s, long before the media and advertising attained their current power. As one woman said, "Magazines play a role in BDD, but they're not the whole story, because everyone sees them but everyone doesn't get BDD." In addition, BDD occurs in societies where the media are less powerful or even absent altogether. A colleague told me about a man with BDD from an isolated village in Africa with no TV, magazines, billboards, movies, or computers. Yet he had classic and severe BDD that focused on his nose.

Cultural Influences

BDD occurs around the world, in Western as well as non-Western countries and cultures. One study found that a similar percentage of American and German students—4% versus 5%, respectively—had BDD. Other studies indicate that BDD appears about equally common in people in Italy, Turkey, and the United States, although these studies didn't directly compare BDD's prevalence in these countries. Still, we don't really know whether BDD is more common in some countries than others, or whether it's more likely to develop in countries or cultures where beauty is more valued or physical imperfections more maligned.

Might sociocultural factors influence the specific BDD symptoms that develop—for example, which body parts are disliked or what aspect of them is disliked? Do Western's societies' obsession with youth contribute to BDD concerns involving aging? When I compared case reports and small case series of BDD from different countries, there were more similarities than differences. Similarities included the proportion of women versus men and other demographic features, which body areas were disliked and what aspects of them were disliked, compulsive BDD behaviors, and levels of BDD-related distress and impairment in social and occupational functioning. Moreover, I've seen people with BDD from many countries around the world, and from many racial/ethnic groups within the United States—and their similarities are striking.

Yet, it appears that cultural values and preferences may influence and shape BDD symptoms to some degree. For example, eyelid concerns appear common in Japan but rare in Western countries. Worry about displeasing other people by being unattractive also seems more common in Japan than in the United States. Some people say that their BDD symptoms began when they moved to another culture and felt that they looked different and didn't fit in.

Can culture protect against, or even prevent, BDD? A woman in her late 70s described the following experience: "I've felt very ugly my entire life. The only time I haven't been preoccupied with how I look was for a couple of years when I lived in Fiji. Maybe it was because the culture was different. In that culture, whites were considered attractive and desirable. I wasn't concerned at all when I was there."

■ Triggers: Comments About Appearance, Stress, and Other Possible Precipitants

BDD usually begins gradually, but about 15% to 20% of people report that their BDD began suddenly, going from no concern to a full-fledged concern in less than a week. Some people in the latter group can pinpoint a life event that seemed to acutely trigger the onset of their BDD. Presumably, such events trigger BDD only in people who are already vulnerable to getting the disorder— those who have risk factors such as those described earlier. As a high school teacher said, "My concern about my nose was triggered by a comment about it, in a context of extreme sensitivity and low self-esteem." Most people are exposed to potential BDD triggers, such as negative comments about their appearance, but they don't get BDD because they aren't at risk for developing it.

"I started worrying about my skin when one of my friends in high school called me 'pizza face,'" Patrick told me. "I know he was only kidding, but it stuck in my mind." Sometimes, the comment is more benign, such as "Your hair looks different today." A comment that triggers onset of BDD is often recalled in great detail and with intense emotional anguish. Some BDD sufferers feel extremely angry and resentful toward the person who made the comment.

Scott started worrying about his appearance when his parents were getting divorced. "It was especially rough on me, because my father blamed me for the breakup. I remember when he was really angry about something, he said to me 'You're no longer my son.' I looked in the mirror and my whole face seemed to be sagging."

Precipitating stressors are sometimes related to psychological themes that appear especially relevant to BDD—for example, being rejected by other people. Gail's BDD began right after her boyfriend broke up with her. "I was dating a man five years younger than me, and I was worried about being older than him. Shortly after he found out I was five years older, he broke up with me. I started being preoccupied with my appearance after that—that I looked too old."

Cosmetic surgery and other cosmetic procedures can also trigger the onset of BDD. My research suggests that this happens in about 2% of people with BDD. However, in a small study from France, three of eight patients who didn't have BDD before cosmetic surgery developed BDD after the surgery.

There are other possible triggers as well. A 28-year-old man started obsessing about his face after he'd been hit by a softball, which he thought permanently indented his cheek. It seems likely that for some people, the physical changes that occur during adolescence might trigger BDD.

■ What Doesn't Cause BDD

Some things clearly *don't* cause BDD. One is vanity. Another is moral weakness. People do **not** get BDD because they are morally defective or weak; BDD is a mental disorder with many complex causes, some of which are, very likely, genetic and neurobiological. It's also highly unlikely that BDD is really a "displacement" for some other problem (an unconscious way to avoid a more emotionally troubling issue). It also isn't simply a "personality problem." BDD is in and of itself a serious disorder that needs to be treated.

■ Concluding Thoughts

In this chapter, I've reviewed some possible risk factors for developing BDD. There are almost certainly many others. Some people who develop BDD probably have many risk factors, whereas others probably have fewer. It wouldn't be necessary for an individual person to have all of the BDD risk factors in order to develop BDD. If someone has a very strong genetic predisposition to developing BDD, environmental factors might play a relatively small role in bringing on BDD, whereas if a person has less genetic vulnerability, powerful environmental factors might be needed for BDD to develop.

Like other mental disorders, a complex chain of steps involving a broad array of risk factors is almost certainly required for BDD to develop. Genetic and environmental risk factors, such as childhood experiences, likely lay the foundation for additional risk factors to subsequently develop, such as certain personality traits or abnormalities in visual processing, serotonin, or other neurotransmitters. The various risk factors likely interact with one another in complex ways over a person's lifetime. For example, whereas certain genes might directly increase the risk of getting BDD, other genes might confer an unusual sensitivity to the effects of stressful life events or negative comments about appearance, which might in turn make a person biased toward misperceiving their environment as threatening. Some likely risk factors, such as neuroticism, aren't specific to BDD, as they increase the risk for developing many different mental disorders. Other risk factors, however, may be specific to BDD.

To answer the critically important question of what causes BDD, much more scientific research is needed to confirm the research findings discussed in this chapter and to explore other possible causes. Research is also needed to understand why BDD usually begins during adolescence, a time when dramatic bodily, social, and brain changes occur. Such research will discover more pieces of the puzzle and put the puzzle together to provide a coherent, integrated picture of how BDD develops. Ultimately, this knowledge should lead to more effective treatments and perhaps even prevent this devastating illness from ever occurring.

10. Getting Better: A Brief Treatment Guide

In this chapter, I'll give an overview of treatments and a brief treatment guide. In the following chapters I'll describe effective treatments, and how they're done, in more detail.

The treatment recommendations in these chapters are general guidelines that should work well for most people, but they need to be tailored to some degree to each person. I'd suggest that you become familiar with the basic treatment strategies in this book and then get the input of a doctor or therapist who's knowledgeable about BDD and has met with you for a face-to-face evaluation. It's best to work as a team with a knowledgeable professional to tailor these treatments to you.

■ Christina: Improvement with Medication

When I first met Christina, she was worried that her skin wasn't clear enough. "It has red blotches on it and too many pimples," she said. "I've gotten depressed because of it. Every time I talk to someone they look at my skin, and they're thinking how bad it looks. It's really hard for me to be around other people at work and school."

Christina was indeed depressed. She thought about her skin for more than 8 hours a day and believed that other people took special notice of how bad it looked. She'd missed several days of school in recent weeks and was having trouble doing her part-time job because she felt so self-conscious and didn't want people to see her.

Christina was reluctant to take medication but decided to give it a try. She started taking a serotonin-reuptake inhibitor (SRI) medication. For the first few weeks nothing much happened. But during the third week, Christina thought that she was starting to obsess a little less and that she wasn't quite as depressed or anxious. During the fourth week, she called me. "I just want you to know how much better I'm feeling," she told me. "I went out with friends instead of staying home, and I had a great time!"

Over the next few weeks Christina continued to improve. After 8 weeks of treatment, her symptoms were essentially gone. "I can't believe this has happened!" she said. Christina had had BDD for 10 years, and this was the first time in 10 years that she'd felt so well. She was now thinking about her skin for only 5 minutes a day. Her emotional pain and depression were gone. She was going out with friends, dating, and doing very well in school and in her job.

Christina also realized that she'd been distorting how bad she looked. Her skin looked fine to her now. "I just wasn't seeing myself clearly before," she said. "I feel like I've been blind, and now I have my sight back! I feel calmer, happier, and more confident. It's hard to believe the medication has made this much of a change, but it has. I feel the way I used to feel, before the BDD ever got started. I feel great!"

■ Jason: Improvement with Cognitive-Behavioral Therapy

Jason had tried several SRI medications but hadn't given them a good enough try because he was reluctant to take them regularly. He'd also tried cognitive-behavioral therapy (CBT) but hadn't really given this a good try either. He'd had BDD for 20 years and had been disabled by his symptoms.

Jason's concern focused on his lips. He thought they were large and ugly and that they offended other people. He frequently licked them to try to make them look better, covered them, checked them in mirrors, and tried to keep them in a more attractive position. He also avoided other people as much as possible. He came for treatment because he wanted to improve his social life and return to work. He wanted to give CBT another try. He was a good candidate, because he was highly motivated to do CBT.

Jason's therapy consisted of several key CBT techniques. First, with his therapist's help, he gradually cut down on his mirror checking, from hours a day to only minutes a day. He also gradually cut down on licking his lips and covering them with his hand. Jason also did behavioral experiments to test his belief that his lips offended other people. These experiments helped him learn that other people weren't bothered by his lips and didn't even seem to notice them. He also learned how to identify and correct errors in his thinking that made him think he was ugly and that other people thought so too. With his therapist's help, he gradually started going places that he feared and avoided. He began talking more with other people, speaking up in groups, and even went to some parties.

After 5 months of treatment, Jason felt much better. He was much less self-conscious and more relaxed around other people. He had better control over his thoughts. He was very pleased with his progress and felt he'd learned skills he could use in the future if his BDD ever flared up. "I really feel better after the CBT," he told me. "The BDD isn't controlling me anymore!"

■ David: Improvement with Medication Plus
   Cognitive-Behavioral Therapy

David was feeling desperate. A 32-year-old disc jockey, he was at the point of quitting his job. He couldn't focus on his work because of his hair obsessions, and he was often late because he couldn't tear himself away from the mirror in the morning. Even the expensive new hairpiece he'd bought to hide his slightly receding hairline didn't help.

"I don't like going out in public, and I've given up on dating," he said. "I don't want to date because someone will run their fingers through my hair and know it's a hairpiece. I can't focus on conversations because I think people are looking at my hair. At times I stay in completely; I don't even food shop."

In the week before he first saw me, David had missed work three times and had considered going to an emergency room because he was so panicked about his hair. "I hate myself and how I look. I've even had thoughts of ending my life. I can't live the rest of my life like this."

David started taking an SRI medication right away. David was receiving supportive psychotherapy (a non-CBT therapy that's described in Chapter 12), which helped him cope better but didn't improve his BDD symptoms. When he started the medication, it didn't work immediately (it usually takes a little time), and the first month of treatment was rocky. David and I considered hospitalization several times. But with the support of his friends, family, and therapist, he maintained his will to live. About a month after starting medication, David started to feel better. His hair preoccupation began to wane, and the thoughts were less emotionally painful. He was more willing to see his friends. He didn't check mirrors all the time, and he sought reassurance less often. He was no longer considering suicide.

He then started CBT while continuing the medication. His therapist helped him cut down and eventually stop mirror checking and reassurance seeking. He started going out more and seeing friends. Finally, he even gave up his hairpiece. He received many compliments on his new hair style (without the hair piece), and his self-confidence greatly improved.

■ Overcoming Barriers to Treatment: The Critical
   First Steps to Success

Before they overcame BDD, David, Christina, and Jason all took important initial steps, which made successful treatment possible. First, they acknowledged that they had a problem—that they worried too much about their appearance and that their worrying was a problem for them. They also recognized that they needed professional help and that other approaches—like surgery and hair clubs—hadn't worked. Although they may not have liked the idea of seeing a psychiatrist or therapist, they realized they had nothing to lose—and potentially much to gain.

There are, unfortunately, many barriers to getting effective treatment for BDD, which need to be overcome. Here are some solutions to some common barriers:

Try to learn about BDD: Many people are uninformed or misinformed about BDD. Some are even unaware that it exists and that most people improve with the right treatment.

Suggested Approach: Learn about BDD and its treatment. In addition to reading this book, you may want to look at some of the suggested reading in Chapter 16.

There's no need to feel embarrassed or ashamed: Embarrassment and shame can prevent people from getting effective treatment. Many BDD sufferers are so ashamed that they never mention their BDD symptoms to anyone, even a mental health professional.

Suggested Approach: See if you can get up your courage and let someone know that you have BDD. It may help to first confide in a family member or friend. Then try to see a mental health professional who's knowledgeable about the disorder and tell him or her that you worry a lot about how you look and think you have BDD. Some people say it's helpful to bring an article about BDD or this book to their appointment to break the ice when raising the topic. Don't just say you're anxious or depressed, because you may get the wrong treatment.

Try to move beyond guilt, anger, and blame: Some people are bogged down in guilt, anger, and blame. They feel guilty and blame themselves because they think they caused their appearance problem or wasted their life by being so focused on their looks. Others blame other people, such as a surgeon who operated on them or people they think made fun of how they look. For some people, the guilt, blame, and anger are so paralyzing that they don't even try to get better.

Suggested Approach: Can you move beyond your guilt, blame, and anger and focus instead on making positive changes for yourself? You aren't responsible for having BDD. BDD isn't anyone's fault. Focusing on feelings of guilt just unnecessarily adds to your distress. And blaming others doesn't help you fix the problem, either. It's far better to acknowledge that you have these feelings and then see if you can move beyond them. Instead of focusing on the past, try to focus on the present and future—and how you can make your life better.

Accept BDD as a "real" problem: It's easy to trivialize BDD. Sometimes sufferers are told that it isn't their "real" problem. It can be mistaken for vanity or a character flaw. When a person with BDD hears this, they feel misunderstood. As one person said to me, "I've been told that BDD isn't my real problem. It's very frustrating, and I get angry over it—they don't get it! There's no mystery about what my problem is—my nose is what bugs me." Or, to be compliant, the person may no longer discuss their BDD and even leave treatment. As one patient said, "If you treat BDD as something other than the real problem, the patient will never bring it up again."

Suggested Approach: Treat BDD as a real problem. Realize that it isn't just a bad hair day or the kind of normal appearance concerns so many people have. Realize that BDD isn't vanity. Treat it as the serious mental illness it is.

Although people with BDD may have other problems as well, it's important to recognize BDD itself as a real problem that requires accurate diagnosis and adequate treatment. If you have BDD and someone tells you that it isn't your real problem, you don't have to accept this. If a doctor or therapist tells you this, and won't focus on BDD in treatment, he or she may not be the right clinician for you. Keep in mind, though, that if you do have other problems, it may help to get treatment for those problems too.

There's no need to accept stigma: To some extent, mental illness is still unfortunately associated with stigma, which may make some people reluctant to seek treatment. However, this view is rapidly changing. Increasingly, psychiatric problems are being recognized as medical problems that deserve treatment, thanks in good part to the advocacy of consumer groups. People with BDD aren't "crazy"—they have a treatable medical problem.

Suggested Approach: Why do you need to buy into stigma? Stigma is decreasing anyway, as people are increasingly willing to accept that psychiatric disorders are real conditions just like medical problems, except that they happen to involve the brain. Would you feel stigmatized if you got treatment for a heart attack? I hope not! BDD really isn't any different. It just happens to involve the brain rather than the heart.

BDD needs to be accurately diagnosed: This is a necessary step before you can get effective treatment. If BDD isn't accurately diagnosed, it probably won't be successfully treated. Unfortunately, some health professionals are still unfamiliar with BDD. Perhaps most important, secrecy about BDD often prevents the diagnosis from being made.

Suggested Approach: You can get a good sense of whether you have BDD by filling out the Body Dysmorphic Disorder Questionnaire (BDDQ), which is in Chapter 3. The additional information in Chapters 3 and in Chapters 4 to 7 can also help you figure out whether the diagnosis applies to you. Then I'd suggest getting an evaluation from a mental health professional familiar with BDD and telling them you think you have this disorder and want treatment for it (see Chapter 16 for how to find help).

Try to accept that you might have BDD: In some cases, other people (such as friends, family members, or a health-care professional) realize the person has BDD, but the BDD sufferer doesn't. Many people with BDD think they truly are ugly and therefore don't have BDD.

Suggested Approach: Realize that someone can have BDD even if they think they don't. It's typical for people with BDD to think they're truly ugly and don't have the disorder. But if other people tell you that you look fine, and they think you have BDD, why not give them the benefit of the doubt? They might be right. If you're worrying a lot about how you look, and this worry is causing problems for you, you may benefit from BDD treatments regardless of how you think you look. Effective treatment will probably help you worry less, feel less depressed and anxious, and give you more control over your thoughts and compulsive behaviors. As one patient said to me, "It's hard to accept it's an actual illness. Once you can accept it and get the right treatment, you'll get your life back." So give the BDD diagnosis a chance! There's nothing to lose.

■ Some Key Points about Recommended Treatments

Cognitive-behavioral therapy (CBT) that specifically focuses on BDD and serotonin-reuptake inhibitors (SRIs, or SSRIs) appear to often be effective for BDD. Research has shown that they significantly diminish symptoms in a majority of people with BDD. Despite recent advances in finding effective treatments for BDD, much less treatment research has been done on BDD than for many other serious mental disorders, and more treatment research is urgently needed.

In the meantime, we already know a lot about treatments that work. Table 10–1 provides a brief summary of what we know at this time. These are some of the key points I'll be making about treatments in the next three chapters.

■ Should I Try CBT, an SRI, or Both for My BDD?

This very important question really hasn't been studied, so at this time there are no definitive answers about whether one of these treatments is more effective than the other or what kind of person does best with each of them. Also, no one knows whether getting both an SRI and CBT at the same time works better than getting just one of these treatments alone.

Until we have scientifically rigorous studies that use standard and accepted scientific methods to directly compare CBT to SRIs in a head-to-head comparison, it can't be concluded which treatment is more effective. Studies like these are also needed to determine whether combining the two

TABLE 10-1 *Key Points about Treatment*

- **Serotonin-reuptake inhibitors (SRIs, or SSRIs) are antidepressant medications that also diminish obsessional preoccupations and compulsive repetitive behaviors.** With these medications, appearance preoccupations, compulsive behaviors (such as mirror checking and comparing), and other BDD symptoms usually improve. People feel better—less depressed and anxious. Symptoms often diminish partially but may resolve completely. They are currently the medications of choice for BDD.

- **The following medications are SRIs:** citalopram (Celexa), escitalopram (Lexapro), fluoxetine (Prozac), sertraline (Zoloft), paroxetine (Paxil), fluvoxamine (Luvox), and clompramine (Anafranil).

- **In studies of SRIs, between 53% and 73% of people with BDD improved significantly with a particular SRI; among those who completed the study, improvement rates were even higher.** In my clinical practice, about 80% of people eventually improved with an SRI (some had to try more than one). These improvement rates were achieved by following guidelines for SRI dosing and treatment recommended in this book.

- **Be sure to take a high enough dose of an SRI for a long enough time.** Often, too low a dose is used, which may not work. Don't give up before trying a high enough dose. Also, you should try the medicine for at least 12–14 weeks (and be on a high enough dose for at least 3 of these 12–14 weeks) before concluding that an SRI won't work for you. A briefer try may be inadequate to see if an SRI will work for BDD.

- **If an SRI alone doesn't work well enough, even after you've tried a high enough dose for a long enough time, you may improve by adding another medication to the SRI or by switching to another SRI.** Also, one SRI may work better than another for you, so trying another SRI may work. There's no way to predict which one will be best for you—you just have to try them.

- **A majority of people with BDD substantially improve with CBT that specifically focuses on BDD symptoms.** This treatment, too, can help people with BDD feel and function much better. Appearance preoccupations, compulsive behaviors (such as mirror checking and comparing), and other BDD symptoms often improve. The encouraging results discussed in Chapter 12 were achieved by CBT-trained therapists who are familiar with BDD and used CBT techniques like those described in this book. It's important to find a therapist who does this treatment and is familiar with BDD (see Chapter 16).

- **CBT is a practical, "here-and-now" treatment that teaches you skills and focuses specifically on improving BDD symptoms.** CBT approaches usually include cognitive restructuring, behavioral experiments, exposure, and response prevention. Additional approaches, such as mirror retraining, may also be helpful.

- **If CBT doesn't work well enough for you, you may need to have more sessions or talk with your therapist about modifying the CBT approach.** Like medication treatment, CBT has to be tailored to the individual person and sometimes needs to be modified during treatment to make it more effective.

(continued)

TABLE 10–1   *Key Points about Treatment (continued)*

- **SRIs and cognitive-behavioral therapy—what I consider the "core treatments" for BDD—may be successfully combined.** These two treatments can work well together.

- **Regardless of whether you try an SRI or CBT or both, it's important to find a doctor and/or therapist who's knowledgeable about BDD, takes your appearance concerns seriously, and is willing to focus treatment on BDD.** Simply focusing treatment on depression, anxiety, or other symptoms may not work for BDD. My website (which can be reached at www.BodyImageProgram.com or through the Butler Hospital or Care New England web sites) lists doctors and therapists who treat BDD. There are many other professionals not listed on this website who can also treat BDD.

- **Surgery and other cosmetic treatments (e.g., dermatologic treatment) generally don't appear helpful for BDD and may even make it worse.** As best we know, it's best to avoid such treatments and to try CBT and/or an SRI instead. There's an exception to this, however: people who compulsively pick their skin and damage it as a result may need dermatologic treatment in addition to an SRI or CBT.

- **Give an SRI or CBT a try!** You have nothing to lose by trying these treatments. Most people tolerate them very well, and a majority get much better. You deserve to feel better and have a better life. These treatments can make this possible.

- **Don't give up!** It may take a while to find the exact approach that works for you, but most people with BDD eventually get better with an SRI or CBT. Some people improve with the first SRI they try, whereas others have to try another one, or even many of them, to find one that works for them. Some people respond to CBT fairly quickly, whereas others need more intensive and longer treatment. But if you persist, and keep trying the recommended treatments, you'll probably get better: you'll be less obsessed, less distressed, will function better, and will enjoy your life a lot more.

treatments is better than using one of them alone. An equally important question that needs to be studied is which treatment works best **for whom**. CBT and SRIs might, on average, be roughly equally effective, but one may work better for certain people (for example, someone who has severe depression or anxiety).

The good news is that there are two treatment options that seem to help a majority of people with BDD! Here are my views about how you can think about which treatment to try. They are based on my experience treating many hundreds of patients with BDD over the years.

I'd suggest taking the following factors into account. Keep in mind that you'll need to evaluate **all** of the issues below when thinking through your options. Also keep in mind that these are just general guidelines, and that it's important to get the input of a knowledgeable doctor or therapist when considering your options.

How severe is your BDD? You can get a rough sense of the severity of your BDD by using the BDD-YBOCS scale, as described in Chapter 3. If your BDD is mild, I'd suggest starting with CBT (although it's fine to take an SRI if you prefer). If your BDD is in the moderate or severe range, you could try either an SRI or CBT or both together. If your BDD is extremely severe, I would strongly recommend an SRI; BDD can be life-threatening, and an SRI can be life-saving. Also, if you're ill enough to be hospitalized, you'll need an SRI. For very severe BDD, it would be ideal to do CBT in addition to taking an SRI. As I discuss in the next two chapters, other medications and types of therapy may also be helpful in some circumstances.

What symptoms do you have in addition to BDD, and how severe are they? This is a complicated issue, and you'll definitely need the input of a qualified professional on this one. Here are just a few general guidelines. (1) If you have attention-deficit disorder (ADHD) or have other attentional or cognitive problems, you may need to get these problems treated before you try CBT. It's fine to take an SRI for BDD and a medicine for ADHD at the same time. (2) If you have severe depression, I would strongly recommend an SRI, as it often improves depression as well as BDD. Some people who are severely depressed find it hard to get up the energy or motivation to do CBT, or to focus on the therapy sessions or do the homework. In this case, trying an SRI first may help you improve to the point where you can do CBT. (3) If you have a number of other psychiatric disorders that an SRI typically works for (such as social phobia, obsessive compulsive disorder [OCD], bulimia, or panic disorder), an advantage of an SRI is that it may effectively treat all of these problems within several months. (4) If you have bipolar disorder, it's very important to be stable on a medication for this disorder before taking an SRI for BDD.

Are you having thoughts of suicide or have you recently attempted suicide? If you're having fairly strong or frequent thoughts of suicide, or have recently attempted suicide, I would recommend an SRI plus CBT. In this situation, an SRI is essential, and CBT may be additionally helpful.

Which treatment do you prefer, and how motivated are you? Your preference should also play a role in your decision, although the more severely ill or suicidal you are, the more I would say that medication is necessary. Your motivation for the treatment is another important consideration. CBT requires good motivation and effort on your part, because you'll need to be an active participant in your treatment (although a good therapist can help you get more motivated). For medication treatment, you need to be willing to take the medication as prescribed and to work collaboratively with your doctor if you develop problems with side effects.

What treatment have you tried in the past, and how did you do with it? If a treatment worked well for you in the past but you're no longer getting it, it probably makes sense to try it again. But if you've tried a lot of the recommended medications for BDD and haven't improved enough or had problematic side effects, you may want to try CBT. Or, if you've tried CBT but haven't improved enough, you may want to try an SRI. One SRI may work much better for you than another SRI. And CBT with a different therapist, or a somewhat different approach, might work better than CBT you had in the past.

Keep in mind, though, that many people have "tried" these treatments but haven't given them an adequate try (I say much more about what adequate treatment is in the next two chapters). If you haven't tried them sufficiently, definitely don't give up on them!

What treatment does your clinician (doctor or therapist) recommend? You need an individualized assessment to be sure you have BDD, diagnose other disorders or problems that need treatment, assess your treatment history, and so on. When coming up with a treatment plan, there are lots of nuances that require the input of a qualified professional.

■ Why Not Give the Right Treatment a Try?

Most people with BDD will need treatment with a professional to get better. The good news is that there are treatments that work. I hope that if you suffer from BDD, you'll be willing to try the recommended treatments after reading this book (please read the next two chapters!). Most people get better if they give the right treatment a good try. There's a good chance you'll get more control over your obsessions and compulsive behaviors, get your life back on track, and be relieved of worry, anxiety, and depression.

You've already put in a huge effort just putting up with BDD—so you probably also have the ability to overcome it. With the right tools—the right treatment—you **can** do something to solve the problem and start feeling better! Why not take steps to get control of your life, rather than continuing to be controlled by your BDD symptoms?

Yet, some people are reluctant to try treatments that are likely to help them, perhaps because they fear stigma or feel ashamed. But as I discussed earlier, you don't need to buy into any of this. Some people misunderstand BDD and its treatment. Other people insist that surgery is the solution. Still others desire to get better "on their own." By the time you finish reading this book, I hope you'll agree that none of these reasons should get in the way of getting effective treatment and feeling better.

Why deny yourself treatment that's likely to help you feel better? What do you have to lose by trying it? While SRIs can have side effects and CBT can be challenging, most people do well with these treatments and easily tolerate them. There are lots of misconceptions about both of them (see the "frequently asked questions" in the next two chapters). You shouldn't feel or look "drugged" while taking an SRI, and these medications aren't addictive. If medication side effects occur, or CBT is too hard, a good doctor or therapist will work with you and probably succeed in making them tolerable.

Even if you think you don't have BDD, because you think you're truly ugly, what's the down side of giving the BDD diagnosis and treatment a chance and find out if they work for you? If you think you might **possibly** have BDD, or if other people think you do, why not read the rest of this book to become more informed about BDD?

Unless you give treatment a try, you can't know how good you might feel. One option is to try an SRI or CBT as an "experiment" to see how it affects you. You can usually tell if an SRI will work within three months (assuming it's being dosed correctly), and CBT often starts working within this amount of time as well. If you give the medicine a good try, you can see how you feel. Then you'll be in an excellent—and much more informed—position to decide whether to continue the treatment or not, or whether to give another one a try. You always have the option of going back to the way things are now if you want. Trying treatment doesn't mean that you have to continue it for the rest of your life.

Some people are reluctant to try treatment because a friend or family member tried it and didn't get better, or because they read about someone on the internet who didn't like it. But is this really a good way to make a decision for yourself? You're a different person from them, and you may have a different outcome with the treatment. Also, they may not have really gotten the right treatment (which I describe in more detail in the next two chapters)—many people with BDD don't. A better way to make a decision is to read the next two chapters to become knowledgeable about the treatment options, and then discuss these treatment options with a qualified professional. You owe it to yourself to make an intelligent decision and to choose for yourself.

If you still have reservations about getting treatment, you can make a list of the pros (advantages) and cons (disadvantages, or costs) of your BDD. Are there any advantages to having it? Maybe you can think of some and maybe not. What about disadvantages? Is BDD causing problems for you? Are you living the life you want to be living, and, if not, is this because your symptoms are getting in the way? Are you experiencing disadvantages from BDD like the following:

- Feeling depressed, sad, ashamed, angry, frustrated, guilty, or stressed?
- Not being able to be in a relationship?
- Not being able to go to school or work?

- Fighting with your partner or your family because of your appearance problems?
- Spending too much money on beauty products, clothes, or cosmetic treatments such as electrolysis or surgery?
- Scarring from skin picking?
- Loneliness and isolation?
- Self-hatred or low-self-esteem?
- Stress on your relationships?
- Being late for things?
- Not being able to participate in activities or see friends because of your BDD?
- Wasting time on rituals?
- Not managing your household well?
- Not focusing enough on your children's needs?
- Using street drugs or alcohol to try to cope with your problem?
- Are there other disadvantages for you? (you may want to look back at Chapter 7 for additional disadvantages of BDD that may apply to you)

Next you can ask yourself whether you want to change. Do you want to overcome these problems? You can make a list of potential pros (positive consequences) and cons (negative consequences) of getting treatment. You might feel that there are some cons, such as taking the time for appointments or the cost. You'll also need to make an effort and participate in the treatment. Maybe there are others for you.

If you're reluctant to try treatment, you've probably given the potential cons of treatment more thought than the pros. You owe it to yourself to take a little time to think through what advantages there could be. You may want to ask friends or family to help you think this through.

Might there positive consequences, like the following?

- Feeling happier and less anxious and stressed
- Having better self-esteem and feeling more confident
- Feeling more comfortable around other people
- Starting to date
- Getting along better with your partner or your family
- Making new friends
- Being able to go out and do things you'd like to do (like shopping, eating out, or seeing friends)
- Doing things with family and friends
- Concentrating better on school or work
- Going back to school or work
- Being on time for things and not keeping people waiting for you
- Stopping problematic use of alcohol or drugs

- Saving time and money
- Letting your skin heal (by not picking any more)
- Being a better parent
- Managing your household and life better

Are there other potential advantages for you? List as many as you can.

Might there be advantages for your friends and family members if you get better?

Some of the patients I've worked with have been reluctant to try treatment, but most are very glad that they did. Anne, who got much better with an SRI, told me, "I'm feeling terrific, for the first time in 30 years." And after CBT, Jason felt that he—not the BDD—was in charge of his life.

Cassandra described herself as a caged animal—her obsessional thinking locked her in a place where she had no freedom or pleasure. Effective treatment freed her; it allowed her to regain control of her life.

Here's what other patients told me, after they got the right treatment:

Jorge: "The treatment I got was very freeing—it's lifted an amazing burden. I regret that I put it off for so many years." He hadn't been interested in psychiatric treatment and had put it off for 20 years. He finally got tired of trying to treat himself; his approaches weren't working, and he was worn out and not living the life he'd hoped for. He decided he had nothing left to lose.

Nathaniel: "I can talk to people without feeling they're staring at me. I'm better able to resist mirror checking. I spend less time obsessing. It comes into my mind less and it's easier to get rid of the thoughts. I can argue with myself that my obsession is irrational—I tell myself, 'just shrug it off!' I'm not so self-conscious around people anymore. It's not a life or death problem for me now."

Sandy: "The medication definitely curbs the obsession. It released a logjam. My life felt like a stream that had thousands of huge boulders and logs in it—the water couldn't flow through smoothly. Now it flows with ease. I feel full of energy and creativity."

Christina: "I just wasn't seeing myself clearly before. I feel calmer, happier, and more confident. It's hard to believe the medication has made this much of a change, but it has. I feel the way I used to feel, before the BDD ever started. I feel great!"

Jason: "I really feel better after the CBT. The BDD isn't controlling me anymore! Tell people, 'Don't be afraid to get help!'"

11. How to Successfully Treat Body Dysmorphic Disorder with Medication

You might wonder why a body image problem would be treated with medication. Well, there are a number of reasons to think it might help. Some of the core features of body dysmorphic disorder—obsessional preoccupation and compulsive, repetitive behaviors (such as mirror checking)—are similar to those of OCD (see Chapter 14), a disorder for which serotonin-reuptake inhibitors (SRIs) often work very well. BDD also has similarities to social phobia and depression, also disorders for which SRIs are often effective.

In addition, chemical changes in the brain and other biological factors likely play an important role in causing BDD (see Chapter 9). These biological factors can produce profound changes in the way you view yourself and in your behavior. So it makes sense that SRIs, which correct problems in brain functioning, might help BDD.

■ Serotonin-Reuptake Inhibitors: The Medication of Choice for BDD

Many people I've described in this book improved with a serotonin-reuptake inhibitor (SRI). These are prescription medicines that are also known as SRIs or SSRIs. SRIs are the best-studied medications for BDD, and at this time they appear to be the most effective medications for BDD. Research done by our program and others indicates that a majority of people with BDD improve if they take these medications correctly.

As shown in Table 11–1, seven SRIs are currently available in the United States: citalopram (Celexa), escitalopram (Lexapro), fluvoxamine (Luvox), fluoxetine (Prozac), paroxetine (Paxil), sertraline (Zoloft), and clomipramine (Anafranil). The first six SRIs in Table 11–1 are also called SSRIs (**selective** serotonin-reuptake inhibitors). Like other psychiatric medications, the SRIs are prescribed by psychiatrists, other physicians, and, in some states, nurses.

TABLE 11–1 *Serotonin-Reuptake Inhibitors*

	Medication	
Generic Name	**Brand Name**	**Typical Dose Range (milligrams per day)***
Citalopram	Celexa	20–60
Escitalopram	Lexapro	10–20
Fluvoxamine	Luvox	100–300
Fluoxetine	Prozac	20–80
Paroxetine	Paxil	20–60
Sertraline	Zoloft	50–200
Clomipramine	Anafranil	100–250

* This is the usual dose range for a variety of disorders. Later in this chapter I discuss the average doses I've used for BDD.

Currently, no medications are approved by the Food and Drug Administration (FDA) for the treatment of BDD. This is because there aren't enough research studies that have been designed to obtain FDA approval in BDD (this is also the case for many other medications and disorders, not just BDD). However, doctors are free to prescribe medications for BDD and other disorders even in the absence of such approval.

The SRIs are a type of antidepressant medication that—unlike other antidepressants—also diminish obsessional thinking and compulsive behaviors such as mirror checking and skin picking. The SRI type of antidepressants appear more effective for BDD than other types of antidepressants because they diminish obsessions and compulsive behaviors as well as depression.

The SRIs are effective for many other symptoms and psychiatric disorders, including depression, obsessive-compulsive disorder (OCD), panic disorder, bulimia, binge eating disorder, social phobia, and hypochondriasis. The SRIs can also be helpful for aggression, impulsivity, and anxiety, and they're used for nonpsychiatric conditions such as headache and pain syndromes.

Antidepressants have been safely used for nearly half a century, and SRIs have been prescribed for decades. SRIs are one of the most commonly prescribed classes of medication, and they've been taken by many millions of people around the globe, often for many years.

The SRIs affect the brain chemical serotonin. Serotonin is one of the brain's natural chemicals, or neurotransmitters, that transmits signals between nerve cells, allowing them to communicate with one another and function (also see Chapter 9). SRIs increase the amount of serotonin available at the junction between nerve cells by preventing its reuptake, or reabsorption, into the nerve cell that released it into the junction. As a result, more serotonin is then available to act on nerve cells that are "downstream." Thus, the SRIs increase serotonin availability in key brain areas. They correct a "chemical imbalance" in the brain and promote the healthy functioning of serotonin. A healthy balance of serotonin is important in many bodily functions, including mood, thinking, sleep, and appetite.

Because different neurotransmitter systems in the brain are highly interconnected, the SRIs also have "downstream" effects on other neurotransmitters, such as dopamine. The SRIs' influence on neurotransmitters triggers a subsequent cascade of effects within brain cells, including effects on DNA and the synthesis of new proteins.

Research on the effect of SRIs in disorders that are similar to BDD sheds some light on how these medicines may work for BDD. In patients with OCD or depression whose symptoms improve with an SRI, the SRI **normalizes** abnormal brain functioning. For example, in OCD, before treatment, brain scans show that fronto-striatal brain regions (the brain's "worry loop") are overactive (see Chapter 9). After treatment, brain scans show that this brain circuit becomes normal (no longer overactive). SRIs may also make the amygdala, the brain's "panic button," function normally and stop overreacting to perceived threats.

So studies like these show that an SRI actually makes the brain more **normal**. Some people worry that medications will somehow disrupt their brains or create an artificial change or state. But research studies indicate that the opposite is true. The SRIs correct a "chemical imbalance" in the brain; they alleviate symptoms by normalizing an abnormal state. Patients who improve with an SRI say that they feel like themselves again—the way they used to—or the way they'd like to feel. SRIs aren't "happy pills"—that is, they don't create an artificial state of happiness.

■ What's the Evidence That SRIs Work?

A number of research studies demonstrate that SRIs substantially improve BDD symptoms in a majority of people. In addition, SRIs appear more effective than other medications for BDD. It's important, however, to use a high enough SRI dose for a long enough time to give the medicine a chance to work.

Before the late 1980s, no one really knew whether BDD got better with medication and, if so, which medications might work. At that time, a colleague and I started treating our patients with SRIs and found that many, both adults and adolescents, improved. It made sense at the time to try these medications because they reduce obsessional preoccupations and compulsive behaviors in OCD. SRIs even helped some severely ill and chronically hospitalized patients after many other medications hadn't worked. In my clinical practice (in 90 patients), I found that 63% of the time, an SRI substantially improved BDD symptoms.

"I'd say I got 95% better on Prozac," one of my patients told me. He'd had severe BDD for 30 years and had been hospitalized more than 10 times for his symptoms. He had also tried 13 non-SRI medications, without results. "My obsessions mostly went away, and I could stay out of the mirror. I stopped being hospitalized. I was so impressed that I bought stock in the drug company!"

Comments like this from my patients spurred me and other researchers to do more rigorous studies of SRIs, which provided more scientifically credible information about these medications' effects. These studies (summarized in Table 11–2), included patients with varying degrees of BDD severity—ranging from milder BDD to extremely severe BDD. On average, study patients had moderate-severe BDD.

The first two research studies in Table 11–2 were "randomized," "double-blind," and "controlled." These are the most scientifically rigorous and convincing type of treatment study, because there is a comparison treatment, and neither patients nor doctors know which treatment patients are getting. Thus, judgments about the treatment's effectiveness aren't biased by expectations of whether the medicine will work or not. "Random assignment" minimizes differences in patient characteristics (for example, symptom severity) in the two treatment groups that could affect treatment outcome. The "open-label trials," also shown in Table 11–2, were also rigorously done; however, there was no comparison treatment, and both doctors and patients knew that they were taking the SRI. There are many other published reports of individual patients or a small number of patients successfully treated with an SRI.

As you can see from the "Study Results" column in Table 11–2, all of the studies found that an SRI was often effective for BDD symptoms. In the fluoxetine (Prozac) study, fluoxetine was more effective than placebo (a sugar pill) for BDD symptoms and daily functioning. In the clomipramine (Anafranil) study, the SRI clomipramine was superior to the non-SRI antidepressant medication desipramine. In the open-label studies, escitalopram (Lexapro), citalopram (Celexa), and fluvoxamine (Luvox) were effective for most patients. These results include all study participants who started taking medication. If only those people who completed the studies are included, the improvement rates are even higher than those shown in Table 11–2.

Another positive result from these studies is that SRIs often help delusional BDD (see Chapter 3). In fact, people with delusional BDD appear as likely as those with nondelusional BDD to improve with an SRI (without taking any other type of medication in addition). That is, people who are **completely** convinced that their view of the defect is accurate, and who can't be talked out of this belief, have a high rate of improvement with an SRI. In other disorders, delusional beliefs are usually treated with an antipsychotic (neuroleptic) medication, which often aren't as well tolerated as the SRIs.

SRIs appear equally likely to help milder BDD and more severe BDD. They also appear effective regardless of how long you've had BDD, and regardless of your gender or whether you also have major depression, OCD, or a personality disorder in addition to BDD.

TABLE 11–2 SRI Studies in BDD[a]

Medication Tested	Study Design	Number of Patients Who Received Treatment	Length of Study and Average Medication Dose (mg/day)[b]	Study Results[c]	References
Fluoxetine (Prozac) versus placebo (sugar pill)	Randomized, double-blind, placebo-controlled, parallel group study[d]	67	12 weeks 77.7 ± 8.0 (range: 40–80)	Fluoxetine was significantly more effective than placebo for BDD symptoms (response rate of 53% vs 18%) and daily functioning	Phillips, 2002
Clomipramine (Anafranil) versus desipramine	Randomized, double-blind controlled crossover study[e]	29	16 weeks (8 weeks on each medication) Clomipramine: 138 ± 87 Desipramine: 147 ± 80	Clomipramine was significantly more effective than desipramine for BDD symptoms (response rate of 65% vs 35%) and daily functioning	Hollander, 1999
Citalopram (Celexa)	Open-label study[f]	15	12 weeks 51.3 ± 16.9 (range: 10–60)	73% of subjects responded to citalopram; quality of life and functioning also significantly improved	Phillips, 2003
Escitalopram (Lexapro)	Open-label study[f]	15	12 weeks 28.0 ± 6.4 (range: 10–30)	73% of subjects responded to escitalopram; quality of life and functioning also significantly improved	Phillips, 2006
Fluvoxamine (Luvox)	Open-label study[f]	30	16 weeks 238.3 ± 85.8 (range: 50–300)	63% of subjects responded to fluvoxamine	Phillips, 1998
Fluvoxamine (Luvox)	Open-label study[f]	15	10 weeks 208.3 ± 63.5 (range: 100–300)	67% of subjects responded to fluvoxamine	Perugi, 1997

[a]These are all of the prospective/controlled and open-label BDD medication studies that had been published in scientific journals at the time this book was written (excluding case reports, case series, and chart review studies).

[b]The "±" sign indicates the standard deviation. In 68% of cases, the dose was within 1 standard deviation of the average dose.

[c]In all of my studies, "response" was defined as 30% or greater improvement on the BDD-YBOCS scale (see Chapter 3); while a 30% decrease in BDD symptoms may seem relatively small, this degree of improvement corresponds well to a rating of "much improved" by both patients and clinicians. Dr. Hollander defined "response" as 25% or greater improvement on the BDD-YBOCS; Dr. Perugi defined "response" as "much" or "very much" improved on the Clinical Global Impressions Scale.

[d]Half of the patients were randomly assigned to fluoxetine and half to placebo; neither the doctor nor the patient knew which treatment the patient was receiving.

[e]Half of the patients were first treated with clomipramine and then desipramine; the other half received desipramine first and then clomipramine. Neither the doctor nor patient knew which treatment the patient was receiving.

[f]Only one treatment (the SRI) was given; both the doctor and patient knew they were receiving it.

■ What Gets Better With an SRI?

People who respond to an SRI generally improve in a variety of ways. The extent of improvement varies for different people. Some people improve only partially, whereas others get completely well. One of my patients said that she felt "wonderful—like a new person." She had stopped worrying about her nose and hair for the first time in 30 years.

Let's take a closer look at what symptoms improve with an SRI.

Preoccupation: Preoccupation with appearance decreases. With SRI treatment, some people spend only minutes a day—or no time at all—instead of hours a day obsessing about how they look. Others are still preoccupied, but less so; for example, they may now worry about their appearance for only 3 hours a day instead of 6. The thoughts come into the person's mind less often, and, when they do, it's easier to let them go and think about other things. Concentration improves because the distracting thoughts aren't present as often.

Ability to resist and control the obsessional thinking: People who get better with an SRI find it easier to ignore and control the distressing thoughts, keeping them in the background or out of one's mind completely. It's easier to focus on other things. The BDD sufferer regains control over their thinking and mind. They—not the obsessions—are in charge.

Emotional pain: The emotional pain and suffering that BDD causes usually diminish as well. The distress may become more tolerable or even vanish. The thoughts are no longer as depressing, anxiety-provoking, or tormenting. In part, this is because they occur less often. In addition, when they do occur, they're less distressing. As one person said to me, "They've lost their punch. Now it's just a twinge."

Compulsive and safety-seeking behaviors: These BDD behaviors usually improve as well. Less time is spent checking mirrors, comparing, skin picking, hair cutting, reassurance-seeking, and performing other BDD rituals. Compulsive rituals are easier to resist and control, and the anxiety caused by doing them, or not doing them, diminishes. "The main thing Prozac did for me was help me stay out of the mirror," one person told me. "I go into the bathroom, and my heart races, but I have the fortitude not to look. It's a very important change. The mirror no longer controls me."

Daily functioning: Functioning also often improves. It becomes easier to go to work or school and to concentrate. It's easier to be around other people or leave the house. BDD sufferers may repair wounded relationships, start socializing more, or begin dating. "Our social life improved dramatically every time my wife took Prozac," an engineer told me. "Every time she stopped it, our social life stopped too."

Several studies in Table 11–2 evaluated whether people treated with an SRI were able to function better in their daily life. All of the studies found that functioning improved in numerous areas: work and school, managing the household, relationships with family and friends, and recreational activities. Some people make these improvements fairly slowly and make smaller gains. Habits can become very ingrained and take time to change. But for others, these changes can occur rapidly and may be dramatic. A woman I treated started school again within several weeks of responding to fluvoxamine, a change she'd wanted to make for 10 years.

Avoidance: Avoidance usually lessens. It's easier to do things, go places, and be around other people. BDD sufferers become more active—their life becomes more colorful and interesting. It's easier to do things when the thoughts and compulsions are less time-consuming, distressing, and powerful. In addition, self-consciousness and fear around other people often diminish, making it easier to socialize. It's interesting that animal research shows that enhancement of serotonin with medications like Prozac leads to more "social" behavior in animals—decreased avoidance, vigilance, and social solitude.

Insight: Many SRI responders experience improved insight, becoming more aware that their view of the defect was distorted. As one woman said, "I used to be 97% convinced that I looked horrible. Now I'm 97% convinced that I don't. I realize I was distorting." In addition, many no longer feel that people are staring or laughing at them.

Summary of improvement in these areas: Table 11–3 illustrates changes in the preceding areas among medication responders in my studies of fluoxetine, escitalopram, citalopram, and fluvoxamine. Keep in mind that these are **average** scores on a BDD severity scale—some SRI responders had less of a response and others more. Each item is rated on a five-point scale (0–4), with higher scores reflecting more severe symptoms. So, for example, before SRI treatment, patients on average experienced moderate to severe interference in functioning, whereas after treatment, those who responded to the medication experienced no interference to mild interference in functioning.

The following areas also often improve with an SRI:

Quality of life: SRIs often improve quality of life. People tend to not only function better but also enjoy their lives more and get more satisfaction from life. In my citalopram (Celexa) and escitalopram (Lexapro) studies, quality of life improved significantly. In these studies, the more BDD symptoms improved, the more quality of life improved. In my study of fluoxetine (Prozac), quality of life improved somewhat more with fluoxetine than with placebo (in a statistical sense, this occurred at a "trend level").

Depression and anxiety: Depression and anxiety often improve. This includes depressed or irritable mood, lack of interest and motivation, poor energy, impaired concentration, low self-esteem, and problems with sleep and appetite. Anxiety symptoms, such as worrying, being on edge, and feeling tense, usually improve as well. Self-consciousness often decreases, and self-esteem and self-confidence get a boost.

TABLE 11-3 *BDD-YBOCS Scores Among SRI Responders Before and After Treatment with an SRI**

BDD-YBOCS Item	Average Score Before Treatment with an SRI	Average Score after Response to an SRI*
BDD Preoccupations		
Preoccupations due to thoughts	3.1 hours a day	1.7 hours a day
Interference in functioning due to thoughts (social, occupational/academic, other)	2.3 (between moderate and severe)	0.5 (between none and mild)
Distress due to thoughts	2.7 (between moderate and severe)	1.2 (between mild and moderate)
Resistance of thoughts	2.1 (between some effort and little effort)	0.9 (between always makes an effort and makes an effort most of the time)
Ability to control thoughts	3.1 (between little control and no control)	1.3 (between much control and moderate control)
BDD Compulsive Behaviors		
Time spent on behaviors	2.7 hours a day	1.5 hours a day
Interference in functioning due to behaviors (social, occupational/academic, other)	2.1 (between moderate and severe)	0.6 (between none and mild)
Distress if behavior prevented	2.6 (between moderate and severe)	1.2 (between mild and moderate)
Resistance of behaviors	2.8 (between some effort and little effort)	1.1 (between makes an effort most of the time and some effort)
Ability to control behaviors	3.1 (between little control and no control)	1.2 (between much control and moderate control)
Insight	2.9 (between fair and poor)	1.5 (between good and fair)
Avoidance (due to thoughts or behaviors—e.g., other people, work/school, going places, doing things)	2.0 (moderate)	0.4 (between none and mild)
Total Score	31.5 (moderate to severe BDD)	13.1 (some appearance concerns but not meeting DSM-IV criteria for BDD)

* Scale items are from the BDD-YBOCS, described in Chapter 3; scores after treatment would be higher if nonresponders were included

Suicidal thinking: In my escitalopram and citalopram studies, **thoughts of death or suicide significantly decreased with treatment**. In the fluoxetine (Prozac) study, no patient treated with fluoxetine had worsening of suicidal thinking between the beginning and end of the study; in contrast, six patients treated with placebo (sugar pill) had worsening of suicidal thinking—a statistically significant difference. This suggests that fluoxetine treatment protected against suicidal thoughts.

Hostility and anger: In my study of fluvoxamine (Luvox), **hostility and anger significantly diminished** with treatment. This result is consistent with studies of SRIs in other disorders.

Body image: Some people have improvement in body image. In my fluoxetine (Prozac) study, fluoxetine was more effective than placebo in diminishing the importance of appearance and behavioral investment in appearance (for example, excessive grooming).

In my studies of fluoxetine (Prozac) and fluvoxamine (Luvox), I asked participants whether their perceived physical flaws changed when taking the SRI. Sixty percent of those who responded to the medication said their flaws had improved. One-third of the 60% said that the defect visually looked the same, but **it wasn't as distressing or anxiety-provoking** as it used to be, and two-thirds said that the defect **actually looked different (and better) visually**. Some patients said things like "The marks on my face are gone. I don't **see** them anymore." One woman told me, "My features seem to have fallen into place. I look more attractive." She said that her appearance had **physically and visually** changed—it wasn't just that she could cope better with it. Another person told me that the "hair mask" on her face disappeared every time we increased her SRI dose and reappeared every time we lowered the dose. Some SRI responders actually **like** their body! After treatment, a woman who improved with escitalopram (Lexapro) told me, "I used to think I looked hideous! But now when I look in the mirror I say to myself: 'you look pretty darn cute!'" About half reported that both kinds of changes occurred—both a change in visual perception and in their emotional reaction to their appearance.

This raises the fascinating question of whether SRIs can actually improve visual perception. As discussed in Chapter 9, serotonin appears to play an important role in vision in animals and may do the same in humans. The SRIs may correct problems in brain functioning that cause faulty perception or interpretation of visual images, overfocusing on tiny details, or overreacting to minor flaws.

Visual discrimination ability: In a study my colleagues and I did of visual discrimination abilities, people with BDD didn't perform as well as healthy control participants in a task in which they were asked to discriminate different objects (e.g., snowflakes, faces) from one another. This seemed to be due to problems paying attention to the task rather than a problem with visual processing. However, BDD participants who were taking a SRI tended to perform more like healthy control participants.

Concern with more noticeable appearance problems: Sometimes the SRIs decrease an obsessional preoccupation with a noticeable aspect of appearance, such as obesity. For example, some people who are quite overweight become less consumed by their weight obsessions. They're still not happy with their weight, but they're no longer obsessed with it. Both their BDD-related concerns and their concern with a more noticeable appearance problem improve.

In a way, this makes sense. The medication can't distinguish between a nonexistent or slight appearance problem (i.e., BDD) and one that's more noticeable. The medication doesn't have eyes! The SRIs probably work by decreasing excessive, obsessional thinking, regardless of what someone actually looks like.

■ Frequently Asked Questions about SRIs

Some people have concerns about taking an SRI. Here are questions they ask.

Shouldn't I Be Able To Feel Better about Myself Without Taking Medication?

Some people want to get better on their own, without medication. Being motivated to get better is very important, but it isn't realistic to try to recover from BDD on your own. As discussed in Chapter 7, BDD is a serious illness with sometimes-devastating effects. It isn't vanity, and it doesn't reflect weakness of character. BDD needs to be treated with approaches shown by scientific studies to work (an SRI or cognitive-behavioral therapy [CBT]). You and the medication work "hand-in-hand" and are on the same team. The right medicine can make it easier for you to make positive changes in your life.

Are SRIs Addictive? Will I Get "High?"

Serotonin-reuptake inhibitors aren't addictive or habit forming, and you won't get "high" from them. Some people have transient (and usually quite tolerable) symptoms when an SRI is stopped abruptly, but these symptoms don't reflect an addiction to the medication.

Do SRIs Cause Side Effects or Serious Problems?

Serotonin-reuptake inhibitors are generally well tolerated. Many people have no side effects; when they occur, they're usually tolerable and may resolve simply with the passage of time. Side effects that don't resolve with time can sometimes be minimized or avoided by trying various strategies, which I discuss below. It's important for you and your treating clinician to work collaboratively to try to minimize side effects if they occur. I say more about side effects below.

Will the Medication Change My Personality?

Some people worry that taking an SRI will make them behave abnormally or look like a zombie. While occasional patients feeling tired or agitated while taking an SRI, they act normally and don't look as though they're "drugged." Patients who get better on an SRI usually say they feel more normal, or that they feel more like themselves again.

Is There a Connection Between SRIs and Suicide?

While some studies suggest that, rarely, people who take an SRI may have increased thoughts about death or suicide, or even attempt suicide, other studies have found that SRIs often decrease suicidal thinking or attempts. There is no evidence whatsoever that these medicines actually make people kill themselves. In fact, in BDD, research shows that suicidal thinking typically improves significantly when people are correctly treated with an SRI (see preceding text). However, all people with BDD—whether they're taking an SRI or not—need to be carefully monitored for suicidal thinking and behavior, as they are common in people with this disorder.

How Will an SRI Affect My Brain and Body?

When they work, SRIs have positive effects on the brain. As discussed earlier, they normalize overactive brain areas and correct a "chemical imbalance," by promoting the healthy functioning of the natural brain chemical serotonin. There's no evidence that psychiatric medicines such as SRIs will harm your brain. In fact, they appear to make the brain healthier by protecting brain cells from damage or death, and by stimulating the healthy growth of new brain cells.

When it comes to other parts of your body, such as your heart, patients treated with SRIs have a lower rate of heart attacks and death from heart disease than those who don't take an SRI.

I've Taken an SRI Before and I Didn't Get Better. Should I Try Another?

There are many reasons you might not have gotten better:

1. You might not have taken a high enough dose—if you didn't, this might be why you didn't get better. In fact, my research studies indicate that the majority of SRI treatment that people with BDD receive isn't even minimally adequate to successfully treat this disorder. Most people don't receive a high enough SRI dose for a long enough time (I say more about adequate treatment below).

2. You might have stopped the medicine before it had enough time to take effect. It's important to take the SRI every single day for 3 to 4 months to see if it will work.

3. The medication needs to be taken as prescribed. It may not work effectively if it isn't taken every day or if less is taken than prescribed.

4. People can respond differently to different SRIs. One may work better than another for you. There's no way to predict which one may be best. Perhaps the one you tried before wasn't a good match for you.

5. Many people who don't get better with one SRI, even if they gave it an adequate try, will get better with a different SRI. So it's definitely worth trying a different one. Sometimes, adding another medicine to the SRI will help the SRI work better (I say more about this later).

How Long Will It Be Before I Feel Better?

It may take anywhere from 2 weeks to up to 3 or 4 months before SRIs start to improve BDD symptoms, and they may not reach their maximum effect for several more weeks or months. Below, I say more about this and also provide some guidelines on how to successfully treat BDD with an SRI.

■ How to Treat BDD with an SRI

The recommendations below are based on all of the research studies published in scientific journals to date, as well as my extensive clinical experience treating patients with BDD. These recommendations are general guidelines for how to successfully treat BDD. It's important, however, to keep several things in mind:

(1) Your treatment will need to be individually tailored to you, in consultation with your doctor. The medication dose you need may differ from what someone else needs. You may do best with one SRI, whereas your friend may do best with a different one. The treatment that's best for you will depend to some extent on your individual situation, such as what other psychiatric disorders you have and past treatment response, and other factors (I say more about this later). Weighing such factors and making prescribing decisions may require considerable clinical judgment and expertise.

(2) Don't try to treat yourself with medication. This can lead to errors, and might even be harmful, even if the guidelines below are followed. It's important to be treated by a doctor who is knowledgeable about BDD and its treatment.

(3) If you think your treatment isn't following the general guidelines or being appropriately treated, be sure to discuss this with your doctor to see if a change should be made.

1. Use an SRI as the first-choice medication for BDD, including delusional BDD: SRIs are effective for a majority of people with BDD, and they may be more effective than non-SRI medications (although more research is needed to be certain about this). They appear equally effective for "delusional" and "nondelusional" BDD (see Chapter 4 and the Glossary for definitions).

2. You can try any SRI: All of the SRIs appear effective for BDD. As you can see from Table 11–2, fluoxetine (Prozac), clomipramine (Anafranil), escitalopram (Lexapro), citalopram (Celexa), and fluvoxamine (Luvox) have been best studied, but clinical experience suggests that sertraline (Zoloft) and paroxetine (Paxil) are also effective.

No studies have compared one SRI to another to see if one might be better than another. In my studies of escitalopram (Lexapro) and citalopram (Celexa), a somewhat higher percentage of patients improved than in my other SRI studies. In addition, a higher percentage were "very much improved" (as opposed to only "much improved"). And many patients responded earlier (within 2–6 weeks) than in my fluoxetine or fluvoxamine studies. While we can't conclude from these few studies that escitalopram (Lexapro) or citalopram (Celexa) are more effective than other SRIs, or work faster, these data are encouraging. Clomipramine would generally not be used first, because it's a little more likely to cause side effects and can be toxic if a patient overdoses.

At this time, there's no way to predict which SRI (or SRIs) will work (or work best) for you. The only way you'll know is to try them. It's best to discuss the options with your doctor.

3. Gradually work your way up to the maximum SRI dose that's recommended by the manufacturer for other disorders, or that you can tolerate, unless you find that a lower dose sufficiently helps your symptoms: The SRI dose that's needed to effectively treat BDD varies for different people. There's no way to predict ahead of time which dose will be best for you. **However, BDD appears to usually require higher SRI doses than those typically used for depression and for many other disorders. It's very important to use a high enough SRI dose.** If your dose is too low, you may not improve, or you may improve only a little. Taking a low dose of an SRI for BDD (for example, 10 mg or 20 mg per day of citalopram) can be like taking only one aspirin for a severe migraine headache.

Table 11–4 shows the average SRI doses I've used in my clinical practice for patients with BDD. You can see that the average BDD doses in Table 11–4 are at the high end of the typical dosing ranges for other disorders—or even

TABLE 11–4 *Average Doses Used in My Clinical Practice to Treat BDD*

Generic Name	Brand Name	Average Dose (mg per day)*	Standard Deviation (mg per day)*
Citalopram	Celexa	66	36
Escitalopram	Lexapro	29	12
Fluoxetine	Prozac	67	24
Fluvoxamine	Luvox	308	49
Paroxetine	Paxil	55	13
Sertraline	Zoloft	202	46
Clomipramine	Anafranil	203	53

* mg = milligrams. The standard deviation indicates the typical range of doses used. In about two-thirds of cases, the SRI dose used was within one standard deviation of the average. For example, for fluoxetine, about two-thirds of people received between 43 mg/day (67–24) and 91 mg/day (67 + 24), with an average dose of 67 mg per day. (However, for clomipramine, the dose never exceeded 250 mg per day.)

exceed these ranges (Table 11–3). Some people worry about taking a high dose of an SRI. But as long as you're tolerating it, and if a lower dose isn't working well, it makes sense to take a higher dose if that works better. *The most important thing is to find the SRI dose that works best for you.* It doesn't make sense to take too low a dose and not feel any better—if you're taking the medication anyway, why not take a dose that works, even if it's on the "high" side?

Some people need an SRI dose that's even higher than the typical maximum dose. I've treated many patients with 30 to 60 mg per day of escitalopram, 80 to 100 mg per day of citalopram or paroxetine, 100 mg per day of fluoxetine, or 400 mg per day of sertraline or fluvoxamine. The higher the dose, the more likely you are to have side effects, but many people tolerate these higher doses well and have minimal or no side effects. The main reason to try such doses is if you're tolerating the medicine well but haven't improved, or if you've only partially improved, with the highest dose recommended by the manufacturer for other disorders. A higher dose may work even better for some people with BDD. One important caveat is that doses of clomipramine (Anafranil) should never exceed 250 mg per day.

If you try a dose that's higher than the maximum recommended dose for at least 3 weeks or so, and find that it doesn't work any better than a lower dose, it makes sense to decrease the dose back down to the lowest dose that worked equally well for you.

However, not everyone with BDD needs a high dose. Some people get better with a low dose or an average dose. You won't need to try a high SRI dose if a lower dose is working well enough for you.

But if a low or average dose doesn't work for you, don't give up on the medicine—and assume it won't work for you—until you've reached (1) the highest dose recommended by the manufacturer (see Table 11–1 for these doses) or (2) the highest dose you can tolerate, if the highest recommended dose causes side effects you can't handle.

I've seen countless people who didn't improve with an SRI—but they never reached a high enough dose to give it a good enough try! Often, this is because BDD wasn't diagnosed, so it wasn't focused on in treatment. Typically, such patients were diagnosed with depression while their BDD went undiagnosed. This can lead to several problems: (1) an SRI dose is used that typically works for depression but is typically too low for BDD, or (2) the doctor doesn't ask to see if BDD symptoms are improving or not and thus can't adjust the dose appropriately to get them better.

If you've already tried an SRI at a low dose, without improving, it can be worthwhile to try the same SRI again at a higher dose. Sometimes this works. You may be better off, however, first trying an SRI you haven't tried before.

4. How to dose an SRI: There's no one-size-fits-all formula; dosing will depend on a number of factors. The most tolerable dosing strategy is to start with a low dose and gradually increase the dose while monitoring for side effects. So, for example, if you try escitalopram (Lexapro), the usual starting dose is 10 mg a day. After 2 weeks or so, assuming you're tolerating it well, you could raise it to 20 mg a day. After 2 to 3 weeks on 20 mg a day, you could then raise it to 30 mg a day, unless you're already starting to improve or are having problematic side effects. For fluoxetine (Prozac), the usual starting dose is 20 mg per day. After taking this dose for 2 weeks or so you could raise the dose to 40 mg a day. After another 2 to 3 weeks you could raise it to 60 mg/day, and then raise it to 80 mg a day after another 2 to 3 weeks, unless you're getting better on a lower dose or are having trouble with side effects.

But these dosing schedules are only general guidelines. Generally, I recommend raising the dose more quickly for people who are severely ill and are tolerating the medicine well. Patients who are closely monitored during hospitalization can also have their dose raised more quickly than described above. Conversely, it makes sense to raise the dose more slowly if you start substantially improving on a lower dose (because you may not need to raise it further) or if you're having trouble with side effects. Your preference also matters. *A reasonable goal, however, is to reach the maximum dose that the manufacturer recommends (if a lower dose isn't already working) within 4 to 9 weeks of starting the medicine.*

This dosing strategy has several potential advantages: (1) you're less likely to undertreat BDD because you'll probably reach a high enough dose, and (2) you'll probably improve more quickly than if you raise the dose more slowly. If the dose is raised very slowly, it can take a long time to reach an effective dose, especially if you end up needing a relatively high dose. On the other hand, the faster the dose is raised, the more likely you may be to get side effects. Also, you may end up on a higher dose than you really need, since a lower dose wasn't used long enough to see if it would work. However, once you've felt better for a while (at least several months), you and your doctor could consider very slowly and gradually lowering the dose (over several months) to see if a lower dose works equally well for you.

If, while the dose is being raised, a particular dose seems to be working, and you aren't severely ill, you and your doctor might opt to stay at that dose for a few more weeks to see what happens before increasing it further. For example, if you're feeling better with 10 mg a day of escitalopram 2 weeks after starting it, you may want to stay at that dose for another few weeks to see if you improve even further. If you do improve, you may want to stay on that same dose for yet another few weeks, to give it even more time to work. However, if your improvement seems to plateau at that dose, and you still have some symptoms, you can then try raising it. This is an individualized decision that's best made with your doctor.

5. Don't give up on an SRI until you've tried it for at least 12 to 16 weeks, while reaching a high enough dose (the maximum dose shown in Table 11–1, if possible) during that time: To see if a particular SRI will work for you, it's important to try it for a total of at least 12 to 16 weeks, while reaching a high dose if possible (unless a lower dose works for you) for at least 3 of those weeks. This is called an "adequate" trial. The trial is considered "inadequate" if you don't reach a high enough dose or if you try the medicine for less than a total of 3 months. An inadequate trial may not be sufficient to successfully treat BDD. Unfortunately, my research studies indicate that the vast majority (nearly 90%) of SRI treatments that people with BDD receive aren't optimal (reaching the highest dose) for this disorder. And two thirds of SRI treatments that are received aren't even minimally adequate for BDD.

In most published BDD studies and in my clinical practice, people needed to take an SRI, on average, for 4 to 9 weeks before their BDD symptoms substantially improved. In my study of fluoxetine (Prozac), two-thirds of people substantially improved (i.e., "responded") between the 4th and 11th week of treatment. In my study of fluvoxamine (Luvox), two-thirds improved between the 3rd and 10th week of treatment. In my studies of citalopram (Celexa) and escitalopram (Lexapro), people responded a little more quickly, with two-thirds responding between weeks 1 and 2 and 7 and 8.

Some people respond to an SRI within several weeks, whereas others have to try it for as long as 12 to 14 weeks—or occasionally even 16 weeks—before they substantially improve. This means you'll need to be patient and wait for the medicine to work. But don't get discouraged: it often does work!

The response rates, and time needed to respond, that I describe in this book are based on studies that increased the SRI dose, and reached the high end of the dosing range, fairly quickly (see the previous examples). If you raise your SRI dose more slowly (i.e., if it takes longer than 9 weeks or so to reach the maximum recommended dose), you may need to try it for more than 12 to 16 weeks to get better. If you haven't gotten to a high enough dose by week 12 to 16 of treatment, it's usually advisable to try to raise your dose at that point, and try the medicine a little longer to see if a higher dose works.

But if you've already reached the highest dose recommended by the manufacturer, or the highest dose you can tolerate, after 12 to 16 weeks of taking it—and you've been on that highest dose for at least 3 weeks—then it's probably best to make a change by switching to another SRI or adding another medicine to the SRI. (I'll say more about these options later in this chapter.) *In my experience, it doesn't make sense to just continue taking the same SRI, if it isn't working for you, after you've had an adequate trial.*

I often see patients who've tried lots of SRIs without getting better. A common problem is that they tried the SRI for too brief a time (for example, only 4 to 8 weeks). In my study of fluoxetine, nearly half of the people who eventually responded to the medication still hadn't responded by the 8th week of treatment. This was the case for one-third of the people in my study of fluvoxamine. These people generally didn't improve until 8 to 12 weeks after starting medication.

6. You need to take the medicine every day as prescribed: It's very important to take the medication every day, exactly as prescribed, even if it doesn't seem to be helping. *If you take less than prescribed, or you take it sporadically, it may not work as well or at all.* If you have trouble remembering to take it every day, try using a pill box (which you can buy at a pharmacy), setting an alarm, or finding another way to remember. If you don't want to take the medicine as prescribed because of side effects or because you have concerns about it, it's better to discuss your concerns with your doctor, rather than stopping the medicine or not taking it as prescribed.

7. Try to be patient; SRIs usually begin to work gradually: Occasionally, the medication begins to work suddenly. Some people can pinpoint the day, or even the hour, that it starts working. But typically, it starts working gradually. People say things like "I felt a little better three days ago and today, but not for very long, so I don't know if it's really working." Don't get discouraged if the medicine takes a while to work and you get off to a slow start. With more time on the medicine, these brief intermittent spurts of improvement gradually develop into more sustained periods of well-being. Good hours gradually turn into entire good days. Good days then become good weeks, months, and years.

8. If you improve with an SRI, you're likely to continue to feel well for as long as you take it: In my clinical experience, the vast majority of people who improve with an SRI continue to feel well over months and even years while taking the medication. Some patients I've treated have done well on the medication for more than a decade. In fact, many people say that the longer they take the SRI, the better they feel. I've found that about 40% of people who improve with an SRI in the first 3 months of treatment continue to improve even more over the next 6 months. I've also found that fewer than 10% of people who respond to an SRI experience a full return of their BDD symptoms while continuing to take the SRI.

9. Continue an effective SRI for a year or two, or even longer: Based on my clinical experience, I'd generally recommend staying on an effective SRI for at least a year or two, even if you're feeling better. You may want to stay on it longer than that, especially if you've tried stopping an SRI in the past and your symptoms returned, or if your BDD has been severe. A year or more of decreased symptoms can allow you to get back to work or do your job more effectively, socialize more, and start enjoying your life.

After a year or two, my patients and I discuss their options. Some people decide they'd like to try to stop the medication to see what happens. In my clinical experience, about 85% of people who stop an effective SRI experience some return of their symptoms, although sometimes they're less severe than they were originally. If your symptoms return, you can always start the SRI again, and in my experience the symptoms usually will improve again. (Occasional people however, don't improve quite as much as they did the first time.) But since it appears that many people—if not the majority—experience symptom return after discontinuing an effective SRI, some people opt to stay on it over the longer term. They don't want to risk a recurrence of their symptoms. For people with very severe BDD, especially those who've attempted suicide because of their symptoms, this is probably the wisest choice.

10. If you decide to stop an effective SRI, plan this carefully with your doctor: There's no way to predict whether your symptoms will return if you stop an SRI. Some people assume that if they've had CBT while taking an SRI that they can safely stop the SRI, but this shouldn't be assumed to be true; this, too, can't be predicted, and your symptoms could return.

Because your BDD symptoms may return if you stop an effective SRI, I'd suggest taking the following steps if you and your doctor decide to discontinue one:

(a) Lower the SRI dose slowly and gradually over months rather than stopping it abruptly. (However, if you switch immediately to another SRI, you can stop the first SRI more quickly). The more severe your BDD symptoms were in the past, the more slowly I'd suggest lowering the dose. This way, if the symptoms return and you decide to increase the dose again, some medication is already "on board," which may help you improve again more quickly. It's also possible (although not really known) that BDD symptoms may be less likely to return at all if the SRI is slowly tapered over a number of months rather than abruptly stopped.

(b) Try discontinuing the SRI when you aren't very stressed and your life is relatively stable. This way, if BDD symptoms return, you may be able to handle them better. It makes sense, for example, that you could deal with returning symptoms better if your job and relationships are stable and going well than if you're looking for a new job and ending an important relationship.

11. What to do about side effects, if they occur: Like all medications, the SRIs have the potential to cause side effects. In general, however, the SRIs are well tolerated. If side effects occur, they're often quite minimal, and they may improve or disappear on their own with the passage of time. Most people have no side effects or fairly minimal and tolerable ones.

Side effects are most likely to occur early in treatment (for example, within the first few weeks). This can be frustrating, because often the medicine hasn't had a chance to work yet. It helps to be patient! But with more time, they may disappear. Side effects are also more likely to occur when the dose is raised.

Reviewing lists of all of possible side effects can lead to unrealistic worry. Some lists contain side effects that occur only rarely or no more often than with a placebo (sugar pill), in which case they probably shouldn't be considered side effects. In medication studies, every physical symptom that a patient has during the study may be listed as a "side effect," even if the symptom has nothing to do with the medicine; this can lead to falsely elevated side effect rates.

Nonetheless, side effects can occur. Some of the more common ones are nausea, insomnia, feeling jittery, fatigue, sweating, decreased appetite, and decreased sex drive and sexual functioning (although sometimes sex drive and functioning improve with an SRI because people are no longer as depressed or self-conscious about their body). Clomipramine (Anafranil) can cause dry mouth and constipation. These side effects are tolerable for many people, and they go away after stopping the medication. None of the SRIs have life-threatening side effects. In my experience, people with BDD who experience side effects are often willing to tolerate them because they so appreciate the symptom relief they obtain.

When side effects do occur, they can often be reduced. Here are a few possible approaches that you and your doctor can consider:

(a) **Keep taking the medicine and wait:** Often, side effects diminish or disappear simply with the passage of time, as your body adjusts to the medicine.

(b) **Change the time the medicine is taken:** Certain side effects may improve by doing this. For example, if an SRI makes you tired (which is pretty uncommon), this side effect may go away—and possibly improve your sleep—if you take it at bedtime instead of in the morning.

(c) **Slow down the rate at which the dose is being raised:** If your doctor is in the process of trying to raise your dose to get it high enough to work, one alternative is to slow down the rate at which the dose is being increased. This will give your body more time to adjust to the medicine. If and when the side effects become more tolerable, you can try raising the dose again.

(d) **Lower the dose:** If side effects are more problematic and not tolerable on the current dose, your doctor can slowly decrease the dose (while watching carefully for worsening of BDD or depressive symptoms) to see if side effects disappear. If they do, an attempt can then be made to increase the dose again if BDD symptoms are still present.

(e) **Add other medications to try to counteract side effects:** There are many potentially helpful options, depending on the side effect you're experiencing.

(f) **Try other options:** Depending on the side effect, there are other options that may help. For example, if the medicine makes you feel jittery, lowering caffeine intake may help. Of if it causes some nausea, it may help to take the medicine with some food.

Often, such strategies are helpful. If they aren't, you and your doctor can consider trying another SRI. You may tolerate one better than another.

12. An important reminder: Be sure your doctor knows you have BDD. Don't just tell him or her that you have just depression or anxiety. A common clinical error is to focus treatment on depression rather than BDD. This often leads to use of an antidepressant other than an SRI, too brief an SRI trial, or an SRI dose that's too low for BDD. In such cases, BDD (and the depression) may not improve. *An effective medication regimen for depression won't necessarily effectively treat BDD. However, an effective medication regimen for BDD will often effectively treat depression, whether or not the depression is due to BDD.*

■ What If an SRI Doesn't Work Well Enough?

If an SRI doesn't work well enough for you, there are several approaches that you and your doctor can try. There's very little research data on what approaches work best, but my clinical experience suggests that several may be effective.

Optimize the SRI You're Already On

This means following the above guidelines to the extent that you can, taking a high enough dose for a long enough time. As I've mentioned, some people benefit from exceeding the maximum dose recommended by the manufacturer (excluding clomipramine [Anafranil]) and tolerate it well. If optimizing the SRI doesn't work for you, there are two major approaches you can take (1) *Augmenting* the SRI or (2) *Switching* to another SRI.

"Augment" the SRI or "Switch" to Another SRI

With **augmentation**, you continue taking the ineffective or partially effective SRI and add another medicine to boost the SRI's effect. With **switching,** you discontinue the SRI and try another SRI. It isn't really known which approach is better, as this question hasn't been well studied. In my clinical practice, however, I found that among patients who hadn't improved sufficiently with an adequate SRI trial, augmenting the SRI was successful in 33% of cases, whereas switching to another SRI was successful in 44% of cases.

When choosing one of these approaches, it may be helpful to consider how much the SRI has improved your symptoms. I found that among people who'd had partial improvement with the SRI (i.e., were "much improved" or "very much improved"), 41% got substantially better when I added an augmenting medicine to the SRI. However, among those people who hadn't improved with an SRI, only 18% substantially improved when an augmenting medicine was added to the SRI. Thus, you may be better off augmenting an SRI if you've partially improved with it, and it may be better to switch to another SRI if you haven't improved at all (or only minimally) to the first SRI. However, this important question needs further research.

There are other things you and your doctor might want to consider. If you've had several adequate SRI trials (for example, three or more) without substantial improvement or any attempt at augmentation, it would make sense to try augmentation. Conversely, if you haven't improved after trying to augment a particular SRI with several different augmenting medicines, it may be best to switch to another SRI.

Here's another important consideration: The more you've improved with an SRI, the less appealing it is to switch to a different one, especially if you were very ill before you took the SRI. The reason is that your symptoms could get worse after stopping the helpful SRI and while waiting for the new one to work; you and your doctor have to consider whether this is an acceptable risk to take. Furthermore, the new SRI might not work as well as the one you're on now (although this can't be predicted). For example, if you're taking an SRI and no longer have thoughts of suicide, and your BDD and depression are a lot better, it may be too risky to discontinue the helpful SRI and try a new one. You might want to augment the SRI instead; continuing the same SRI and adding another medicine to it allows you to maintain your improvement with the SRI, whereas if you stop the SRI you risk losing this improvement. But for some people, a switch isn't particularly risky and may make sense.

So, when deciding whether to augment or switch, there are several things to consider, including your individual situation and your and your doctor's preference. The approach you take needs to be tailored to you.

Augmenting an SRI

To the best of my knowledge, the only data on the effectiveness of SRI augmentation in BDD comes from my clinical practice and my study of augmentation of fluoxetine (Prozac) with pimozide (Orap), which I'll discuss later. So it really isn't known which augmentation approaches are best. However, a number may be worth trying. Table 11–5 shows the augmenting medications I've most often used for BDD, typical dosing ranges, and average doses.

Often, I augment the SRI only after I've tried it for at least 12 weeks and at a high enough dose. I do this because the SRI may work well enough by itself. This approach can keep the medication regimen simple. Sometimes, however, it makes sense to augment the SRI sooner, before the SRI alone has been adequately tried. This may be reasonable, for example, for someone with very severe BDD. Or the augmenting medicine may be more helpful than an SRI alone for certain symptoms (e.g., agitation) or a co-occurring disorder other than BDD.

TABLE 11–5   *Potential SRI Augmentation Medications for BDD*

Medication				
Generic Name	Brand Name	Type of Medication	Common Dosing Range for BDD (mg per day)	Average Dose Used in My Clinical Practice (mg per day)
Busiprone	Buspar	Antianxiety	30–80	57 ± 15
Levetiracetam	Keppra	Antiepileptic	750–3,000	2,118 ± 1,046
Clomipramine	Anafranil	SRI	Therapeutic blood level	128 ± 76
Venlafaxine	Effexor	Antidepressant	150–450	365 ± 89
Bupropion	Wellbutrin	Antidepressant	150–400	400 ± 0
Olanzapine	Zyprexa	Psychotropic agent (Neuroleptic)	5–20	8.3 ± 2.9
Ziprasidone	Geodon	Psychotropic agent (Neuroleptic)	10–180	60 ± 67
Risperidone	Risperdal	Psychotropic agent (Neuroleptic)	1–6	3.8 ± 1.7
Methylphenidate	Ritalin	Stimulant	10–60	32 ± 7
Lithium	Lithobid, Eskalith	Mood stabilizer	Therapeutic blood level	825 ± 568

Based on my clinical experience and augmentation studies of other disorders, I'd suggest trying an augmenting agent for about 6 to 8 weeks, and reaching the higher end of the dosing range in Table 11–5 if possible during that time, before making a final decision about whether it's working or not.

Buspirone

Buspirone (Buspar), an antianxiety medication with effects on serotonin, is sometimes used as an augmenting agent for depression and OCD. Unlike other antianxiety medications, buspirone is generally not sedating and has no potential for causing physical dependence or addiction.

In my clinical practice, adding buspirone to an SRI has been effective for about one-third of patients. The amount of improvement is fairly large. People with delusional BDD appear as likely to improve with buspirone as those with nondelusional BDD. Buspirone augmentation is appealing because this medicine typically has so few side effects. It may also improve coexisting anxiety and possibly depressive symptoms as well.

I've also treated a small number of patients with buspirone alone who preferred not to take an SRI. Several experienced some improvement in BDD symptoms, although none had the robust response that can occur with an SRI.

Levetiracetam

I recently did a small pilot study with levetiracetam (Keppra), a medication that's marketed for the treatment of seizures. In this 12-week open-label study of 17 people, 53% substantially improved. Of the five patients who had levetiracetam added to an SRI that they were already taking, two got better. Of the 12 patients who took levetiracetam without an SRI, 7 got better. While the effectiveness of this medication for BDD needs further research, these preliminary findings are encouraging and suggest that levetiracetam may be worth trying in addition to an SRI (or without an SRI; see further discussion below).

Clomipramine

I sometimes combine the SRI clomipramine (Anafranil) with one of the selective SRIs (SSRIs: fluvoxamine [Luvox], fluoxetine [Prozac], paroxetine [Paxil], citalopram (Celexa), escitalopram (Lexapro), or sertraline [Zoloft]) if improvement isn't sufficient with an adequate trial of an SSRI alone. Some patients do better with an SSRI/clomipramine combination than with either medication alone.

However, the dosing must be done very carefully. The SSRIs can greatly increase clomipramine blood levels, which can be highly toxic at very high levels. Therefore, a lower dose of clomipramine should generally be used when it's combined with an SSRI than when clomipramine is used without an SSRI. If a patient is already on an SSRI, I usually begin by adding only

25 mg a day of clomipramine and then gradually raising the dose, depending on the response and clomipramine blood level. Clomipramine levels should always be checked when this medication is combined with an SSRI to ensure that the dose isn't too high. Also, patients should be monitored for a rare syndrome called serotonin syndrome.

In my clinical practice, 44% of patients substantially improved when I added clomipramine to an SSRI or vice versa. This response rate was somewhat higher than for other augmentation strategies, although the magnitude of the response wasn't quite as large as for some other strategies. Nonetheless, because clomipramine is an excellent antidepressant, it may be an appealing augmentation choice for people who are severely depressed. Although I generally recommend trying an augmenting agent for 6 to 8 weeks, I'd recommend trying clomipramine for 12 weeks before deciding whether it's working well enough. I generally wouldn't combine clomipramine with an SSRI without first attempting to optimize a trial with just one of them.

Other Antidepressants

Antidepressants other than clomipramine can be added to an SSRI. These medications include venlafaxine (Effexor) and bupropion (Wellbutrin). Some patients do well with this approach. Some of my patients with severe depression who hadn't responded to lots of medications did particularly well on 400 mg per day of bupropion (Wellbutrin) plus 60 to 100 mg per day of citalopram (Celexa). It's possible that adding bupropion (Wellbutrin), which doesn't directly affect serotonin, is more effective for people whose depression doesn't seem to be largely due to BDD, but this is speculative at this point. Care should be taken when combining venlafaxine with an SSRI because of the risk of serotonin syndrome (although the risk is low, and I've never seen it occur with this combination of medications).

Neuroleptics

The neuroleptics (antipsychotics) are a class of medicines often used to treat psychotic symptoms; they are also effective for a broad range of other symptoms (e.g., agitation and anxiety). (Because some of the newer ones are effective for so many different kinds of symptoms, they are now officially classified "psychotropic agents"—meaning they have effects on psychiatric symptoms). These medications are potentially promising SRI augmenters for BDD. First, they are effective SRI augmenters in OCD and depression. Second, many people with BDD have prominent delusions of reference and delusional conviction about the perceived appearance defect; neuroleptics are the best treatment for delusional thinking in other disorders.

There are two types of neuroleptics: "typical" (or "first generation") and "atypical" (or "second generation"). Although neither type has been well studied in BDD, the atypicals appear more promising. Some of my patients have responded well when we added atypical neuroleptics such as ziprasidone (Geodon), olanzapine (Zyprexa), or risperidone (Risperdal) to an SRI. Ziprasidone (Geodon) seems especially promising.

These medications can diminish severe distress and agitation resulting from BDD. For patients with these kinds of severe symptoms I may combine an atypical neuroleptic with an SRI from the beginning of treatment. Using an atypical neuroleptic early in treatment can provide quicker relief than the SRI alone—producing a calming effect (but not usually a sedating effect if the dosing is done correctly). This can help the person function better, and in some cases prevent hospitalization.

However, only one study has adequately studied a neuroleptic as an SRI augmenter. This study tested pimozide (Orap), a typical neuroleptic that is effective for Tourette's disorder (characterized by repetitive, uncontrollable verbal utterances or physical movements known as tics, which are similar to the compulsive behaviors of OCD). Pimozide is an effective SRI augmenter in OCD, and it has long had the reputation (which was based more on word of mouth than scientific studies) of being uniquely effective for delusional BDD and certain other types of delusional disorder.

In the pimozide study, patients who hadn't had a good response to an adequate trial of fluoxetine (Prozac) were randomly assigned to receive treatment with either pimozide or placebo, while remaining on fluoxetine. Pimozide wasn't more effective than placebo, even for people with delusional BDD. Nor did pimozide improve insight more than placebo. At the time of this writing, I would tend not to augment an SRI with a typical neuroleptic, such as pimozide, but I would consider augmenting an SRI with an atypical neuroleptic for certain patients. However, much more research is needed.

Methylphenidate

Some patients (10%–20% in my experience) improve significantly when methylphenidate (Ritalin) or another stimulant is added to an SRI. I'm more likely to use this approach when patients are severely depressed and fatigued, because the stimulant can improve depressed mood and energy as well as BDD. One concern, however, is that stimulants are potentially habit forming and are best not used in people at risk for substance abuse or dependence. Because stimulants can potentially worsen tics, there's a theoretical concern that they might worsen skin picking (which has some features in common with tics), but I haven't seen this happen.

Lithium

Lithium is a natural substance that's best known as a treatment for bipolar disorder (manic depressive illness). However, it's also effective for a broad range of other disorders and symptoms (e.g., mood swings, depression, aggressive behavior, suicidal thinking). In my clinical experience, about 20% of BDD patients substantially improve when lithium is added to an SRI.

Benzodiazepines

Benzodiazepines (e.g., clonazepam [Klonopin], lorazepam [Ativan]) are used primarily to treat anxiety and insomnia. Strictly speaking, I don't consider them augmenting agents, because I add them to an SRI at any point during treatment—whenever they're needed. Benzodiazepines can be very helpful for severe distress, anxiety, or agitation if an SRI doesn't adequately diminish these symptoms or before an SRI has had a chance to work. Benzodiazepines can also greatly improve poor sleep. They can be used temporarily or over the longer term. Temporary use of benzodiazepines during the first few weeks of treatment (while waiting for an SRI to work) can be especially valuable for people who are severely anxious, agitated, unable to sleep, or suicidal. Benzodiazepines are potentially habit forming, but in my experience, few people with BDD abuse them. I tend not to prescribe them, however, for people who've abused alcohol or drugs. For these individuals, an atypical neuroleptic may be a helpful alternative.

Cognitive-Behavioral Therapy

If medication doesn't work well enough, you should strongly consider adding CBT to the medication. Cognitive-behavioral therapy (CBT) can also be used along with medication from the start of treatment. Most of the next chapter is devoted to CBT.

Switching to Another SRI

If you don't improve with an adequate trial of one SRI, you may improve with another. My approach is, if necessary, to try one SRI after another, in the hope that one will work better than others. You may have to try several SRIs before you find one that works.

It appears that all of the SRIs are about equally effective for BDD (although this is not well studied). This means that **on average** they all appear about equally likely to work. However, this doesn't mean that they will all work equally well **for you**. One (or several) may be more effective than another for a given person. There's no way to predict which SRI (or SRIs) will work best for you. If you don't improve with one, it's worth trying another (although you might want to first try SRI augmentation). I've treated many patients who responded to an SRI after they didn't improve with many others. In some cases, the sixth one worked after five had failed! In my clinical practice, 43% of patients who didn't improve with an initial adequate SRI trial improved with at least one subsequent SRI, and 44% of subsequent adequate SRI trials received by these patients were effective.

What if you've improved with an SRI but want to try another one because of side effects, or to see if another SRI works even better? The good news is that if one SRI has worked for you, other SRIs appear highly likely to also work. In my clinical practice, among people who substantially improved with one SRI and then switched to a different one, 92% of subsequent SRI trials also led to improvement. The subsequent SRI may work a little better than the earlier one, about the same, or not quite as well. There's no way to predict the outcome.

■ Other Medications

The SRIs are by far the best-studied medications for BDD and have been shown to be effective in all studies that have tested them. However, there are some other options to consider if an SRI, and the strategies discussed earlier, don't work for you. So far, I've focused on trying SRI augmentation or switching to another SRI if an SRI doesn't work well enough. But there are a few other approaches that may also help.

Venlafaxine

Venlafaxine (Effexor), an antidepressant with potent effects on serotonin, may possibly work for BDD when used by itself (I mentioned earlier that it can potentially be helpful when combined with an SRI). In a recent 12-week open-label study of 17 people, BDD symptoms significantly improved with venlafaxine treatment. However, the degree of improvement was less than has been found in open-label studies of SRIs. For this reason—and because available research consists of only this one small pilot study and no controlled studies—venlafaxine should **not** be considered a first-choice medication for BDD at this time. The SRIs have been much better studied. I would recommend venlafaxine only for people who haven't improved sufficiently with a number of adequate SRI trials. Further research on this promising medication is needed.

Levetiracetam

As I discussed earlier, this medication seems promising for BDD when taken with or without an SRI. In my pilot study, 7 of 12 patients who weren't taking an SRI substantially improved with levetiracetam (Keppra) treatment. Several people decreased the dose or stopped the medication after they'd improved, and their symptoms got worse again. When they restarted levetiracetam, their symptoms got better again. For several people, this pattern was repeated a number of times, suggesting that the medication was having a real effect.

The response rate (7 of 12 people, or 53%) isn't as good as in open-label SRI studies. In addition, the degree of improvement for the participants as a whole wasn't as great as in most SRI studies—although among those who did improve, the amount of improvement was large. Also, several people who'd had SRIs in the past did better with levetiracetam than they had with an SRI.

Because only this one small pilot study and no controlled studies have been done, levetiracetam should not be considered a first-choice medication for BDD at this time. I would recommend it only for people who haven't improved sufficiently with a number of adequate SRI trials or who can't tolerate an SRI. Further research on this promising medication is needed.

Other Antiepileptic Medications

Medications such as valproic acid (e.g., Depakote), gabapentin, and lamotrigine (Lamictal) are sometimes helpful for anxiety or depressive symptoms. Valproic acid and lamotrigine can be very helpful for mood swings in people who have bipolar disorder in addition to BDD. At this time, however, these medications shouldn't be used by themselves to treat BDD because relevant research hasn't been done.

MAO Inhibitors

The MAO inhibitors (MAOIs) (phenelzine [Nardil], tranylcypromine [Parnate], selegeline [Deprenyl]) are older but very effective antidepressants that seem to sometimes be effective for BDD. Although most available data comes from patient reports of past treatment rather than more rigorous treatment studies, they appear effective in about 30% of cases. I haven't used them much for BDD because so many SRIs are now available, which are much better studied for BDD and are generally better tolerated. However, an MAOI may be worth trying if many other medications haven't worked.

A very important caveat: The MAOIs must be taken exactly as prescribed. They can't—under any circumstances—be combined with certain foods or certain other medicines, including SRIs. If not taken exactly as prescribed, MAOIs can have very toxic effects, so it's critically important to follow prescribing directions and to **never** combine an MAOI with an SRI, venlafaxine, or certain other medicines and foods.

Opioids

I know a few people who took a prescription opioid (opiate) medication (e.g., Percocet) for a medical problem and unexpectedly experienced relief from severe BDD symptoms. I also know several who unfortunately became addicted to an illegal opioid (e.g., heroin) because it alleviated intolerable BDD symptoms. I don't routinely recommend opioids or prescribe them, because they're potentially highly addicting. Also, I know of only a few cases in which they've been tried. Nonetheless, they remain an option for a severely ill person who has failed all standard treatments. Treatment with an opioid is preferable to life-long hospitalization, living in a nursing home for the rest of your life because you're so ill, or suicide.

Other Medications

A number of other medications appear less promising for BDD, although it's important to highlight that they've barely been researched, so not much is known about their effects on BDD.

In a study I did in the early 1990s, before we knew how to treat BDD, I asked my patients what medications they'd taken in the past, and which ones had worked. With a class of antidepressant medications known as tricyclics (excluding the SRI clomipramine [Anafranil], which is a tricyclic), only 15% of 48 treatments resulted in improvement. In a similar study done by Dr. Eric Hollander, tricyclic antidepressants (excluding clomipramine) led to no overall improvement in BDD symptoms, whereas SRIs did improve BDD symptoms. The tricyclic medications sometimes improved depression but usually not accompanying BDD symptoms.

Only 2% of neuroleptic (antipsychotic) treatments were effective (in most cases, they weren't used in combination with an SRI). However, at the time of this study, only the typical (not the atypical) neuroleptics were available, so this result may not apply to the atypicals. There are a few published case reports in which an atypical neuroleptic (olanzapine [Zyprexa]) was effective for a patient with BDD. Certainly, more research on the effectiveness of these medications for BDD is greatly needed, especially because so many people with BDD have delusional thinking about their appearance.

Other types of medications—such as stimulants and benzodiazepines—don't seem effective for BDD when used without an SRI (although as I've discussed earlier, some may help in combination with an SRI).

■ Electroconvulsive Therapy, Neurosurgery,
   and Other Treatments

In published case reports, electroconvulsive therapy (ECT) (also known as shock therapy), was reported to be effective for BDD in two of eight patients. My research data suggests a similarly low response rate, with 0 of 8 people responding. I'm aware of approximately 10 additional people with BDD who had ECT; this treatment wasn't effective for BDD for any of these patients, although several of them had temporary improvement, primarily in depressive symptoms. These findings, while limited by the very small number of patients, suggest that this treatment isn't promising for BDD. Nonetheless, because ECT is the most effective treatment for depression, it may be worth considering for someone with BDD who is also severely depressed, especially if the depression doesn't appear largely due to BDD. Because ECT has the potential to be lifesaving for people with severe depression, it should remain an option for someone with BDD who is very depressed and suicidal.

While brain surgery might seem like a drastic measure, some people are so severely tormented and incapacitated by their BDD symptoms that they seriously consider it or actually have it done. In a report published in a scientific journal, one patient had improvement in BDD symptoms with a brain surgery procedure known as a modified leucotomy. A colleague told me about a young woman with debilitating and intractable BDD who had an excellent response to a similar procedure (bilateral anterior cingulotomy and subcaudate tractotomy). Procedures like these interrupt fronto-striatal brain circuits, which function abnormally in OCD and may also be involved in BDD (see Chapter 9).

I know of four people with unusually severe BDD who, after not improving with countless treatments, had a neurosurgical procedure known as an anterior internal capsulotomy, a type of brain surgery that's being studied in severe treatment-resistant OCD. Two of the four patients substantially improved. One woman had been completely devastated by BDD concerns that focused on her hair. She lost her job and friends, was housebound, and had many lengthy psychiatric hospitalizations. She'd tried countless times to electrocute herself and kill herself in other ways. Even though she was young, her family was planning on sending her to live in a nursing home, because she was too ill to care for herself and her family was exhausted. Her husband told me, "Before the surgery, her life was desperation and despair; the procedure was miraculous and lifesaving." However, in a study of this procedure in people with intractable OCD, those who also had BDD-like symptoms (BDD per se wasn't assessed) tended not to improve as much as people without BDD-like symptoms.

It's hard to know what to make of these somewhat conflicting reports. The main thing to consider is that the research data available on neurosurgery is still extremely limited. While I don't at this time recommend brain surgery for BDD, it's worth considering for extremely severe, life-threatening BDD for which many other treatments haven't worked. It's a better alternative than committing suicide or living in a nursing home or being hospitalized for the rest of your life because you're so ill.

Other new treatments known as neuromodulation (such as vagal nerve stimulation and deep brain stimulation) are being pioneered and tested in a variety of psychiatric disorders. I've heard about one patient with BDD who improved with deep brain stimulation. But none of these treatments have been studied in BDD, so we don't know whether they're effective for this disorder.

■ A Suggested Approach to Treating BDD with Medications: A Proposed Algorithm

In this section, I'll discuss a proposed "algorithm" for treating BDD with medications, which summarizes and visually presents some of the information in this chapter. The algorithm is shown in Figure 11–1. It's a visual flow diagram that you can follow when treating BDD.

(1) **Treat with an SRI:** If you follow the arrow down from the top of the algorithm in Figure 11–1, you can see that if BDD is present, the next step is to treat with an SRI, whether you have delusional or nondelusional BDD.

(2) **Response to an SRI:** If you have a good response to the SRI, you then follow the line that goes to the right. In this case, the algorithm suggests continuing the effective SRI for at least 1 to 2 years or longer. If you haven't had a good response to the SRI, you follow the line to the left, which asks if you had an adequate trial.

(3) **Have you had an adequate SRI trial?** I've discussed in the text what an adequate SRI trial is; footnote "c" of Figure 11–1 briefly reminds you of this.

(4) **Be sure you have an adequate SRI trial:** If you **haven't** had an adequate SRI trial, you follow the line that goes over to the left and down, which indicates that the next step is to have an adequate SRI trial (see footnote "d" of Figure 11–1 and the above text for a description). If you **have** had an adequate SRI trial, you follow the line to the right and down. At the fork, you then go to the right or the left, depending on whether your BDD has partially responded (follow the line to the left) or not responded (follow the line to the right) to the SRI.

(5) **Augment or switch:** If your BDD has **partially** improved with an adequate SRI trial, the algorithm suggests that you try SRI augmentation. However, the information in parentheses indicates that switching to another SRI is also an option. If your BDD **hasn't** partially improved with an adequate SRI trial, you follow the line to the right. The algorithm suggests that you can switch to another SRI. However, trying SRI augmentation is also an option.

(6) **Augmentation options:** You then continue to follow the lines of the algorithm, depending on your response.

The algorithm doesn't include non-SRI medication options that you can try if adequate SRI trials haven't helped your symptoms enough. These options are discussed in the text.

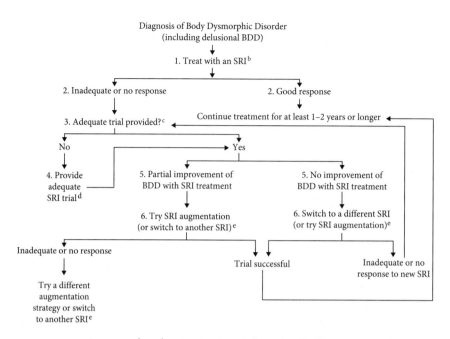

Diagnosis of Body Dysmorphic Disorder
(including delusional BDD)

↓

1. Treat with an SRI[b]

2. Inadequate or no response ← → 2. Good response

3. Adequate trial provided?[c] ← Continue treatment for at least 1–2 years or longer ←

No → Yes

4. Provide adequate SRI trial[d]

5. Partial improvement of BDD with SRI treatment

5. No improvement of BDD with SRI treatment

6. Try SRI augmentation (or switch to another SRI)[e]

6. Switch to a different SRI (or try SRI augmentation)[e]

Inadequate or no response

Try a different augmentation strategy or switch to another SRI[e]

Trial successful

Inadequate or no response to new SRI

FIGURE 11–1 A proposed medication treatment algorithm for BDD[a]

[a]This is an abbreviated version of a proposed medication treatment approach to BDD; see the text for more detail. This algorithm incorporates and is consistent with scientific evidence, but because such evidence is currently limited, the algorithm is also based on clinical experience. The algorithm focuses on SRI treatment only and does not include other medications (see text) or CBT. CBT appears effective for BDD (see the next chapter).

[b]In some cases (e.g., for severe anxiety and suicidal thinking), consider combining a benzodiazepine or neuroleptic with an SRI as initial treatment.

[c]Has the highest SRI dose recommended by the manufacturer or that you can tolerate been reached and used for a minimum of 3 weeks, and has the total SRI trial duration been at least 12 to 16 weeks?

[d]Try to reach the highest dose recommended by the manufacturer or the highest dose you can tolerate for at least 3 weeks; be sure that you take the SRI for a total duration of 12 to 16 weeks.

[e]Options include buspirone, clomipramine (Anafranil), venlafaxine (Effexor), bupropion (Wellbutrin) and others.

■ Individualized Treatment Is Important

This algorithm and the medication guidelines in this chapter shouldn't be used in a cookbook fashion or in place of your doctor's clinical judgment. The algorithm contains general treatment suggestions and may need to be modified to reflect your unique situation. For example, you may also have non-BDD disorders or symptoms that will influence the medication you take. If you have another disorder, such as bipolar disorder, for example, you'll need additional medications that aren't shown on the algorithm. For people with an alcohol or drug problem, it may be unwise to use a benzodiazepine or a stimulant. Other factors may influence the treatment decisions that you and your doctor make. They include medication side effects, your treatment preference, or a need for immediate symptom relief. If you're pregnant or thinking of getting pregnant, it's very important to talk with your doctor about how this might influence your treatment choices.

I recommend a comprehensive evaluation by a psychiatrist and development of an individualized treatment plan. Creativity and expertise in psychopharmacology are needed for people with more treatment-resistant BDD. So is persistence. With enough tries, in my experience most people eventually improve with medication. Don't give up!

There are still relatively few treatment studies of BDD. Much more treatment research on BDD is urgently needed, and such research will likely modify and improve the algorithm and treatment guidelines in this chapter. I'm optimistic that this research will eventually yield a broader range of treatment options, and even more effective treatments, for BDD.

12. COGNITIVE-BEHAVIORAL THERAPY FOR BODY DYSMORPHIC DISORDER

Cognitive-behavioral therapy (CBT) is the best-studied and most promising type of psychotherapy for body dysmorphic disorder (BDD). It's a practical "here and now" treatment that focuses on changing problematic thoughts and behaviors. CBT is effective for many other mental disorders, such as depression, phobias, panic disorder, obsessive compulsive disorder, and eating disorders.

This chapter provides an overview of CBT for BDD. The goal of this chapter is to convey some of the basics of CBT for BDD, including what CBT for BDD basically consists of, the evidence that CBT works for BDD, what symptoms often improve, the rationale for using it, frequently asked questions, and an overview of how it's done. I also briefly discuss other types of therapy. However, I wouldn't recommend that you try to treat yourself using just the information in this book, because it isn't detailed enough for this purpose. There isn't enough room for a comprehensive description of how to actually do the therapy—that's an entire book itself! My colleagues (Drs. Sabine Wilhelm and Gail Steketee) and I have written a treatment manual for therapists that provides a detailed guide for how to actually do CBT for BDD. Dr. Wilhelm has also written a CBT guidebook for people with BDD. (See Chapter 16 for more information.)

Unless you have very mild BDD, I'd suggest that you get CBT from a therapist who is trained to do CBT and is familiar with treating BDD.

■ A Few CBT Basics

The **cognitive** aspect of CBT focuses on thoughts and beliefs (cognitions). The goal is to identify, evaluate, and change unrealistic and self-defeating ways of thinking. The **behavioral** aspect of CBT focuses on problematic behaviors, such as mirror checking and avoidance of social situations. The goal is to stop such behaviors and substitute healthier behaviors. Usually, cognitive and behavioral approaches are combined—hence, the term "cognitive-behavioral therapy."

CBT for BDD usually consists of the following core techniques: (1) cognitive restructuring, (2) exposure and behavioral experiments, (3) ritual (response) prevention, (4) perceptual (mirror) retraining, and (5) relapse prevention. I'll very briefly describe each of the core techniques here and then discuss them in more detail later in this chapter.

Cognitive Restructuring (Evaluating and Changing Self-Defeating Thoughts)

What it is: You learn to identify and evaluate negative thoughts and beliefs you have about your appearance, as well as "errors" in your thinking (like thinking you can predict the future). You learn how to figure out whether your BDD thoughts are accurate and helpful, and you learn to develop more accurate, helpful, and healthier beliefs.

Goal: The goal is to develop more accurate and helpful beliefs about your appearance and yourself, rather than automatically assuming that your BDD beliefs are true.

How it's done: You first learn to notice and identify "negative automatic thoughts" that you have about your appearance. Negative automatic thoughts (for example, "Everyone will laugh at me if I go out tonight") happen so quickly and automatically that you may not even be aware of them. You then learn to objectively evaluate whether these thoughts and beliefs are true or not. You do this by examining the evidence for and against them, and by determining whether the thoughts involve distorted thinking (also known as "thinking errors"). You then use this information to generate more accurate and helpful appearance-related beliefs.

CBT also teaches skills to help you work on "deeper" level beliefs about yourself (for example, "I'm inadequate" or "no one will ever love me"). This involves cognitive restructuring, self-esteem exercises, and other approaches.

Why it's important: People with BDD have very negative beliefs about their appearance and themselves as a person. Most people just assume their beliefs are true. It's important to objectively evaluate the accuracy of these beliefs, and to develop more accurate, helpful, and healthier beliefs.

Exposure and Behavioral Experiments

What it is: You gradually face situations that you avoid (for example, social situations) because of your BDD.

Goal: The goal is to stop avoiding situations because of BDD and to feel more comfortable in those situations.

How it's done: First, you make a list of situations you avoid (for example, the grocery store) and number them from 0 to 100 according to how anxious you feel in them and how much you avoid them. You start by going into one of the easier situations (one that's rated about a 30) and staying there until you feel less anxious. The more you do this, the easier it will get, and you can then face harder situations.

Exposure for BDD also includes doing behavioral experiments which test your predictions about what will happen to see if they're true (for example, whether people will laugh at you in the grocery store). During the exposure, you collect actual evidence while you're in the situation to see if your belief is true.

Why it's important: Avoiding anxiety-provoking situations (like social situations or school) just feeds BDD symptoms and keeps them going. Avoidance also prevents you from living a fulfilling and enjoyable life. Learning how to do exposure will make your life more normal, happier, and more productive.

Ritual (Response) Prevention

What it is: You decrease and eventually stop doing excessive, compulsive BDD rituals, such as mirror checking, excessive grooming, and reassurance seeking.

Goal: The goal is to stop doing certain compulsive behaviors (such as reassurance seeking) altogether and to do others (such as grooming) only a normal amount.

How it's done: First, start with the easier rituals, trying to cut them down. Then move on to behaviors that are harder to control, and try to cut those down too.

Why it's important: Doing BDD rituals over and over again doesn't really help. Even if you feel a little better right after you do them, the relief doesn't last for very long. Plus, these behaviors just feed BDD and keep it going. Even worse, for some people rituals immediately increase obsessions, anxiety, and depression. Ritual (response) prevention helps you get better control over these time-consuming and problematic behaviors.

Perceptual (Mirror) Retraining

What it is: You learn to (1) look at your entire face or body (not just the disliked areas) in a "holistic" way in the mirror without excessively checking disliked areas and (2) describe your body in a nonjudgmental way, rather than in a negative, critical way.

Goal: The goal is to develop a healthy relationship with mirrors, so you don't check them excessively or avoid them, and to view yourself less negatively and more realistically.

How it's done: You look in the mirror from a normal distance and describe your body parts in a nonjudgmental way, going from head to toe. You don't say negative things to yourself about how you look or zero in on disliked areas. You start with easier mirrors and then move on to harder ones.

Why it's important: Mirrors and reflecting surfaces are part of everyone's life. Because you'll sometimes unexpectedly encounter them, or need to look in them, it's good to be able to do it without getting upset or "stuck" in the mirror.

Relapse Prevention

What it is: You prepare for the ending of treatment.

Goal: The goal is to help you maintain the gains you made in treatment and prevent relapse (return) of your symptoms.

How it's done: You review which techniques were most helpful for you and how to keep practicing them in the future. You also do other things, such as anticipating possible future stressors and how you can manage them using CBT skills.

Why it's important: It's important to prepare for the end of treatment to keep your skills sharp in the future.

Although I've listed the first four techniques separately, in reality they overlap to some degree and are usually combined in treatment. Several other cognitive and behavioral techniques are sometimes also used for BDD, usually in combination with the core techniques I just described. They include habit reversal for skin picking and hair pulling, mindfulness, activity scheduling, and scheduling pleasant activities. I'll describe these techniques later in this chapter.

■ More CBT Basics

1. CBT teaches helpful skills: These skills help you cope with and overcome BDD. As with any kind of learning, it's important to take an active role in your treatment. CBT isn't something that's done to you; rather, it's something you learn how to do, and it requires work on your part. In many ways, your therapist is like a coach or guide who teaches you skills and helps you master them. Eventually, you learn to be your own coach.

2. Number of sessions: The number can vary, depending on the severity of your symptoms, how motivated you are for the treatment, and other factors. The optimal number is unclear; published studies have used from 8 to 60 sessions. The treatment manual written by my colleagues and I contains 22 weekly sessions plus 3 "booster" sessions after treatment ends. Occasional people need fewer sessions than this, whereas others will need more. The number of sessions will need to be tailored to you and your individual needs.

3. Frequency of sessions: Often, CBT is done once a week. It's possible (although not known) that it will work faster and better if it's done more frequently (for example, several times a week or daily). Patients with more severe BDD may benefit from more than one session a week.

4. Length of sessions: Typically, CBT sessions last for 50 minutes to an hour, but they can be longer. Most published studies have used 90-minute sessions (see further discussion below).

5. Individual or group treatment: CBT can be done with just you and your therapist, or in a group (with one or two therapists and 4 to 10 other people with BDD). Some people participate in both individual CBT and group CBT.

6. Homework is important: Homework (skills' building assignments) is done between sessions. It involves practicing skills you learn in your therapy sessions. At various stages of the treatment, you'll do cognitive restructuring, exposure/behavioral experiments, and ritual prevention as homework (in addition to doing these things during your therapy sessions). Doing homework is an essential ingredient of getting better.

7. Stages of treatment: Treatment typically begins with an evaluation by a clinician to confirm that you have BDD, assess other problems or disorders you may have, and discuss treatment options. If you decide to do CBT, you'll then have another few sessions to lay important groundwork for treatment—for example, learning more about BDD and CBT, setting your goals for treatment, and developing an understanding of how your BDD developed and what factors seem to keep your symptoms going. Then you'll move on to learning and practicing the core techniques, and perhaps other techniques, listed earlier. Toward the end of treatment, you'll learn "relapse prevention," which will help you maintain your gains after you end treatment. "Booster sessions," in which you check in with your therapist from time to time after you end treatment, can also help you maintain your gains and keep your CBT skills sharp.

8. You need a therapist trained in CBT: For CBT to work, you need to find a clinician with training in CBT who is also knowledgeable about treating BDD with CBT.

■   What's the Evidence that CBT Works?

Research studies indicate that CBT that specifically targets BDD symptoms substantially improves BDD in a majority of people. Most of these studies, which are summarized in Table 12–1, used a combination of cognitive and behavioral techniques. These CBT techniques were tailored for BDD specifically; they didn't focus simply on anxiety or depressive symptoms. Many other reports of individual patients successfully treated with CBT have been published. Studies

TABLE 12–1 *Published Studies of Cognitive-Behavioral Therapy (CBT) for BDD* [a,b]

Study Design	Individual or Group Treatment [c]	Number of Patients	Number and Length of Treatment Sessions	Study Results	Reference
Patients were randomly assigned to CBT or a no-treatment control condition [d,e]	Individual	19	• 12 weekly sessions • Each session was 60 minutes	BDD symptoms improved significantly more with CBT than no treatment	Veale, 1996
Patients were randomly assigned to CBT or a no-treatment control condition [d]	Group (four to five members per group)	54	• 8 weekly sessions • Each session was 2 hours	CBT was significantly more effective than no treatment; significant improvement occurred in 82% of the CBT group at the end of treatment, and in 77% at follow-up 4.5 months later	Rosen, 1995
Case series [f]	Individual	Five in the first series; 17 in the second	• First series: 4 weeks of daily CBT (20 total sessions), 12 weeks of daily CBT (60 sessions), or 8 or 12 weeks of weekly sessions • Second series: 4 weeks of daily sessions • All sessions were 90 minutes	Four of five patients in the first series improved; in the second series BDD severity decreased by 50% or more in 12 of 17 patients	Neziroglu, 1993, 1996

| Case series[f] | Group | 13 | • 12 weekly sessions
• Each session was 90 minutes | BDD symptoms significantly improved | Wilhelm, 1999 |
| Case series[f] | Individual | 10 | • 6 initial weeks of daily sessions (30 total sessions)
• Each session was 90 minutes
• The 6 months of relapse prevention sessions occurred every other week | BDD symptoms significantly improved by 6 weeks and remained stable at follow-up after another 6 months. Relapse prevention treatment resulted in stable gains for anxiety and depression, which worsened in the control group during the 6-month follow-up, although the groups did not differ in BDD symptom severity at the end of the 6-month follow-up. | McKay, 1997, 1999 |

[a] These are the prospective controlled studies and large case series published in scientific journals at the time of this writing. Single case reports, small case studies, and chart-review studies are excluded. However, it's worth noting that in a retrospective chart-review study of 30 patients with BDD, Drs. Juan Gomez-Perez, Isaac Marks, and Juan Gutierrez-Fisac reported improvement in about half of the 21 patients who completed CBT treatment. Also excluded are studies of body image dissatisfaction that did not determine whether participants had the disorder BDD per se.

[b] All of the studies except for McKay's used a combination of cognitive and behavioral techniques; McKay and colleagues used only behavioral techniques.

[c] Patients who received individual treatment met alone with their therapist; those treated in a group received treatment with other patients with BDD.

[d] Patients were randomly assigned to CBT or to a waiting list; those on the waiting list didn't receive treatment. This study design has some advantages over a case series, because the no-treatment condition controls for changes in BDD that might occur simply with the passage of time or for other reasons.

[e] In this study, no patients were delusional.

[f] In the case series design, all patients received CBT.

haven't yet compared CBT to non-CBT types of therapy, so it still needs to be proven that CBT is more effective than other therapies. In the meantime, however, CBT is considered the psychotherapy of first choice for BDD.

The first two studies in Table 12–1, which were "controlled" studies, are the most scientifically rigorous studies done so far. These studies compared people who got CBT to people on a waiting list who received no treatment. Another advantage of these two studies is that they randomly assigned patients to one of the two treatment conditions, which minimizes differences in the patients in each group (such as BDD severity) that might affect how they do with treatment. The other studies in the Table were "case series" in which patients were treated with CBT (but weren't compared to another group, such as patients on a waiting list who got no treatment).

All of the studies found that CBT was often effective for BDD. Only one study has looked at who CBT is most likely to work for. It found that the better the person's insight before treatment (i.e., the less delusional their BDD beliefs), the better they did with CBT. It also seems likely that people who are more motivated to work hard in CBT, and who do lots of homework, are more likely to improve. This may be the best predictor of who gets better with CBT.

■ What Gets Better with CBT?

Many aspects of BDD, as well as related symptoms such as depression, improve with CBT that is focused on treating BDD. These improvements are generally similar to those found in medication studies (see Chapter 11). The studies in Table 12–1 found improvement in the following areas with CBT treatment for BDD:

BDD symptoms: In all studies, core BDD symptoms significantly improved by the end of treatment. Treated patients spent less time obsessing about their appearance and less time performing BDD rituals. In addition, they were better able to control their obsessions and rituals. After treatment, BDD obsessions and behaviors caused less distress and less interference in day-to-day functioning. Treated patients also avoided situations less because of BDD.

Depressive symptoms: Some studies looked at change in depressive and anxiety symptoms, and found that these symptoms also significantly improved.

Insight: In Dr. Neziroglu's case series, insight tended to improve, with people developing more realistic and accurate beliefs about their body defects.

Body image: In one study, women with BDD who received CBT felt more physically attractive and more satisfied with their appearance compared to those on a waiting list who didn't receive CBT. Feelings of low self-worth in connection with weight and shape also improved.

Self-esteem: One BDD study looked at self-esteem, finding that it improved more in women who received CBT than in those on a waiting list who didn't get CBT.

Social anxiety: Another BDD study, which measured social anxiety, found that it diminished significantly more in people treated with CBT compared to those on a waiting list who didn't get CBT.

Daily functioning: Studies have shown that CBT reduces impairment in functioning specifically due to BDD obsessions and rituals.

Taken together, these results are very promising and encouraging. They indicate that CBT often improves not only the core BDD features of preoccupation, distress, and impairment in functioning but also many other important aspects of the disorder. In brain imaging studies of similar disorders, such as obsessive compulsive disorder (OCD), CBT (like serotonin-reuptake inhibitors [SRIs]) has been shown to normalize brain function. An advantage of CBT is that you learn helpful skills that you can implement for the rest of your life.

■ Rationale for Using CBT for BDD

The rationale for using CBT is that (1) as I just discussed, available research studies indicate that it's often effective for BDD; (2) CBT is the first-choice psychotherapy for disorders that are similar to BDD, such as OCD and social phobia; and (3) the "model" of how CBT works (which I discuss below) provides a theoretical rationale for why CBT should work for BDD.

Figure 12–1 shows a simplified "CBT model" for BDD symptoms. The model starts with ordinary appearance concerns. These are very common.

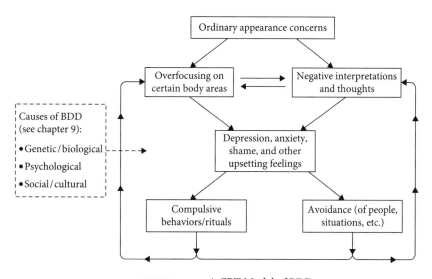

FIGURE 12–1 A CBT Model of BDD

We all have some minor physical flaws, or things about our appearance that we don't really like, and we may occasionally think about them. People who don't have BDD disregard the flaws and don't consider them very important. They let the thoughts go and get on with their day. People with BDD, however, **overfocus** on minor flaws or imperfections, paying lots of attention to them. They also **interpret and react** *to* things they don't like about their body differently than people without BDD do. People with BDD evaluate flaws—or even normal-looking body parts—very negatively, considering them to be ugly and important. They may also think that the flaws mean that they're defective as a person—even inadequate or worthless. This overfocusing, preoccupation, and negative interpretation, shown in Figure 12–1, probably develops from some of the risk factors discussed in Chapter 9, such as a biological vulnerability, perfectionism, or certain childhood experiences.

As Figure 12–1 shows, this negative thinking in turn triggers distressing feelings such as depression, anxiety, fear, and shame. To try to reduce, or cope with, these negative thoughts and feelings, people with BDD do rituals like skin picking and mirror checking, and they avoid situations where they feel anxious, such as being around other people.

Unfortunately, these behaviors have a rebound effect and actually keep negative thinking going. As Figure 12–1 shows, rituals (such as mirror checking) keep the person focused on how they look. They reinforce selective attention, overfocusing on minor flaws, and the negative thinking and feelings that triggered the rituals in the first place. By doing rituals and avoiding anxiety-provoking situations, the person never learns that things would go okay if they just faced the situation without doing any rituals.

CBT techniques target different pieces of this model (Figure 12–1). Cognitive restructuring focuses on changing negative thinking and negative interpretations of minor or nonexistent flaws. It also helps you develop more accurate and helpful beliefs. Perceptual retraining helps you change your negative thinking about your body and helps you stop overfocusing on physical details and tiny flaws. Ritual (response) prevention helps decrease rituals (such as mirror checking), and exposure/behavioral experiments help you stop avoiding situations that cause anxiety and increases comfort in those situations.

■ Frequently Asked Questions about CBT

Some people have concerns about CBT. Here are questions they ask:

Shouldn't I Be Able to Feel Better about Myself Without Being In Therapy?

It isn't realistic for most people to try to recover from BDD on their own. As discussed in Chapter 7 and throughout this book, BDD can cause major problems for people. You can try CBT techniques yourself, and if your symptoms are very mild and you're highly motivated, this may be helpful. But it isn't sufficient for most people. Most people with BDD (just like people with other disorders for which CBT is often used) need professional help. There's no need to feel badly about this; BDD is a serious illness. In CBT treatment, you and the therapist work together as a team, and you learn how to become your own therapist after the treatment ends, so you can keep your skills sharp.

Will CBT Just Mask My Real Problems?

No. BDD symptoms themselves are the "real problem" that needs to be fixed, and this is what CBT focuses on. Some people who've experienced childhood abuse or other life stressors think this is why they have BDD, and that this is what they should focus on in treatment. While such experiences may contribute to why a person gets BDD, they aren't the only cause (see Chapter 9). It's important for your therapist to know if you've had troubling life experiences, or have other major problems, but CBT works for BDD without extensively discussing or resolving these issues.

Exposure Sounds Scary—Is It Too Hard?

With exposure, you will face situations that will make you somewhat anxious. But exposure goes step-by-step so the anxiety isn't overwhelming. You start with easier situations and gradually face harder ones, as you become more comfortable and start to master your fears. Your therapist should only go as fast as you can handle. You and the therapist work as a team, so you'll have a lot of input about the exposures you do.

I'm Busy–Will CBT Take A Lot of Time?

CBT sessions usually take about 50 minutes to 1 hour each week. This might sound like a lot, but there are about 112 waking hours in a week, so this is less than 1% of your waking time. Even with some travel to your therapist added in, it isn't a lot. You'll also need to do about 45 to 60 minutes of homework a day, but this is often integrated into your daily life, so it may not take a lot of extra time.

By doing CBT, you'll probably **save** time. Probably one of the reasons you're busy (if you are) is that you're wasting time by doing BDD rituals and being distracted by your obsessions. CBT will help you cut down on these things, which will free up time for other (more enjoyable!) activities.

I'm Too Depressed to Do CBT—What Can I Do About That?

CBT often improves depression. So it's worth making your best effort to do CBT, even if you're depressed. But if you're severely depressed, it will be harder—and maybe not possible—to do CBT. Depression can sap your motivation and concentration, and can make it hard to do even the simplest task, even getting out of bed.

If you're very depressed, it may help to try an SRI medication along with CBT. The SRI is likely to improve your depression, which may make it easier to do CBT. You could also try an SRI first and then start CBT after the SRI improves your mood, energy, concentration, and motivation.

I've Done CBT Before But I Didn't Get Better. Should I Try It Again?

There are many possible reasons for why you didn't get better. Here are just a few: (1) You might not really have had CBT. Perhaps your therapist wasn't really trained in CBT or didn't stay focused on CBT techniques. (2) You might not have been motivated enough at the time to really learn CBT skills, or you might not have done enough homework to learn them. (3) There may have been a problem in the treatment—for example, the exposures may have been too hard, or not challenging enough. (4) You might have been too depressed (see the earlier question). (5) You might not have had frequent enough sessions or continued the treatment for long enough.

If you had one of these problems, or another problem that interfered with CBT, it's worth trying it again. Even if you had good CBT, it may still be worth trying again, perhaps with more frequent or longer sessions, a different therapist, or some other change, to see if it works better this time.

■ Doing CBT for BDD

The CBT approach discussed in this book has some things in common with CBT for disorders that are similar to BDD, such as social phobia, OCD, and depression. But because BDD differs from these other disorders (see Chapter 14), CBT for BDD differs too. It's likely that as more treatment research is done, some of the currently recommended techniques will be modified to make them even more effective.

The First Steps

Before you start CBT, it's important to take a few essential steps.

(1) **First, you need to find a therapist who's specifically trained in CBT and is familiar with treating BDD:** Most therapists and counselors aren't trained to do CBT. You can ask over the phone, before you even make an appointment,

whether the therapist does CBT and has treated patients with BDD. If you have trouble finding a CBT-trained therapist, some of the resources listed in Chapter 16 may be helpful. You'll need to meet with the therapist for an evaluation to confirm that you have BDD and discuss treatment options.

(2) You need to be motivated for treatment and willing to do homework between sessions: CBT isn't just done **to** you. You aren't a passive recipient of the treatment, which magically makes you better. Rather, you learn specific skills with your therapist's guidance. It's like learning to play soccer or play the piano. You need to be motivated to learn, and you need to practice! If you aren't sure whether you want to do CBT, you can meet with the therapist to learn more about the treatment. I'd encourage you to give it a try—it can really turn your life around!

(3) Is this the right time to focus therapy on BDD? For some people, it may be best to work on another problem first. For example, if you also have an eating disorder and your weight is dangerously low, this may need attention first. Or if you have a serious problem with alcohol or drugs, it's probably best to get this problem under control before you do CBT for BDD. Or if you're going through a major life crisis that isn't BDD related, you might want to resolve this problem first.

Starting CBT for BDD: A Few Essential Building Blocks

Once you decide to start CBT, there are a few things you and your therapist will do to lay the groundwork for learning the core CBT skills:

(1) Learning more about BDD and CBT: Your therapist will discuss BDD and CBT with you (i.e., provide psychoeducation) and answer your questions.

(2) Developing a model of your BDD: You need to discuss your BDD symptoms in some detail, so you and your therapist can develop a "model" (understanding) of your CBT. You can use Figure 12–1 as a guide, filling in some of your negative thoughts, what rituals you do, what situations you avoid, and so on. You and your therapist will then use this model to help tailor the treatment specifically to your symptoms.

(3) Setting goals: It's important to set goals for the treatment. For example, one goal might be to return to school. Another might be to cut back on mirror checking, develop friendships, or start dating. The more specific you make your treatment goals, the better.

You'll then begin to learn the core CBT skills discussed in this chapter: cognitive restructuring, exposure, and ritual (response) prevention. Usually, CBT involves all of these skills. Some of the additional skills I discuss subsequently, such as mirror retraining and habit reversal (if you pick your skin or pull/pluck your hair), may also be helpful.

Cognitive Restructuring (Evaluating and Changing Self-Defeating Thoughts)

We're thinking all the time, even though we aren't always aware of our thoughts. They can run through our head so quickly, or "automatically," that we hardly notice them. Sometimes our thoughts are pleasant, sometimes they're neutral, and sometimes they're upsetting. The thoughts that constantly pop into our minds are very powerful. They're so powerful, in fact, that they determine how we feel. They can make us feel happy, anxious, irritated, or upset. Our thoughts also affect how we behave.

Here's an example. If you hear a loud noise in the middle of the night and think it's a burglar, you'll feel frightened and probably call the police and maybe hide under the bed. But what if you think the noise was caused by your cat knocking a book off a shelf? You might simply feel a little annoyed and go back to sleep. So what you **think** is happening—how you **interpret** the situation—will affect how you feel (frightened versus annoyed) and how you behave (calling the police and hiding vs. going back to sleep). So it isn't the situation itself that determines what you feels, but how you interpret and perceive the situation.

Most people assume that their interpretation of situations or events is true. You may not even be aware that you're making an interpretation, because this happens so automatically and quickly. The problem is that some of our interpretations aren't accurate. Sometimes they assume the worst. This can make us feel terrible. If you assume the burglar is in the house—even if he isn't—you'll have a very unpleasant night.

The situation is similar for BDD. If you interpret a minor or even nonexistent flaw as something that's terrible or horrendous, you'll feel bad. But if you don't interpret it as something terrible, you'll feel better. As I discussed earlier in this chapter and as shown in Figure 12–1, everyone has ordinary negative thoughts about their appearance, at least occasionally. But people with BDD evaluate the flaw very negatively, and they consider it to be very important. It isn't how they **actually look** that's the problem—instead, it's their **interpretation and evaluation** of how they look. Figure 12–1 shows how this negative interpretation starts a cascade of negative feelings and problematic behaviors.

Let's use Keisha as an example (see Figure 12–2). Keisha filled out the previously discussed CBT model shown in Figure 12–1 for herself. Her CBT model is shown in Figure 12–2. While looking in the mirror, she thought, "I have a pimple on my face today." Instead of letting the thought go, Keisha zeroed in on the pimple and thought, "Oh, no—everyone's going to notice it and think I look really bad!" Then she focused on it even more and started thinking that people wouldn't want to be with her because she looked so bad. She started feeling upset, nervous, and ashamed. Then she scrutinized the pimple with a magnifying mirror, which made it look much worse to her and also made her notice some tiny bumps she hadn't seen before. She started picking at them. Because she was so upset and ashamed, she was late for school and didn't sit with her friends at lunch.

When she saw the pimple, what if Keisha hadn't zeroed in on it and had such a negative interpretation of it? What if she hadn't had the thought that everyone would notice the pimple, think she looked really bad, and wouldn't want to be with her? What if, instead, she'd thought something like, "I have a little pimple; it will probably be gone by tomorrow"? She probably wouldn't have felt so upset. Nor would she have stared in the mirror, picked at her skin, and avoided lunch with her friends. She wouldn't have gone down the BDD road of rituals and avoidance.

With cognitive restructuring, you learn how to stop simply assuming that your negative thoughts and interpretations are true. You learn how to rationally examine and evaluate your self-defeating thinking, identify errors in your thinking, and develop more accurate and helpful beliefs. This, in turn, will diminish the unpleasant feelings that your negative thinking causes.

Filling Out a Thought Record

Cognitive restructuring is done by filling out a form called a "**thought record**" (shown in Box 12–1). It's best to fill out a thought record right after you've

---

BOX 12–1	*Thought Record for Cognitive Restructuring*			
Triggering Situation	**Negative Thoughts**	**Feelings**	**Thinking Errors**	**Rational Response**

You can also use this form for core beliefs (see text).

had a negative thought (or as soon as possible). Or you can fill one out before you go into a situation that you anticipate will be difficult to prepare yourself and cope better with the situation. The more thought records you fill out, the more helpful this exercise will be.

It's important to actually fill out the thought record on paper; this process clarifies your thinking. But once you get the hang of it, you can "fill out the form" in your head, while you're actually in a triggering situation, so you can cope with the situation better at the moment it's occurring.

Box 12–1 is a blank thought record you can use. You can carry blank forms with you, so you can fill them out whenever you have a upsetting thought about how you look. Keisha's thought record has been filled out as an example (Box 12–2). (Her thought record is taken from the top of her CBT model, which is shown in Figure 12–2.)

Here are the steps involved in filling out a thought record:

Step 1: Triggering situation (column 1): Write down the situation you were in when you had the negative thought. This is the "triggering situation."

BOX 12–2   *Keisha's Thought Record*

Triggering Situation	Negative Thoughts	Feelings/ Emotions	Thinking Errors	Rational Response
Getting ready for school and looking in the bathroom mirror	Everyone's going to notice it and think I look really bad! No one will want to be with me	Upset, nervous, ashamed	Fortune-telling Mind reading All-or-nothing thinking	I can't be sure what will happen; my friends are always happy to see me

---

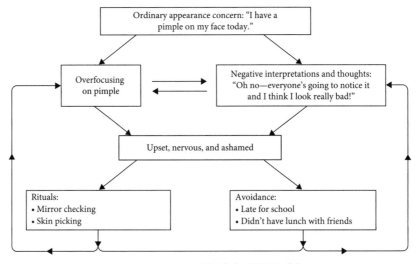

FIGURE 12–2 Keisha's CBT Model.

To identify a triggering situation, ask yourself: "What situation was I in when I felt upset?" For Keisha, this was looking in the mirror in her bathroom when she was getting ready for school.

Step 2: Negative thought (column 2): Write down your negative thought. For Keisha, this was "Everyone's going to notice it and think I look really bad! No one will want to be with me."

It can take a lot of practice to learn how to identify your negative thoughts. They can be so "automatic" that we hardly realize we're thinking them. They're like a thinking "habit." To identify the negative thought it can help to first notice that you felt upset or anxious or worried. Then ask yourself, "What was just going through my mind? What thought made me feel upset?" Here are some examples of negative BDD thoughts:

- She must be thinking I look hideous.
- I'll never have a good time at the party because everyone will be staring at me.
- No one will want to talk with me because of my ugly jaw.
- This haircut is a total disaster! I definitely can't go out tonight.
- Those boys must be laughing at me because my skin is so bad.

Step 3: Feelings/emotions (column 3): Then write down how the thought made you feel. Did it make you feel sad, unhappy, anxious, panicked, worried, frightened, ashamed, nervous, disappointed, angry, frustrated, guilty, envious, annoyed, or irritable?

Step 4: Thinking errors (column 4): The next step in filling out a thought record is to identify whether your thoughts contain any "thinking errors." (These are also called "**cognitive errors**" or "**cognitive distortions**"). Thinking errors are faulty ways of thinking. We all make thinking errors every day in our normal thinking—not all of our thoughts are actually accurate! Some common thinking errors are shown in Box 12.3.

For each negative thought, you may be able to identify one thinking error or many. Keisha's negative thoughts had at least three: fortune telling, mind reading, and all-or-nothing thinking (see Box 12–2). Tom's thought record, shown in Box 12–4, shows that his negative thought about his haircut included three thinking errors: catastrophizing, all-or-nothing thinking, and fortune telling. His negative thought about buying groceries involved mind reading, black and white thinking, labeling, and discounting the positive.

Step 5: Rational response (column 5): Now that you've identified your negative thoughts and the thinking errors they involve, try to answer them with a rational response. A rational response is a more realistic or helpful way of thinking; it's sometimes called a **rational alternative thought**. To come up with a rational response, you take the approach of a scientist or detective and ask yourself the following kinds of questions:

BOX 12-3   *Common Thinking Errors*

- **All-or-nothing (black or white) thinking**: You see yourself or the world in extremes—all good or all bad, or black versus white. The subtle shades of gray get lost. A BDD example: "With hair like this, I'll always look **totally** ugly."

- **Mind reading:** You believe you know what other people are thinking—and you assume they're having negative thoughts about you—without having sufficient evidence or without considering other, more likely, possibilities. A BDD example: "I **know** that person is thinking my teeth look funny."

- **Fortune telling:** You predict that things will turn out badly. A BDD example: "I know everyone will laugh at me if I leave the house and they see me."

- **Thinking with your feelings:** You think something must be true because you feel it so strongly, and you ignore evidence to the contrary. You take your emotions as evidence for the truth. A BDD example: "I **feel** unattractive, so I must look that way."

- **Labeling:** You put a fixed, global, and negative label on yourself without considering evidence to the contrary. A BDD example: "I'm just an ugly loser!"

- **Discounting the positive:** You claim that positive things you do or positive aspects of yourself, don't count. You transform neutral or even positive experiences into negative ones. A BDD example: "I know that I'm nice and smart, but that doesn't matter! All that matters is my stomach." Or when someone tells you that you look good, you don't believe them, and you think they're just being nice. This is why people with BDD have trouble accepting compliments.

- **Negative filtering:** This is similar to "discounting the positive." You focus on the negatives and ignore the positives and the bigger picture. A BDD example: "The only feature anyone notices is my ugly chin."

- **Personalization:** You believe that other people are reacting to **you**, without considering other, more likely, explanations for their behavior. A BDD example: You assume that a look of disgust on someone's face is directed toward you rather than something else.

- **Overgeneralization:** You make far-reaching, global conclusions on the basis of a single interaction or event. A BDD example: "I didn't get asked out this weekend. I'm **never** going to go out on a date. No one in the **whole world** likes me!"

- **Catastrophizing:** You exaggerate the negative aspects of an event and view negative events as catastrophic, without considering other possibilities. A BDD example: "This haircut is such a disaster that life's not worth living anymore."

- **Unfair comparisons:** You have unrealistically high standards and focus primarily on the few people who meet those standards, finding yourself inferior in comparison. A BDD example: You compare yourself with airbrushed models in magazines and feel upset that you don't look as good as they do.

		BOX 12–4	Tom's Thought Record		

Triggering Situation	Negative Thoughts	Feelings/ Emotions	Thinking Errors	Rational Response
Getting a haircut	This haircut is a total disaster. I won't be able to go out tonight	Panic and shame	Catastrophizing All-or-nothing thinking Fortune telling	This haircut isn't perfect, but it isn't the end of the world. I may not like it, but I can live with it and go out tonight. I can't predict how my friends will react, anyway. Besides, they like me for who I am (sense of humor, friendliness), not because of my hair.
Buying groceries	That woman must be looking at me and thinking I'm totally ugly because my jaw's so wimpy.	Humiliation, anxiety, anger	Mindreading Black and white thinking Labeling Discounting the positive	She might be thinking I'm ugly, but how do I know for sure? She probably has lots of other things to think about, like whether she's buying the right groceries. I really can't read people's minds. People tell me how smart I am and what a good personality I have. Maybe they're right!

- What's the evidence that my thought is true? What's the evidence against it?
- Is there an alternative view or explanation?
- Is my thought logical? Is there another way of thinking that might be more rational?
- Is this thought helpful right now? If not, is there a more helpful thought?

The thinking errors you identified can help you come up with a rational response. For example, if you were mind reading, your rational response might include something like this: "I don't have special powers, and I can't really read people's minds...." Or, if you identified "fortune telling," your rational response might be "I really can't predict the future; this (fill in feared event) could happen, but it might not." Some people find it helpful to identify at least one rational response in response to each thinking error.

Your rational response needs to be at least somewhat believable and credible. When he was buying groceries, Tom's rational response included, "She might be thinking I'm ugly, but how do I know for sure? She probably has lots of other things to think about." His rational response wasn't "I know she's thinking I look great"—because he didn't have any evidence that this was true.

Also, your rational response shouldn't just be positive thinking. With positive thinking, you simply try to convince yourself of something positive. The problem is that this often doesn't help you feel much better. In contrast, with cognitive restructuring you objectively evaluate the evidence for and against your belief, and you come up with a more realistic thought. It should be more helpful than positive thinking because it's based on evidence, not on what you wish or hope is true.

After you complete a thought record, you can check in on how you're feeling. Are you still as anxious, fearful, or worried? If you came up with a good rational response, these upsetting feelings shouldn't be quite as strong.

Additional Approaches for Healing Negative Core Beliefs

The negative thoughts I've been focusing on so far are thoughts about appearance like "This haircut is a total disaster," or "I know that person was staring at my fat legs." Now I'm going to discuss "deeper" types of negative thinking and beliefs. These are more complex thoughts about appearance and deeper beliefs that we have about ourselves as a person.

We all have "deeper" level beliefs that underlie our negative automatic thoughts. The deeper beliefs can also be unrealistic and trigger distressing feelings. One type is called "intermediate level" beliefs. These are negative, rigidly held "rules" or assumptions that you have about your appearance—for example, "All that matters is my hair; my personality and talents aren't as important." Often, these beliefs are expressed as "should statements"—for example, "I should look perfect." Or they can be expressed as "if-then" statements—for example, "If I can't make my skin look better, then I'll never go on a date." These beliefs often confuse appearance with happiness. Here are some intermediate-level beliefs:

- "If I looked better, my life would be fine."
- "If my appearance is defective, I'm inadequate as a person."
- "I have to look perfect."

Core beliefs are the "deepest level" beliefs. They are global beliefs about yourself, your future, and the world around you. People with BDD usually have very negative core beliefs about their worth as a person, such as "I'm inadequate," "I'm worthless," or "No one will ever love me."

Here are some examples:

- "I'm unlovable and worthless."
- "No one will ever accept me."
- "I'll always be alone."
- "I'm defective."

To identify core beliefs, you examine your negative thought (one you put on your thought record) and ask yourself questions like the following:

- "What does this negative thought mean about me?
- "And if that were true, what would that mean about me?"
- "What's so bad about that"?

Keisha could ask herself: "What does my thought about my pimple mean about me?" What she came up with is the belief that she'd always be alone. Some of the thought records you've done already might contain some core beliefs.

It's important to try to identify these deeper negative beliefs and to develop healthier, more accurate beliefs. This will have a positive effect on how you view yourself and feel about yourself. You can start working on core beliefs after you've done a lot of thought records with more automatic types of thoughts, like the ones I discussed earlier, and after you've done some exposure, ritual prevention, and perceptual (mirror) retraining.

Here are some approaches for developing more accurate and healthier core beliefs:

(1) Thought record: You can include core beliefs in your thought record. In column 2, Keisha could have also written the following under the thought about her pimple: "I'll always be alone." Then she would have completed the rest of the thought record for this core belief (just as she did for the negative automatic thought). On her thought record, she wrote down the feelings caused by her core belief: sad and lonely. Then she identified the thinking errors her core belief involved: fortune telling, catastrophizing, and over-generalization. Then she came up with a rational response: I don't know for sure that I'll always be alone; I don't have any evidence that this will really happen. Plus, people say they like me because I have a good personality and I'm a loyal friend.

(2) Self-esteem pie: Often, core beliefs reflect low self-esteem—feelings of inadequacy or worthlessness. Doing the self-esteem pie exercise with your therapist can help you develop a more realistic picture of your self-worth. First you draw a circle (a "pie") and divide it into different pieces that reflect what you base your self-esteem on. The size of each piece should reflect how important each item is. For most people with BDD, their first pie shows that they base their self-esteem mostly on their appearance—and mostly **negative** aspects of their appearance.

Then work with your therapist to try to identify some positive things about yourself, or, at least, things that other people would consider your positive traits. For example, is there anything you like about your appearance, do you do a good job at work, are you smart, do you have any positive personality traits, do you have any talents, do you manage your money well, are you creative, are you loyal, and so on? Then redraw your self-esteem pie, first filling in your positive characteristics. Fill in as many things as you can. Then fill in your weaknesses and appearance last. The goal is to come up with a more balanced and accurate pie—and one that doesn't involve the thinking error of discounting the positive!

This self-esteem exercise can also help you come up with a rational response for your thought records. You may have noticed that on his thought record, Tom wrote down some of his positive traits.

(3) Turning the tables: When doing this exercise with your therapist, you try to change your perspective by asking yourself questions like, "If I noticed that one of my friends had a few pimples on his face, what would I think of him?" "Would I respect him less?" "Would I like him less?" Answering questions like these can help you realize that having a few pimples isn't that important and doesn't affect what you think of other people. In fact, research has shown that people with BDD judge other people on the basis of many things, not just their looks. So why assume that everyone else is judging **you** based on how you look? Think about what kinds of things you like and value in your friends. This might also help you fill out your own self-esteem pie and rational responses on your thought records; maybe you have some of the same positive traits.

(4) Writing a letter to your imagined children: In this exercise, you pretend to have a son or daughter who has the same beliefs you do about their looks, and you write a letter to them in which you give them guidance and advice about their appearance worries. Keisha's letter started with, "Dear Daughter, Please don't worry so much about one small pimple—it will probably go away in a day or two! You're a wonderful girl. You have so many talents, and your parents and friends think you're wonderful. They really won't care if you have a little pimple on your face . . . So don't spend so much time in the mirror, and please sit with your friends when you go to school. They like spending time with you! . . ." If you say things like this to your imagined child, why wouldn't they also apply to you?

Exposure and Behavioral Experiments

Once you've learned some of these cognitive exercises, you can move on to exposure (while continuing the cognitive exercises). Exposure involves gradually facing situations that you fear and avoid because of BDD. For many people, these are social situations. The goal of exposure is to feel free to go into various situations and feel more comfortable in them, rather than avoiding them. You learn to face your fears.

As we've discussed (see Figure 12–1), avoidance is an understandable result of your negative thoughts and feelings. If you worry that everyone's laughing at you, and you feel ashamed as a result, you might want to avoid being around other people. You might also engage in other types of avoidance, such as turning your head or body away from people. The problem with avoiding things—like social situations, dating, school, work, or trips—is that it robs you of pleasure, satisfaction, and a more productive life.

Avoidance also prevents you from seeing how things might have turned out if you didn't avoid the situation. For example, if you always wear a hat or heavy makeup when you go out, you don't have a chance to see if people react to you in an unusual way if you go out without them. Or if you never go to a party, you never have a chance to find out that you might enjoy going. If Keisha had sat with her friends at lunch, she would have found that nothing bad happened. In fact, her friends were always happy to see her, and they liked talking with her. When she avoided lunch, she was just left with her worries, and she assumed they were true.

Exposure does cause a little anxiety—in fact, it has to in order to work. But if you do exposure right, the anxiety won't be overwhelming. You do it step-by-step so you first master easier exposures and then move onto harder ones when you're ready. You can do cognitive restructuring before exposure so you go into the situation with more realistic and accurate thinking; this can make exposure more tolerable.

It can also help to first imagine yourself in the anxiety-provoking situation (this is called **imaginal exposure**). After doing this, you can actually go into the feared situation (in vivo exposure). In vivo exposure is more effective, so you'll want to be sure you do this.

It's important to stay in the feared situation until your anxiety decreases. This way, it will be easier to go into the situation the next time. And you'll need to do exposures repeatedly—ideally, every day—so you feel more comfortable and confident in various situations. Doing exposures is a little like watching a scary movie. The first time you see it, you'll be on edge and maybe even a little frightened. But if you see it over and over again, you calm down and might even find it boring.

While you're doing the exposure, it helps to test your prediction about what will happen in the situation and see whether it comes true. This is called a **behavioral experiment**. It's like cognitive restructuring, in the sense that you take the perspective of a scientist or detective and gather evidence about the accuracy of your thinking. However, cognitive restructuring is initially done primarily with pen and paper, by filling out thought records (later it can be done in your head). In contrast, behavioral experiments are done primarily in a real-life situation, during exposure.

To do exposure you follow a number of steps. It's important to follow all of the steps and to fill out the exposure/behavioral experiment form. An example of this form is shown in Box 12–5. You fill out the first half of the form **before** the exposure and the second half **after you've completed** the exposure.

The Basic Steps

(1) Make an exposure hierarchy: With your therapist's assistance, you first develop a list of situations that you avoid or that make you anxious. (See blank Hierarchy for Exposure form [Box 12–5].) You rank order the situations according to how anxious you think you'll feel in the situation and how much you avoid the situation. Use a rating of 0 to 100, where 0 reflects no anxiety or no avoidance, and 100 reflects a state of panic or complete avoidance. A rating of 50 reflects moderate distress or avoidance. The number assigned often reflects such factors as the number of people in the situation, familiarity of these people, the distance of the exposed body part from others, and how bright it is.

When selecting situations for your hierarchy, think back to your goals for the treatment. For example, if one of your goals was to be able to attend a party at school, you can include this on your hierarchy form. On her form, Keisha included sitting with friends at lunch. Try to make the situations specific, and only list situations that will be feasible for you to actually enter at some point.

Lorenzo's exposure hierarchy is shown in Box 12–6. He rated going out to the mailbox a 10 for anxiety and 5 for avoidance on a scale of 0 to 100. He gave

---

BOX 12–5   *Hierarchy for Exposure*

Feared/Avoided Situation	Anxiety Rating (0–100)	Avoidance Rating (0–100)
#1 (most difficult situation):		
#2:		
#3:		
#4:		
#5:		
#6:		
#7:		
#8:		
#9:		
#10 (least difficult situation):		

BOX 12-6   *Lorenzo's Hierarchy for Exposure*

Feared/Avoided Situation	Anxiety Rating (0–100)	Avoidance Rating (0–100)
#1 (most difficult situation): Giving a toast at a social gathering	100	100
#2: Going to a party	90	90
#3: Speaking up in class	80	80
#4: Talking to a classmate or stranger face-to-face from a foot away for at least 5 minutes	70	80
#5: Talking to a classmate or stranger face-to-face for at least 5 minutes	60	60
#6: Going to class and sitting near classmates	50	50
#7: Asking a store clerk about an item	40	45
#8: Shopping—for example, grocery shopping	30	30
#9: Jogging around the neighborhood	20	20
#10 (least difficult situation): Going out to the mail-box	10	5

shopping a higher rating, because this involved being around more people, who might notice his "beet-red" face and "really weird" hair. He rated talking to a classmate or a stranger face-to-face for at least 5 minutes a 60, whereas talking with them from only a foot away was a 70 and 80 because they'd get a closer look at his face and hair.

(2) Select a situation from your hierarchy and prepare for the exposure: The next step is to plan your first exposure, using an Exposure/Behavioral Experiment Form (Box 12–7). Box 12–8 shows a form that has been completed for Lorenzo. To start, **select a situation** with a relatively low number (around 30 or 40). Starting with an activity rated a 5 or 10 is probably too easy. Lorenzo decided he would start by going grocery shopping (Box 12–8).

Then, as shown in Box 12–7, ask yourself **what aspect of the situation causes you the most distress**. For Lorenzo, the most distressing thing was thinking that people would be disgusted by his looks and move away from him (Box 12–8).

Then make a **specific prediction** about what you think will happen in the situation. This is an important part of exposure for BDD. If you don't test out a prediction during exposure, to see whether your prediction comes true or not, the exposure might not be as effective. A few guidelines for coming up with a prediction:

a) Make your prediction very specific, rather than vague: This way, it will be much easier to confirm or disconfirm it. It can help to use specific numbers

BOX 12–7   *Exposure Form/Behavioral Experiment Form*

Fill Out the Top Part *Before* **The Exposure**

My Exposure Situation (be specific)

What aspect of the situation causes me the most distress?

Negative thoughts/predictions

Preparing My Thoughts

Negative thoughts/predictions   **Rational Response**

What kinds of avoidance behaviors or rituals do I need to watch out for?

Goals for the Exposure—How will I know I did well?
1.
2.
3.

Fill This Part Out *After* **the Exposure**

Distress Rating   Beginning_____ Middle_____ End

Evaluating My Efforts:

Did I reach my goal?

Did my negative thoughts/predictions come true?

What did I learn?

How will I reward myself?

This form is based on a form developed by Dr. Sabine Wilhelm.

Fill Out the Top Part Before the Exposure

My Exposure Situation (be specific)
I'll go to the grocery store on a Saturday afternoon when it's busy to buy groceries with Juanita.

What aspect of the situation causes me the most distress?
People will be disgusted by my looks and move away from me.

Negative thoughts/predictions
80% of people will look at me with disgust (at least briefly) and move away from me within 5 seconds because I look so bad.

Preparing My Thoughts:

Negative thoughts/predictions	**Rational response**
People will be disgusted by my looks (mind reading, fortune telling)	I don't know for sure what people are thinkings, and I can't predict what will happen. Maybe they'll be focusing on other things.
People will move away from me (fortune telling)	

What kinds of avoidance behaviors or rituals do I need to watch out for?
Shopping in uncrowded aisles
Wearing my hat

Goals for the Exposure—How will I know I did well?
1. Buy everything on my grocery list
2. Stay in the store for at least 30 minutes (don't rush)
3. Don't wear my hat

Fill This Part Out After the Exposure

Distress Rating   Beginning _60_ Middle _50_ End _40_

Evaluating My Efforts:

Did I reach my goal?
Yes!!

Did my negative thoughts/predictions come true?
No. About 30% of the people didn't move at all; they seemed busy picking out food or watching their kids. About 30% moved away from me. But no one looked disgusted. They were mostly looking at other things and hardly seemed to notice. About 40% moved toward me. Juanita and I agreed on this.

What did I learn?
Maybe people aren't disgusted by my looks or taking special notice of me. Maybe I don't look really weird or disgusting.

How will I reward myself?
Watch a movie with Juanita.

This form is based on a form developed by Dr. Sabine Wilhelm.

for percentages and distances. As shown in Box 12–8 Lorenzo predicted that people who saw him in the grocery store would think he looked ugly, and that at least 80% of them would look at him with disgust (at least briefly) and move away from him within 5 seconds because he looked so bad. At first, Lorenzo wasn't sure that people would react with a look of disgust, but after he gave it more thought he realized that if he really looked that strange, people wouldn't be able to totally suppress a reaction of disgust. Notice that Lorenzo specified the percentage of people he thought would look at him with disgust, and he identified a specific amount of time within which they would move away from him. If you have a vague prediction (for example, "people will look at me in the store"), it will be hard to collect good evidence, because it isn't clear how many people "some" is (is it only 1 or 50?).

b) *Come up with a prediction that won't be "confirmed" for reasons that have nothing to do with your appearance:* For example, if you predict that 20% of people will leave the checkout line in the grocery store because you look so bad, the problem is that this could happen for reasons that have nothing to do with you. People might leave the line to get some food they forgot, because they noticed that another line was shorter, because they realized they're in the "cash only" line and don't have any cash, and so on. Lorenzo's prediction—that 80% of people would look at him with disgust and move away from him within 5 seconds—would be unlikely to occur for other reasons. Before the exposure, Lorenzo and his therapist discussed the fact that some people would have to move away from him so they wouldn't bump into him. What Lorenzo needed to check out was whether **most** people (80%)—not just some of them—would move away from him within 5 seconds with a look of disgust on their face.

c) *Make a prediction that you'll learn something from:* To benefit from the exposure, choose an experiment that's likely to influence your thinking to at least some degree. If your prediction doesn't come true but your reaction is "so what," then it probably wasn't worth doing the experiment in the first place.

d) *Specify your prediction before the experiment, not after it:* To collect believable evidence, you need to plan beforehand exactly what you're testing.

The next step, before actually doing the exposure/behavioral experiment, is to **do some cognitive restructuring on paper,** focusing on the negative thoughts you think you'll have in the exposure situation. This will help you get your thinking straight before you actually do the exposure. It will make the exposure easier, because you'll be prepared with a more rational way to think when you're in the situation. As shown in Box 12–8, Lorenzo examined his negative thoughts, and he realized that they involved several thinking errors: mind reading and fortune telling. He then wrote down a rational response. You can additionally do cognitive restructuring in your head

during the exposure, while you're actually in the situation, by identifying your negative thoughts and thinking errors, and developing rational responses.

Then you write down on the Exposure/Behavioral Experiment Form **what kinds of avoidance behaviors or rituals you need to watch out for.** These are things you might be tempted to do so that you feel less anxious in the situation. Some people try to sneak these behaviors in during the exposure, but doing this unfortunately sabotages the exposure exercise. For Lorenzo, subtle avoidance behaviors were shopping only in uncrowded aisles. Another was wearing his hat so people couldn't see his hair. Doing this would sabotage his exposure by making it too easy. Also, even if Lorenzo successfully completed the exposure, he might think that it "didn't really count" because there weren't too many people around and they couldn't see his hair.

The final preparation step is to write down your **goals for the exposure.** Make sure they're very specific and achievable. Don't write down feelings— for example, not feeling anxious—as a goal. It isn't realistic to not feel anxious in the exposure situation. Also, your goal shouldn't be to do something perfectly, because most people don't do things perfectly. Also, don't have your goal be to get someone else to do something (like give you a compliment), because it's hard to control other people's behavior. Instead, focus on your own behavior. Lorenzo's goal was to buy everything on his grocery list, stay in the store for at least 30 minutes (not rush through it), shop in crowded aisles, and not put on his hat while he was in the store.

(3) Do the exposure: Now that you've filled out the first part of the exposure form as preparation, the next step is to actually do the exposure. For Lorenzo, this was actually going to the grocery store. Here are a few guidelines:

a) Don't act in an unusual way while collecting your evidence: For example, don't stare at people or follow them around to see how they're reacting to you, since this could make people uncomfortable. For this reason, they might even move away from you or look at you in an unusual way.

b) Don't distract yourself from feeling anxious: Don't try to think about something neutral or pleasant, sing a song in your head, or reassure yourself that you'll be able to do your rituals (like combing your hair) after the exposure. (It's fine, however, to do cognitive restructuring while you're in the exposure situation.) Remember not to do the subtle avoidance behaviors that you wrote down on your form—such as camouflaging or any avoidance behaviors—and don't do any rituals. These kinds of behaviors will make exposure less effective. If it's too hard to stop using camouflage right away, you can cut back on it more gradually.

c) Stay in the situation long enough to try to reach your goals and for your anxiety to diminish: This will make it easier to face the situation again. Your anxiety will initially rise, but then it will fall. It won't last forever.

Lorenzo and his girlfriend, Juanita, went to the store at a busy time. They observed that about 30% of people didn't move at all when they were around Lorenzo. They seemed to be busy deciding what food they wanted to buy. About 40% of people moved away from Lorenzo, and about 30% moved toward him. Neither Lorenzo nor his girlfriend observed any looks of disgust, even fleeting ones.

(4) After the exposure: To get maximum benefit from the exposure, be sure to complete the form as soon as you've finished the exposure. **Write down how much distress you experienced** while you were in the situation, using the 0 to 100 scale, at the beginning, middle, and end of the exposure. Did your distress diminish? If not, you'll need to consider planning the exposure differently the next time you do one. The more you do exposure in that same situation, the lower your distress levels should be.

Then write down **whether you reached your goals and whether your negative predictions came true.** Be careful not to discount any parts of the exposure that you did successfully. Then write down **what you learned from the exposure.** Lorenzo learned that maybe people weren't disgusted by his looks, and maybe they didn't particularly notice him at all. In fact, they seemed much more interested in checking the food prices or ingredients, looking at their shopping list, or keeping their children well-behaved. Lorenzo also realized that perhaps he had initially believed his prediction because he went to the grocery store only when it was nearly empty, and he barely looked at people because he was so worried that they were staring at him. So he'd never had much of an opportunity to really see if his prediction was true.

Finally, **reward yourself**—even if you didn't do the exposure perfectly! Exposure can be challenging, so if you made a good effort, do something enjoyable. Lorenzo rewarded himself by watching a movie that night with Juanita.

It's important to **review the experiment and your Exposure/Behavioral Experiment Form with your therapist.** Review whether the expected outcome occurred and what you learned. It's also important to get your therapist's feedback.

Additional Guidelines for Exposure

For exposure to work, you need to enter avoided situations repeatedly, until your anxiety diminishes. One exposure won't be enough. Work on it every day if possible, and spend at least 45 to 60 minutes a day doing exposure. With enough practice, your anxiety and fear will gradually decrease.

Once you feel more comfortable in the situation you've tried, you'll need to challenge yourself more by facing a situation with a higher rating on your exposure hierarchy. Next, Lorenzo planned an exposure in which he asked a store clerk about a grocery item, and then he did one in which he sat near a classmate in class. Eventually he did everything on his exposure hierarchy. As you move up your list, remember that you still need to keep doing the easier exposures on your list.

You can do exposure alone or with your therapist or a friend. It can be advantageous to take someone with you, because you can get their input on what happened during the exposure.

If an exposure makes you too anxious, do an exposure on your hierarchy with a lower rating. If you find that you underestimated how anxious you'd actually feel in the situation, you'll need to reevaluate your anxiety and avoidance ratings. The important thing is not to give up! If you do it right, exposure will initially make you somewhat anxious, but the more you do it, the easier it will get. And the rewards can be enormous: you'll be able to live a much freer and more enjoyable life.

Ritual (Response) Prevention

Ritual (response) prevention is preventing yourself from doing your compulsive behaviors (rituals), which are discussed in Chapter 6. The goal is to cut down on and eventually stop checking mirrors, asking for reassurance, comparing yourself with other people, measuring your body, excessively changing your clothes, or engaging in any other compulsive BDD behaviors.

The rationale for ritual prevention is that these behaviors are usually time consuming and take you away from doing more enjoyable things. They can cause other problems, like making you late for things, or keeping family or friends waiting for you while you're doing them. Even if these behaviors decrease anxiety, the relief is usually only temporary, if it occurs at all. Sometimes rituals immediately increase anxiety. And rituals just keep you focused on your appearance (as shown in Figure 12–1). For example, the more you look in the mirror, the more you feed your thoughts about not looking right. In addition, rituals can keep you from learning that nothing terrible will happen if you don't do them. For example, if you always comb your hair for an hour before you leave the house, you'll never learn that people won't shun you if you go out without doing this.

Some BDD experts focus on ritual prevention after the patient has already learned cognitive restructuring and exposure. In this case, ritual prevention should be started very soon after starting to learn exposure, because doing rituals during exposure will dilute the effectiveness of the exposure. Other experts start ritual prevention before cognitive restructuring and exposure, because bringing rituals under control quickly may possibly diminish your preoccupation and distress earlier in treatment. Regardless of when you learn ritual prevention, the most important thing is to make sure it's a key component of your treatment.

There are a number of ways to cut down on rituals:

1. Do the ritual fewer times during the day. For example, instead of checking the mirror 30 times a day, try to cut it down to 25, and then gradually cut it down even further.

2. Spend less time each time you do a ritual. For example, when you do look in the mirror, spend 10 minutes each time if you now spend 15. Gradually, spend less and less time.

3. Delay doing your rituals. For example, if you get the urge to ask someone how you look, put it off. See how long you can put it off for— the longer, the better! Eventually you'll want to stop the ritual entirely.

4. Eliminate rituals in certain situations. For example, if you do a lot of comparing, see if you can stop doing it during meetings at work, so you can focus on the meeting. Then start cutting back in other situations.

5. Make changes in your environment so it's harder to do the ritual. If you use tweezers to compulsively tweeze your eyebrows, throw them out, or let your husband keep them for you. If you compulsively shop for beauty products, get rid of your credit and debit cards.

Be creative, and try to come up with other ways to resist your rituals. One woman posted reminder signs outside her bathroom door which said "Are you SURE you really want to go in there???" This reminded her that if she did go in, she'd probably pick her skin and end up feeling much worse. She told me, "Reading the sign reminded me that I'd regret it; it got me to stop, turn around, and do something else instead."

It can help to make a list of enjoyable activities to do if you feel the urge to do a ritual. Some people put this list on the refrigerator, where they can easily find it. Also, when you do cut back on your rituals, you'll have lots more time on your hands, and you'll want to fill it with healthy, enjoyable, and productive activities.

Cutting down on your rituals will probably make you anxious initially, and you'll feel the urge to do your ritual. But don't give in! If you keep going without doing the ritual, your anxiety will eventually diminish. Cutting back gradually will make ritual prevention easier to do. And the more you practice, the easier it will get. And keep in mind that for many people, rituals often immediately increase anxiety—so by not doing them, you won't have to experience that.

If you're having trouble getting motivated to do ritual prevention, you could make a list of the advantages and disadvantages of each of your rituals, rating each advantage and disadvantage from 1 (not very important to me) to 10 (very important to me). This might help you better recognize the problems that your rituals cause you.

When you do exposures, it's important to incorporate ritual prevention into them. You'll want to cut down on—and eventually completely stop doing—rituals during your exposures. If you don't, you won't learn that things will turn out fine in the exposure situation without doing your rituals. On your Exposure/Behavioral Experiment Form (Box 12–7), you can list rituals you might be tempted to do under "What kinds of avoidance behaviors or rituals do I need to watch out for?" You can also make not doing a ritual one of the goals for an exposure. For example, an exposure goal could be to go to a party without going into the bathroom to check your hair.

Of all of the CBT techniques, ritual prevention is probably the easiest to do without the assistance of a professional therapist. Even if you don't do CBT with a therapist, I'd encourage you to try it on your own. The key to success is to be consistent in cutting down the behaviors and to watch out for subtle rituals. Once you cut down, don't let yourself start doing them more again. The more consistent you are, the more relief you'll experience and the more time you'll free up for other things.

The Basic Steps

Start by making a list of your rituals using the Ritual Form (see Box 12–9). Rate each ritual from 0 to 100 according to how hard it would be to stop it. Susan's Ritual Form is shown in Box 12–10.

Also record how much time you spend on your rituals each day. You can also keep a diary of situations that seem to trigger or worsen the ritual. This can help you become more aware of triggering situations, anticipate difficult situations, and devise techniques for dealing with them.

Once you fill out this form, try to start cutting back on your rituals, using one or more of the techniques described earlier. Start with the ritual with the lowest rating (the least anxiety-provoking one). Challenge yourself to cut

---

BOX 12–9   *Ritual Form*

Behavior/Ritual	How Hard It Would Be to Stop the Behavior
#1 (most difficult):	
#2:	
#3:	
#4:	
#5:	
#6:	
#7:	
#8:	
#9:	
#10 (easiest):	

BOX 12-10 *Susan's Ritual Form*	
Behavior/Ritual	**How Hard It Would Be to Stop the Behavior**
#1 (most difficult): Using lots of makeup (camouflaging)	100
#2: Grooming (spending too much time in the morning)	80
#3: Buying lots of beauty products	65
#4: Checking mirrors	60
#5: Changing my clothes lots of times in the morning	50
#6: Comparing myself with other people and models in magazines	40
#7 (easiest): Asking my mother for reassurance	30

back as much as you can, but be realistic with what you expect from yourself. Keep track of how much time you're spending on the ritual each day, and try your hardest to make it less and less.

After you've had some success with cutting down on the easiest one, gradually move up your Ritual Form, trying to cut back on or stop harder rituals. You can start to cut down on one ritual at a time or on several simultaneously. Eventually, the goal is to stop all of them or do them only a normal amount. If you can stop a compulsive behavior cold turkey, rather than cutting it down gradually, that's great (but this usually isn't possible).

Susan rated reassurance seeking the lowest, so she started with this behavior, gradually doing it less and less (Box 12–10). For the first week, she asked her mother for reassurance only 10 times instead of 20 times a day. For the second week, she asked only 5 times a day, and for the third week only 2 times a day. Then she stopped altogether. You could cut down on your behaviors faster or slower than this, depending on what you think you can challenge yourself to do and successfully accomplish.

Susan then moved up the list on the Ritual Form, cutting down on comparing, then clothes changing, and so on. For example, over time she gradually cut her grooming time down from 5 hours a day to only 30 minutes a day.

Here are some examples of how you can try to decrease your rituals, but keep in mind that, as I already discussed, there are many approaches you can try (for example, decreasing the time you spend, changing your environment).

Reduce and eventually stop excessive mirror checking: Checking mirrors and other reflecting surfaces (e.g., windows, backs of spoons) is one of the most important behaviors to control. Many people say they quickly feel better when they cut back or stop this behavior. Mirror checking is time consuming and often increases anxiety. Also, when you look at yourself for so long, and in such minute detail, you get a very distorted view of yourself and may feel even worse about how you look.

The goal is to have a normal relationship with mirrors (perceptual retraining, which I'll describe later, can also help you achieve this). This means not going out of your way to check mirrors, not checking them many times a day or for long periods of time, not staring in them from only an inch or two away, and being able to look in them briefly when necessary (for example, when grooming each morning). It's probably also a good idea to take down extra mirrors if you don't really need them.

Reduce and eventually stop asking for reassurance: Getting reassurance that you look okay may decrease your anxiety, but only temporarily; soon the anxiety returns, along with the urge to ask again. And quite often, a reassuring reply isn't believed anyway. The best thing is to stop asking people how you look or if you look okay.

Reduce and eventually stop excessive grooming: Try to limit grooming activities to a reasonable amount of time, for example, 15 minutes a day. Use time, rather than how you feel, to decide when to stop. Or stop excessively grooming in certain situations—while you're at work or in your car, for example.

Reduce and eventually stop getting cosmetic treatments: Many people with BDD compulsively get cosmetic procedures, which usually doesn't make them feel any better. Try stopping this altogether, but if you can't, try to delay getting it. If you're planning to get a nose job in 6 months, try putting it off for 9 months. Then when the time arrives, try putting it off for another 6 months. Instead, use the money for something that you'll value or enjoy.

Reduce and eventually stop compulsive spending: If you're spending lots of money on clothes or beauty products, make a budget that you stick to or throw out your credit cards. These products never really help you feel any better, so why waste your money on extra products you don't really need?

Reduce and eventually stop touching: Compulsively touching disliked body areas can be a problem in and of itself by distracting you and taking up lots of time. But it can also trigger other BDD behaviors, like picking at your skin if you feel a bump, shaving or plucking hairs if you feel some stubble, or rushing to the mirror to check out something that doesn't feel right. Try cutting back on this behavior. Habit reversal, which I describe subsequently, may also help.

Reduce and eventually stop comparing: Try to stop comparing yourself with perfect images on TV and in magazines. Consider canceling your subscription to beauty magazines, especially if you read lots of them. When you're talking with other people, try to notice other things about them, like what they're saying and what kind of a mood they seem to be in—rather than how they look. If you're in class, try to listen to the lecture rather than comparing yourself to the teacher or other students.

Reduce and eventually stop other compulsive BDD behaviors: Stop measuring yourself, frequently weighing yourself, and frequently changing your clothes. Get rid of the tweezers and pins you use to pick your skin. Stop any other rituals you're doing. Tell yourself that these are BDD rituals—not things you **have** to do.

Perceptual (Mirror) Retraining

Mirrors and reflecting surfaces are part of everyone's life. Because you'll sometimes unexpectedly encounter them, or need to look in them to do a normal amount of grooming, it's good to be able to do so without getting "stuck" or very upset. The goal is to be able to look in them when you need to, but to not excessively check them or gaze in them.

Ritual prevention is a very helpful technique for getting mirror checking under better control. What I'll describe here—perceptual (mirror) retraining—is an additional technique for developing a healthier relationship with mirrors and learning to see yourself more "holistically" and realistically.

The rationale for perceptual retraining is that when people with BDD look in the mirror, they usually zoom in on the disliked body areas and examine these areas in excruciating detail. They also say very negative things to themselves about the disliked areas, like "I have millions of ugly hairs all over my face!" As shown in Figure 12–1, this behavior feeds negative BDD thoughts by keeping you focused on the perceived flaws and on tiny details that other people don't notice.

Perceptual retraining interrupts this overfocusing and selective attention to appearance that feeds BDD obsessions. So when you have to look in the mirror during the day (for example, when washing your face in the morning) or when you happen to catch a glimpse of yourself in a reflecting surface, you can call upon your perceptual retraining skills so you see yourself more accurately.

With perceptual retraining, you look in the mirror from a normal distance—3- to 4-feet away for a view of your entire body and about a foot away for a view of your face. You can start with either a full-length mirror or a hand-held mirror, whichever makes you less anxious. You then describe your body in a nonjudgmental and uncritical way, going from head to toe (if using a full-length mirror). So you could describe your height, the color and length of your hair, the color of your eyes, the approximate shape of your face and breadth of your shoulders, and so on. It's probably best not to describe tiny details, as it seems that people with BDD already overfocus on tiny details and can't see the forest for the trees. The point is to learn to see **all** of you—the "big picture"—the way other people see you.

It's also important to not describe the body areas negatively (this type of "labeling" is one of the thinking errors I described earlier). So you would describe your hair as "medium brown, straight, and down to my shoulders" rather than saying it's "mud colored and stringy."

The hardest part of perceptual retraining is to not zero in on and scrutinize the areas you don't like. This is the impulse most people have. The problem is that this is mirror checking—a ritual you're trying to overcome! It gives you a very distorted view of yourself, because you overfocus on that one area and don't "see" all the rest of your body, including areas you like. You also need to avoid any urges to "fix" your appearance, like putting on more makeup, picking at your skin, or plucking hairs.

Perceptual retraining is usually done twice a day for about 5 to 10 minutes each time. You'll want to first practice it with your therapist. It's probably best to start with "easier" mirrors (those you think you look better in) and then move on to "harder" mirrors. You can also start doing this in a darker room, and then gradually do it in brighter rooms. As with exposure and ritual prevention, a gradual approach is best, because your anxiety will be more manageable. With practice, your anxiety will gradually diminish.

Other Potentially Helpful Techniques

The techniques below may be combined with the core techniques described earlier.

Habit Reversal

This is an established treatment for trichotillomania (hair pulling) that is increasingly being used for other problematic habits, such as skin picking. In BDD, it can help skin picking, hair plucking, and body touching. You first write down detailed information about your picking behavior (or hair plucking or touching) in a diary so you become more aware of your picking (this is called "**awareness training**," or "**self-monitoring**"). This can be the situation in which you picked and the length of the picking episode. Then you learn to substitute other behaviors (a "competing response") for the picking, plucking, or touching by doing something else with your hands for at least several minutes, if not longer. You could clench your fist, squeeze a soft ball, or knit. You also learn relaxation techniques, how to reward yourself for not picking, and how to use habit reversal in a wide range of situations.

Mindfulness

Mindfulness skills are psychological and behavioral versions of meditation practices from Eastern spiritual training that are increasingly being used to treat medical and mental health problems. Mindfulness involves a particular way of observing and being aware of your thoughts and emotions by focusing on them "in the moment." Rather than actively resisting your thoughts, you just watch them float by, like clouds across the sky, and gently let them go without engaging them. You also observe your thoughts in a nonjudgmental way, without criticizing them or yourself. You also become fully involved in what is happening in the moment (e.g., what your friend is saying to you, or the feel, smell, and taste of the plum you're eating). When you notice your thoughts straying to BDD (e.g., "She looks so good and I look really ugly"), you gently bring your attention back to what is happening in the moment—for example, what your friend is saying to you. You don't try to actively fight the thoughts or push them out of your mind.

This approach can potentially help you disengage from the powerful BDD obsessions that grip your mind. The perceptual (mirror) retraining exercise that I just described includes some elements of mindfulness (nonjudgmental awareness and description).

Activity Scheduling and Scheduling Pleasant Activities

This approach is often used in the treatment of depression. It consists of scheduling activities throughout the day by writing them down in an appointment book and then doing them. This includes pleasant and enjoyable activities, as well as activities that help you feel better about yourself. This approach doesn't directly target BDD symptoms, but it minimizes idle time, leaving less time for BDD obsessions and rituals. It can also improve your mood. Activity scheduling may be especially useful for people with severe BDD and depression who may find it hard, for example, to even get out of bed.

Relapse Prevention

Once you've reached your treatment goals, you'll move on to relapse prevention, which will take the last few sessions of the treatment. The goal is to help you maintain the gains you made in treatment and prepare for becoming your own therapist after treatment ends. In these sessions, you review which CBT techniques were most helpful for you and how to keep practicing them in the future. You also plan ahead for challenging situations you anticipate you'll face after you finish CBT and how you can manage them. Some ups and downs in BDD symptoms are to be expected; recognizing your vulnerable times (for example, when you're stressed) and being sure to use your CBT skills at those times will help keep your symptoms under control. It's also important to make sure that you have plenty of enjoyable and rewarding activities to do so you don't have lots of idle time that your rituals can start to fill up again. If your BDD symptoms return and persist despite using relapse prevention strategies, you'll want to see your therapist for some booster sessions (see below).

Booster Sessions

It may help to have some "booster sessions" with your therapist after you finish the treatment. This consists of checking in with your therapist to brush up on your CBT skills and to trouble shoot any rough spots you may be experiencing. You can look back at notes you wrote down during your sessions and practice your skills even more. Even if you don't have booster sessions, you're more likely to do well if you keep practicing your CBT skills after your therapy has ended.

■ What You Can Try if CBT Doesn't Work

If CBT doesn't work for you—or doesn't work as well as you'd like—the following approaches may be helpful:

1. Talk with your therapist: If you're discouraged about lack of progress, let your therapist know. He/she may be able to modify the approach to make it more successful. Also, be patient, especially at the beginning of the treatment when you're building the foundation for the treatment.

2. Try to figure out if you're doing CBT skills right: CBT skills can be challenging to learn and keep using correctly. Some people learn them well but then backslide a little (usually because they aren't practicing them enough). Faulty ways of thinking can creep into your rational response when doing cognitive restructuring. It can be challenging to design a good exposure. And some people compulsively check the disliked body areas during perceptual (mirror) retraining. If you don't seem to be doing the skills correctly, work with your therapist to learn them or get back on track if you mastered them in the past.

3. Are you practicing your CBT skills enough?: Are you doing enough homework every day? Are you frequently practicing and using all of the skills you've learned? If not, this may be why treatment isn't working. If the treatment is too hard, tell your therapist so he or she can make it more doable for you. Remind yourself that it's worth it to work hard at CBT—most people get better with CBT!

4. Consider more frequent or longer treatment sessions: More intensive treatment may be more effective for you. Longer sessions, in particular, may allow you to learn things in your session by actually doing them with your therapist (e.g., longer exposures).

5. Consider involving a family member or friend in your treatment: Sometimes it helps to have a family member or good friend learn something about CBT and help out by being an "ancillary coach" at home. They won't be able to take your therapist's place, but they may be able to help by encouraging you to do your homework and practice your skills. They can also help with such things as coming up with rational responses when doing cognitive restructuring, or helping you cut down on rituals. Having a friend or family member come to one or a few of your sessions with your therapist may be all that's needed for them to help.

6. Consider taking an SRI: If CBT has helped you somewhat, an SRI may help you improve even more. Or if you're too depressed to do CBT, an SRI can make it possible to do CBT by improving your mood, energy, concentration, and motivation. If your BDD is very severe, an SRI can also make you less anxious and make it easier for you to leave the house and try exposure and behavioral experiments. SRIs and CBT work very well together.

■ Other Kinds of Therapy

Non-CBT types of psychotherapy haven't been studied to determine whether they help BDD. This type of research is greatly needed. In the meantime, given the lack of evidence that they work, they aren't currently considered "first-choice" therapies for BDD. Nonetheless, some people may benefit from them, depending on the specifics of their situation. Some of these therapies/treatments (for example, a self-help group or family therapy) can be used at the same time a person is getting CBT or an SRI.

Insight-Oriented Psychotherapy

Insight-oriented psychotherapy, also known as psychodynamic or exploratory psychotherapy, is a type of "talking therapy." This approach focuses on increasing self-understanding and bringing about behavioral change (e.g., improving relationships with others) through exploration of one's perceptions and interactions with others. Better understanding of yourself, awareness of your inner life and motivations, and improvement in your problems may result.

Available research evidence, although it's extremely limited, suggests that this type of treatment alone—as well as psychoanalysis alone—is generally ineffective for BDD symptoms. However, if you have other problems, such as long-standing problems in relationships or a crisis in your life, this treatment may be helpful.

Supportive Psychotherapy

Supportive psychotherapy is another type of talking therapy that emphasizes the creation of emotional support and a stable, caring relationship with patients. The therapist focuses more on providing support than on increasing patients' understanding of themselves. Components of this approach often include advice, learning new social skills, and assistance in problem solving.

The goal is to help patients attain the highest possible level of functioning. In reality, many therapists combine elements of supportive psychotherapy and insight-oriented psychotherapy.

For people with BDD, this kind of therapy offers understanding and support for their struggles with the disorder. It can help BDD sufferers cope better with life. Often, at least a little supportive therapy is provided as part of medication treatment, and a good CBT therapist will offer some support as well. Currently, however, given the lack of evidence that this type of therapy helps BDD, it isn't recommended as the only treatment for BDD or as a first-choice treatment for BDD. However, it may help people with BDD cope better with BDD or deal with other problems such as life stressors.

Couples and Family Therapy

Family meetings and couples or family therapy also aren't recommended as a first-choice or only treatment for BDD, but they may be helpful in combination with CBT and/or medication treatment. It can be helpful for the treating clinician to meet with family members, at least once, to get to know them and hear their view of the problem. Family members often find it helpful to learn about BDD—what it is and what the treatment options are. If family members participate in BDD rituals, family meetings can include coming up with ways to avoid being part of them.

More extended family meetings or formal couples or family therapy may be helpful for selected individuals, particularly families of children and adolescents with BDD. This approach may increase understanding of BDD's effect on the patient and the family, provide a forum for devising coping strategies, and teach family members how to assist in CBT. Other family problems, if present, can also be addressed. Parents or guardians will need to be involved to at least some extent in the treatment of their children or adolescents, regardless of what type of treatment they receive.

Group Therapy

The therapies described earlier—CBT, insight-oriented psychotherapy, supportive psychotherapy, or family therapy—can be provided in a group rather than individually. Based on current knowledge, group CBT is probably more likely to help BDD symptoms than other types of group therapy.

Eye Movement Desensitization and Reprocessing

Eye movement desensitization and reprocessing (EMDR) is a newer therapy that's being used to treat a variety of mental disorders. It still isn't clear how effective this treatment is. One small report was published in which EMDR was used to treat seven patients with BDD, six of whom improved. This report is intriguing; however, it is anecdotal, in the sense that standard rating scales weren't used to assess BDD severity and other symptoms. It also lacked a control group. Given these limitations, as well as the small number of patients and the fact that there is, to my knowledge, only one report on EMDR, it's premature to recommend EMDR for BDD. Also, I'm not aware of a convincing theoretical rationale for why this treatment should work for BDD. Nonetheless, non-CBT therapies like EMDR need to be studied to determine whether they might be effective for BDD.

Hypnosis

Hypnosis hasn't been studied for BDD, so it isn't recommended to treat this disorder. Some of my patients tried hypnosis for BDD but were too anxious, tense, and preoccupied to be successfully hypnotized.

Vocational Rehabilitation

Some people—particularly those who've been underemployed or unemployed for a long time—may benefit from a formal vocational rehabilitation program. Improvement with CBT or medication may get them to the point where they can usefully participate in such a program. For someone who hasn't been working, the first step may be a volunteer job, with gradually increasing hours, then perhaps a part-time paying job. Some people may be able to start working immediately with the support of a vocational rehabilitation program.

Drug and Alcohol Treatment

It's generally best for people with BDD who abuse drugs or alcohol to also be in a treatment program that focuses specifically on their drug or alcohol problem, even if they think their substance abuse is caused by BDD. It's important, however, that the treatment program's philosophy supports treatment with an SRI and/or CBT for BDD symptoms.

Self-Help Groups

The effectiveness of self-help groups for BDD hasn't been studied. However, it's unlikely that, by themselves, they would be adequate treatment for most people with BDD. BDD is a serious disorder that requires professional treatment. However, depending on the nature of the self-help group, they may potentially offer helpful support and advice, assuming the group members are knowledgeable about BDD and endorse CBT and medication treatment (see Chapter 16 for resources).

■ Tailoring Treatment to You

Your treatment plan needs to be tailored to your individual needs and life situation. I recommend that everyone with BDD be treated with an SRI and/or CBT. I'd suggest that the CBT you get generally follow the guidelines in this chapter, but it will need to be tailored to your specific symptoms and needs.

Some patients benefit from some of the other types of therapy I've described, as an additional treatment. If you're severely ill, you may benefit from more intensive treatment in a day hospital setting or a residential setting (see Chapter 16). If you have other disorders, in addition to BDD, they may require additional medications or a different kind of therapy. You should get the advice of a psychiatrist, a clinical psychologist, or other licensed mental health professional to make this determination.

Additional research on psychotherapy for BDD is greatly needed. More research will enable us to better determine how well CBT works, which CBT treatment components are most effective, and whether other components should be added. Research is also needed to find out for whom CBT works best and how to tailor it specifically to children and adolescents. Scientific research may also lead to the development of other types of therapy for BDD.

In the meantime, I encourage you to find a therapist who does CBT for BDD and to give the treatment a good try. It can be very helpful for BDD, and you'll learn excellent skills that you can use for the rest of your life.

13. Cosmetic Treatments: Surgery, Dermatologic, Dental, and Other Treatments

Even though there are effective treatments for body dysmorphic disorder (BDD), most people seek and receive treatments that don't seem to work. These treatments include surgery, dermatologic treatment, and other cosmetic treatments, such as dental treatment to fix "ugly" teeth. Other people get electrolysis to remove unwanted facial or body hair, join hair clubs, and try other remedies. This can waste lots of time and money. Even more concerning, people with BDD often end up bitterly disappointed when these procedures don't give them the relief they're so desperately seeking.

While more scientific research is needed to further confirm that these treatments don't work for BDD, on the basis of current knowledge I'd recommend that you avoid them: they don't seem to help, and they can even make BDD worse. Instead, I'd recommend that you try a serotonin reuptake inhibitor (SRI) or cognitive behavioural therapy (CBT), both of which appear far more effective for BDD.

■ Sophie's and Kate's Experiences

At first, Sophie was happy with her nose surgery. But after several months she became increasingly dissatisfied and had another operation. This time, she thought the surgeon ruined her nose. She even considered suing him even though other people told her how nice her nose looked (it had also looked fine before surgery).

"I don't care what other people say," she said. "He made me look like an idiot!" A third nose operation was also unsuccessful. "People still look at my nose and think it's ugly," she said. "They're thinking I look like a dog." Sophie believed this even though she'd often been asked to work as a model. "They ask me to model because they feel sorry for me because of my atrocious appearance," she said.

Kate spent thousands of dollars on skin remedies and had seen many dermatologists and plastic surgeons as well as countless cosmetologists and aestheticians for her freckle problem. She'd even managed to buy liquid nitrogen through a mail-order catalog to remove freckles from her face. "I felt desperate for treatment—I'd try anything. I constantly called the doctor when the treatment didn't seem to be working. I was an obnoxious patient."

■ How Many People Get Cosmetic Treatment for BDD and What Procedures Do They Get?

Studies have found that 3% to about half of people who seek cosmetic surgery have BDD. One study found that 7% of women seeking cosmetic surgery had BDD, whereas 33% of the men did. A study from France found a high rate of BDD in 132 people who were seeking cosmetic surgery: BDD was present in 9% of all people seeking surgery, in 25% of the men, and in 40% of those who had no defect or only a slight physical defect. Studies have also found that 9% to 14% of those who seek treatment from a dermatologist have BDD. Thus, it appears that a substantial proportion of people—especially men—who have cosmetic procedures have BDD.

What about the flip side of this question: the percentage of people with BDD who seek and receive cosmetic treatment? In two studies I conducted, which included a total of 450 people with BDD, three-quarters had sought surgery or other cosmetic treatments from doctors or other health professionals for their perceived appearance flaws. Two-thirds of the 450 people had received at least one of these treatments. Most people had received more than one treatment. One woman had sought 35 different cosmetic treatments! So people with BDD seek and receive a lot of cosmetic treatment. It's especially concerning that about 40% of children and adolescents with BDD receive cosmetic treatment for their BDD concerns.

Figure 13–1 shows these results. As you can see, dermatologic treatment was the type that was most often sought and received. This makes sense when you consider that skin and hair preoccupations are the most common BDD concerns. Topical and oral anti-acne agents such as antibiotics were the most common dermatologic treatments. These medications were followed by isotretinoin (Accutane), which is of concern because of this medicine's association with birth defects. Other treatments included dermabrasion for perceived or minimal acne, and finasteride (Propecia), minoxidil (Rogaine), and hair transplants for hair problems.

Figure 13–1 also shows that 34% of people requested surgery, and 22% actually had surgery for their BDD concerns. Smaller studies have found that an even higher percentage—26% to 40%—of people with BDD have

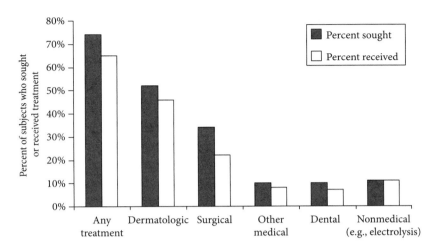

FIGURE 13–1 Dermatologic, Surgical, Dental, and Other Cosmetic Treatment Sought and Received by 450 Adults with BDD.

had surgery for BDD concerns. In my study, people who received surgery had an average of two to three surgeries, so multiple surgeries were the rule. Rhinoplasty (a nose job) was the most common procedure; other common procedures are jaw/chin surgery, breast augmentation, and liposuction.

Some people even have surgery on a body part that looks acceptable to them. They undergo the surgery to try to make the body part even more attractive and thereby "distract" peoples' attention from the "defective" body part. A handsome man was planning to have a total facial reconstruction, even though his face looked fine to him, because he thought that if his face looked even better, people might not notice his supposedly thinning hair. A beautiful young woman had a cheekbone implant so that people would look at her cheekbones instead of her "ugly" lips.

As Figure 13–1 shows, people in my study also received dental treatment, such as tooth whitening or braces; other medical treatments, such as hormones for perceived body hair problems; and treatments provided by nonphysicians, such as electrolysis.

About 30% of all requested cosmetic treatments, and nearly half of all requested surgeries, weren't actually received. The most common reason is that the doctor considered the treatment unnecessary and didn't provide it. In a survey of cosmetic surgeons, 84% had refused to operate on people with BDD. So some people had to see a lot of doctors before they could find one who agreed to provide the requested treatment.

It can be very difficult, though, to turn down requests for surgery or other cosmetic treatment because people with BDD suffer so much. "The doctors and my friends and family tried to talk me out of surgery," Andrew told me.

"But they couldn't turn me down because I was so miserable." Another man said, "I can't believe the doctor did liposuction because now I know I look fine before I ever had it done. But I was so unhappy back then that he gave in and did it."

Carlos thought he looked like an "alien" and believed he was one of the ugliest people in the world. He'd sought treatment from 3 dentists, and 16 plastic surgeons, all of whom turned him down. Finally, the seventeenth surgeon agreed to do a nose job, but Carlos hated the result so much that he sued the surgeon. When I saw him, he was so desperate for more surgery that he was planning to get into a massive car accident that would destroy his entire face.

Some people with BDD are so desperate for cosmetic treatment—but can't afford it or can't find a doctor willing to do it—that they do it themselves. One man cut into his forehead with surgical instruments to try to change its shape. (See Chapter 7 for more examples.) People who try doing surgery on themselves are unhappy with the outcome.

■ What's the Effect of Cosmetic Treatment in People with BDD?

Effect on BDD Symptoms

Cosmetic treatment doesn't appear to usually help BDD symptoms. In my studies, 81% of the treatments that were provided resulted in no change in overall BDD severity. Table 13–1 shows this.

The table also shows that, considering all types of cosmetic treatments combined ("any treatment"), only 8% of all treatments were followed by improvement in overall BDD symptoms, and 11% were followed by worsening of overall BDD symptoms. In my prospective study of BDD, in which 200

TABLE 13–1   *Outcome of Cosmetic Treatment for 450 People with Body Dysmorphic Disorder*

Treatment type	Improved (%)	Same (%)	Worse (%)
Any treatment	7.9	81.0	11.1
Surgery	10.9	70.8	18.2
Dermatologic treatment	7.4	86.6	6.0
Dental	10.0	55.0	35.0
Other medical treatment	0.0	88.9	11.1
Nonmedical (e.g., electrolysis) treatment	3.1	87.5	9.4

Total number of treatments received = 890.

people were interviewed annually, those who had cosmetic treatment during the follow-up period were not more likely to have improvement in BDD symptoms than those who didn't have cosmetic treatment.

Sometimes, after a cosmetic procedure the person thinks the treated body part looks better, and they may obsess less about that specific part. But usually, they obsess just as much about the other body areas they disliked before the procedure. Or they start to obsess about a new body part. As a 50-year-old business executive said, "My obsession stayed regardless of my appearance. After surgery, it just moved on to something else." Other people worry more about smaller imperfections. As Elena told me, "I've seen six dermatologists, and I think they made my skin look better, but I don't worry any less, because I worry just as much about small pimples as big ones. And now I'm hypervigilant. I worry my skin will get bad again." Some patients are happy for a while with the treated body area, but over time they start to dislike it again.

It makes sense that cosmetic treatment wouldn't work because in BDD the problem isn't with actual appearance—it's a problem of distorted body image. Changing a surface, physical characteristic doesn't cure the tendency to worry, obsess, and overfocus on minor details and imperfections, and to see oneself in a distorted way.

What about surgery, which is generally the most extreme and expensive treatment? Table 13–1 shows that 71% of surgeries resulted in no change in BDD symptoms, and 18% worsened BDD symptoms. This result differs from how people without BDD feel about cosmetic surgery; most of them are satisfied.

Another study similarly found that 81% of 50 BDD patients were dissatisfied or very dissatisfied with the outcome of medical consultation or surgery. Repeated surgery tended to fuel increasing dissatisfaction. A study from Japan found that of 274 patients with BDD who requested cosmetic surgery many were dissatisfied with the results. The researchers concluded that performing surgery on people with BDD is risky because they often have unrealistic expectations, are often unhappy with the outcome, and may become angry with the surgeon.

Of the 265 members of the American Society for Aesthetic Plastic Surgery who participated in a survey, 84% said they had operated on a patient who they thought was appropriate for surgery, only to realize after the surgery that the patient had BDD. Of these surgeons, 82% said the patient had a poor outcome with surgery: 43% said the patient was more preoccupied with the perceived defect, and 39% said the patient was now preoccupied with a different perceived defect.

"I hated the results of my surgery," Nicole told me. "Too much bone was taken off one side of my nose. Now you can see a shadow on the smooth side and a bump on the other side. It was the biggest mistake of my life. It took all of my looks away." Some people feel temporarily better, but the improvement usually doesn't last. "My nose looked better for a while after I had surgery," a 35-year-old salesclerk told me. "But then it seemed to grow back after six months, and I wasn't happy with it anymore." One man thought that braces had pulled his ears down. Another man became more preoccupied with his hair after trying minoxidil. "I was much more obsessed," he said. "I kept wondering, 'Was it growing?' I spent even more time in the mirror."

Some people with BDD seem to have very high and unrealistic expectations from surgery, expecting the outcome to be perfect. This was the case with Darrel: "The surgeries I had helped a little, but they weren't good enough. I'm a perfectionist." Some people have surgery after surgery, seeking perfection and ending up disappointed. Others with BDD have a very particular idea of how they should look after surgery, which may not conform to conventional views of beauty, including the surgeon's view. As Marissa's husband said, "The surgeons always focus on something different than my wife wants them to."

There is, however, a group of people with BDD who may benefit from a combination of mental health and dermatologic treatment: people who have damaged their skin by picking it. Resulting infections, wounds, or scarring may need or benefit from dermatologic care to heal the damage. This treatment, however, won't help the BDD symptoms that damaged the skin in the first place. Psychiatric treatment is needed to control the BDD obsessions and picking. In one study, I found that 85% of 20 people with BDD who picked their skin had no improvement in their skin obsessions or picking with dermatologic treatment but that 75% improved with an SRI.

Anger, Violence, and Suicidal Thinking

Sometimes the outcome of cosmetic treatment is extremely poor—even life-threatening. One man who had multiple ear surgeries became suicidal and violent each time the bandages were removed after surgery, necessitating repeated emergency hospitalization. Another young man's surgeon refused to do forehead surgery but gave him some facial cream; the patient thought the cream created huge, dark spots on his face. He became so enraged that he went on a rampage around his parents' house, threatening them with a hammer and splintering their furniture, and he needed to be hospitalized to keep himself and others safe.

Most of the people I've seen aren't litigious, physically aggressive, or violent. Most are reasonable, nonviolent, and law-abiding people. Some, however, have threatened to sue, or expressed fantasies of harming, their surgeon. Even when the treatment outcome is good by other peoples' standards, which it usually is, some people blame the surgeon or dermatologist for ruining their looks. Some are angry because they feel their request wasn't followed.

A 30-year-old man told me, "I wanted my nose shorter, but the surgeon changed the whole shape because he thought it would look better that way. I feel I lost my identity, and I'm sorry I ever had it done."

In the surgeon survey I previously mentioned, 40% of the surgeons said that a patient with BDD had threatened them; 39% were threatened legally and 12% physically. This is a terribly unfortunate outcome for the surgeon and BDD sufferer alike, and it's yet another reason to avoid surgery.

Rarely, people with BDD are so angry about the procedure that they actually become violent toward the doctor. There are several well-known cases of surgeons who were murdered by people who appeared to have BDD (see Chapter 7).

Occasional people with BDD become seriously depressed and consider suicide because they're so devastated by the results of a cosmetic procedure. "My life has never been the same since my surgery," Ahmed said. "I went to have my nose done, and the surgeon volunteered that I could use an implant in my chin, even though my chin had never bothered me. It ruined my life. I was horrified by the surgery. My nose was ruined—I have awful scar tissue there. I was very angry and upset. I got suicidal because of it. I also got swallowing and saliva problems because of the chin implant. I had to go to the emergency room because I was so upset." A woman lawyer, who had many unsuccessful surgeries, told me that she might ultimately kill herself over the results of future cosmetic surgery.

Recently, studies have found that women who have cosmetic breast implants, or any type of cosmetic surgery, are more likely to commit suicide than women who don't have these surgeries. It isn't known how many of these women had BDD, but I wonder whether some did and whether they committed suicide because surgery worsened BDD.

I've treated many patients who were suicidal over their belief that Accutane (a powerful acne medication) caused irreversible damage, such as dry and flaky skin, or a change in skin color. "In using the Accutane, I threw gasoline onto the fire," one patient told me. "I've caused irreparable damage to myself. Because of this, I prefer not to live." Accutane treatment more generally has been associated with depression and even suicide; I wonder how many of these people actually had BDD and to what extent BDD—rather than the medication itself—may have been responsible for their depression and suicidal thinking or behavior.

■ Other Ineffective Treatments for BDD

- Diet—I once saw a magazine article on my research that blazoned the headline "Feeling ugly? Eat a banana." The author recommended that

BDD sufferers eat chicken, avocado, corn, and bananas to cope with their symptoms because these foods may affect serotonin levels. While it's true that certain foods contain building blocks of serotonin, there's no evidence whatsoever that foods affect serotonin levels enough to diminish BDD symptoms. I don't recommend diet alone to treat BDD.

• Natural remedies—Some people try "natural remedies," such as homeopathic approaches, megavitamins, St. John's wort, and other substances found in health food stores or on the internet. There is no evidence that these treatments work. Just because substances like tryptophan and 5-hydroxytryptophan (5-HTP) are natural and have links to serotonin doesn't mean they effectively treat BDD. While some natural substances promoted as remedies are harmless, others may be harmful. In fact, many years ago the U.S. Food and Drug Administration withdrew the supplement tryptophan from the U.S. market because a toxic variant of this compound was inadvertently produced, which caused at least 37 deaths and 1,500 cases of a severe syndrome called eosinophilia myalgia syndrome. 5-HTP, too, may be dangerous. The weight loss herbal supplement ephedra (ma huang) has been linked to heart attacks, strokes, and even deaths.

Herbs and dietary supplements can be marketed without proof of safety or effectiveness. Some are contaminated with toxins like mercury, lead, or dangerous pesticides. Prescription medicines, such as SRIs, in contrast, must undergo extensive and rigorous scientific testing to demonstrate that they're both safe and effective before they can be marketed. You're much better off trying an SRI, since they've been extensively tested for safety, safely taken by many millions of people, and shown by research studies to often effectively treat BDD.

■ Try Treatments That Work!

Instead of trying the treatments discussed in this chapter, why not try an SRI or CBT? These treatments are often very helpful for BDD and can even be lifesaving.

Some people who initially consult surgeons, dermatologists, or dentists may be reluctant to see a psychiatrist or other mental health clinician. If this is true for you, keep in mind that as best we know, cosmetic treatments usually don't work. Seeing a psychiatrist or therapist doesn't mean you're "crazy." It simply means that you have a potentially treatable illness that in many ways is no different from heart disease or any other medical illness. Mental health treatment is likely to help you feel a lot better. There's a good chance it will give you more control over your obsessions, help you get your life back on track, and relieve your mind of worry, anxiety, and depression.

It may be hard for you to accept this advice if you think your defect is real and truly looks bad, as almost all people with BDD do. But look back at what my patients have told me about how they wish they'd never had surgery. And keep in mind that regardless of what you actually look like, if you're obsessing about an appearance problem that's upsetting you a lot or causing problems in your life, the right mental health treatment is likely to quell your obsessions, alleviate your suffering and distress, and help you have a happier and more productive life.

14. ANOREXIA NERVOSA, OBSESSIVE COMPULSIVE DISORDER, AND OTHER PSYCHIATRIC DISORDERS—WHAT'S THEIR RELATIONSHIP TO BODY DYSMORPHIC DISORDER?

The question of whether body dysmorphic disorder (BDD) is related to certain other psychiatric disorders—or is even the same as another disorder—is important. If it is, treatments that work for those disorders might also work for BDD, which would expand treatment options for BDD. And because related disorders tend to run together in families, we could predict that relatives of people with BDD would be at increased risk for a related disorder, and vice versa. But, if BDD isn't exactly the same as other disorders, that makes it important to diagnose BDD as a separate disorder and to treat BDD specifically.

In this chapter, I'll discuss several disorders and how closely related to BDD they seem to be. While some have similarities to BDD—and are probably related to BDD—they all differ from BDD in some significant ways. For this reason, it's important to consider BDD a distinct disorder and to provide treatment for BDD specifically.

■ Obsessive Compulsive Disorder

Nina constantly worried that she'd throw her children out the window or cut them with a knife. She frequently checked to make sure she hadn't harmed them and that they were okay. "The thoughts don't make any sense to me," she said, "I would never hurt anyone, especially my children, but I can't stop my thoughts." Mark worried that he'd get sick from dirt or germs. He washed his hands for hours a day so he wouldn't get sick or contaminated. He refused to allow visitors into his home, and whenever he, his wife, or his children entered the house he made them change their clothes and take a shower.

Nina and Mark had obsessive compulsive disorder (OCD), a disorder characterized by obsessions, which are intrusive, recurrent, unwanted ideas, thoughts, or impulses that are difficult to dismiss despite their disturbing nature. OCD is also characterized by compulsions (rituals), which are repetitive behaviors, either observable or mental, that are intended to reduce the anxiety caused by obsessions. The most common OCD obsession is fear of contamination, and the most common compulsion is checking.

Similarities

Obsessions (which focus on appearance) and compulsive behaviors (such as reassurance seeking and mirror checking) are also hallmarks of BDD. In addition, the content of thoughts in BDD and OCD can overlap. Both disorders can involve a desire for symmetry (of a body part in BDD and other things in OCD), a concern that something "isn't right" (a body part in BDD and other things in OCD), and a need for perfection. Compulsive checking and reassurance seeking are symptoms of both.

Additional similarities include the ratio of females to males who get the disorder, average age when the disorder begins, the tendency for both disorders to be chronic (without the right treatment), similar family history of psychiatric disorders, and poor functioning in daily activities (although functioning may be somewhat worse in BDD). BDD may involve some of the same brain circuits as OCD (see Chapter 9). And both BDD and OCD often improve with serotonin-reuptake inhibitors (SRIs). (OCD has been convincingly shown to respond better to SRIs than to other medications.) Cognitive-behavioral therapy (CBT) for these disorders has some elements in common, including a focus on exposure and ritual prevention.

There are a few other clues that BDD and OCD are probably related. First, many people have both of them (when disorders commonly coexist, this indicates that they may be related to each other). Studies have found that 3% to 37% of people with OCD also have BDD (the average is about 17%); conversely, about one-third of people with BDD also have OCD. And a study done at Johns Hopkins University found that BDD and OCD tend to run together in families.

Differences

But BDD and OCD also have some differences. One is that people with BDD focus specifically on appearance, believing that they look ugly or abnormal, whereas people with OCD have nonappearance-related obsessions and beliefs, such as fearing that the house will burn down if they don't check the stove

20 times. People with BDD tend to think their belief is true, whereas those with OCD tend to realize that their belief is irrational. On average, insight into the accuracy of the belief is poor in BDD but fair to good in OCD.

Another difference is that BDD appears to often involve core beliefs that the person is defective, worthless, or unlovable, whereas OCD beliefs typically have other themes, such as a fear of being responsible if something bad happens. I mentioned in Chapter 9 that a study found that people with BDD tend to have negative and threatening interpretations for appearance-related and social information, whereas people with OCD don't. This finding points to a fundamental difference in the way people with BDD and OCD process information from their environment.

People with BDD appear more likely to have major depressive disorder, abuse drugs and alcohol, and have suicidal thinking and behavior. When it comes to treatment, in BDD there's more of an emphasis on cognitive approaches, behavioral experiments, and perceptual retraining. And while medication approaches for BDD and OCD are similar, sometimes people with both disorders find that the medicine helps either their BDD or their OCD symptoms, but not both, indicating that they aren't the same disorder.

Finally, in my prospective interview study, when OCD symptoms improved, BDD symptoms often immediately got better. This finding suggests that these disorders may be causally linked to each other. However, among those study participants whose OCD remitted (went away), about half remained symptomatic with BDD. This suggests that BDD isn't the same disorder as OCD, because if it were we'd expect BDD to always remit when OCD does.

It's revealing to hear what patients with both disorders say about similarities and differences between them. Like many people, Renee saw some differences as well as similarities. "My BDD concerns seem more reasonable to me, whereas my OCD concerns have no basis in reality. They seem crazy and senseless....Even though my OCD is more severe than my BDD, the BDD hurts me more socially because people can see the problem. Bill's comparison was similar: "They're alike in a lot of ways, but the OCD is irrational and senseless. The BDD is true; it makes sense. The BDD made me suicidal."

Practical Implications

So BDD and OCD have many similarities but also some differences. It's likely that they're closely related but aren't the same disorder. Because people with BDD seem more likely to be depressed, suicidal, and abuse drugs or alcohol, it's especially important to look for and treat these symptoms in people with BDD. It's also very important to treat BDD as a separate disorder—and not simply as OCD—using the treatments recommended in this book. However, because of their poor insight, it may be harder to convince people with BDD to try mental health treatment.

■ Depression

Because so many people with BDD are depressed, it's reasonable to consider whether BDD is a symptom of depression, rather than a separate disorder. However, this doesn't appear to be the case. BDD and depression share some features and may be related conditions, but they have important differences that must be kept in mind when treating BDD.

Similarities

BDD and depression share features such as sadness and gloominess, poor self-esteem, rejection sensitivity, and feelings of unworthiness and defectiveness. And like many people with depression, some BDD sufferers have prominent feelings of guilt. BDD and major depression also commonly co-occur, with about three-fourths of those with BDD having a major depressive episode at some point during their life. Conversely, people with major depression—especially those with "atypical depression"—not uncommonly have BDD.

In my prospective study, when major depression improved, BDD tended to immediately improve—and vice versa. This suggests that they may be related conditions. However, among those study participants whose depression went away, about half continued to have BDD, which suggests that BDD isn't the same disorder as major depression.

Differences

One important difference is that people with BDD have prominent obsessional preoccupations and repetitive compulsive behaviors. People with depression may not like how they look (or anything else about themselves), but they aren't obsessionally preoccupied with perceived appearance flaws. Nor do they perform time-consuming, repetitive, compulsive behaviors. Many depressed people focus less, not more, on their appearance when they're depressed, even neglecting it. Additional differences include, in BDD, a higher male-to-female ratio, an earlier age of disorder onset, more chronic illness, and perhaps poorer functioning.

These disorders also respond somewhat differently to treatment. First, while research is still limited, BDD and accompanying depressive symptoms appear to not respond as well to non-SRI antidepressants as to SRIs. Depression responds well to both. In addition, BDD often takes longer to respond to an SRI and appears to typically require higher SRI doses than depression. And BDD may not respond as well to electroconvulsive therapy as depression does. Importantly, studies have shown that BDD often improves with an SRI regardless of whether depression improves, suggesting that BDD isn't simply a symptom of depression. And CBT for BDD focuses on exposure, response prevention, and perceptual retraining, unlike CBT for depression.

Practical Implications

While BDD and depression are probably related disorders, and many people with BDD are depressed, BDD isn't simply a symptom of depression. Unfortunately, BDD symptoms are often considered to simply be a symptom of depression. But for BDD and associated depressive symptoms to improve, BDD should be specifically identified and focused on in treatment.

■ Eating Disorders

People with anorexia think they're too fat and lose too much weight. People with bulimia have disturbed body image as well as binge eating and compensatory behaviors (such as self-induced vomiting) to prevent weight gain. Might BDD be related to these disorders? I've received letters and phone calls from young women who assume they have BDD—yet, they appear to actually have anorexia or another eating disorder. Occasionally, BDD and eating disorder symptoms closely overlap, making them hard to differentiate.

Similarities

The eating disorders anorexia and bulimia share with BDD a preoccupation with appearance, body dissatisfaction, distorted body image, and an excessive influence of appearance on self-esteem. One study found that people with BDD and those with an eating disorder have equally severe body image symptoms, such as similar levels of body dissatisfaction and feelings of unattractiveness.

Some people with BDD fixate on body areas that are typically disliked in anorexia and bulimia, such as their weight or the size of the stomach, hips, or thighs. Both disorders involve compulsive behaviors such as mirror checking and body measuring. BDD sometimes involves unusual eating or excessive exercise or dieting. Furthermore, BDD and eating disorders often co-occur, which suggests that they may be related.

Differences

First, BDD doesn't involve markedly abnormal eating behavior, such as binging on food, inducing vomiting, or taking laxatives or water pills to lose weight.

Also, BDD may involve a broad array of body areas, typically facial features and other non–weight-related concerns, whereas eating disorders focus on weight and body shape (the fatness of certain areas, such as the thighs and stomach). In addition, people with BDD actually look normal, whereas people with anorexia don't. As women with anorexia lose weight, many feel more satisfied and in control of their body and their life. In contrast, people with BDD nearly always feel distressed and out of control.

One study found that compared to women with an eating disorder, people with BDD evaluate themselves more negatively because of how they look, and they avoid activities more because of feeling self-conscious about their appearance.

BDD and eating disorders also have a strikingly different male-to-female ratio (more than 90% of people with eating disorders are women). Furthermore, effective treatments for BDD and eating disorders differ in some important ways. People with anorexia don't improve as often or as robustly with SRIs as those with BDD do. And while bulimia responds well to the SRIs, it also improves with a wide range of antidepressant medications, which doesn't appear to be the case for BDD.

Practical Implications

Because of their differences, it's important to differentiate BDD from eating disorders and diagnose them as different disorders. Usually, it's easy to differentiate them, but occasionally it isn't. Jean, for example, obsessed about the size of her hips. She sometimes dieted but didn't have other symptoms of an eating disorder. Did she have BDD, or did she have what's called an "eating disorder not otherwise specified" (an eating disorder that doesn't fulfill all of the DSM diagnostic criteria for anorexia or bulimia)? In the absence of abnormal eating behavior, it's probably reasonable to diagnose BDD. However, research is needed to better understand what the correct diagnosis is in cases like this. Most of the people I've diagnosed with BDD who had weight-related concerns also had nonweight-related concerns, such as preoccupation with facial features.

■ Social Phobia

Social phobia (also known as social anxiety disorder) is another disorder that's probably closely related to BDD. In Japan, in fact, BDD is considered a type of social phobia (taijin kyofusho). Social phobia is characterized by an excessive fear of social or performance situations in which the person is exposed to unfamiliar people or to scrutiny by others and fears they'll do something embarrassing or humiliating.

Similarities

Studies have found that people with BDD tend to be introverted and have high levels of social anxiety, distress, fear, avoidance, and physiological arousal in social situations. In addition, both disorders involve feelings of inadequacy, shame, preoccupation with what other people think of them, and fear of being negatively evaluated, embarrassed, humiliated, rejected, and unlovable. Several studies discussed in Chapter 9 suggest that people with BDD are similar to those with social phobia in their tendency to misinterpret social situations and other situations as threatening, and to have amygdala hyperreactivity. Additional similarities include the ratio of females to males who get the disorder, the chronicity of the disorder (without the right treatment), and poor functioning in daily activities.

Furthermore, many people have both BDD and social phobia—another clue that they may be related disorders. In fact, more than one-third of people with BDD also have social phobia (unrelated to their appearance concerns).

Differences

One difference is that BDD preoccupations focus specifically on perceived physical flaws whereas social phobia doesn't. Also, compulsive behaviors (rituals) are a prominent feature of BDD but not social phobia. In fact, some people with BDD consider these behaviors (e.g., skin picking) to be their most distressing and problematic symptom.

In my prospective interview study, when social phobia symptoms improved, BDD symptoms didn't immediately improve—or vice versa—suggesting that these disorders may not be closely causally linked. And among those subjects whose social phobia went away, about half remained symptomatic with BDD, suggesting that BDD isn't the same disorder as social phobia.

BDD and social phobia may also respond somewhat differently to medication treatment. Social phobia often improves with SRIs, but also with certain other medications. While these other medications haven't been well studied in BDD, they appear less promising for BDD. And while CBT for BDD and social phobia have some elements in common, CBT for BDD focuses more on response prevention and perceptual retraining.

Practical Implications

Although BDD and social phobia have many similarities and are probably closely related, they appear to have some differences and aren't identical disorders. So when a person has prominent social anxiety, it's important to not simply assume they have social phobia. Instead, ask what makes them anxious and whether their anxiety is triggered largely by appearance concerns. If it is, BDD is the more accurate diagnosis and needs to be treated.

■   Other Disorders and Concluding Thoughts

Considering all available evidence, BDD has many similarities to—and is probably related to—several disorders, most notably OCD, social phobia, depression, and eating disorders. However, BDD doesn't appear to be identical to, or simply a symptom of, any other disorder.

There are yet other disorders to consider, which I discuss at greater length in my other book on BDD (*The Broken Mirror: Understanding and Treating Body Dysmorphic Disorder*). Because some people with BDD (about one-third currently and one half at some point in their life) have delusional beliefs and referential thinking, they can be misdiagnosed with schizophrenia. But BDD and schizophrenia have many important differences. They definitely aren't the same disorder and probably aren't even closely related.

The ICD-10 **Classification of Mental and Behavioural Disorders** (the international classification manual of disorders) classifies BDD as a type of hypochondriasis. But this disorder, too, seems to differ from BDD in some important ways, and it's very doubtful that they're the same illness.

This means that BDD should be identified and diagnosed when it's present, rather than assumed to just be a symptom of another disorder. As best we know, effective treatment for BDD differs in some ways from treatments for other disorders. If BDD isn't correctly identified and focused on in treatment, it may not get better.

But it's important to be aware that a person can have both BDD **and** another mental disorder. Major depressive disorder, alcohol or drug abuse/dependence, social phobia, OCD, and eating disorders commonly co-occur with BDD. **All** disorders that are present should be diagnosed and treated. Treating just one of them won't necessarily make the others better. This is the same situation as for medical disorders. You wouldn't assume that when high blood pressure is treated, Lyme's disease will also improve. This is additionally important because research generally indicates that people with multiple psychiatric disorders tend to be more severely ill than those with fewer disorders. For example, a study of women with anorexia found that those who also had BDD were more likely to have problems in daily functioning and to attempt suicide. I and my colleagues found that people with both BDD **and** an eating disorder have greater body image dissatisfaction and more psychiatric hospitalizations than those with just BDD. We also found that those with both BDD **and** OCD function more poorly and have more suicidal thinking and suicide attempts than those with just BDD or OCD.

In the future, when we better understand what causes BDD and other disorders, we'll have a clearer understanding of their relationship to one another. This understanding should ultimately lead to even more effective treatments and may even prevent these disorders from ever developing in the first place.

15. ADVICE FOR FAMILY MEMBERS AND FRIENDS

BDD has far-reaching effects. Family members, friends, and significant others usually suffer, too. Sometimes, BDD causes relationships to end. Also, it's stressful and painful to watch a loved one struggle with such a difficult disorder. You may feel helpless, frustrated, angry—because no matter how hard you try, you can't get the BDD sufferer to stop worrying about their looks or stop their rituals. You may feel isolated and alone, thinking no one else in the world is struggling with a similar problem. But there are some things you can do.

■ "The Selfish Disease": A Husband's Perspective

"There aren't enough days on a calendar to tell you how many times I've wanted to leave my wife," Sam told me. "I'm a very loyal person, and I love her. But at times it gets to be too much. She's late when we go out, and sometimes she won't go at all. She can get so wrapped up in her obsessions that she ignores me completely. She doesn't give the children the attention they need. BDD is the selfish disease."

Sam sometimes accompanied his wife, Beth, to her sessions with me and told me about how he tried to cope with her illness. "My wife has had this problem for decades," he said. "No one knew what it was." I heard about Beth's fixation on her nose and the many unsuccessful surgeries she'd had. Her preoccupation had made it difficult to raise her children. She also had a hard time focusing on a job; she wanted to work, but had been mostly unemployed. "This is a problem that affects family members, too," Sam told me. "I hope this doesn't sound too selfish, but sometimes I think I've suffered as much as my wife!"

Sam and Beth had been married for 10 years. Beth's previous husband had left her because of her symptoms. "You might be skeptical that it was because of my nose obsession," she told me. "But it was. I hounded him all day long. I'd plead with him to help me find another surgeon, and I'd constantly talk about how surgery would solve my appearance problem. We hardly had a social life. Sometimes I wouldn't go to social events at all because I thought I looked so bad. That really drove him crazy."

Like Beth's first husband, Sam had gotten very involved in her BDD. At her insistence, Sam held magnifying mirrors and bright lights so she could get a better look at her nose, a ritual that could take more than an hour a day. Beth talked to him incessantly about her nose, saying she wanted surgery and asking if her nose looked okay. "The questioning is especially hard," Sam told me. "No matter what I say, she doesn't really believe me." They'd missed family get-togethers and had few friends because his wife felt too ugly to be around other people. A few times Sam even took her to an emergency room because she'd looked in the mirror and considered suicide.

"There's no worse illness on earth than BDD," Sam told me many times. "People who haven't lived with it probably wouldn't understand, but this is the most devastating thing in the world. I've seen death. I've seen murder. This is as bad....Maybe it's harder for me than my wife, because I'm more helpless than her. I can't do anything about it."

One of the hardest things for Sam was the isolation. "I've felt very alone because friends and family don't understand. I've mostly dealt with this on my own. I took a risk and told a few relatives, but they don't understand it; they think it's strange." But Sam resolved to stand by Beth. Eventually, she got much better with treatment, and the strain on their marriage diminished.

Sam's story isn't unusual. Sometimes friends and family members don't know that BDD is the root of their loved one's problems, because the symptoms are kept secret—but they experience its effects nonetheless.

The "selfish disease"—Sam's description of BDD—reflects many family members' experience. The person with BDD can be so wrapped up in their obsession that family members are ignored. BDD sufferers seem to put their needs first—missing the social engagement, forgoing a wedding, spending too much money on beauty products, talking about their appearance instead of showing interest in others. They may seem distant, preoccupied, and self-absorbed. But if people with BDD could take their mind off their appearance, they would. BDD may seem selfish to other people, but it isn't a selfishness problem. Effective treatment often puts an end to the "selfishness"—what appeared to be selfish behavior turns out to have been symptoms of BDD.

■ "I Knew Something Was Wrong with My Daughter": A Parent's Perspective

"I knew something was wrong with my daughter when she'd be in the bathroom for an hour and was upset when she came out." This mother had tried very hard to help her daughter cope with BDD. Some of the approaches she tried—such as reassuring her—weren't successful, but others were. Her daughter finally agreed to see a psychiatrist and improved with treatment.

Parents often suffer a lot. They may have to cope with their daughter's dropping grades and avoidance of friends and activities. They may care for a

35-year-old son who's unable to support himself or live on his own. They may finally, in desperation, take their handsome adolescent son for a chin implant, because they can no longer tolerate his relentless pleas for cosmetic surgery, only to find he's even more desperate after surgery.

Coping with BDD can be especially hard for parents because they may feel responsible for their child's difficulties. Did they cause the problem? Did they overemphasize the importance of appearance? Should they have raised their child differently? Blaming themselves only compounds their suffering.

One mother felt helpless when she tried to help her son cope with his hair, and she blamed herself. "He's so upset over his hair that he can't function because of it. We try not to reassure him, but he's so desperate, we have to. He's having temper tantrums because he thinks his hair is getting worse. We don't know what to do!"

Her son felt badly, too. "I can't enjoy being with them, because I'm so upset over how I look," he said. "I can't even have a good Christmas with them. I have to ask them 'Does my hair look okay? Does it look thin?' And they say to me, 'Don't ruin the day.' But I do. And I feel bad about how much unhappiness I've caused them. I've put them through hell."

I heard from the mother of a boy who had killed himself because he thought he was so ugly. He'd seen many doctors, but BDD hadn't been diagnosed. "For many years I lost patience with my son for always staring in the mirror and saying he was ugly when he was a quite handsome boy," she wrote. "He used to say to me, 'What's this thing that's taking me over, mom?' The night before he died, he said I didn't understand him, which was true, and that there was no hope for him.

"I know that it's almost impossible to sway the mind of someone with body dysmorphic disorder, but at least one can be patient, understanding, and loving, and prevent them from feeling isolated.... My tragedy will always be that I didn't know and couldn't tell him that it wasn't his fault."

■ Suggested Guidelines for Family Members and Friends

Most of the guidelines I'll discuss in this chapter won't actually treat BDD; that's the role of cognitive-behavioral therapy (CBT) and medication. But these coping strategies may increase the odds of a good outcome and make BDD easier to live with.

Recognize BDD Symptoms, Take Them Seriously, and Talk Openly About BDD

This is the first critical step. It's easy to mistake BDD symptoms for normal appearance concerns or even vanity (see Chapter 3). It's easy to ignore the warning signs, thinking your loved one is simply self-centered or self-absorbed. You may mistakenly assume that an adolescent with BDD is simply going through a "phase." BDD can also be mistakenly diagnosed as another psychiatric disorder (see Chapter 3). Don't ignore BDD warning signs.

If you think a loved one may have BDD, try not to get angry or critical, tease the person because they're so focused on their looks, or reassure them that they look okay. Instead, in a calm and nonjudgmental way, tell them that you've noticed that they seem very worried about how they look, and mention any clues you've noticed, like their spending lots of time in the mirror. Ask them to talk with you about their concerns. Tell them that you think they might have BDD, a common and treatable body image problem. Suggest that they read this book. Talk with them about the next step they'd like to take, and let them know you're willing to help. The sooner you and your loved one recognize the problem, the sooner the recovery process can begin.

Some people don't want to hear that they have BDD, but many others are relieved to learn that they may have a treatable condition and that they aren't alone. Identifying BDD is the first step to helping both you and the BDD sufferer cope with the illness.

Encourage and Support the Mental Health Treatment Recommended in This Book

Getting the right treatment is essential. Don't tell your loved one to just "snap out of it," try harder," or "just stop worrying." You wouldn't take this approach if they had cancer. Saying such things will just alienate them and make them feel you don't understand.

Give them information about BDD and its treatment, and encourage them to try a serotonin-reuptake inhibitor (SRI), CBT, or both and to stick with the treatment. Offer to make an appointment with a qualified professional and accompany them to an evaluation. Your encouragement and support can make a big difference.

If they agree to get treatment, encourage them to give it a really good try by keeping their appointments, doing their CBT homework, and taking all of the medicine as prescribed. If you want, you can help out with CBT once the therapist shows you how to do this.

While many people with BDD welcome the option of treatment because it offers them hope of relief, others are reluctant. If they're reluctant, encourage them to try it. Ask them what they have to lose and what worries them about the treatment. You can remind them that they won't necessarily get side effects from medication. If side effects occur, they may be relatively mild and temporary. In my SRI treatment studies, hardly anyone stopped treatment because of medication side effects. CBT is challenging but doable.

It's important to support mental health treatment rather than surgery or other cosmetic treatment. This can be hard. People with BDD may be desperate to get cosmetic procedures, and may beg and plead with you to agree to the treatment or pay for it. Encourage them to avoid these treatments and try the right mental health treatment instead. Most BDD sufferers are disappointed with the results of cosmetic treatments. Many say they wish that someone—including their family members—had talked them out of it.

If the Person with BDD is Reluctant to Get Mental Health Treatment, Focus on Their Suffering and Problems with Functioning; This Makes Treatment Worth Trying

It's especially distressing when someone with BDD won't accept the diagnosis or get help. Because most people with BDD have little or no insight, this difficult situation is unfortunately fairly common. Here are some approaches to try:

- Without haranguing them, continue to gently provide information about BDD and support psychiatric treatment. Encourage them to read this book (see, especially, if they're willing to read Chapter 10).
- Emphasize how much the appearance concerns are ruining their life. Rather than arguing with them about how they look, focus on the fact that:
  - they're overly preoccupied and spending too much time on BDD thoughts;
  - they're worrying too much, which is stressful for their mind and body;
  - they're suffering too much because of their appearance concerns;
  - their worries are causing problems with their functioning, relationships, and other important things in their life;
  - their preoccupation has too much power over them and is depriving them of what they want and deserve in life. They may not like how they look, but this shouldn't control their life or cause them so much anguish.
- Emphasize that effective treatment is the way they can gain control of their thoughts and feelings. It can greatly diminish their suffering and improve their functioning and quality of life. They, not the appearance preoccupation, should be in charge. They should be able to think about whatever they want to think about and interact comfortably with other people, free of gnawing, painful thoughts. What do they have to lose by trying treatment?
- Point out that trying the right treatment doesn't mean they have to continue it for the rest of their life. Many people try to stop their medication at some point to see how they do (See Chapter 11). And CBT is time limited. By giving a try, they can see how it affects them.
- Periodically remind the sufferer that you are willing to help and that with the right treatment, most people with BDD get better.

Don't Discuss Appearance at Length, Argue About It, or Try to Talk the Person Out of Their Beliefs about Their Looks

Trying to talk the person with BDD out of their belief is understandable. They look fine, so why not just explain this to them? However, this approach is unlikely to help. It can also consume endless amounts of your time and is especially likely to fail with someone with delusional BDD (someone who is completely convinced that their view of their appearance is accurate). Usually, everyone ends up feeling frustrated. Following the suggestions in the preceding section are more likely to help.

In general, the less you discuss appearance at all, the better. For example, if someone is obsessed with their nose, don't tell them their nose is fine but they might want to change their hairstyle. Or if their face is slightly round, don't say it's a tiny bit round but really looks fine. Such well-intentioned comments generally aren't helpful. Even if you think they're benign or helpful, they can trigger severe distress and even new appearance obsessions.

Nonetheless, certain individuals—those who have some insight and acknowledge that their view of their looks is distorted—may benefit from an occasional reminder that their view is exaggerated and is due to BDD. But don't do this a lot, argue about it, or try to convince someone who can't acknowledge their faulty thinking.

As CBT or medication start to work, insight may improve. As it does, it may be helpful to occasionally remind the BDD sufferer that their view isn't accurate—that it's very negative and different from how other people see them.

Offer Support and Help

Because BDD can be so hard to cope with, it's easy to criticize and express anger toward someone who has it. But this isn't helpful. Instead, do your best to offer support and to create a supportive home environment. Help the BDD sufferer talk about their feelings of anxiety, depression, shame, and isolation. Let them know that you care and that you'll try to understand and support them through the recovery process.

There are many more specific things you can do to help, although this will depend on your specific situation and your relationship with the person. You might offer to help them get to their doctor's or therapist's appointment, help them pay for treatment, or help them keep track of taking their medication. You can also offer to help with their CBT homework—for example, go out with them to do exposure exercises. If you offer to help with the treatment, it's a good idea to meet at least occasionally with the therapist or doctor for some guidance.

Limit Your Involvement in BDD Rituals

A major pitfall is being drawn into BDD rituals. You may be asked to hold mirrors to allow multiple views of the defect, shine lights on it while it's inspected, measure a body part, or cut, groom, or style hair. The person with BDD may beg you to pay for expensive items, such as wigs, clothing, beauty products, or surgery.

It's best for both you and the BDD sufferer not to participate in BDD rituals. Doing rituals never has and never will cure the disorder. It just feeds the BDD and can even make it worse by reinforcing those behaviors (see Chapters 6 and 12). Assisting with rituals also drains your time and energy—and, in some cases, your pocketbook.

It's important to first calmly explain that you won't participate in rituals because it isn't good for the person. Say that you know they're upset but that participating in rituals can actually make their preoccupations and fears worse. It won't defeat BDD and, ultimately, keeps it going. Even if anxiety improves by doing a ritual, the relief is only temporary. Resisting the behaviors is better in the long run (see Chapter 12). It's often hard to hold the line, but it's best to do so. All family members need to agree on this. Try to convey understanding and support rather than anger and hostility.

If you're already participating in rituals, you may have to back out of them gradually, rather than cold turkey (see the section on ritual prevention in Chapter 12).

Be consistent, and kind, in your resolve! Consistency is crucial so the person with BDD learns that the behaviors aren't acceptable or helpful. Help them develop alternative activities—such as going for a walk, listening to music, or doing a hobby—that they can do instead when they get the urge to do rituals. Consulting with the person's clinician may help you come up with useful strategies to try.

Fortunately, treatment with medication or CBT often diminishes the rituals as well as requests that other people participate in them. If your loved one is getting mental health treatment, it may help to meet with the clinician to develop a plan for how to stop participating in rituals.

Don't Give Reassurance

Reassurance seeking is the BDD ritual that most often involves other people, and it's one of the most frustrating for family members and friends. The typical—and understandable—response is to provide the reassurance the BDD sufferer seeks. After all, they look fine, so the natural tendency is to say so. Common responses include "You look fine!" "I can't see it at all," "I can hardly see it," or "It's not as bad as you think." The problem is that these responses don't stop the questioning for long, if at all—and they don't put an end to the appearance concerns. The best response to this ritual—as to all others—is not to participate.

Paradoxically, responding to questioning with a reassuring reply can actually perpetuate the reassurance-seeking behavior. If the response does temporarily decrease the BDD sufferer's anxiety, this transient relief fuels their attempt to obtain more relief by asking the question again.

Occasionally, because they're so frustrated, family members say that the defect really looks bad. They don't actually believe this, but they say it in anger, or because the BDD sufferer hasn't accepted reassurance that they look fine. I recommend not saying such a thing, because it can greatly distress the BDD sufferer and even worsen BDD symptoms.

I often meet with family members, along with the person with BDD, to discuss BDD more generally and this behavior in particular. We all agree that providing reassurance benefits no one. The person with BDD can usually acknowledge that they aren't reassured very much by the responses they get, and family members can readily acknowledge that no matter what they say, it really doesn't help. We then agree that, for the benefit of the BDD sufferer, family members will no longer respond to requests for reassurance. Instead, if necessary, they will remind the person with BDD that this behavior is a BDD ritual—and that it isn't helpful for them to respond.

Different families come up with their own helpful responses. Responses that may be helpful are "I'm sorry; I know you're suffering, but it doesn't help for me to respond to your question," "We agreed it isn't helpful for me to reassure you," "Your need for reassurance is a symptom of BDD, and it won't help if I give it to you," or "I know you're anxious, but reassuring you won't help." The main point is to avoid commenting in any way on the person's appearance as part of the response. After giving this response it may help to do something with the person—for example, go for a walk, play a game, or watch a movie.

If possible, **always** avoid giving reassurance. Providing reassurance only occasionally—for example, only 20% of the time—may seem like very little, but it may be frequent enough to reinforce and maintain the behavior. Keep in mind, though, that if you've been used to giving reassurance, you may have to cut down gradually rather than stopping cold turkey (see ritual prevention section in Chapter 12).

Encourage Better Functioning but Also Recognize the Person's Limitations

You may be in the position of urging the BDD sufferer to be on time for work or school, go out of the house to do errands, get a job or go to school, or see their friends. In some cases, the person with BDD lives with and is supported by family members long after the time has come to live independently.

In my experience, family members often give this kind of support willingly, yet providing it may be a significant strain. You may wonder whether you're doing an adult BDD sufferer a disservice by having him or her live with you or be financially dependent on you. Are you "enabling" the disorder in some way?

Alexandra's parents expressed this dilemma. "Our daughter is 33 years old. She should be on her own by now. But we're afraid that if we ask her to leave she won't be able to support herself. We've tried it before, and it didn't work. But we wonder if we're doing the right thing by having her continue to live with us."

It's best to encourage better functioning. If the BDD sufferer is an adult, the goal is eventual self-support. Encourage them to get out of the house and socialize, attend family events, see friends, get a job, or go to school. Encourage your loved one to push themselves as much as possible so they function at their highest level.

At the same time, recognize their limitations. Don't apply too much pressure. This process can be a delicate balancing act and will require some judgment on your part. The gradual approach that's used in exposure therapy (described in Chapter 12) is best. Encourage them to try things step-by-step—from easier to harder to hardest—and to do these things often. Encourage them to keep doing things they've successfully done before. For someone who hasn't been able to work, moving to a volunteer job and then to part-time and then full-time work can be an effective strategy. It can be very helpful to get advice from the clinician who is treating the BDD sufferer, or from a vocational rehabilitation counselor, so you can tailor your approach to your individual situation.

Also encourage the BDD sufferer to keep busy. You can suggest activities or help create lists of activities that they can engage in when idle or preoccupied.

For people with severe BDD, simply insisting that the person function better is likely to be fruitless. For them to make progress, it's crucial that they receive treatment from a qualified professional. Don't try to care for the person on your own. Adequate treatment with medication and CBT can be critical to success. Vocational rehabilitation (see Chapter 12) can also be helpful. If possible, meet with professionals who are providing treatment to discuss ways in which you can facilitate the BDD sufferer's transition to better functioning. Your support and encouragement can be extremely helpful.

Encourage Participation in Family Events

People with BDD may avoid family get-togethers or important events such as graduations, weddings, or funerals. They may dread these events because they fear facing other people and worry they'll be judged negatively because of how they look. "I'm petrified about my brother's wedding," one man told me. "If my hair doesn't start growing back by then, I'm not going. My family will be incredibly upset, but I refuse to go."

It's best to encourage the person with BDD to participate in family events. Remind them that the focus won't be on them; at a wedding, it will be on the bride and bridegroom. Encourage them to face their fears by being around other people. If they do this enough, their fears will eventually diminish. They may even feel better afterward because they didn't miss the event. Avoiding social situations only reinforces BDD symptoms.

But also consider if it's realistic at this time for the person to attend events like this—this depends on their current level of functioning. It's best to take a step-wise approach to facing feared and avoided situations (See exposure section in Chapter 12.) The eventual goal is to not avoid any social situations like family events. A clinician who is knowledgeable about BDD can provide you with helpful guidance.

Give Praise for Even Small Gains

Resisting the urge to comb their hair in the mirror for an hour or ask for reassurance for a day may not seem like big feats, but they can be major accomplishments for someone with BDD. Recognize this, and praise your loved one for even small gains. Praise works better then criticism.

Recognize and support each step the BDD sufferer takes toward resisting BDD rituals, participating in activities, leaving the house, socializing more, and improving functioning at work or school. Don't expect BDD symptoms to disappear overnight. Praise any improvement, no matter how minimal it may seem. Encourage the BDD sufferer to keep going and not to give up, even if they're having a bad day or week.

Don't compare the BDD sufferer to other people who are functioning well. This will only make them feel worse. It's important to judge progress according to their current level of functioning. If a person is housebound, they probably won't be able to go to a baseball game the first time they leave the house. Going to the mailbox to get the mail may be the most they can initially do (see Chapter 12).

When Assessing Progress, Look at the Big Picture

When someone is working to overcome BDD, look at the big picture. Are they generally moving in the right direction? Try not to judge progress on a day-to-day basis; instead, look at the big picture. Rather than asking if the person is better today than yesterday, ask if on average the past few weeks have been better than 6 months ago or when they were at their worst.

It's common to have setbacks along the way. Don't be too discouraged by this. BDD symptoms typically wax and wane, and a period of improvement can be followed by some bad days. Don't fall into the trap of assuming that a bad day means all gains have been lost. However, if a setback persists or is severe, it's wise to let the treating clinician know, as a change in treatment may be needed.

During Times of Stress, You May Need to Modify Your Expectations

BDD symptoms can increase at times of stress. Virtually any type of change can be stressful—positive events as well as negative ones. At these times, you may need to lower your expectations a little, keeping in mind that progress may be slower, or even temporarily stop, during stressful times. At times like these, your encouragement, support, and understanding may be especially helpful.

Be Patient

Patience is enormously helpful! It's especially needed when waiting for your loved one to agree to get treatment or improve with treatment. Medication and CBT can take some time to work. Sometimes, with the right treatment, functioning improves quickly, but some people need more time to get back on track, especially if they've been ill for a long time. It doesn't help to argue or get angry.

On the other hand, don't be so patient that you drop all of your expectations and stop your encouragement. Keep encouraging the person to get the right treatment, stick with it, and keep up their hope that they'll improve.

Try to Limit Angry Outbursts

Angry outbursts, or what some of my patients refer to as temper tantrums, can seriously disrupt the family. They're a particularly difficult aspect of BDD. The outbursts usually reflect frustration and anger over the psychological pain, isolation, and disruption of life that BDD can cause.

Sometimes, angry behavior is precipitated by an upsetting event, such as the perception of being mocked by other people. Some of my patients routinely become very angry after getting a "bad" haircut. Unfortunately, you may bear the brunt of this frustration and anger.

If this behavior is related to BDD, try to understand this, and try to identify what triggers outbursts. If getting into discussions or arguments about how the person looks triggers anger, then do everything possible to avoid these discussions (try the approaches recommended earlier in this chapter).

Try not to respond to anger with anger. This usually only escalates the problem. Instead, try to stay calm. Encourage the person to "take time out" and do something soothing or relaxing. Then, after they calm down, say you'd like to talk with them about the problem. Try to do this calmly, without being angry or threatening yourself. Point out your concerns about their anger, and explain that it doesn't help solve anyone's problems.

Set limits on destructive behavior. Firmly but nonangrily let the person know that it isn't acceptable to damage property or take out their anger on another person—and this never solves the underlying problem. It just creates more problems. Urge them to talk about how they feel, rather than expressing their feelings in angry behavior or words. If violent behavior has the potential to harm others or already has, let any treating clinicians know about your concerns and consider involving law enforcement personnel to protect people and help you manage it.

If anger and violence are a problem, it's critical to get treatment for your loved one. Try to meet with the treating clinician to discuss strategies for dealing with anger and to get this problem under control.

If the Person with BDD is Considering Suicide, Get Immediate Professional Help

Nothing is more likely to precipitate a family crisis than suicidal thinking or behavior. Usually, suicidal thinking and behavior are associated with an underlying psychiatric disorder, such as depression, bipolar disorder, substance abuse, or BDD. In fact, suicidal thinking and behaviors are common in BDD (see Chapter 7). Other factors, such as stressful life events, can also contribute.

Suicidal thoughts and behaviors are serious warning signs that the person is suffering greatly. Furthermore, they may culminate in actual suicide. It's a serious mistake to ignore or minimize such signs or to assume they'll simply pass.

If a person with BDD appears depressed or expresses self-destructive thoughts, gently ask if they've had thoughts that life isn't worth living, thoughts of harming themselves, or a plan to end their life. Ask questions like how often they have the thoughts, how strong the feelings are, how likely they are to act on them, and whether there's anything that makes them want to live. Asking such questions won't put thoughts of suicide in their head; it may even be life saving.

If your loved one expresses any thoughts like these, get them professional mental health care right away. You shouldn't deal with suicidal thoughts or behavior on your own. Contact a psychiatrist or therapist, a primary care doctor, a local hospital or clinic, or a community mental health center. If your loved one is already getting treatment, it's important for the treating clinician to know about the suicidal thoughts. If the situation seems urgent, immediately contact the treating clinician if there is one, and if necessary take your loved one to a hospital emergency room or an emergency health care clinic so they can be evaluated. In an emergency it's sometimes best to have law enforcement personnel intervene and transport the person there if they're unwilling to go or to ensure their safety en route.

Keep Your Family Routine as Normal as Possible

If BDD upsets your family routine, try to get it back to normal. No one benefits when BDD takes over and disrupts your life. It's best for both you and the BDD sufferer to live as normal a life as possible. For example, if you're planning on having relatives over for Thanksgiving, go ahead with it and encourage (but don't force) your daughter to participate, even if she's going through a bad spell and doesn't want to. Do this without expressing anger or criticism, and don't feel guilty about it.

Take Time for Yourself

It's important to have some time for yourself—for your responsibilities and the things you enjoy. By overprotecting the BDD sufferer and being overly involved in their life, you can inadvertently communicate to them that they're incapable of better functioning. This can undermine their sense of confidence and self-worth. At the same time, don't avoid them or give up on them!

Let them know that you care and support them—but also take some time for yourself. It's important to do some enjoyable things each day. You'll probably feel better by taking a break from the BDD. There's no need to feel guilty about this. If this isn't sufficient, you can consider joining a support group, or even seeing a therapist yourself for support and help with coping.

If you can't do any of these things or take enough time out because your loved one requires such intensive care and close monitoring (for example, because they're so impaired, depressed, or suicidal), this is a clue that they may need more intensive psychiatric care (see Chapter 16).

Don't Blame Yourself

Some family members—parents in particular—wonder if they're responsible for BDD. We don't know what causes it, but it probably has many causes, and it's unlikely to result largely—if at all—from something you've done wrong (see Chapter 9). We also don't know how to prevent BDD, so don't blame yourself for not preventing it.

Instead of looking back and blaming yourself, focus on the present and future. Accept that the person has a problem, and do what you can now to help the BDD sufferer overcome their symptoms.

Remember That You Aren't Alone

You may feel isolated or feel a sense of stigma because a loved one has a psychiatric problem. Some people may find BDD symptoms hard to understand. But BDD is a legitimate disorder that's getting better known, and it isn't rare. Millions of family members around the world are trying to make sense of it and cope with it. Consider sharing your struggles with someone you trust; support from other people can be helpful. Remember that you aren't alone!

Maintain Hope!

Most people with BDD improve with the right treatment. So don't give up hope! If your loved one refuses to get the right treatment, keep encouraging them to do so. With treatment, symptoms often get much better. Sometimes the first treatment is helpful; other times it's the third, fourth, or fifth. Keep in mind that time and patience may be needed to find the treatment that works best for a particular person. I have no doubt that in the coming years we'll find more and even better treatments for BDD.

16. Getting Help for Body Dysmorphic Disorder

■ What Kinds of Clinicians Can Treat BDD?

It's important to get treatment from a licensed health care professional who is knowledgeable about BDD and can provide the treatments recommended in this book. There are a variety of licensed professionals who may have training and experience in treating BDD.

Several different types of licensed professionals can prescribe medication. Psychiatrists are medical doctors who have at least four additional years of specialized training in psychiatric disorders and their treatment following medical school. Primary care doctors, any other type of physician, and in some states nurses with an advanced degree can also prescribe medication.

A number of different types of professionals are trained in psychotherapy. Clinical psychologists have specialized training in psychiatric disorders and psychotherapy; they have a doctoral degree (a Ph.D., a Psy.D., or an Ed.D. degree). Psychiatrists also have specialized training in psychotherapy. Clinical or psychiatric social workers, who have a master's degree, and in some states nurses with an advanced degree in mental health can also provide therapy. Counselors may or may not have formal or accredited training in psychotherapy. The term "therapist" is very broad and can refer to any of these professionals. Only some of these professionals have training specifically in CBT.

It's ideal to be evaluated by a psychiatrist to consider the option of taking medication. People who haven't improved after trying several medications may benefit from seeing a psychiatrist with particular expertise in psychopharmacology (prescribing medication). If you can't find a psychiatrist with expertise in BDD, you may want to see one with expertise in obsessive compulsive disorder (OCD) because of its similarities to BDD.

Seek out a therapist who is familiar with BDD and has training in and experience with cognitive-behavioral therapy (CBT). Most therapists aren't trained to do CBT. If you can't find a therapist with expertise in doing CBT for BDD, seeing a CBT therapist with expertise in treating OCD or social phobia is a good approach. Keep in mind, though, that CBT for BDD differs in some ways from CBT for OCD or social phobia. The CBT treatment manual written by Drs. Wilhelm, Steketee, and myself (see below) is a guidebook that CBT-trained therapists can follow when they treat patients with BDD.

■ What "Level of Care" Is Best?

Treatment is offered at different "levels of care." Below I describe them from least "intensive" (i.e., a "lower level" of care) to more intensive (a "higher level" of care). Most mental health treatment these days is received at the lowest level—as an outpatient—which is often appropriate for BDD. The availability of treatment, the cost, and how much of it you can get differs by country (much of what I say in this section pertains primarily to the United States); it also differs by state, region, whether you have health insurance, and the type of health insurance you have.

The level of care that's best for you will depend on several factors. The more severely ill you are, the more intensive the treatment you may need. Also, if you've given a lower level of care a really good try, and it didn't work for you, you can consider a higher level of care. A higher level of care is essential if you're feeling violent or suicidal and think you might act on your violent or suicidal thoughts.

- **Outpatient treatment:** With outpatient treatment you live at home. Visits for outpatient CBT usually occur once a week or in some cases twice a week. Booster sessions, if needed after the treatment ends, are less frequent than this (see Chapter 12). Visits for medication usually occur from once a week to a few times a year. The frequency will depend on how you're doing, whether your medicine is being changed, and other factors. This is the setting where most BDD treatment occurs.

- **Intensive outpatient treatment:** Some clinics or hospitals may offer intensive outpatient treatment, which is similar to outpatient treatment except that it offers more frequent visits and closer monitoring of your status.

- **Partial hospital treatment (day hospital):** In terms of intensity, this treatment is "between" outpatient and inpatient treatment. Sometimes, people are treated in this setting after an inpatient stay so they can transition more gradually back to home. Partial hospital treatment lasts for much of the day, but you return home in the evening. It usually takes place from several days a week to 7 days a week. This treatment might last for a week or up to several months. Most partial hospital programs don't provide specialty treatment for BDD (a few exceptions are listed below), but they may provide useful support and structure if you're very distressed and having significant difficulty with daily functioning. Medication treatment can be monitored more closely than as an outpatient.

- **Inpatient treatment:** You stay overnight in the hospital. Inpatient hospitalization can last for as little as a day or two to as long as several months. Usually, in the United States, inpatient hospitalization is very brief and generally available only for people who pose a danger to themselves (are suicidal) or others (are violent), or who are unable to care for themselves

or be cared for by others at home because they're so ill. The vast majority
of inpatient units don't provide specialty care for BDD, although medication can be started or adjusted in this setting. Usually, as soon as people
are stabilized and safe, they go to a "lower level" of care, typically a partial
hospital or outpatient setting.

- **Residential treatment:** Residential treatment provides more intensive
  and longer-term treatment for more chronically and severely ill people,
  who live in the treatment setting. Residential treatment may not be widely
  available.

■ Should I Try to Treat Myself?

I'd recommend that you not try to treat yourself. Some people with mild BDD
may improve if they treat themselves with CBT techniques. But most people
will need professional care. Getting professional care is especially important
if you have severe symptoms, are very depressed, or are suicidal.

I strongly recommend that you not try to treat yourself with medication. The first-choice medicines for BDD (SRIs) are prescription medications.
Even though prescribing these and other medications might seem simple and
straightforward, it actually requires lots of training and skill to do it right.
The guidelines in this book are only general guidelines that can't be applied in
a cookbook fashion. It can even be harmful to treat yourself with medication.
Herbs and supplements that can be obtained without a prescription aren't
recommended for BDD.

■ Some More Advice When Seeking Treatment for BDD

- To find a licensed professional with expertise in BDD, you can try calling
  a professional organization in your state. For example, to find a psychiatrist, you can call your state psychiatric society for a referral. The websites
  listed below may also be helpful.

- If you live near a medical school, you can call the department of psychiatry to see if they have any faculty or staff with experience treating BDD.
  If you're a college student, contact your student health service to see what
  kind of treatment they provide. Or you can contact a local hospital to see
  if they have mental health clinicians on their staff. You can also try your
  local mental health center. Your primary care doctor may also be able to
  make a referral to a mental health professional.

- If you can't find a clinician with expertise in BDD, finding one with
  expertise in OCD or social phobia is the next best step. If your symptoms
  overlap a lot with an eating disorder (see Chapter 14), a clinician with

expertise in eating disorders is another option. But be sure to tell them that you think you have BDD!

- If you think you need treatment, but your insurance plan doesn't cover it, or doesn't offer enough treatment sessions, you can always ask the company for information on how to appeal their decision so you can get treated.

- If you don't have health insurance, ask a local medical school or doctors, therapists, or health care clinics in your area if they charge less, or nothing at all, for uninsured patients. Your local community mental health center may be a particularly good place to try. Many medical schools offer treatment by supervised trainees at a lower fee.

- If you can't afford medication, there are several options. First, your doctor may be able to give you free samples (although this often isn't possible). Some pharmaceutical companies offer patient-assistant programs that provide free medication to people with a limited income, although eligibility criteria are often stringent. At the time of this writing, several web sites, both nonprofit (e.g., www.needymeds.com) and supported by pharmaceutical companies (e.g., www.rxassist.org and www.pparx.org), offer centralized access to application forms for patient assistant programs. Alternatively, Wal-Mart and Target stores currently charge very little for 30-day supplies of certain medications.

- It's okay to ask over the phone, before you see a clinician for the first time, or when you see them in person, if they're familiar with BDD and the treatment described in this book.

- Tell the professional you see that you've read this book and think you may have BDD. Tell them about your body image concerns, not just your depression, anxiety, or other symptoms or problems. This way, you're more likely to get the right treatment.

- Keep this book's treatment guidelines in mind while also recognizing that your treatment will need to be individually tailored to you (See Chapters 10, 11, and 12).

- Some internet websites provide useful and accurate information on BDD and its treatment (I've listed some of these below). Others don't. Some recommend treatment approaches that have no scientific basis or evidence to support them, and they're unlikely to be helpful.

- Be persistent in getting and trying the treatments recommended in this book. Most people with BDD can get better!

■ Some Treatment and Research Programs

Here are some BDD programs where you may be able to find treatment or get more information on where to get help. Their websites offer useful information about BDD. Please note that I am familiar with some of the individuals and programs listed here, but I've made no independent investigation or assessment of the skills, experience, expertise, or credentials of all of them or their personnel. If you contact them, I'd suggest that you inquire further about their current program and current experience and expertise in treating BDD. To get additional names of people who treat BDD, please visit my website at www.bodyimageprogram.com. Some of the other websites below also list professionals who treat BDD.

BDD and Body Image Program

Butler Hospital and Brown University
345 Blackstone Boulevard
Providence, RI 02906
Phone: 401–455–6466 and 401–455–6490

Website: www.BodyImageProgram.com or www.butler.org/body.cfm?id=123. My website can also be reached through the Butler Hospital website and the Care New England website.

I founded this program at Butler Hospital/Brown University, which specializes in BDD, in 1994. Our mission is to do research to learn more about BDD and develop better treatments, to provide treatment, and to provide education and information about BDD. My website, which I periodically update, includes lots of information about BDD, a referral list of professionals around the world who have experience treating BDD, and references for scientific articles on BDD. My website also describes my program's ongoing research studies, which include treatment studies, both therapy and medication studies, for adults with BDD. We also offer a medication study for children and adolescents. We offer currently recommended treatments and new treatments for BDD. All participants receive actual treatment for BDD. Qualifying individuals receive free study treatment and monetary compensation for their participation.

BDD Clinic and Research Unit

Massachusetts General Hospital and Harvard Medical School, Simches Research Building, 185 Cambridge Street, Boston, MA 02114
Phone: 617–726–6766

Website: www.massgeneral.org/bdd/

This program is headed by Dr. Sabine Wilhelm, Associate Professor of Psychiatry at Harvard Medical School. She is a leading expert on BDD and CBT for BDD. Her website provides useful information about BDD and information about ongoing BDD treatment studies. Dr. Wilhelm and I are doing several BDD treatment studies together, and we coauthored the CBT treatment manual for therapists that is listed below.

Compulsive, Impulsive, and Anxiety Disorders Program

Mount Sinai School of Medicine, One Gustave L. Levy Place, P.O. Box 1230, New York, NY 10029
Phone: 917–492–9449

Website: www.mssm.edu/psychiatry/ciadp/index.shtml

This program is headed by Eric Hollander, M.D., Professor of Psychiatry at Mount Sinai Medical School, who is a leading expert in BDD. This program specializes in treating BDD, OCD, and related disorders as well as impulse control disorders. This program is participating in our child/adolescent treatment study.

Los Angeles Body Dysmorphic Disorder and Body Image Clinic

10850 Wilshire Blvd., Suite 240, Los Angeles, CA 90024
Phone: 310–741–2000

Website: www.bddclinic.com

This program, headed by Arie Winograd, L.M.F.T., offers outpatient treatment and a support group for BDD.

UCLA Body Dysmorphic Disorder Research Program

Semel Institute for Neuroscience and Human Behavior, David Geffen School of Medicine, 300 Medical Plaza Los Angeles, CA 90095
Phone: 310–206–4951

Website: www.npi.ucla.edu/bdd

This BDD research program is headed by Jamie Feusner, M.D. Dr. Feusner is also affiliated with the Los Angeles Body Dysmorphic Disorder and Body Image Clinic, described earlier.

UCLA OCD Intensive Treatment Program

Resnick Neuropsychiatric Hospital, UCLA, 300 UCLA Medical Plaza, Box 956968, Los Angeles, CA 90095–6968
Phone: 310–794–7305

Website: mentalhealth.ucla.edu/projects/anxiety/ocd

This 6-week OCD partial hospitalization program also provides treatment for BDD.

University of California at San Diego OCD Program

8950 Villa La Jolla Drive, Suite B225, La Jolla, CA 92037
Phone: 858–534–6200

Website: http://health.ucsd.edu/specialties/psych/adult_outpatient/ocd.htm

This program is headed by Sanjaya Saxena, M.D., Professor of Psychiatry, UCSD. The program offers treatment with both medications and CBT.

Menninger Clinic OCD Treatment Program

2801 Gessner Drive, Houston, TX 77080
Phone: 800–351–9058

Website: http://www.menningerclinic.com/p-ocd/index.htm

This program, under the direction of Thröstur Björgvinsson, Ph.D., Assistant Professor at Baylor College of Medicine, offers residential treatment for adolescents and adults with OCD and related disorders, including BDD.

BDD Treatment Programme

The Priory Hospital, North London, England
Grovelands House, Southgate, London N14 6RA, United Kingdom
Phone: 020 8882 8191

Website: www.veale.co.uk/index.html

This hospital's BDD program is overseen by Consultant Psychiatrist David Veale, M.D., who is a leading BDD expert. It offers inpatient, partial hospital, and outpatient treatment.

Centre for Anxiety Disorders & Trauma

99 Denmark Hill, London SE5 8AF, United Kingdom
Phone: 020 3228 2101 or 020 3228 3286

Website: www.psychology.iop.kcl.ac.uk/cadat/

Bio-Behavioral Institute

935 Northern Blvd, Suite 102, Great Neck, NY 11021
Phone: 516–487–7116

Website: www.bio-behavioral.com

This program is overseen by Fugen Neziroglu, Ph.D., Associate Professor at Hofstra University and Clinical Professor of Psychiatry at New York University, and Jose Yaryura-Tobias, M.D., Professor of Psychiatry at New

York University, who have expertise in BDD. The program offers an intensive outpatient program and an inpatient program for BDD.

Massachusetts General Hospital/McLean Hospital
OCD Institute at McLean Hospital

McLean Hospital, 115 Mill Street, Belmont, MA 02478
Phone: 617–855–3279

Website: www.mclean.harvard.edu/patient/adult/ocd.php

This program is under the direction of Michael Jenike, M.D., Professor of Psychiatry at Harvard Medical School. It provides partial hospital and residential treatment, primarily for OCD. This program also provides treatment for BDD.

Rogers Memorial Hospital OCD Center—Oconomowoc

34700 Valley Road, Oconomowoc, WI 53066
Phone: 800–767–4411

Website: www.rogershospital.org/obsessive_compulsivedisorders.php

Rogers Memorial Hospital—Milwaukee

11101 W. Lincoln Avenue, Milwaukee , WI 53227
Phone: 1–800–767–4411

Website: www.rogershospital.org/obsessive_compulsivedisorders.php

This program is directed by Bradley C. Riemann, Ph.D., Assistant Professor at Chicago Medical School, Marquette University, and the University of Wisconsin-Milwaukee. The program provides partial hospital and residential treatment for OCD and related disorders, including BDD.

■ Organizations and Websites

BDD Central

Website: www.bddcentral.com

This website, directed by Britney Brimhall, provides information about BDD as well as treatment resources, support groups, and links to other BDD resources.

Obsessive Compulsive Foundation

112 Water Street, Suite 501, Boston, MA 02119
Phone: 617–973–5801

www.ocfoundation.org.

The OCF educates the public and professional communities about OCD and related disorders, provides assistance to individuals with OCD and related disorders, and supports research into the causes and effective treatments of OCD and related disorders. This foundation keeps a referral list of clinicians who treat OCD and related disorders, including BDD.

Association for Behavioral and Cognitive Therapies

305 7th Avenue, New York, NY 10001
Phone: 212–647–1890

Website: www.aabt.org

This organization (formerly the Association for Advancement of Behavior Therapy) can help with a referral to a therapist who specializes in OCD or social phobia.

OCD Action

Davina House, Suite 506–507, 137–149 Goswell Road, London EC1V 7ET United Kingdom
Phone: 020 7253 5272

www.ocdaction.org.uk

National Alliance on Mental Illness

Colonial Place Three
2107 Wilson Blvd., Suite 300, Arlington, VA 22201–3042
Phone: 703–524–7600

Website: www.nami.org

While not focusing on BDD specifically, this organization is an effective and helpful self-help, support, and advocacy organization for people with severe mental illness. Their support groups may be helpful for people with BDD.

▪ Books and Other Reading

- *The Broken Mirror: Understanding and Treating Body Dysmorphic Disorder, Revised and Expanded Edition,* by Katharine A. Phillips, M.D. Published by Oxford University Press, 2005 (the first edition was published in 1996). This is my first book on BDD. It's longer than the current book, and it provides more detailed and comprehensive information about BDD.

- *Cognitive–Behavioral Therapy for Body Dysmorphic Disorder,* by Sabine Wilhelm, Ph.D., Katharine A. Phillips, M.D., and Gail Steketee, Ph.D. Published by Guilford Publications, 2009. This book provides a detailed guide for clinicians who want to treat BDD with CBT. Its approach to CBT is similar to that outlined in this book.

- *The Adonis Complex: How to Identify, Treat, and Prevent Body Obsession in Men and Boys,* by Harrison G. Pope, Jr., M.D., Katharine A. Phillips, M.D., and Roberto Olivardia, Ph.D. Published by The Free Press, 2002. This book reveals the many types of body image obsessions that affect boys and men, including muscle dysmorphia, other forms of BDD, and eating disorders. It offers practical approaches to overcoming these problems.

- *Feeling Good About the Way You Look,* by Sabine Wilhelm, Ph.D. Published by Guilford Press, 2006. This self-help book complements the clinician treatment guide referenced above. It focuses on CBT for BDD, using an approach that's similar to the one described in this book.

- **Scientific research articles published in journals:** Researchers like myself are constantly doing scientific research on BDD to increase knowledge of this disorder and how to effectively treat it. The results of research studies are published in scientific journals. While these reports are geared toward other scientists and clinicians, you may want to look at them to stay abreast of new knowledge on BDD. To find some of these articles you can check out PubMed, a service of the National Library of Medicine. It provides access to over 17 million citations for professional articles in life science journals. Increasingly, you can access complete articles for free. The address is www.pubmed.com. Once you get to the site, if you type in "body dysmorphic disorder" in quotation marks, you'll find citations for many published articles reporting research findings on BDD. I periodically update my website (www.bodyimageprogram.com), which includes a list of recent articles on BDD that you can find on PubMed.

■ Concluding Thoughts

I hope I've conveyed what my patients would want you to know about BDD. This disorder affects many lives, and it causes great suffering. Certain treatments are very helpful and offer much hope for BDD sufferers.

BDD is a common but underdiagnosed disorder. Sufferers often keep their emotional pain a secret, even from their loved ones. Courage is often needed to tell others about it. Despite the suffering it causes, BDD is often overlooked and trivialized. Many people feel isolated and alone.

The voices in this book speak as strongly and as clearly as the facts. I hope that readers with BDD and their friends and family will take comfort in knowing they aren't alone.

Have hope! The treatments I've discussed can make a tremendous difference—in some cases, a lifesaving difference—in the lives of people with BDD. In the future, we will know more and probably have even more and better treatments.

Luke's and Pat's words echo what many patients have told me:

"Suicide is the furthest thing from my mind now. I have a great life. Thank God I got treatment. I owe my life to it."

"Tell everyone you know with BDD never to give up! I almost did. Thank God I didn't. Finally, after all these years, I feel really good! Tell them there's hope."

GLOSSARY

Agoraphobia   Anxiety about being in places or situations from which escape might be difficult or embarrassing, or in which help might not be available, in the event of having a panic attack or panic-like symptoms. Typically, people with agoraphobia feel anxious in or avoid being outside of their home alone, in a crowd, on a bridge, or traveling in buses, cars, or trains.

Amygdala   A small almond-shaped structure deep in the brain. The amygdala is the command center for the body's fear system. It communicates potential threats (e.g., perceived environmental threats) to other relevant brain areas so the threat can be quickly responded to. The amygdala is also involved in processing and reacting to emotional facial expressions.

Anafranil   The brand name for the SRI medication clomipramine (see clomipramine).

Anorexia nervosa   A type of eating disorder in which the person refuses to maintain body weight in the normal range and has an intense fear of gaining weight or becoming fat despite being underweight. Anorexia nervosa also involves a disturbance in the way one's body weight or shape is experienced, undue influence of body weight or shape on self-evaluation, or denial of the seriousness of the low body weight. Amenorrhea (the absence of at least three consecutive menstrual cycles) also occurs.

Antidepressant   A class of medications effective for treating major depressive disorder. Antidepressants are also effective for a variety of other disorders, such as dysthymia, panic disorder, social phobia, bulimia, generalized anxiety disorder, obsessive compulsive disorder, and others. Certain antidepressants are also used to treat nonpsychiatric disorders, such as headache and pain syndromes. There are many different types of antidepressant medication. The serotonin-reuptake inhibitors (SRIs, or SSRIs) are a specific type of antidepressant medication.

Augmentation   Adding a second medication to a medication that's already being taken in order to boost the first medication's effectiveness. This approach is commonly used for depression and other disorders. In BDD, the augmenting medication is usually added to an SRI.

Behavioral experiment   This is a component of cognitive-behavioral therapy. It's often integrated with exposure. A behavioral experiment is an experiment that a person designs and carries out to collect evidence for and against a particular prediction. The purpose is to objectively find out whether the prediction comes true.

Benzodiazepine   A type of medication used primarily to treat anxiety and insomnia.

Brain circuit   Interconnected neurons in the brain which influence one another's activity and specialize in certain tasks (such as interpreting visual images).

Bulimia nervosa   A type of eating disorder in which the person has recurrent episodes of binge eating, recurrent compensatory behaviors to prevent weight gain (e.g., self-induced vomiting), and a disturbance in body image (self-evaluation is unduly influenced by body weight and shape).

Buspirone (Buspar)   A type of antianxiety medication with effects on serotonin. It's sometimes used to augment an SRI when treating BDD or depression.

Caudate   The caudate is a C-shaped structure deep in the brain's core (the striatum), which regulates voluntary movements, habits, learning and cognitions (e.g., memory). It may be involved in BDD.

CBT   See cognitive-behavioral therapy.

Celexa   The brand name for the SRI medication citalopram (see citalopram).

Citalopram (Celexa)   A type of serotonin-reuptake inhibitor, a class of medications that diminish obsessional thoughts and compulsive behaviors (rituals) as well as depression and other symptoms (e.g., anxiety).

Clomipramine (Anafranil)   A type of serotonin-reuptake inhibitor, a class of antidepressant medications that diminish obsessional thoughts and compulsive behaviors (rituals) as well as depression and other symptoms (e.g., anxiety).

Cognitive-behavioral therapy (CBT)   A practical, "here-and-now" type of therapy that encompasses a number of specific therapeutic approaches. The **cognitive** aspect of CBT focuses on cognitions—that is, thoughts and beliefs. The goal of cognitive therapy is to identify, evaluate, and change distorted, unrealistic, and unhelpful ways of thinking. The **behavioral** aspect of CBT focuses on problematic behaviors (rituals and avoidance), such as excessive checking and social avoidance. The aim is to stop performing rituals, no longer avoid situations, and substitute healthier behaviors. Often, cognitive and behavioral approaches are combined—hence, the commonly used term "cognitive-behavioral therapy," or CBT. CBT is used to treat disorders such as depression, phobias, panic disorder, obsessive-compulsive disorder, and eating disorders, among others. It is currently the psychotherapy of choice for BDD.

Cognitive restructuring   A component of cognitive therapy and, more broadly, of cognitive-behavioral therapy. Cognitive restructuring involves learning to identify and evaluate negative thoughts and beliefs as well as thinking (cognitive) errors. This process generates more accurate and helpful beliefs.

Cognitive therapy   Cognitive therapy is a practical, here-and-now treatment that is part of cognitive-behavioral therapy (CBT). Cognitive therapy teaches specific skills and uses cognitive approaches to learning. It's used to treat a host of mental disorders, including BDD. It includes cognitive restructuring. In BDD and many other disorders, cognitive therapy is combined with behavioral techniques—hence, the term cognitive-behavioral therapy.

Compulsion   Also known as a ritual. A compulsion is an excessive repetitive behavior (such as hand washing or checking) or mental act (such as counting) that's performed to try to decrease anxiety caused by an obsession (repetitive thought). Compulsions are usually difficult to resist or control. They are characteristic of obsessive compulsive disorder and BDD. Examples of compulsions in BDD are mirror checking, excessive grooming, reassurance seeking, and skin picking.

Controlled study   A type of study in which the treatment being investigated is compared to another type of treatment received by a "control group." The control group may receive a standard and proven treatment, a competing experimental treatment, no treatment (for example, they may be on a treatment waiting list), or a placebo. A placebo in a medication study is an inert substance (also known as a "sugar pill") that physically resembles the treatment being studied. If a controlled study shows that a treatment is as effective as a proven treatment, or more effective than placebo, this is strong evidence that the treatment works.

Delusion (delusional thinking)   A false belief based on incorrect assumptions about external reality that is firmly sustained despite what almost everyone else believes.

Delusional BDD   A form of BDD in which negative, inaccurate beliefs about appearance are held with absolute conviction and certainty (for example, a normal-looking person is 100% certain that their head is "gigantic"). This form of BDD is probably the same disorder as the nondelusional form of BDD, in which the person can acknowledge that their view of their appearance may be distorted or inaccurate.

Dopamine   One of the brain's many neurotransmitters (brain chemicals that are transmitted between nerve cells). Dopamine plays an important role in certain movement disorders and in many psychiatric disorders, especially those characterized by delusional thinking and hallucinations. It may play a role in BDD.

DSM   DSM stands for Diagnostic and Statistical Manual of Mental Disorders. This manual contains the official classification system for psychiatric disorders used in the United States. Disorders in DSM are defined by "diagnostic criteria" that describe their essential features. DSM-IV is the current version of DSM. DSM-IV-TR (TR stands for "text revision") contains the same disorders and the same diagnostic criteria as DSM-IV, but supplementary explanatory text has been updated.

Dysmorphophobia   An older term for BDD that's occasionally still used. It's occasionally used in a broader sense than BDD, to refer not only to the specific disorder BDD but to any excessive preoccupation with a minimal or nonexistent defect in appearance.

Electroconvulsive therapy (ECT)   Also known as shock therapy. ECT is a very effective treatment for depression. It's usually reserved for more severe depression that hasn't improved with antidepressant medication.

Escitalopram (Lexapro)   A type of serotonin-reuptake inhibitor, a class of antidepressant medications that diminish obsessional thoughts and compulsive behaviors (rituals) as well as depression and other symptoms (e.g., anxiety).

Exposure   Also known as exposure therapy. Exposure is a component of cognitive-behavioral therapy that's effective for obsessive compulsive disorder and certain other disorders, especially anxiety disorders. **Exposure** consists of facing feared and avoided situations. In BDD, these situations typically involve being around other people. Exposure is combined with ritual prevention, which consists of not performing compulsive behaviors (rituals). When treating BDD, exposure is usually combined with behavioral experiments.

Exposure hierarchy   A method used in exposure therapy. It's a list of situations that cause anxiety. The situations are rated according to how much anxiety they produce and how much they're avoided.

Extrastriate body area   An area of the brain that responds to visual images of human bodies and nonface body parts. This area is located toward the back of the brain between the occipital and temporal lobes.

Fluoxetine (Prozac)   A type of serotonin-reuptake inhibitor, a class of antidepressant medications that diminish obsessional thoughts and compulsive behaviors (rituals) as well as depression and other symptoms (e.g., anxiety).

Fluvoxamine (Luvox)   A type of serotonin-reuptake inhibitor, a class of antidepressant medications that diminish obsessional thoughts and compulsive behaviors (rituals) as well as depression and other symptoms (e.g., anxiety).

Fusiform face area   An area of the brain that responds selectively to visual images of human faces. The fusiform area is located in a region toward the back of the brain between the occipital and temporal lobes.

GABA (gamma-aminobutyric acid)   One of the many neurotransmitters (chemical messengers) in the brain that transmits messages between nerve cells. GABA is ubiquitous in the brain and is the primary inhibitory neurotransmitter.

Genetics   Genetics studies characteristics of living organisms that are inherited, and which genes are responsible for passing certain characteristics from one generation to the next. Genetic information is carried by DNA.

Habit reversal   This is an established treatment for trichotillomania (hair pulling) that's increasingly being used for other problematic habits, such as skin picking. It consists of awareness training (becoming more aware of when the behavior occurs, triggers for the behavior, etc.), learning a competing response (doing something else with your hands), relaxation, rewarding yourself for not doing the behaviors, and learning to use habit reversal in a wide range of situations. In BDD, habit reversal is used to help people get control over compulsive skin picking, hair pulling or hair plucking, and touching disliked body areas.

Hypochondriasis   Preoccupation with fears of having, or the idea that one has, a serious disease based on a misinterpretation of bodily symptoms. The preoccupation persists despite appropriate medical evaluation and reassurance, and it causes clinically significant distress or impairment in functioning.

ICD-10   The current international classification and nomenclature system for medical and psychiatric disorders published by the World Health Organization. Its psychiatric classification system is very similar to that of DSM-IV.

Insight   This term has several meanings, even within psychiatry/psychology. In this book, it's used to mean that a person recognizes that an inaccurate belief they have isn't really true and that their belief is due to a mental illness.

Insight-oriented psychotherapy   Also known as psychodynamic or exploratory psychotherapy, this is a type of "talking therapy." It focuses on increasing self-awareness and bringing about behavioral change (e.g., improving relationship with others) through exploration of one's perceptions and interactions with others.

Insomnia   Difficulty sleeping.

Lexapro   The brand name for the SRI medication escitalopram (see escitalopram).

Luvox   The brand name for the SRI medication fluvoxamine (see fluvoxamine).

Major depressive disorder   Also known as major depression. A depressive disorder characterized by depressed mood or loss of interest or pleasure, as well as other symptoms. These include abnormal sleep or appetite (too much or too little), fatigue, low self-esteem or feelings of worthlessness, guilt, difficulty concentrating, and thoughts that life isn't worth living.

    Atypical subtype   A type of major depression in which mood is reactive (that is, it brightens in response to actual or potential positive events) as well as two or more of the following features: significant weight gain or increase in appetite, an increase in sleep, heavy feelings in the arms or legs, and sensitivity to rejection by others leading to difficulties in social or occupational functioning.

MAOI (MAO inhibitor)   A class of antidepressant medication that is very effective but no longer widely used.

Mindfulness   Mindfulness skills are psychological and behavioral versions of meditation practices from Eastern spiritual training. They involve a particular way of observing and being aware of your thoughts and emotions by focusing on them "in the moment" in a nonjudgmental way. Mindfulness is used in the treatment of certain psychiatric disorders and is a potentially useful addition to the core CBT approaches for BDD.

Minoxidil   The generic name for Rogaine. A medication taken to promote hair growth.

Morphometric magnetic resonance imaging (MRI)   This is a brain imaging technique used commonly in medicine. It provides a picture of the brain's structure. Functional MRI provides a picture of the brain's activity.

Muscle dysmorphia   A form of BDD in which people—usually boys and men—think they're too small, thin, or inadequately muscular, even though they look normal or even unusually muscular.

Neuroleptic   A type of medication used to treat Tourette's disorder, delusional disorder, schizophrenia, bipolar disorder (manic depressive illness), and other disorders. Neuroleptics may also be used in combination with other medication to treat obsessive compulsive disorder and major depressive disorder. They are sometimes used to treat nausea. They're also known as antipsychotics, even though they're commonly used to treat symptoms other than psychosis.

Neuropsychological studies   Studies that use neuropsychological tests to assess brain function. These tests often consist of cognitive (e.g., language, memory, or attention) or sensorimotor (e.g., perception, ability to draw a line, finger tapping) tasks.

Neurotransmitter   A type of chemical messenger in the brain that transmits messages between nerve cells. There are many types of neurotransmitters, including serotonin, norepinephrine, GABA, and dopamine. Abnormal functioning of brain neurotransmitters is implicated in many neurological and psychiatric disorders.

Nondelusional BDD   A form of BDD in which the person realizes that their inaccurate beliefs about their appearance may not be true. This form of BDD is probably the same disorder as the delusional form of BDD, in which the person is completely convinced that their view of their appearance is accurate.

Obsession   A recurrent, persistent, and intrusive thought, impulse, or image that's difficult to dismiss despite its disturbing nature. Obsessional thinking is characteristic of obsessive-compulsive disorder and BDD.

Obsessive compulsive disorder (OCD)   OCD is characterized by obsessions or compulsions (usually both) that cause marked distress, are time consuming (take more than 1 hour a day), or significantly interfere with functioning. Obsessions are recurrent, persistent, and intrusive thoughts, impulses, or images. Compulsions are repetitive behaviors (e.g., hand washing or checking) or mental acts (e.g., counting) that are performed in response to an obsession and are aimed at preventing or reducing distress or a dreaded event.

Occipital lobe   The occipital lobe is the visual processing center of the brain. It's located at the back of the brain.

OCD   See obsessive-compulsive disorder.

Open study   Also known as an open-label study. This is an uncontrolled study (one with no comparison group) in which both the patient and doctor know what treatment the patient is receiving.

Orbitofrontal cortex   An area on the bottom of the front part of the brain that's involved in memory and social functioning. This area plays an important role in OCD and may also be important in BDD.

Orbitofrontal-striatal-thalamic circuit ("worry loop")   This brain circuit connects the orbitofrontal cortex with the striatum (which includes the caudate), thalamus, and other nearby brain structures. This circuit is overactive in obsessive compulsive disorder. It may also be involved in BDD.

Panic attacks   Panic attacks consist of a discrete period of intense fear or discomfort that peaks within 10 minutes of onset and is accompanied by a number of physical symptoms, such as heart palpitations, sweating, trembling or shaking, shortness of breath, chest pain or discomfort, feeling dizzy, and fear of dying.

Panic disorder   Panic disorder consists of recurrent panic attacks that come out of the blue. At least one of the attacks has been followed by one month or more of one (or more) of the following: concern about having more attacks, worry about the consequences of the attacks, or a significant change in behavior related to the attacks.

Parietal lobe   An area on the upper side of the brain toward its back that has many functions. It plays a key role in body image and may be important in BDD.

Paroxetine (Paxil)   A type of serotonin-reuptake inhibitor, medications that diminish obsessional thoughts and compulsive behaviors (rituals) as well as depression and other symptoms (e.g., anxiety).

Paxil   The brand name for the SRI medication paroxetine (see paroxetine).

Perceptual (mirror) retraining   A technique used in cognitive-behavioral therapy for BDD that focuses on (1) learning to look at your **entire** face or body (not just the disliked areas) while looking in the mirror, and (2) learning to **nonjudgmentally and objectively** (rather than negatively) describe your body while looking in the mirror. The ritual of mirror checking shouldn't be done during this exercise.

Pimozide (Orap)   A type of neuroleptic medication.

Placebo   In a medication study, an inert substance, sometimes called a **"sugar pill,"** that physically resembles the medication being studied. The patient is unable to discriminate between the placebo pill and active treatment, and doesn't know which treatment he or she is receiving. In a "double-blind" study, the physician also doesn't know whether the patient is receiving placebo or active treatment. This study design guards against bias in assessing treatment outcome. If the treatment being studied is more effective than placebo, this is strong evidence that it's effective.

Post-traumatic stress disorder (PTSD)   PTSD develops following exposure to a traumatic event. PTSD is characterized by persistent reexperiencing of the traumatic event (e.g., recurrent distressing dreams), persistent avoidance of stimuli associated with the trauma and numbing of general responsiveness, and persistent symptoms of increased arousal (e.g., difficulty falling or staying asleep or an exaggerated startle response).

Prospective study   A study that is done "forward over time." In other words, such studies measure characteristics or events as they occur, after the study has started. In contrast, retrospective studies are done "backwards over time," in that they collect data about events that have already occurred.

Prozac   The brand name for the SRI medication fluoxetine (see fluoxetine).

Referential thinking   Casual incidents and events are misinterpreted to have a special meaning that is specific to the person. An example in BDD is thinking that someone is staring at you because you're ugly rather than just glancing in your direction while thinking about something else. "Referential thinking" includes ideas of reference and delusions of reference. When the person is certain the events are referring to them, the phenomenon is called **delusions of reference**. When they think this is happening but aren't certain that it is, the phenomenon is called **ideas of reference**.

Retrospective study   A study done "backwards over time"; in other words, data are collected about events that have already occurred. This is in contrast to a prospective study, in which data are collected about events or characteristics at the time they actually occur.

Ritual   Also known as a compulsion. A ritual is an excessive repetitive behavior (such as hand washing or checking) or mental act (such as counting) that's performed to try to decrease anxiety caused by an obsession (repetitive thought). Rituals are usually difficult to resist or control. They are characteristic of obsessive compulsive disorder and BDD. Examples of rituals in BDD are mirror checking, excessive grooming, reassurance seeking, and skin picking.

Ritual (response) prevention   A component of behavioral therapy in which repetitive ritualistic behaviors (compulsions), such as excessive mirror checking or excessive grooming, are stopped.

Schizophrenia   Schizophrenia consists of symptoms such as delusions, hallucinations, disorganized speech, behavior that is grossly disorganized or abnormal (e.g., purposeless agitation), and symptoms such as lack of emotion or motivation. The symptoms cause impairment in functioning.

Selective serotonin-reuptake inhibitor (SSRI)   A type of serotonin-reuptake inhibitor (SRI) that has prominent effects on serotonin but little direct effect on other neurotransmitters. The SSRIs currently marketed in the United States are fluoxetine (Prozac), fluvoxamine (Luvox), paroxetine (Paxil), sertraline (Zoloft), escitalopram (Lexapro), and citalopram (Celexa). Clomipramine (Anafranil), an SRI, has fairly prominent effects on the neurotransmitter norepinephrine in addition to serotonin. SRIs are currently the medication of choice for BDD.

Serotonin   One of the many neurotransmitters (chemical messengers) in the brain. Serotonin plays an important role in mood, sleep, appetite, pain, impulsivity, and other bodily functions. Abnormal functioning of serotonin is involved in a wide variety of psychiatric disorders, including depression, obsessive compulsive disorder, and eating disorders. It probably plays an important role in BDD.

Serotonin-reuptake inhibitor (SRI)   A class of antidepressant medication with prominent effects on serotonin. This is a broader term that encompasses the narrower term SSRI. Unlike other antidepressants, SRIs diminish obsessional thoughts and compulsive behaviors, and they effectively treat obsessive compulsive disorder as well as depression and a broad range of other disorders. The SRIs currently marketed in the United States are clomipramine (Anafranil), fluoxetine (Prozac), fluvoxamine (Luvox), paroxetine (Paxil), sertraline (Zoloft), citalopram (Celexa), and escitalopram (Lexapro).

Sertraline (Zoloft)   A type of serotonin-reuptake inhibitor, a class of medications that diminish obsessional thoughts and compulsive behaviors (rituals) as well as depression and other symptoms (e.g., anxiety).

Social phobia   Also known as social anxiety disorder. A marked and persistent fear of one or more social or performance situations in which the person is exposed to unfamiliar people or to possible scrutiny by others. The person fears appearing anxious or doing something humiliating or embarrassing in front of others. The fears may occur in most social situations (generalized type) or in a specific situation (e.g., fear of public speaking).

SRI   See serotonin-reuptake inhibitor.

SSRI   See selective serotonin-reuptake inhibitor.

Striatum   A part of the brain that consists of the caudate and an area called the putamen. This area is involved in regulating voluntary movements, habits, and cognitions (e.g., memory). It's important in OCD and other disorders, and may be important in BDD.

Substance use disorder   Problematic use of alcohol or street drugs (abuse or dependence). This includes cocaine, marijuana, opioids (e.g., heroin), hallucinogens (e.g., LSD), and other illicit drugs.

Supportive psychotherapy   A type of talking therapy that focuses on the creation of emotional support and a stable, caring relationship with patients. The therapist focuses more on providing support than on increasing patients' understanding of themselves. Advice, learning new social skills, and assistance in problem solving are often components of this approach.

Temporal lobe   The temporal lobe is an area on the side of the brain that's important in speech, hearing, and memory. It also plays a role in vision.

Thinking errors   Also known as cognitive errors or cognitive distortions. These are faulty or distorted ways of thinking that fuel negative thoughts and beliefs. Examples of thinking errors are mind reading, fortune-telling, and catastrophizing. During the cognitive restructuring part of CBT, thinking errors are identified, which helps to generate more rational and helpful thoughts and beliefs.

Thought record   A form used in cognitive restructuring (see Chapter 12 for examples).

Trichotillomania   Recurrent pulling out of one's hair, resulting in noticeable hair loss as well as clinically significant distress or impairment in functioning.

Zoloft   The brand name for the SRI medication sertraline (see sertraline).

INDEX

Accidents, 16, 77, 91, 107, 109, 236
Accutane, 111, 234, 239. *See also* Isotretinoin
Acne, 15, 65
   and appearance preoccupation, 118, 120
   facial, 48
   mild, 19, 49, 50, 62, 64, 83
   perceptions about, 64
   and skin picking, 76, 79, 80
   and suicide, 111, 113
Acne medication and products, 84, 107, 108,
   234, 239
   Accutane, 111
Acral lick syndrome, 130
Activity scheduling, 226
Adjunctive therapy, 231
Adolescents. *See* Children and adolescents
   with BDD
*Adonis Complex: How to Identify, Treat, and
   Prevent Body Obsession in Men and
   Boys* (Pope, Philips, Olivardia), 274
Aesthetics, 135
Age of onset, 116–118. *See also* Children and
   adolescents with BDD
Aging, BDD and, 124–125
Agoraphobia, 39, 277
Alcohol abuse, 105, 121, 180, 230
Algorithm for medication treatment,
   185–186, 187
American Society for Aesthetic Plastic
   Surgery (ASAPS), 108, 237

Amygdala, 131, 133, 157, 277
Anabolic steroids, 51, 106, 113, 136
Anafranil. *See* Clomipramine
   (Anafranil)
Anger and hostility, 107–108
   SRIs in treatment of, 163
   support of family and, 257, 261–262
   toward surgeons, 108, 238–239
Animal research, 161
Anorexia nervosa, 18, 250, 277
Anterior internal capsulotomy, 184
Antidepressants, 156. *See also* Monoamine
   oxidase inhibitors; Serotonin-
   reuptake inhibitors (SRIs)
   defined, 277
   MAOIs, 24, 182, 186, 281
   tricyclic, 183
Antipsychotic drugs. *See* Neuroleptics
Anxiety, 22, 104, 112, 161, 177
   and appearance concerns, 84
   and camouflage, 78
   and CBT, 196, 217, 218
   and compulsive behaviors, 70-1, 72
   and distress, 70–71
   and exposure therapy, 210
   medications to treat, 176, 180
     benzodiazepines, 180
     SRIs, 151
   and mirror checking, 70, 72, 222
   and ritual prevention, 219, 220

Anxiety disorder:
  agoraphobia, 39, 277
  panic disorder, 25, 40, 112, 149, 156, 189,
    277, 278, 283
  post-traumatic stress disorder, 283–284
  social phobia, 25, 38, 104, 197, 200,
    248–249, 285
Appearance concerns, 26–27, 49–50. *See also*
    Body image; Hair concerns; Skin
    concerns
  and actual vs. ideal self, 134
  and BDD by proxy, 52–56
  and BDD Diagnostic Module, 20, 21–22,
    25, 28, 113
  in children and adolescents, 16,
    118–119, 123
  differentiating BDD from normal
    concerns, 32–35
  dissatisfaction, 33, 134, 135
  normal, and BDD compared, 34
  obsessive, 51
  and overfocusing, 18
  preoccupation with, 17–20, 44–46, 58
  and self esteem, 103
  society's focus on, 136
Association for Behavioral and Cognitive
    Therapies, 273
Attractiveness:
  and body image, 10, 18, 237
  self-evaluation, 61, 100, 118
  societal messages, 127
Augmentation, of SRIs, 175, 176–180,
    185, 278
Avoidance behaviors, 91, 93–94, 95,
    97, 98–99, 100, 161, 191,
    198, 205–206, 211

Baldness, 48, 52, 53, 54, 74, 75, 90, 118.
    See also Hair loss/thinning
Barbie (toy), 136
BDD. *See also individual entries*
  definition, 17
  by proxy, 52–56, 134
BDD and Body Image Program, 269
BDD Central, 272
BDD Clinic and Research Unit, 269–270
BDD Diagnostic Module, 28, 30, 31, 33, 35,
    38, 124

BDD Treatment Programme, 271
BDD-YBOCS. *See* Yale-Brown Obsessive-
    Compulsive Scale Modified for BDD
Beauty products, 83–84, 223, 252
Behavioral experiments, in CBT:
  defined, 278
  and exposure therapy, 190–191, 210–218
Behaviors, in BDD, 68. *See also* Avoidance;
    Compulsive behaviors; Rituals
  camouflaging, 68–69, 77, 78
  clothes changing, 84
  combing, 67
  comparing, 73–74
  compulsive shopping, 84
  control of, 70
  dieting, 61, 84–85
  distraction techniques, 87
  and distress, 70–71
  doctor shopping, 82–83
  exercise, 85–86
  grooming, 75–76
  hand washing, 87–88
  information seeking, 86
  and interference in functioning, 70
  measuring, 86
  of men with muscle dysmorphia, 51
  mirror checking, 14, 15, 35, 60, 70, 71–73,
    119, 198, 224
  personal experience (cases), 90–91
  reading, 86
  reassurance seeking (questioning),
    80–82, 279
  resistance, 70
  skin picking, 78–80
  tanning, 83
  time spent on, 70
  touching, 86–87
  weight lifting, 85–86
Benzodiazepines, 180, 186, 278
Bio-Behavioral Institute, 271–272
Bipolar disorder (manic-depressive illness),
    118, 149, 179, 182
Bodily damage, 107
Bodily symmetry, 130
Body checking, 86. *See also* Mirror checking
Body Dysmorphic Disorder Questionnaire
    (BDDQ), 28, 29, 30, 31, 33, 35,
    122–123, 145

Body hair, 48, 75, 82. *See also* Hair concerns

Body image, 18, 22–23, 28, 43–49, 55. *See also*
  Appearance concerns; Eating disorders
  and attractiveness, 14, 18, 235
  and CBT, 196
  and cosmetic surgery, 237
  dissatisfaction, 250
  and SRIs in treatment of, 163

Brain and BDD, 131–132
  and adolescent development, 138–139
  amygdala, 131, 133, 157
  caudate, 132, 278
  dopamine, 130, 279
  extrastriate body area, 280
  fusiform face area, 280
  GABA (gamma-aminobutyric acid),
    129, 280
  hyperactivity in, 133
  occipital lobe, 282
  orbitofrontal-striatal-thalamic circuit
    ("worry loop"), 283
  parietal lobe, 133, 283
  serotonin hypothesis, 133
  striatum, 133, 285
  temporal lobe, 131, 285
  visual processing, 132, 133, 163

Brain circuit, 278

Breast concerns, 16, 23, 48, 54, 61, 74, 77,
    120, 239

Bright lights, avoiding, 99

*The Broken Mirror: Understanding and
  Treating Body Dysmorphic
  Disorder*, 273

Bulimia nervosa, 21, 247, 248, 278

Bupropion (Wellbutrin), 178, 186

Buspirone (Buspar), 278
  augmentation of SRI with, 177

Camouflage, 68, 69–70, 76–78, 84, 98, 116, 217
  body parts, 78
  body position as, 78
  clothing as, 51, 69, 77–78
  hair/wigs as, 77, 78
  hats as, 69, 77, 98
  makeup as, 69, 77, 78, 116
  masks as, 77

Care levels, of treatment, 266–267

Caring, for children, 98

Caudate, 278

Causes of BDD, 127–139. *See also* Triggers
  aesthetics, 135
  brain-based, 131–133
  childhood maltreatment, 134
  cultural influences, 136–137
  evolution and animal models, 130
  genetic and neurobiological risk factors,
    128–133
  life experiences, 134
  neurotransmitters, 133
  noncauses, 138
  overfocusing and selective attention,
    130–131
  patients' perspectives, 127
  personality traits and values, 135
  psychological risk factors, 134–136
  serotonin hypothesis, 133
  society's focus on appearance, 136–137
  teasing and life experience, 134
  threat misperception, 131–132

CBT. *See* Cognitive-behavioral therapy

Celexa (citalopram). *See* Citalopram

Centre for Anxiety Disorders & Trauma, 271

Childhood maltreatment, 134–135

Children and adolescents with BDD,
    118–119
  BDD behaviors in, 118–120
  characteristics of, 119–120
  diagnosis in, 122, 123, 254–255
  diagnostic questionnaire, 28, 29, 30, 31,
    33, 35, 122–123, 145
  diagnostic scale, 28, 30, 31, 33, 35, 38, 124
  and mirror checking, 119
  parents' perspective, 229
  and puberty, 116
  and self-esteem, 121
  suicide attempts, 120–122
  and teasing, 134
  treatment for, 122–125, 157, 247

Citalopram, 155, 158, 161, 167, 168, 170,
    177, 278
  dosage, 167, 168
  effectiveness of, 158, 161, 167
  study of, 170, 178

Clinical psychologists, 265

Clinical settings, 25

Clinicians, 265

Clomipramine (Anafranil), 155, 177–178,
        186, 278
    augmentation of, 178
    dosage, 168
    effectiveness of, 167
    side effects, 167, 173
    study of, 158
Clonazepam (Klonopin), 180
Clothing, 84
    as camouflage, 77–78
Cognitive-behavioral therapy (CBT), 59, 114,
        130–131, 142, 189
    activity scheduling, 226
    and anxiety, 196, 216, 217
    an approach, 200–227
    behavioral experiments, 190–191, 210–218
    body image and, 196
    cognitive errors, 205, 206
    cognitive restructuring, 190
    defined, 278–279
    depression and, 199–200
    effectiveness, 183–186
    exposure therapy, 190–191, 199, 210–218
    family and friends and, 254–255, 256,
        258–259
    FAQs about, 198–200
    goal-setting for, 201
    group therapy, 229
    habit reversal, 225
    improvement with, 196–197
    and insight, 196
    medication, 143, 146–150, 180, 259
    mindfulness, 225–226
    model to treat, 197–198
    perceptual (mirror) retraining, 191–192,
        224–225
    rationale for, 197–198
    relapse prevention, 196, 226
    ritual prevention, 191, 218–220
    sessions, 192, 227
    stages of, 200–201
    strategies in case of non-effectiveness,
        226–227
    therapist, 200, 265
    thought record for, 204, 208, 209
*Cognitive-Behavioral Therapy for Body
        Dysmorphic Disorder,* 265
Cognitive errors, 205, 208

Cognitive restructuring, 190–201, 202
    and cognitive errors, 205
    to correct negative core beliefs, 198,
        208–209, 216
    defined, 279
    and negative thinking, 202–203
    thought record with, 202, 203–208, 209
Cognitive therapy, 279. *See also*
        Cognitive-behavioral therapy
Comparing behavior, 73–74
Compulsion. *See* Compulsive behaviors;
        Rituals
Compulsive behaviors, 10, 51, 68, 70, 71,
        119, 120, 146, 147, 150, 157, 162, 179,
        197, 244, 246, 247. *See also* Obsessive
        compulsive disorder; Repetitive
        behaviors; Rituals
    in animals, 130
    brain circuitry and, 128
    camouflaging, 68–69, 77, 78
    clothes changing, 84
    compulsive shopping, 84
    dieting, 61, 84–85
    doctor shopping, 82–83
    exercise, 85–86
    grooming, 75–76
    hand washing, 87–88
    information seeking, 86
    mirror checking, 11, 35, 71–73, 81, 87, 222
    reading, 86
    reassurance seeking (questioning),
        80–82, 279
    and ritual prevention, 219
    shopping as, 84
    skin picking, 78–80
    and SRIs, 157
    tanning, 83
    touching, 86–87
    weight lifting, 85–86
Compulsive, Impulsive, and Anxiety
        Disorders Program, 270
Controlled study, 279
Cosmetic (plastic) surgery, 223, 234–242. *See
        also* Nose job (rhinoplasty); Surgeons
    BDD patients and, 234–241
    BDD symptoms, 236–238
    dissatisfaction with, 237
    unnecessary, 106

Cosmetic treatment, 69, 106, 108, 233–241
Couples and family therapy, 229
Culture and BDD, 136–137. *See also*
      Sociocultural theories

Day treatment, 231, 266. *See also* Partial hos-
      pital treatment
Delusional BDD, 120
   defined as, 279
   neuroleptic drugs in treatment,
      178–179
   and schizophrenia, 250
   SRIs to treat, 133, 158, 167, 177, 185
Delusional thinking, 64–65, 279. *See also*
      Insight
Dental treatment, 233, 235
Depression, 16, 35, 60, 61, 246–247
   atypical subtype, 37, 246, 281
   BDD misdiagnosed as, 28, 38, 250
   and CBT, 200
   differences with BDD, 246–247
   hospitalization for, 76
   and low self-esteem, 102–103
   and mania (bipolar disorder), 118, 179
   misdiagnosis avoidance, 38
   similarities with BDD, 246
   and SRIs, 161
   and suicide attempt, 111–112
Dermatologic treatment, 78, 79, 115, 233,
      234, 238
   dermabrasion, 234
   dissatisfaction with, 108, 237–238
   and skin picking, 78, 238
Dermatologists, 19, 28, 48, 113, 234
   and hair loss, 82, 90
   shopping for, 106
   violence towards, 107–108
Desipramine, 158
Diagnosis of BDD, 19, 20. *See also*
      Diagnostic instruments
   in adults, 96, 108, 120, 121, 157, 259
   in children and adolescents, 121, 123,
      124, 269
   misdiagnosis, 28, 38, 39–41
   and treatment, 121–124, 157, 247
*Diagnostic and Statistical Manual, Fourth
      Edition* (DSM-IV) criteria, 17–21, 33,
      279–280

differentiation of BDD, from other
      disorders, 21
distress or impairment in functioning,
      20–21
face-to-face interviews, 30
preoccupation, 17–20
useful guidelines, 32
Diagnostic instruments:
   BDD Diagnostic Module for adults, 31
   BDD Diagnostic Module for children and
      adolescents, 124
   BDDQ for adults, 29
   BDDQ for children and adolescents,
      28, 122–123
   BDD-YBOCS, 31, 33, 162
   Structured Clinical Interview for DSM-IV
      (SCID), 31
Dieting, 84–85
Disfigurement, 71, 91, 124
Displacement, 138
Distraction techniques, 87
Distress, 20. *See also* Stress
   and anxiety, 70–71
   clinically significant, 33
   emotional, 41, 71, 78, 87
   over muscle dysmorphia, 50–51
Diuretics, 51
Divorce, 71, 95
Doctor shopping, 82–83, 106. *See also*
      Dermatologists; Surgeons
Dopamine, 130, 133, 157
   defined, 279
Dosage, medication, 167–171. *See also*
      specific medications
Drug abuse, 105–6, 121, 186, 230. *See also*
      Anabolic steroids
Drug and alcohol treatment, 230
DSM-IV. *See Diagnostic and Statistical
      Manual, Fourth Edition* (DSM-IV)
      criteria
Dysmorphophobia, 280

Eating disorders, 30, 116, 201, 247. *See also*
      Weight concerns
   anorexia nervosa, 21, 248
   binge eating, 247
   bulimia nervosa, 21, 247, 248
   and dieting, 247

Economic cost, of BDD, 109–110
Effexor. *See* Venlafaxine (Effexor)
Elderly, BDD in, 125–126
Electroconvulsive therapy (shock therapy), 24, 183–185, 280
Electrolysis, 48, 75, 233
Elephant Man, 59, 89
Embarrassment, 27. *See also* Shame
    in talking about BDD, 48, 52, 79, 80, 144
Emotional distress, 41, 71, 78, 87, 114.
        See also Distress
Emotional pain, 59, 62. *See also* Anxiety;
        Depression; Embarrassment; Guilt;
        Shame
Employment. *See* Work, effects on
Ephedra, 106, 240
Ephedrine, 51
Escitalopram (Lexapro), 155, 160, 161, 167, 168, 170, 177, 280
    dosage, 168, 169, 170
    effectiveness of, 158, 163, 167
    and suicidal thinking, 163
    study of, 161, 167
Evolution and BDD, 130
Exercise, 85–86
    aerobics, 85
    excessive, 85, 107, 247
    weightlifting, 85–86
Exposure hierarchy, 212–213, 218–219, 280
Exposure therapy, 190–191, 199, 210–217, 280
    anxiety, 211
    and behavioral experiments, 190–191, 210–217
    and CBT, 190, 199, 210–218
    guidelines, 217
    hierarchy in, 212–213, 280
    and ritual prevention, 219
    steps in, 212–217
Extrastriate body area, 280
Eye movement desensitization and reprocessing (EMDR), 229

Face concerns, 52–54
Facial hair (beard), 77
Facial surgery. *See* Cosmetic (plastic) surgery
Family and friends:
    anger, response to, 257, 261–262

and CBT, 227, 228–229
coping strategies, 263
and delusional beliefs, 256
encouragement by, 254–256, 259–260
family and genetic link to BDD, 127–129
guidelines for, 253–264
parent's perspective, 252–253
and patience with treatment, 253, 261
praising by, 260
progress assessment by, 260–261
psychiatric treatment encouragement by, 254–256
reassurance and, 71, 81, 257–258
recognizing BDD symptoms, 253–254
ritualistic behaviors and, 257
and routine, 263
and secrecy, 76, 109, 252
and stress management, 261
suicidal thinking, response to, 262–263
support and help and, 256
violence, response to, 262
Family therapy, 125, 228–229, 229
Fear, 54, 104
Feeling Good About the Way You Look (Wilhelm), 274
Femininity, 53, 54. *See also* Women
5-HTP (5-hydroxytophan), 240. *See also* Tryptophan
Finasteride, 234
Fluoxetine (Prozac), 155, 170, 171, 177, 280
    dosage, 168, 169
    effectiveness of, 158, 163, 167
    pimozide (Orap) to augment, 176, 179
    studies of, 163
    suicidal thinking, 163
Fluvoxamine (Luvox), 156, 177, 280, 281
    dosage, 168
    effectiveness of, 158, 163, 167
    patient response to, 161, 163, 170, 177
    study of, 163
Food and Drug Association (FDA), 156, 240
Fragility of body part, 55, 56
Freckles, 53, 65, 73, 234
Friends of BDD patients. *See* Family and friends

Functional impairment. *See* Impairment
functioning
Fusiform face area, 280

GABA (gamma-aminobutyric acid),
129, 280
Gabapentin, 182
Gender and BDD, 112. *See also* Femininity;
Men; Women
age of onset, 116–118
body image satisfaction, 32–33, 102, 163,
196, 250
in children and adolescents. *See* Children
and adolescents with BDD
and hair thinning, 34, 48
similarities and differences, 244–245
Genetic and neurobiological risk factors,
129–133, 280. *See also* Brain
and BDD
Genetics, of BDD, 129, 280
Genital concerns, 48, 77, 86, 98, 115.
See also Penis size
Geodon (ziprasadone), 179. *See also*
Ziprasidone
Germany, 100, 111, 115, 136
GI Joe (action toy), 136
Grooming, excessive, 35, 36, 43, 68, 69, 81,
84, 191, 223
in animals, 130
of hair, 75–76
Group therapy, 193, 229
Guilt, 60–62, 144, 246

Habit reversal, 223, 281
Hair concerns, 34, 60, 253, 260. *See also* Hair
pulling disorder (trichotillomania)
body hair, 48, 75, 82
and camouflage, 77, 78
excessive grooming of, 75–76
facial hair, 77
haircuts, 58, 75
reading about, 86
and school work, 96
symmetry, 52–53
Hair loss/thinning, 34, 75, 88
baldness, 53, 54, 90, 118
and depression, 91, 101, 102
embarrassment about, 91, 109

and gender, 48, 91, 95
and grooming, 75
and hair piece, 48, 75, 77, 143
medication to treat, 234
panic and, 90, 143
Hand washing, 87
Hats, as camouflage, 77
Hopelessness, 23, 60, 71
Hospitalization, 23, 25, 79, 109, 110, 112, 120
for depression, 76
outpatient vs. inpatient, 266
suicide attempts and, 21, 79, 109, 110, 120
Housebound, 83, 100, 260. *See also* Isolation
children, 120
Human growth hormone, 51
Hypnosis, 230
Hypochondriasis, 56, 156, 250, 281

ICD-10 (International Classification of
Disease), 281
*Classification of Mental and Behavioural
Disorders*, 250
Illegal behavior, 108
Imaginal exposure, 211
Imagined defect, of BDD, 17
Impairment in functioning, 20–21, 33, 96,
100. *See also* School, effects on;
Work, effects on
alcohol abuse, 105, 121, 180, 230
anabolic steroids, 51, 106, 113, 136
anger and hostility, 107–108
anxiety, 22, 104, 112
avoidance behaviors, 91, 93–94, 95, 97,
98–99, 100
and BDDQ, 30, 33
camouflage, 98
CBT for, 197
clinically significant, 33
and diagnosis of BDD, 30
and Diagnostic Module, 30
disfigurement, 91
and emotional distress, 20, 33
low self-esteem, 102–103
reducing, 197
self-surgery, 106–107
shame, 98
social phobia, 25, 38, 104, 197, 200,
248–249, 285

Impairment in functioning (*Cont.*)
  and spectrum of severity, 15–17
  and SRIs, 160–161
  suicide. *See* Suicide
  violent behaviors. *See* Violent behaviors
Impotence, 95.*See also* Genital concerns;
     Penis size
In vivo exposure, 211
Inferiority, 60, 130. *See also* Low
     self-esteem
Information seeking, 86. *See also* Resources
     for treatment
Inpatient treatment, 266–277
Insight (degree of delusionality), 65, 281
  and CBT, 196, 256
  and delusional BDD, 64–65, 196
  and SRIs, 161, 179
Insight-oriented psychotherapy, 228, 281
Insomnia, 180, 281
Intensive outpatient treatment, 266
International Classification of Diseases
     (ICD-10), 250, 281
Intensive outpatient treatment, 266
Intimacy problem, 94. *See also* Isolation;
     Marital stress; Social situations
Isolation, 23, 24, 61–62. *See also*
     Housebound
  of adolescents, 122
  from family and friends, 252
  and suicide, 114
Isotretinoin (Accutane), 234, 239
Italy, 108, 136

Japan, 137
  and social phobia, 248
  studies in, 237

Keppra. *See* Levetiracetam

Lamotrigine (Lamictal), 182
Leucotomy, 184
Levetiracetam (Keppra), 177, 181–182
Lexapro. *See* Escitalopram (Lexapro)
Life events, as risk factor for BDD, 137.
     See also Trauma
Lip concerns, 22
Lithium, 179
Lorazepam (Ativan), 180

Los Angeles Body Dysmorphic Disorder and
     Body Image Clinic, 270
Low self-esteem, 102–103, 121, 161
  CBT for, 197
  in children, 121
  and depression, 103
  and life experience, 134
  and personality, 135
  and suicide, 114
Luvox. *See* Fluvoxamine (Luvox)

Ma huang (ephedra), 106, 240
Major depressive disorder, 281
Makeup, 48, 76, 80
  as camouflage, 77, 78
Manic-depressive illness (bipolar disorder),
     118, 179
MAOIs. *See* Monoamine oxidase
     inhibitors
Masculinity, 53, 54. *See also* Gender and
     BDD; Men
Masks, as camouflage, 77
Massachusetts General Hospital/McLean
     Hospital OCD Institute at McLean
     Hospital, 272
Measuring behavior, 86
Media, and attractiveness, 136
Medical evaluation, 104–105
Medication, 155–187, 189–231. *See also*
     Antidepressants; Neuroleptics; *and
     specific medications*
  for acne, 111
  algorithm for, 185–186
  and chemical imbalance, 157
  combined with CBT, 117, 123, 143, 150,
     259, 261
  good response to (Christina's story),
     141–142
  and hospitalization, 143
  SRIs. *See* Serotonin-reuptake inhibitors
     (SRIs)
  SRI boosters, 155–157
  taking as prescribed, 171
Men. *See also* Baldness; Gender differences;
     Hair loss/thinning; Penis size
  masculinity, 53, 54
  muscle dysmorphia, 50–52, 77, 85,
     105–106, 112, 136

Menninger Clinic OCD Treatment
    Program, 271
Mental health professional, 144. *See also*
    Clinical psychologist; Psychiatrist;
    Therapist
    evaluation from, 145
Methylphenidate (Ritalin), 179
Mindfulness, 225–226, 281–282
Minoxidil, 234, 282
Mirror checking, 14, 15, 35, 60, 71–73, 198
    by adolescents and children, 118, 119
    and anxiety, 70, 72, 223
    car accident, 107
    CBT techniques, 198
    and ritual prevention, 222, 224
    and skin picking, 78
    and suicide attempt, 90
    triggering panic attack, 72, 73
Mirror retraining, 191–192, 224–225, 283.
    See also Perceptual retraining
Misdiagnosis of BDD, avoiding, 38,
    39–41
Modified leucotomy, 184
Monoamine oxidase inhibitors (MAOIs),
    24, 182, 281
Moral weakness, 138
Morphometric magnetic resonance imaging
    (MRI), 282
Murder attempts, 108
Muscle dysmorphia, 49, 50–52, 282
    and alcohol and drug abuse, 105
    and anabolic steroids, 106
    and excessive exercise, 51
    and media, 136
    and suicide attempts, 112
    and weight-lifting, 85

National Alliance on Mental Illness, 273
Natural remedies, 240
Negative thinking, 198, 202–203
Neurobiological risk factors, 129–133
Neuroleptics, 178–179, 186.
    defined, 282
    pimozide (Orap), 179
Neuromodulation, 184
Neuropsychological studies, 282
Neurosurgery, 184
Neuroticism, 135

Neurotransmitter, 282. *See also* Dopamine;
    GABA; Serotonin
Nondelusional BDD, 282
Nondiagnosis, of BDD, 169
Nonpsychiatric treatment. *See* Cosmetic
    Treatment; Dental treatment;
    Dermatologic treatment; Surgery
Nose concerns, 22, 34, 49, 55, 233
    and rituals, 252
Nose job (rhinoplasty), 23, 235

Obsessional thinking. *See also*
    Preoccupation
    about appearance, 57–58
    embarrassment and shame about, 58–59
    emotional pain and, 59–62
    and insight, 64–65
    referential thinking and, 62–64
    and SRIs, 160
Obsessions, 57
    defined, 282
    certainty, 64–65
    painful feelings, 59–62
    staring at and mocking one's appearance,
    62–64
Obsessive compulsive disorder (OCD),
    243–246, 282
    BDD misdiagnosed as, 40
    defined as, 244
    and depression, 177
    differences with BDD, 244–245
    linked to BDD, 132
    misdiagnosis avoidance, 40
    similarities with BDD, 244
Obsessive Compulsive Foundation,
    272–273
Occipital lobe, 282
OCD Action, 273
Olanzapine (Zyprexa), 179, 183
Open-label study, 158
    of SRIs, 181
Open study, 283
Opioids, 182–183
Orap. *See* Pimozide (Orap)
Orbitofrontal cortex, 283
Orbitofrontal-striatal-thalamic circuit
    ("worry loop"), 283
Outpatient treatment, 266

Overfocusing, 130–131. *See also* Selective attention

Pain, 59, 60. *See also* Emotional pain
Panic attacks, 62, 283
    and mirror checking, 104
    physical symptoms of, 104
Panic disorder, 40, 283
    BDD misdiagnosed as, 40
    misdiagnosis avoidance, 40
Paranoia, 62
Parietal lobe, 283
Paroxetine (Paxil), 155, 167, 168, 177, 283
Partial hospital treatment, 266. *See also* Day treatment
Penis size, 78, 82, 107
    and impotence, 95
    obsessive measuring of, 86
    and reassurance seeking, 80
Perceived stress, 104–105
Perceptual (mirror) retraining, 191–192, 224–225, 283
Perfectionism, 135
Personality traits, 135
Physical deformity, 91
Pimozide (Orap), 176, 179, 283
Placebo, 283
Plastic surgery. *See* Cosmetic (plastic) surgery; Surgery
Post-traumatic stress disorder (PTSD), 112, 283–284
Preoccupation:
    with appearance, 21, 33, 44–46, 58
    CBT treatment, 131
    and DSM-IV criteria, 17–20
    and emotional distress, 41, 71
    examples of, 44–46
    resistance to, 58
    SRI treatment, 160
Prevalence of BDD, 136
Professional care, 267
Prospective study, 284
Proxy, BDD by, 42–46
Prozac. *See* Fluoxetine (Prozac)
Psychiatric disorder, 28. *See also* Anxiety disorders; Depression; *and specific disorders*
    serotonin and, 132

SRI treatment, 156
Psychiatric hospitalization, 69, 99, 174, 240. *See also* Hospitalization
Psychiatric treatment, 153, 238, 255. *See also* Cognitive-behavioral therapy; Family and friends; Medication; Treatment
Psychiatrists, 265
Psychological risk factors, 134–136
Psychopharmacology, 187, 265. *See also* Medications; Serotonin-reuptake inhibitors
Psychotherapy:
    cognitive behavioral, 189, 228
    couples and family, 229
    group, 229
    insight-oriented, 228
    supportive, 228–229
Psychotropic agents, 178. *See also* Medication
Puberty, 116
PubMed, 274

Quality of life, 100
    and SRIs improving, 161
Quality of Life Enjoyment and Satisfaction Questionnaire (Q-LES-Q), 101
Questioning behavior, 6, 68, 71, 80–82, 258. *See also* Reassurance seeking
Questionnaires, 28–30. *See also* Diagnostic instruments
    BDD Diagnostic Module for adults, 31
    BDD Diagnostic Module for children and adolescents, 124
    BDDQ for adults, 29
    BDDQ for children and adolescents, 122–123
    Q-LES-Q, 101
    quality of life, 100–102
    SAS-SR, 93
    SF-36, 100, 101
    self-report, 30

Rational response, 205
Reassurance seeking, 35, 80–82, 222
    from doctors, 55

from friends and family, 71, 81–82,
257–258
measuring behavior as, 86
response prevention, 219, 222
Referential thinking, 62, 63
defined, 284
in schizophrenia, 250
Relapse prevention, 192, 226
Relationships. *See also* Family and friends;
Intimacy
and BDD behaviors, 71, 73, 74
of children with BDD, 121
and social activities, 73, 92–96
Relaxation techniques, 225
Remission, 245
Repetitive behavior. 67–88, 219–224.
See also Compulsive behavior;
Rituals; Stereotypic behaviors
in animals, 130
brain chemistry and, 132–133
CBT for, 132
Research, 18. *See also* Treatment,
resources for
accessing of, 274
additional reading, 93
animal, 161
on clinical features of BDD, 130
on cognitive-behavioral therapy, 146
cross-cultural studies, 136–137
on gender and BDD, 115–116
need for treatment, 128, 131, 138
pharmacological, 187
twin and adoption studies, 129
Residential treatment, 267
Resistance of BDD behaviors, 69, 70.
See also Ritual (response)
prevention
Resources for treatment, 268–275
Internet websites, 268
symptoms and clinical features
of BDD, 265
Retrospective study, 284
Rhinoplasty. *See* Nose job (rhinoplasty)
Risk factors, 114, 127–137. *See also* Causes
of BDD
Risperidone (Risperdal), 179
Ritalin (methylphenidate), 176, 179.
See also Methylphenidate

Ritual behaviors, 68, 70, 132, 160, 222, 284.
See also Compulsions, Compulsive
behaviors, Repetitive behaviors,
Rituals
Ritual (response) prevention, 191,
219–224, 284
and anxiety, 219
and CBT, 191
and compulsive behavior, 223
defined, 284
and exposure therapy, 219
Ritual Form for, 221
Rituals, 68, 71, 198, 284. *Also see*
Compulsions; Compulsive behaviors;
Repetitive behaviors
Rogers Memorial Hospital—Milwaukee, 272
Rogers Memorial Hospital OCD
Center—Oconomowoc, 272

Sadness, 61
Safety-seeking behaviors, 68
Scarring, 48. *See also* Skin picking
Schizophrenia, 284
BDD misdiagnosed as, 41
misdiagnosis avoidance, 41
School, effects on, 96–98
in adolescents, 16, 118
impairment, 96
Screening for BDD, 28–32, 122. *See also*
Questionnaires
Secrecy:
and shame. *See under* Shame
in skin picking, 80
Selective attention, 130. *See also*
Overfocusing
Selective serotonin-reuptake inhibitor
(SSRI), 284. *See also* Serotonin-
reuptake inhibitors (SRIs)
Self-consciousness, 93
in adolescence, 121
Self-esteem. *See* Low self-esteem
Self-evaluation, 203, 216
Self-help groups, 230–231
"Self-ideal" discrepancy hypothesis, 135
Self-mutilation, 107
Self-portraits, of BDD people, 50
Self-surgery, 106–107
Sensations, tactile, 56

Serotonin, 156–157, 177, 285
  tryptophan, 240
  visual perception, 163
Serotonin hypothesis, 132–133
Serotonin-reuptake inhibitors (SRIs),
    59, 65, 117, 146–150, 155, 285.
    See also specific drugs
  adequate trial of, 170
  and algorithm to treat BDD, 185–186, 187
  augmenting approach, 175, 176–180
  in BDD and depression compared, 169
  brain functioning, 156–157
  controlled studies of, 194, 196, 279
  correcting chemical imbalance, 156–157
  defined, 285
  for delusional BDD, 158, 167
  for depression, 161
  discontinuing, 172–173
  dosage, 169–170
  eating disorders, 248
  effectiveness of, 176–180
  FAQs about, 164–166
  first line medication, 167
  hypochondriasis, 156
  improvement with, 160–164
  individualized treatment, need for, 187
  key points, 146
  and MAOIs, 182
  and OCD, 157
  open-label trials of, 158, 160, 283
  other medications with, 181–183
  and personality problems, 165
  proof of effectiveness of, 155–157
  side effects, 164, 173–174
  for social phobia, 249
  switching approach, 175, 180–181
  treating BDD with, 141, 144, 166–174, 181
  used with CBT, 146, 149
Sertraline (Zoloft), 155, 167, 285, 286
  dosage, 156, 168
  effectiveness of, 177–178
Severity, spectrum of, 15–17, 31
Sexual abuse, 134
Sexual orientation, 115
SF-36 (Medical Outcomes Study 36-Item
    Short Form Health Survey), 100, 101
Shame, 60, 98, 256. *See also* Embarrassment
  camouflage, 98

inferiority, 60
and secrecy, 26–27
sexual abuse, 134
and suicide, 114
and treatment, 144
Shock therapy (electroconvulsive therapy
    [ECT]), 24, 280
Shopping compulsion, 84. *See also* Doctor
    shopping
Side effects, medication, 151
  SRIs, 164–165, 173–174
Single photon emission computed
    tomography (SPECT), 133
Skin concerns, 48, 60
  acne, 79, 87, 107, 124
  color, 48, 83
  defects, 19, 69
  and diet, 85
  freckles, 53, 65, 73, 234
  inability to work, 73
  and response to treatment, 142
  scarring, 31, 80
  SRIs used to treat, 65, 141, 156, 160, 238
  tanning, 77, 83, 87
  wrinkles, 48, 52, 53, 83, 87, 120
Skin picking (neurotic excoriation), 35, 78,
    198, 238
  and acne, 79, 80
  dermatologic treatment for, 78, 233,
    234, 238
  and scarring, 78, 80
  and suicide, 91
  as symptoms, 80
Social Adjustment Scale (SAS-SR), 93
Social and cultural risk factors, 136–137
Social anxiety, 249
  and CBT, 196
Social dominance, and serotonin, 139
Social phobia (social anxiety disorder), 28,
    38, 285
  BDD misdiagnosed as, 38–41, 104
  CBT for, 197, 200
  differences with BDD, 249
  misdiagnosis avoidance, 38
  similarities with BDD, 249
Social situations, 91, 92–93, 95, 104. *See
    also* Avoidance; Family and friends;
    School, effects on; Work, effects on

BDD symptoms and, 20, 93, 260
  marital stress and, 55
  withdrawal from, 121
Sociocultural theories:
  cross-cultural research, 136
  media images, 136
SRIs. *See* Serotonin-reuptake inhibitors
  (SRIs)
Stereotypic behavior, 130. *See also*
  Grooming, excessive; Rituals
  role of dopamine and, 130
Steroids. *See* Anabolic steroids and Muscle
  dysmorphia
Stigma:
  overcoming, 145
Stress. *See also* Distress
  as trigger, 137
Striatum, 285
Stroke, 106, 133
Structured Clinical Interview for DSM-IV
  (SCID), 31
Substance use disorder, 285. *See also* Alcohol
  abuse; Drug abuse
Suffering, 15, 20, 160, 255, 262
Suicide, 79, 112–113, 114, 121, 239, 262
  attempt, 111–112
    by adolescents, 120–121
    BDD/OCD comparison, 245
    and breast augmentation, 120, 235
    delusional BDD, 120
    and depression, 112
    and family, 113, 229
    hospitalization for, 109
    and mirror checking, 71, 90
    and SRIs, 165
  thinking, 110–111, 163, 165, 239
  response by family and friends,
    262–263
Support groups, 24, 263
Supportive psychotherapy, 228, 285
Surgeons:
  anger and violence toward, 107–108
  refusal to operate, 238
  shopping for, 82–83
  threat for, 239
Surgery, 26, 79, 106, 115, 138, 184, 234, 237,
  239, 255. *See also* Cosmetic (plastic)
  surgery

angry reaction to, 238–239
brain, 184. *See also* Neurosurgery
multiple, 235
outcome of, 237–238
self-surgery, 106–107
unnecessary, 52, 106
unrealistic expectations of, 237, 238
Symmetry, body, 52–53
Symptoms of BDD, 43, 62, 65, 80, 84, 87.
  See also Behaviors, in BDD;
  *Diagnostic and Statistical Manual,
  Fourth Edition* (DSM-IV) criteria;
  specific symptoms
  CBT for, 189–231
  in children and adolescents, 118–120
  chronic, 116
  recognizing, 26–28
  remission of, 245
  severity of, 15–17, 31
  SRI treatments of, 166–187. *See also*
    Medication
  and stress, 104–105
  sudden onset of, 137
  treatment plan and. *See* Medication;
    Treatment

Talking therapy, 228, 281, 285
Tanning, 83. *See also* Skin
Teasing as trigger for BDD, 134
Temperament. *See* Personality traits
Temporal lobe, 285
Testosterone, 106. *See also* Anabolic steroids
Theories of BDD. *See* Causes of BDD; *specific
  theories*
Therapist:
  and CBT, 200
  meaning of, 265
  reassurance sought from, 80–81
Therapy. *See* Cognitive-behavioral therapy;
  Cognitive therapy; Couples and
  family therapy; Exposure therapy,
  Insight-oriented psychotherapy;
  Supportive Psychotherapy
Thinking errors, 205, 207, 285–286
Thought record, in CBT, 204–208, 209, 286
Touching behavior, 86–87
Tourette's disorder, 179
Trauma, as cause of BDD, 134

Treatment, 28, 155, 166, 180, 229, 233, 255, 261, 279. *See also* Cognitive-behavioral therapy; Medication; Psychiatric treatment; Serotonin-reuptake inhibitors (SRIs)
  adequate, 117, 145, 150, 165, 230, 259
  for children and adolescents, 122, 123
  effective, 176–180
  family patience with, 253, 261
  guide to, 141–153
  individualizing treatment, 150, 186–187
  ineffective, 109, 228, 239–240
  key points about, 146
  neurosurgical, 184
  overcoming barriers to, 143–146
  plan for, 231
  and remission, 245
  resources for, 268–275
  shopping for, 82–83
  things to consider when seeking, 267–268
  and trivialization, 144
  unnecessary, 106. *See also* Cosmetic treatment
Treatment guide, 141–153
  cognitive-behavioral therapy, improvement with, 142
  medication, improvement with, 141–142
  medication plus cognitive-behavioral therapy, improvement with, 143
  recommendations, 146, 147–148
Treatment studies, 156–161, 163, 165, 166, 170, 177–179, 181–183, 187, 192–197, 254, 269. *See also* Research; *specific medications*
Trichotillomania, 225, 286
  BDD misdiagnosed as, 40
  misdiagnosis avoidance, 40
Tricyclic antidepressants, 183
Triggers, 137–138
  comment about appearance as, 137
  environmental events as, 139
  family and, 261
  life events as, 137
  stress as, 138
  teasing as, 134
Trivialization of BDD, 27, 144

Tryptophan (amino acid), 240
Twin and adoption studies, 129

UCLA Body Dysmorphic Disorder Research Program, 270
UCLA OCD Intensive Treatment Program, 270
Underrecognition of BDD, reasons for:
  confusion with vanity, 27
  lack of familiarity, 27–28
  misdiagnosis, 28
  pursuit of cosmetic treatment, 9–10
  secrecy and shame, 26–27
  trivialization, 27
United States, BDD in, 136
University of California at San Diego OCD Program, 271

Vagal nerve stimulation, 184
Valproic acid, 182
Vanity, 27
Venlafaxine (Effexor), 178, 181, 182, 186
Violent behaviors, 91, 107–108, 121, 238, 262, 266
  murder attempt, 108
Visual perception, 131, 133
  serotonin and, 163
Vocational rehabilitation, 230. *See also* Work, effects on
Vulnerability-stress hypothesis, 226

Weight concerns, 13, 21, 34, 49, 85, 107, 116, 164, 248. *See also* Eating disorders
  dieting and, 85
  SRIs to treat, 164
  of women, 33, 49
Weight-lifting, 85–86, 107. *See also* Muscle dysmorphia
Wellbutin, 176, 178. *See also* Bupropion
Women, 32, 48, 86, 115, 132, 248. *See also* Gender and BDD
  with anorexia, 250
  body image satisfaction of, 33, 163
  breast concerns of, 54, 61, 87, 120
  CBT for, 196
  compared to men, 115, 116, 248
  and femininity, 54

gender differences, 115, 116
weight concerns of, 33, 49
Work, effects on, 96–98
    and disability, 96
    impairment in, 96
    mirror checking, 96
"Worry circuit" of brain, 132

Yale-Brown Obsessive-Compulsive Scale
    Modified for BDD (BDD-YBOCS),
    32, 33, 162. *See also* BDD-YBOCS

Ziprasidone, 179. *See also* Geodon
Zoloft. *See also* Sertraline (Zoloft)
Zyprexa, 179, 183. *See also* Olanzapine